LINCOLN'S PLAN OF RECONSTRUCTION

Lincoln's Plan of Reconstruction

By
CHARLES H. McCARTHY

AMS PRESS, INC.
NEW YORK
1966

AMS PRESS, INC.
New York, N.Y. 10003
1966

Manufactured in the United States of America

CONTENTS

	Page
INTRODUCTION	xv

I
TENNESSEE

Election and Policy of Lincoln	1
East Tennessee	3
Secession	8
Federal Victories	10
A Military Governor	11
Origin of Military Governors in the United States	12
Measures of Governor Johnson	17
Negro Troops	20
Nashville Convention of 1863	21
Proclamation of Amnesty and Reconstruction	23
Steps to Restoration	27
Nashville Convention of 1865	30
Election of William G. Brownlow	32
Nomination of Lincoln and Johnson	32
Presidential Election in Tennessee	34

II
LOUISIANA

Popularity of Secession	36
Financial Embarrassment	37
Capture of New Orleans	38
Lincoln's Advice	38
General Shepley appointed Military Governor	39

	Page
Election of Representatives to Congress	45
Division among Unionists	47
Military Operations	49
Lincoln Urges Reconstruction	51
Political Activity among Loyalists	53
Title of Louisiana Claimants	58
Opposition to General Banks	61
Plan of Reconstruction proposed	66
Election of 1864	70
Inauguration of Civil Government	72
Lincoln's Letter on Negro Suffrage	73
Constitutional Convention	75
Congressional Election	76

III

ARKANSAS

Indifference to Secession	77
The Fall of Sumter	78
Seizure of Little Rock	79
Military Matters	79
Threat of Seceding from Secession	82
General Phelps appointed Military Governor	82
Enthusiasm of Unionists	83
Lincoln's Interest in Arkansas	83
Inaugurating a Loyal Government	84
The Election of 1864	90

IV

VIRGINIA

Secession	93
Physical Features and Early Settlements	94
Society and Its Basis	95

CONTENTS

	Page
The Counter-Revolution	97
Convention at Wheeling	99
Organizing a Union Government	100
Legislature of Restored Virginia	103
The State of Kanawha	105
Attorney-General Bates on Dismemberment	105
Making a New State	107
Compensated Emancipation	108
Formation of New State discussed in Congress	110
Cabinet on Dismemberment	120
Lincoln on Dismemberment	124
Webster's Prediction	126
Inauguration of New State	128
Reorganizing the Restored State	129
Right of Commonwealth to Representation in Congress	131
Rupture between Civil and Military Authorities	133
The President Interposes	135
Congress Refuses to Admit a Senator-Elect	138

V

ANTI-SLAVERY LEGISLATION

Compensated Emancipation in Congress	143
Contrabands	143
The Military Power and Fugitive Slaves	144
Lincoln on Military Emancipation	148
Andrew Jackson and Nullification	151
Lincoln on Compensated Emancipation	152
Compensated Emancipation in Delaware	155
Abandoned Slaves	160
Border Policy Propounded	163
General Hunter and Military Emancipation	168
Slavery Prohibited in the Territories	170

CONTENTS

	Page
Attitude of Border States on Slavery	172
Lincoln Resolves to Emancipate Slaves by Proclamation	177

VI

THEORIES AND PLANS OF RECONSTRUCTION

The Presidential Plan	190
Sumner's Theory of State Suicide	196
"Conquered Province" Theory of Stevens	211
Theory of Northern Democrats	217
Crittenden Resolution	220

VII

RISE OF THE CONGRESSIONAL PLAN

Bill to Guarantee a Republican Form of Government	224
Henry Winter Davis on Reconstruction	226
House Debates on Bill of Wade and Davis	236
Pendleton's Speech on Reconstruction	257
Provisions of Wade-Davis Bill	262
Senate Debate on Bill of Wade and Davis	264
President's Pocket Veto	273
Proclamation concerning Reconstruction	278
Manifesto of Wade and Davis	279

VIII

AN ATTEMPT TO COMPROMISE

President ignores Controversy with Congress	286
Summary of Military and Naval Situation	288
Attempt to Revive the Pocketed Bill	289
House Debates on Ashley's Reconstruction Bill	291
Defeat of Ashley's Bill	311

IX

THE ELECTORAL VOTE OF LOUISIANA

	Page
Resolution excluding Electoral Votes of Rebellious States	314
Amendment of Senator Ten Eyck	315
Senate Debate on Ten Eyck's Amendment	316
Defeat of the Amendment in favor of Louisiana	334
Senate Passes Joint Resolution	338
Counting the Electoral Vote	339
The President's Message	339

X

SENATE DEBATE ON LOUISIANA

Congressmen from Louisiana at the National Capital	341
Proposal to Recognize Louisiana	343
Powell's Speech opposing Recognition	344
Henderson's Argument for Recognition	348
Howard's Argument in Opposition	358
Reverdy Johnson's Speech for Recognition	370
General Discussion on Louisiana	374

XI

INCIDENTS OF RECONSTRUCTION

The Thirteenth Amendment	384
The Freedmen's Bureau	385
Volunteer Diplomats	389
The Hampton Roads Conference	395
Lincoln's Letter to General Hurlbut	401
Lincoln's Letter to General Canby	402
Lincoln's Last Words on Reconstruction	403

XII

CULMINATION OF THE PRESIDENTIAL PLAN

	Page
Lincoln and the South	407
Inauguration of Andrew Johnson	408
Arkansas after the War	409
Condition of Tennessee	412
Louisiana	417
Reorganization of Virginia	425
The Wreck of the Confederacy	431
Andrew Johnson on Reconstruction in 1864	438
Johnson's Speeches after Accession to the Presidency	440
Raising the Blockade	444
The Executive Department Recognizes Virginia	445
Restoration of North Carolina	448
The President Hesitates	458
Executive Policy in Mississippi	460
Restoration of Georgia	465
Texas	466
The Reconstruction Conventions	468
Temper of the South	472
Mississippi Legislation relative to Freedmen	475
Southern Reaction	482
The President's Change of Opinion	487
Examination of Lincoln's Plan	491

APPENDIX A

THIRTY-SEVENTH CONGRESS 499

APPENDIX B

THIRTY-EIGHTH CONGRESS 502

Preface

MUCH of the material included in this volume was collected several years ago while the author was a graduate student at the University of Pennsylvania. The researches then commenced probably first suggested to him the lack in our political literature of an ample and interesting account of the return of the States. Students, librarians, and even professors of history knew no adequate treatise on the era of reconstruction, and their testimony was confirmed by the authority of Mr. Bryce, who happily describes the succession of events in those crowded times as forming one of the most intricate chapters of American history. No apology is offered, therefore, for considering in this essay so important and so long-neglected a theme as the rise of the political revolution that occurred before reunion was finally accomplished.

On the general subject several excellent monographs have recently appeared; these, however, are nearly all employed in discussing the second stage in the process of restoration, and, except incidentally, anticipate scarcely anything of value in the present work, which, so far at least as concerns any logical exposition, conducts the reader over untraveled ground. As the introduction indicates with sufficient accuracy both the scope and method of this study, nothing is required here beyond a concise statement of the author's obligations.

Like many other students of American institutions, the writer cheerfully acknowledges his indebtedness to the works of Brownson, Hurd and Jameson, and, by transferring some of their opinions to his book, has shown a practical appreciation of their researches. In addition to these obligations, in which the author is not singular, he profited for four years by the lectures of Dr. Francis N. Thorpe, his professor in constitutional history. Except in a very few instances, where the name of an author was forgotten, credit for both suggestions and material is uniformly given in the references and footnotes.

For the selection, arrangement, and treatment of topics the author alone is responsible; he desires, however, to take this opportunity of acknowledging generous assistance received from three intimate friends: his colleague, Dr. Charles P. Henry, found time in the midst of arduous literary engagements to read the whole of the manuscript and to make many valuable suggestions, especially in matters of style and diction; the book is not less fortunate in having been critically read by Thomas J. Meagher, Esq., whose extensive and accurate knowledge of public as well as private law contributed to a more clear and scientific statement of many of the constitutional questions discussed; the technical skill and the superior intelligence of Mr. George M. Schell were of considerable assistance to the author in correcting the proofs of the entire book. Nor must he omit to record his appreciation of the courtesy of Mr. L. E. Hewitt, the efficient librarian of the Philadelphia Law Association. Finally the writer gratefully acknowledges his chief obligation to the scholarship of his former teacher, Dr. John Bach McMaster, who kindly interrupted the progress of his great historical work long enough to read a considerable portion of this essay. Indeed, it was the encouragement of that eminent author which first suggested the publication of these pages.

Before concluding his remarks the writer wishes to disclaim any sympathy with the progressive school of historical criticism, which derides the Constitution as a thing of the past and learnedly characterizes all veneration for its authority as the worship of a fetich. This book will have attained one of its principal purposes if, in the language of a distinguished surviving statesman of the war period, it will teach " the constant and ever-important lesson that the Constitution is always a more reliable guide for the legislator than those fierce passions which war never fails to excite."

PHILADELPHIA, September 14, 1901.

INTRODUCTION

SO closely blended with the essential principles of our federal system of government were the causes of the Civil War that a clear understanding of its results appears to require some account of the origin, the independence and the permanent union of these States. Upon the eventful years between the Treaty of Paris and the Declaration of Independence, crowded as they are with work of note, one could linger with pleasure; this epoch, however, has already engaged the pens of so many writers, eminent as well as obscure, that a re-study of the blunders of England's ministers and the revolt of her distant colonies might justly be regarded as a piece of presumption.

Nor does it seem necessary to recite the familiar achievements of the succeeding period; for, perhaps, the portion of American history most attractive to the general reader is included between the 4th of July, 1776, and the 4th of March, 1789. To these years belong the most conspicuous services of that giant race of leaders whose swords relieved a gallant people from oppression and whose wisdom established a form of government not, indeed, in universal harmony with popular prejudice, but admirably designed for the popular welfare.

It was at the outset of what may properly be styled the national era that there appeared the remarkable group of statesmen who guided the infant Republic on its dim and perilous way. On their broad experience gleamed a vision of the future touching all their work with elements of immortality. By them was skillfully established a system of revenue and of finance adequate to all the exigencies of the time, and a foreign policy inaugurated which for generations together preserved unbroken harmony with the world outside. They doubled by wise and peaceful acquisition the area of that Union whose independence had been wrested from George the Third, and with no less wisdom prescribed the procedure and defined the jurisdiction of Federal courts.

The forty years following March 4, 1789, form an epoch with characteristics of its own. This was the period of Virginian ascendency, the Adamses alone breaking the line of illustrious Presidents furnished by the Old Dominion. Introduced by an experiment in government which aroused the slumbering energies of the nation, its conclusion was marked by the disappearance from political life of the splendid ideals and rich traditions of the Fathers.

The election of General Jackson coincides with the beginning of a new phase in American political and industrial development. It was not that the fame of a splendid military record had raised its possessor to an office for which long experience in governmental affairs had hitherto been thought indispensable, or that the selection of Presidents had passed from an intellectual few to the control of a much more numerous class who were willing to bestow on politics the attention and energy requisite for success in trade; but it was about this time that the imperious power of slavery entered upon its career of aggression. Philosophic statesmen of a previous epoch had ardently hoped that the institution would be permitted quietly to disappear; indeed, the greatest among them, though divided upon a multitude of political and economic questions, agreed in encouraging every movement designed for its extinction. These humane efforts, however, were not destined to win immediate success, and even with the coöperation of the General Government served only to demonstrate the difficulty of such an undertaking.

After 1820 all the dangers which menaced the integrity of the Union were, with one notable exception, traceable to this cause. When Mr. Lincoln in his discussions with Senator Douglas declared that it was the sole cause of all the troubles which had disturbed the nation, he meant, probably, to assert no more than that in his own time it had been the most conspicuous one.

Long before slavery became a subject of embittered controversy the doctrine of State Rights had agitated the country. As early as the summer of 1793 it had found in Justice Iredell an able advocate on the bench of the United States Supreme Court. For party purposes it was adopted five years later by Madison and Jefferson in the celebrated Virginia and Kentucky Resolutions, and during the second war with Great Britain these statesmen were startled to find New England Federalism vindicating its unpatriotic, if not treacherous, conduct in the exact language which they had invented to embarrass a former administration. With this instrument, too, Calhoun in 1832 shook the foundations of the Union. Both Northern and Southern statesmen of that generation, however, pushed the principle of State sovereignty as far only as their immediate object seemed to require.

It is a popular mistake to suppose that beyond the limits of the South this erroneous doctrine found little favor in the minds of men; for on the eve of the War of

1812 a Governor of conservative Pennsylvania had armed her citizen-soldiers against Federal power.

The illustrious Marshall could relate how, before the highest tribunal in the land, its champions with unwearied zeal renewed the battle for a hopeless cause. The eloquent voice of Webster hushed for a time the fretful agitation of South Carolina statesmen, and his genius fixed in imperishable literary form that interpretation of the Constitution which called forth the abundant resources of both the Nation and the States. In his conquering words lived those elevated thoughts that in future years sustained the defenders of the Republic.

President Jackson, for the energy and promptness by which he defeated the projects of the Nullifiers, has been justly eulogized; but, when the excitement of the hour had passed away, the calmer judgment of even his admirers perceived that victory inclined rather to the side of Calhoun.

Discussion of the abstract question of State sovereignty might, probably, have long continued without endangering the Union had the principle not been invoked to defend the institution of human servitude; yoked to that powerful interest it was inevitable that both should go down together in undistinguishable ruin.

From the Protean fount of slavery flowed an hundred various streams coloring almost every important question in the tide of events. In the generation between the election of General Jackson and the inauguration of Mr. Lincoln its defeats were few, its triumphs numerous and important. Prosperity revealed its weaknesses and encouraged its experiments. The fruits of its greatest victory, the dismemberment of Mexico, revived those stormy

INTRODUCTION

scenes which thirty years before had for the first time been witnessed in an American legislative hall. Dissolution of the Union was once more threatened, and again averted by the genius and patriotism of the venerable triumvirate, who scarce outlived their noble work; but the compromise from which Clay, Calhoun and Webster expected a restoration of former tranquillity contained within itself the very seed-plot of even graver troubles.

After 1850 the attachment of Southern men to their industrial system was played upon by ambitious politicians more and more, until the final overthrow of themselves and the government which they sought to establish for its preservation. It could be shown how before that time one war was prolonged for the protection, and another undertaken chiefly for the extension, of that aggressive institution; how its existence was supposed to require Federal interference with the mails and an abridgment of even the ancient right of petition. Every power of the national Government and all the resources of the cotton States had been employed for its advantage.

The United States Supreme Court was the last agent within the Union by which its advocates sought to dignify and perpetuate human servitude, and so successful were their efforts that an enlightened and humane Chief Justice was but little misrepresented in language or in sentiment when political opponents ascribed to him the doctrine that "the negro has no rights which the white man is bound to respect."

The moral progress of the United States during the last forty years finds, probably, in no single event a better illustration than the change in public opinion upon the interesting question of human rights. When the majority opinion was delivered in the Dred Scott case it excited among members of the dominant political party but little surprise. The shock which a judicial utterance of such sentiments would give in our time to the ethical notions of the American people affords at once both a measure of the advance that has been made in the interval and an undoubted proof that progress has not been, as is commonly supposed, exclusively or even mainly along material lines. It is singular, too, that the first serious attempt of the Federal Supreme Court to set at rest a dangerous political question should have been followed by effects of so alarming a tendency.

It is not intended to relate in these pages the origin or the fate of those compromises designed to avoid the inevitable conflict already in the closing months of President Buchanan's administration casting ominous shadows in the pathway of the nation, nor to describe the uncertain policy of the General Government or attempt to determine the measure of its responsibility for the fearful rebellion which that hesitation encouraged.

The skill and industry of a multitude of laborers have gathered from the field of conflict a harvest as bountiful as the result was satisfactory. We have general histories and bird's-eye views, military accounts and naval accounts of the Civil War; memoirs and diaries, by actors more or less prominent in the events which they describe, and narratives of battles and of sieges. In this varied and ample field even a belated worker might hope to glean something of value; but this study, whatever it may discuss incidentally, will be chiefly concerned with the subject of Reconstruction, a phase of our political and constitutional

INTRODUCTION

development which, though beginning during the progress, lies mainly beyond the close of the Rebellion.

The organization into a separate government of the late Confederate States, with their resolute struggle for independence, is the chief event in the extraordinary career of this favored nation. The story of their submission to Federal power and the return to their former places in the Union is not inferior either in interest or instruction to any political event recorded in history. This return is what is commonly known as Reconstruction. Though the term on its introduction into political discussion was frequently objected to as inaccurate, it has been generally adopted in the writings of publicists as well as in popular speech. The word "restoration," which was at first preferred, was soon found to be inexact; for while former relations were resumed by the erring States, they came back, one with diminished territorial extent and all with domestic rights greatly abridged. They had, in fact, been *reconstructed*. It is true that even the loyal States did not emerge unscathed from this political revolution. In the South, however, the established industrial system had been swept completely away.

The theme falls naturally under two heads, Presidential Reconstruction and Congressional Reconstruction. An account of the former, which extended from the summer of 1861 to the autumn of 1865, occupies the whole of this volume. Any adequate treatment of the latter, including as it does the eventful period from the meeting of Congress in December, 1865, to the withdrawal of Federal forces from the South in 1877, will require a narrative somewhat more ample.

The conspicuous landmarks of Reconstruction require

no extraordinary talent to recognize and locate. It is the unfamiliar region between that is difficult accurately to map out. The failure hitherto to present in a single view the striking features of these neglected parts is chiefly responsible for the fact that Reconstruction remains one of the most obscure parts of our history. A candid and comprehensive account of the political events of the time appears to divest the subject of much of the difficulty commonly supposed to attend its investigation. From a sufficient body of essential facts the step to an understanding and exposition of every principle of moment is comparatively easy.

Though the general design of this volume will be suggested to the student of American history by an inspection of its principal subdivisions, it may not be unnecessary for the benefit of the general reader to add a brief outline of the plan that has been adopted.

Chapter I. relates the most important political events in the history of Tennessee from its attempted secession to the restoration, in March, 1865, of a civil government loyal to the United States. Military movements in that Commonwealth have been noticed only so far as to render intelligible the successive steps by which that reorganization was accomplished.

Chapters II. and III. bring the affairs of Louisiana and Arkansas, respectively, down to about the same time. Events in those States have been treated, so far as conditions permitted, in the same manner as in the case of Tennessee.

Chapter IV. is concerned with the secession, restoration and dismemberment of Virginia. The formation out of a portion of that Commonwealth of the new State of West

INTRODUCTION

Virginia, both because of the grave constitutional question which arose on a division of the parent State and the intrinsic interest of the subject, has been considered with some degree of minuteness.

In Chapter V., which discusses anti-slavery legislation, it will appear how Mr. Lincoln, though never an Abolitionist or even a radical Republican, became by pressure of military necessity an instrument in the hands of God to destroy an institution opposed by a long line of American statesmen and condemned by the light of the nineteenth century.

The succeeding chapter considers the various theories and plans of restoration presented during the progress of the war. The rise of the Congressional plan, which ultimately prevailed, is treated separately in Chapter VII. Only the first stage of its development, however, falls within the limits of this inquiry, which ends with the meeting of the Thirty-ninth Congress in December, 1865.

Chapters VIII., IX. and X. trace the progress of the controversy between the Legislative and the Executive branches of Government. The culmination of this difference, however, in the impeachment and trial of President Johnson is a phase of Congressional Reconstruction.

The topics treated in the eleventh chapter, having frequently employed the pens of able and popular writers on the Rebellion, are considered in this study merely for the purpose of making it complete in itself; hence that section is little more than an epitome of what has already been said on those subjects.

The twelfth and last chapter brings every part of the narrative up to December 4, 1865. To clearly compre-

INTRODUCTION

hend the arduous task that confronted President Johnson this section includes a rapid survey of the wreck of the Confederate States. The principal part, however, is reserved for an account of the conventions assembled under his authority, the method of instituting loyal governments and the spirit and tendency of Southern legislation relative to freedmen. An examination of the Presidential plan of Reconstruction completes the volume.

Lincoln's Plan of Reconstruction

I

TENNESSEE

WHILE the celebrated joint debates with Senator Douglas in 1858, the Cooper Union and other addresses, marked Mr. Lincoln, in the new political party just rising to power, as the intellectual peer of able and trusted leaders like Sumner, Chase and Seward, his conservative opinions on the subject of slavery made his nomination by the Chicago Convention more acceptable to delegates from the border States. Though his competitors received, in the memorable contest which followed, almost a million votes in excess of the number cast for Mr. Lincoln and his associate, the fierce conflict among fragments of the Democratic party resulted, as is well known, in the choice of a decided majority of Republican electors.[1] This rather unexpected defeat of a political organization that had lost but two Presidential contests since its first success under Jefferson afforded Southern leaders a pretext for urging a dismemberment of the Union. Indeed, there is evidence that the more impetuous among them had, four years earlier, seriously determined, in case of Fremont's election, upon a similar course.[2] Thus the present

[1] McPherson's Political History of the United States, p. 1.
[2] McPherson's Pol. Hist., pp. 389-399; "Parson" Brownlow's Book, pp. 54, 159, 160; Lalor's Cyclopedia of Political Science, Political Economy and United States History, Vol. III. p. 698.

event, so far from being an universal disappointment to members of the defeated party, had been ardently hoped for by many. The choice of a minority party, and not at first possessing the entire confidence of even that minority, Mr. Lincoln, unable to divine the future, was compelled in dealing with the insurrection to proceed with the utmost caution. Washington himself, in organizing the Federal Government, had a task of less magnitude, and the renown of his military achievements silenced for a time even the boldest in opposition. President Lincoln's victories, gained on a different field, gave no such unquestioned authority to his name. This peculiar situation forced him to adopt for the guidance of his administration a policy not altogether free from embarrassment to both himself and his successor. His purpose at that time appears to have been to meet the demands of the moment by the contrivances of the moment. Whether a different course would have been rewarded by earlier or by more complete success is a hazardous subject for speculation. If his theory of our national existence be liable to the multitude of objections which have grown up in these fruitful times of peace, no other has been suggested that is free from criticism. His political doctrine, too, had the advantage of always recommending measures scarcely less distinguished for enlarged views than those enlightened convictions which characterize his first inaugural address. Whatever may be concluded of its merits, the theory embraced at the outset exerted on many administrative acts of President Lincoln an influence that continued to be felt during his entire executive career; and without remembering this fact we shall not easily comprehend either the extent of his "Border Policy," as the plan of compensated emancipation is often called, or his undoubted concern for persecuted Union men in the seceded States.

The sufferings of loyal citizens in East Tennessee had early enlisted the President's sympathies, and almost from the commencement of hostilities measures for their relief formed in his mind part of the plan of operations by the army under General Buell. Writing, January 6, 1862, to that commander he gives reasons for suggesting the occupation of some point there rather than Nashville, and adds: "But my distress is that our friends in East Tennessee are being hanged and driven to despair, and even now, I fear, are thinking of taking rebel arms for the sake of personal protection. In this we lose the most valuable stake we have in the South."[1] The cause of these outrages may be briefly explained in a digression.

In no part of the late Confederate States was the slave interest more feeble than in the thirty counties comprising East Tennessee.[2] That portion of the State contained in 1860 slightly over 300,000 inhabitants,[3] of whom only about one tenth were slaves, while in many counties they formed no more than one in seventeen of the population. Here and there, indeed, were persons of wealth some of whom owned a few negroes. But though a majority of the people looked upon domestic slavery as something foreign to their social life, they had no strong philanthropic impulse to oppose it. While quite willing to allow their countrymen elsewhere to keep bondmen at pleasure, they did not regard it any concern of theirs to assist either in extending or perpetuating human servitude. If the existence of the Union or of slavery was the issue, they would have hesitated little in deciding which should perish. Though, as we shall presently see, they were as intolerant of the Republican party as any community in the South, they were devotedly attached to the Union. The

[1] Letters and State Papers of Abraham Lincoln, Vol. II. p. 112. The edition of Nicolay and Hay is used throughout.
[2] The Loyal Mountaineers of Tennessee, p. 24.
[3] More correctly, 301,056. Ibid.

fact is partly explained by the industrial basis of society in this favored region.

Cut off from Middle Tennessee by lofty ranges of the Cumberland, and from North Carolina by the Great Smoky, the Black and the Stone mountains, this extensive district is traversed in its entire length by the Tennessee and its chief tributaries, the Clinch and the Holston; as the great river flows down to Alabama it receives, before turning west and north to join the Ohio, the waters of many important and beautiful streams, some of which, as the French Broad and Nolachucky, are associated with deeds of note in the War for Independence; indeed, one of its crowning victories was chiefly won by settlers from the banks of the Watauga. Other names, like Hiwassee, are familiar to readers of later events in Tennessee history, and Chickamauga Creek was destined shortly to become more famous than any.

Knoxville, in early times a capital of the State, was, in 1860, the metropolis of East Tennessee; Chattanooga, at the southern extremity of the valley, is separated from Bristol, on the Virginia line, by a distance of more than two hundred and forty miles; Cleveland and Greenville were towns of less importance. The absence of large cities makes it evident that manufacturing had not yet begun to attract serious attention. Like early settlers everywhere in America, the pioneers of Tennessee sought the most immediate returns from the products of the forests and fields around them. The rich mineral deposits, then either unknown or almost untouched, had not given rise to those great extractive operations which in our time have so stimulated the commercial life of East Tennessee. Vast cotton plantations, worked by multitudes of slaves, like those in the western portion of the State, had no existence in these mountain valleys, though occasionally small "patches" were cultivated for domestic use.

Citizens of West Tennessee would naturally place upon the Federal Constitution an interested construction; their industries, they believed, required such an interpretation of that instrument as would place the institution of slavery beyond the reach of Congressional interference. While the people of East Tennessee, too, believed in the several sovereignty of the States, the question of slavery did not touch them so nearly. Indifferent to the subject themselves, they had little sympathy with those who had determined to break up the Union from a mere suspicion that their interests were menaced by the success of a new political party. But to ascribe to the want of interested motives their indifference to the great disturbing question of the time would be to assign but one and that, perhaps, not the chief cause.

Except on its northern and southern boundaries this delightful region is practically isolated from several adjacent States as well as from the remainder of Tennessee. It was in this by-place of nature and amidst such a population that *The Manumission Intelligencer*, a weekly newspaper, made its appearance in 1819.[1] It was followed the next year by *The Emancipator* of Elijah Embree, a Pennsylvania Quaker; this in turn was soon succeeded by a more celebrated publication, *The Genius of Universal Emancipation,* conducted by Benjamin Lundy. While these publications served to perpetuate and to extend, they did not create the sentiment of which they became exponents, for, several years before their appearance, an anti-slavery society flourished in Jefferson County. Its existence is noticed as early as 1814.[2] This anti-slavery feeling was part of the philosophic movement encouraged by nearly all Southern as well as Northern statesmen before the inauguration of General Jackson. A new industrial era, beginning about that time, put an end to the abolition societies in the South; and though Lundy's paper was discontinued in Tennessee after 1824, events of frequent occurrence sustained the anti-slavery sentiments of the people.

[1] The Loyal Mountaineers of Tennessee, p. 32.
[2] Ibid.

6 LINCOLN'S PLAN OF RECONSTRUCTION

The Tennessee valley was a natural thoroughfare from Virginia to the south-west, and when slaves were purchased on the Potomac they were chained together, to prevent escape, and in that condition driven to the homes of their new masters.[1] The plaintive songs of captives as they were marched in lines along the valley highways often caused the free mountaineer to pause in his labors and reflect on what was passing before his eyes. He "saw slavery in its bitterness and without disguise." The remembrance of such spectacles was apt to strengthen in him anti-slavery feelings that had come down from Revolutionary times. But whether Southern leaders ascribed the sentiment to an inherited tendency or regarded it as a consequence of this odious phase of the domestic slave-trade, they did not think it beneath the dignity of attention; for it was, doubtless, to create a sympathy for their institution that a "Southern Commercial Convention" was held at Knoxville in 1857. It was too late, however, to root out the convictions of two generations; the counsels of the wise were soon to be confounded and the

[1] Thirty years before President Lincoln published his Emancipation Proclamation Great Britain abolished slavery throughout her colonies. Naturally this action was viewed in no friendly spirit by the slave interest in America, for it brought the free negro to the very door of the Southern States, and though it was regarded as a menace to the "peculiar institution," it was not until a positive loss was sustained that any controversy arose with England. In October, 1841, the brig *Creole,* of Richmond, with a cargo of 135 slaves left Hampton Roads for New Orleans. The negroes, under Madison Washington, killed one of the owners, took possession of the vessel and steered her into the port of Nassau. There those slaves not expressly charged with murder were set at liberty, and though the administration demanded their surrender they were not given up. The experience of the *Creole* was not singular, several cases of a similar nature being recorded. These facts showed the danger of navigating the Bahama channel after 1833, and at least one reason for preferring the overland route down the Tennessee valley was an expectation of avoiding such accidents.—(See Wilson's Rise and Fall of the Slave Power, Vol. I. pp. 443-444; Lalor's Cyclopedia of Political Science, etc., Vol. I. pp. 709-710.)

fretful agitation of leaders soon to be hushed in the tempest of war.

No Republican electoral ticket was presented in the great political battle of 1860 for the suffrage of Tennessee voters, and had any citizen openly advocated the election of Mr. Lincoln he would have had to endure insult or injury, or to abandon his home. This explains why the successful candidates received no vote in all the State. As "Parson" Brownlow, selecting extreme abolition and secession types, characteristically expressed it, his people were equally opposed to the William L. Garrisons and the William L. Yanceys of politics.[1] In this situation the supporters of Bell, Breckenridge and Douglas were left to contend for victory among themselves. Addresses of the time reveal not only the emotions of individual speakers, but the excited state of public opinion. The attitude of Constitutional Union men was vigorously stated in a debate at Knoxville by Nathaniel G. Taylor, an elector on the Bell and Everett ticket. "The people of East Tennessee," said the orator, "are determined to maintain the Union by force of arms against any movement from the South throughout their region of country to assail the government at Washington with violence, and that the secessionists of the cotton States in attempting to carry out their nefarious design to destroy the Republic would have to march over his dead body and the dead bodies of thousands of East Tennessee mountaineers slain in battle."[2]

When Yancey came up from Alabama to "precipitate" this section into rebellion the intrepid Brownlow made a similar reply.[3] The energy or the elegance of such utterances may be questioned, but the deeds of loyal Tennesseans during

[1] Brownlow's Book, p. 52.
[2] The Loyal Mountaineers of Tennessee, pp. 80-81.
[3] Brownlow's Book, p. 67.

eventful years to follow are evidence alike of the sincerity of the speakers and their insight into the temper of the times.

Except Tennessee, all the States that attempted secession did so by means of revolutionary bodies styled conventions; this description of them is justified both by the general powers of administration and government which they assumed and by the fact that the legislatures in convoking them transcended their authority, the members of every State legislature being "bound by oath or affirmation to support" the Federal Constitution, which forms a part of the fundamental law of each commonwealth. Though the Legislature of Tennessee, following the example of law-making bodies in other disloyal States, passed a "Convention Bill," it was promptly defeated by a majority of 13,204 in a total vote of more than 120,000. Notwithstanding the constitutional prohibition that "no State shall enter into any treaty, alliance, or confederation,"[1] the Legislature on May 1 authorized Governor Harris to appoint commissioners to form a military league with the Confederate States. Six days later the relations entered into by these agents were ratified in a secret session, the State government thereby turning over temporarily to the President of the Confederacy its entire military force. These matters disposed of, the plans of disunionists were completed by the passage on the same day of a declaration of independence and an ordinance dissolving all Federal relations between Tennessee and the United States. Though this measure was to be voted upon a month later, the Legislature, as if anticipating the result, adopted and ratified the Confederate constitution. What was so ardently desired by secessionists was finally accomplished, and on June 24 the Governor declared his State out of the Union, the vote being 104,019 for, and 47,238 against, separation.[2] The Tennes-

[1] Art. I. sec. 10, Constitution of the United States.
[2] McPherson's Pol. Hist., p. 5.

see Legislature did not assume the functions of a secession convention till after the commencement of hostilities; but from that date the forms of law ceased to be seriously regarded. While the disunion party scored a present triumph, loyalist leaders like Horace Maynard, Thomas A. R. Nelson and Andrew Johnson, at the imminent risk of injury or even of death, were speaking and working actively against the spirit of secession. The strong Union feeling thus excited resulted ultimately in local insurrections and in the meeting, June 17, of a convention at Greeneville in which a remonstrance was adopted and a committee appointed to petition the Legislature for the separation of East Tennessee and such counties of Middle Tennessee as were willing to coöperate in the formation of a new commonwealth. But the presence there during the following years of veteran Confederate armies prevented Union men from organizing a separate government, and saved the State from the fate of Virginia. All who were known to have had a connection, or who were suspected of sympathy, with this movement were especially obnoxious to the secession party, and at the hands of soldiers were subjected to many indignities. In various ways the feeling of opposition to the Confederacy was intensified, and it was not long before measures of retaliation were considered. Union people were quick to perceive the advantage which the South derived from the use of railways within the State, and, in expectation of assistance from Federal forces in Kentucky, five railroad bridges were burned. East Tennesseeans, however, were destined to be sorely disappointed in the matter of aid from the Union army; and, without effective organization or arms, were easily captured or dispersed. Of the former, many were sent as prisoners of war to Alabama, hundreds were crowded into loathsome jails in the State and others hanged, with circumstances of deliberate cruelty, near the scenes of their alleged crimes.

These were among the outrages to which Mr. Lincoln referred in his letter to the Federal commander. By Horace Maynard a Representative, and Andrew Johnson a Senator, in Congress the President was kept very accurately informed of events in the State and often importuned to relieve their constituents. This he constantly endeavored to do, but his intentions were effectually defeated by the inactivity of General Buell, who cherished other plans for destroying his antagonist. More than two years were to elapse, from the time President Lincoln urged his policy, before Tennesseeans received any aid from Federal armies; long before that time they had been ruthlessly punished for their patriotism, and then their oppressors were chastised by the hand of an abler warrior than General Buell.

Within a month from the date of President Lincoln's letter of January 6 General Grant had possession of Fort Henry and, ten days later, February 16, received the surrender of Fort Donelson. Nashville, becoming unsafe, was evacuated on February 23, 1862; the State appeared for the first time to be slipping from the grasp of the Confederacy, and a question, hitherto more or less academic, presented itself for practical settlement. In the territory from which hostile armies were reluctantly retiring there would be involved a great derangement in the administration of local civil law from the necessary displacement there of all officials heretofore acting in obedience to the Confederate States.

By other Union victories in the Spring of 1862 the same situation confronted the Federal Government in Arkansas, in North Carolina and in Louisiana. Indeed, this identical question arose as early as 1861 in Virginia and Missouri, but in the former the rebel government was abrogated by a delegate convention that restored a loyal government from which in due time sprang the separate State of West Virginia. In Missouri a lawfully chosen convention appointed a pro-

TENNESSEE

visional government in sympathy with the Union. This subject, however, will be more conveniently discussed elsewhere.

When General Johnston received tidings of the disaster at Donelson he retired with his army to Murfreesboro, leaving Nashville, which he was unable to protect, a scene of panic and dismay, first advising Governor Harris to secure the public archives and convoke the Legislature elsewhere. It was in these circumstances that President Lincoln, on the same day, February 23, nominated, and the Senate, March 5, 1862, confirmed, Andrew Johnson as military governor of Tennessee with the rank of brigadier-general. As the commission antedates the action of the Senate by two days the President, no doubt, consulted the leaders of that body relative to the contemplated nomination, and received assurance of its favorable consideration.

Nothing in any way connected with the appointment of Senator Johnson, who was destined to act so conspicuous a part in the important and difficult work of reconstruction, can fail to be of interest, and any account of the execution of his office would be incomplete without some observations on the nature of his commission of which the following is a copy:

WAR DEPARTMENT, *March 3, 1862.*

To the HON. ANDREW JOHNSON:

SIR: You are hereby appointed military governor of the State of Tennessee, with authority to exercise and perform, within the limits of that State, all and singular the powers, duties, and functions pertaining to the office of military governor, including the power to establish all necessary offices, tribunals, etc.

EDWIN M. STANTON,
Secretary of War.[1]

Quoting the essential part of this document a recent coöperative work has this comment: " The office [that of military governor] was new to the laws and history of the State

[1] Misc. Doc. No. 55, H. of R., 1 Sess. 39th Cong., p. 5.

and country. Its powers and duties were limited only by the will of one man, the occupant." [1] From the commission itself we derive our prime conception of both the nature of the office and the functions which it comprehended. The authority of the incumbent extended to the exercise, within the limits of Tennessee, of all "the powers, duties, and functions pertaining to the office of military governor." Nothing in this language implies that the office was of recent creation. Nor is its nature to be discovered by a perusal of the supplemental authority contained in the President's letter of September 19, 1863, to Governor Johnson, for the official conduct of the latter on his arrival in Nashville can not be seriously thought to have been influenced by instructions received nineteen months later. It is perfectly true, as Mr. Ira P. Jones, author of the chapter on Reconstruction in Tennessee, asserts, that the office of military governor had never been exercised within that State; but it is not a fact that it was new to the laws and history of the " country," if by this indefinite expression he means the United States. During the war with Mexico the American people had been made familiar with military commissions and with military governors. Secretary Marcy prepared, June 3, 1846, for General Stephen W. Kearny the following instructions: " Should you conquer and take possession of New Mexico and Upper California, or considerable places in either, you will establish temporary civil governments therein." [2] To this direction general rules of conduct were added, and the letter authorized the assurance that " It is the wish and design of the United States to provide for them [the people of New Mexico] a free government with the least possible delay, similar to that which exists in our Territories." By virtue of this authority General Kearny appointed Charles Bent governor of New

[1] Why The Solid South? p. 170.
[2] Cutt's Conquest of California and New Mexico, p. 246.

Mexico. Mr. Polk in his Message of July 6, 1848, to Congress maintained that with the termination of war his power to establish temporary civil governments over New Mexico and California had ceased; the legality of their previous existence he justified by the law of nations. By cession to the United States, the government of Mexico no longer pretended to any control over them.[1] President Polk, differing from other leaders of his party, held that "until Congress shall act, the inhabitants will be without any organized government."[2] But Congress, notwithstanding urgent appeals of the Executive, moved very deliberately in the matter of abolishing the office of military governor. In May, 1847, Colonel Richard B. Mason assumed the office of Governor and commander-in-chief of the United States forces in California. Two months after ratification of the treaty with Mexico he received notice of the fact, but no intimation that the civil government instituted by the President was discontinued. Without other instructions than an order to extend over California "the revenue laws and tariff of the United States" he, as well as his successor, General Riley, continued the existing government.

After affirming the legality of its institution the United States Supreme Court (Cross *vs.* Harrison, p. 193, 16 Howard) says that the existing government did not cease as a consequence of the restoration of peace; the President might have dissolved it, but he did not do so. Congress could have put an end to it, but that was not done. "The right inference from the inaction of both is, that it was meant to be continued until it had been legislatively changed." In fact it was so continued until the people in convention formed a government, subsequently recognized by Congress, when California was admitted during the autumn of 1850 as a State.

[1] Statesman's Manual, Vol. IV. p. 1742.
[2] Ibid.

The authority, then, of both political departments, as well as the more deliberate opinion of the judicial branch, of the General Government had established a precedent with which Mr. Lincoln was thoroughly familiar; for, by a singular coincidence, both he and Mr. Johnson were serving together in the Thirtieth Congress, which began its first session in December, 1847. They participated in, or were interested spectators of, all those stirring scenes that marked the beginning of one of the last legislative victories of slavery; so that this portion at least of American history was not strange to either the President or the Senator from Tennessee.

The question whether Tennessee was within or without the Union will be reserved for more ample discussion farther on; it is sufficient to observe here that its territory was held by an adverse party and its government hostile to the national authority. If the administration of Colonel Mason and his successor in California was not regarded by President Lincoln as a sufficient basis for his action there was still left an undoubted foundation. The appointment was deemed an element of strength to the Union forces operating in Tennessee, and, in this view, the act was entirely within the power of the President as Commander-in-Chief of the army and navy of the United States. Though its wisdom may be questioned and its results dismissed with a sneer, it was not a novelty nor can his admirers claim for Mr. Lincoln the merit of its invention; and if in its origin the office had a bearing on the extension, its present application was not wholly unconnected with the abolition of slavery. The remaining pages of this chapter and the two succeeding ones will be employed in tracing rapidly the operation of the system of military governors in those States in which it was seriously attempted to be enforced.

The movements of contending armies had already obliterated in many districts of Tennessee almost every trace of civil government, and when State officials hurried away to Memphis, where Governor Harris had reassembled the Legislature, they left behind them an uncontrolled mob which General Forrest found it necessary to charge with his cavalry to remove a portion of Confederate military stores that had not been distributed among the poor or perished in the prevailing anarchy.[1] General Grant had already, on February 22, from Fort Donelson, issued an order that "no courts will be allowed to act under State authority, but all cases coming within reach of the military arm will be adjudicated by the authorities the Government has established within the State. Martial law is therefore declared to extend over West Tennessee." The order added, "whenever a sufficient number of citizens return to their allegiance to maintain law and order over the territory, the military restriction here indicated will be removed."[2] Union troops under General Nelson having occupied the city on the 25th, Governor Johnson on his arrival, March 12, 1862, from his seat in the United States Senate was not under the necessity of employing the harsh discipline of General Forrest to restore order in the deserted capital. For this part of his career he was, however, severely censured by political adversaries in Tennessee. Detached from their historical settings, indeed, his acts could justly be described as tyrannical. But it is precisely these figures in the back-ground that are necessary to harmonize the whole and set before us in its proper light a truthful picture of the times. As his professions preceded his administrative acts it is proper to introduce this portion of the subject by quoting from a speech which he delivered in Nashville the evening after his arrival. Five days later, March 18, it was printed under the style of "An Appeal to the People" of Tennessee. After some general observations on the tran-

[1] The Lost Cause, p. 209.
[2] Ann. Cycl., 1862, p. 763.

quil and prosperous existence of the State in the Union, and on the honors by which many of her sons had been distinguished, he noticed the fact that the very leaders of secession themselves had been the recipients of Federal bounty and patronage; had taken oaths to support the Constitution and yet labored to overturn Federal authority. Entering fairly upon his theme, he continued:

> Meanwhile the State Government has disappeared. The Executive has abdicated; the Legislature has dissolved; the Judiciary is in abeyance. The great ship of State . . . has been suddenly abandoned by its officers and mutinous crew, and left to float at the mercy of the winds, and to be plundered by every rover upon the deep.

Pausing to enumerate many acts of spoliation, he resumes:

> In such a lamentable crisis the Government of the United States could not be unmindful of its high constitutional obligation to guarantee to every State in this Union a republican form of government, an obligation which every State has a direct and immediate interest in having observed towards every other State. . . . This obligation the national Government is now attempting to discharge. I have been appointed, in the absence of the regular and established State authorities, as Military Governor for the time being, to preserve the public property of the State, to give the protection of law actively enforced to her citizens, and, as speedily as may be, to restore her government to the same condition as before the existing rebellion.

The "regular and established State authorities," to whom Governor Johnson refers, were, of course, none other than those officials who administered affairs in Tennessee before the 6th of May. Of these some had actually abandoned their offices, while others had subordinated their functions to a power hostile to the constitution of the State. He proceeded:

> These offices must be filled temporarily, until the State shall be restored so far to its accustomed quiet, that the people can peaceably assemble at the ballot-box and select agents of their own choice. . . .
> I shall, therefore, as early as practicable, designate for various positions under the State and county governments, from among my fellow-citizens, persons of probity and intelligence, and bearing true allegiance to the Constitution and Government of the United States, who will execute the functions of their respective offices until their places can be

filled by the action of the people. Their authority, when their appointment shall have been made, will be accordingly respected and observed.
. . . Those who through the dark and weary night of rebellion have maintained their allegiance to the Federal Government will be honored. The erring and misguided will be welcomed on their return. And while it may become necessary, in vindicating the violated majesty of the law, and in reasserting its imperial sway, to punish intelligent and conscious treason in high places, no merely retaliatory or vindictive policy will be adopted.[1]

To all who in private and unofficial capacity had assumed an attitude of hostility to the Government amnesty was offered for all past acts and declarations upon condition of yielding obedience to the supremacy of the laws. This the Governor advised them to do. Though the "Appeal," brief, clear and characterized by the best temper, is a state paper of decided merit, there were many classes still residing at the capital upon whom it made little impression. The mayor and the city council were ordered to take the oath of allegiance to the United States, and on their refusal were imprisoned. Of the harshness of this measure it need only be observed that the essence of government is to govern, and had the new executive failed on this occasion to assert authority his administration would have been wrecked at the outset. For printing seditious matter the press was placed under restraint, and within a few months it was found necessary to punish with unusual severity, even ministers of the gospel. Clergymen, with a few exceptions, were not only hostile to the Union but actually encouraged treason from their pulpits. These offenders Governor Johnson summoned to take the oath of allegiance or to depart from the State. They appeared before him, as commanded to, refused compliance, but asked time for deliberation; this being granted, to the full extent desired, and still persisting in their refusal they were placed in confinement. That they were not proceeded against with

[1] Life and Speeches of Andrew Johnson, pp. 451-456. Boston: Little, Brown & Co. 1866.

undue haste appears from an entry in a diary kept by one of Governor Johnson's biographers which fixes the date as June 28.[1] Three months had fully elapsed since the arrival of Mr. Johnson before the ministers were punished for their seditious utterances. To prevent interference with his executive functions he sometimes imprisoned judges. Other measures no less arbitrary have been the subject of much criticism. He declared that whenever a loyal citizen was maltreated five or more sympathizers with the Rebellion should be arrested and dealt with as the nature of the case appeared to require. When the property of Union men was destroyed remuneration should be made them from the property of the disloyal. The President seems to have approved of these reprisals. Nothing more clearly shows the demoralized condition of society in Tennessee than the necessity of adopting measures similar to those employed eight centuries before by the Danish and Norman conquerors of England to protect their followers from private assassination by the natives. With the natural leaders of the people, including bankers, physicians and clergymen, encouraging treason, men of inferior intelligence and station could not be expected to remain peaceful and contented citizens, and as preachers of sedition seldom lack numerous and sympathetic audiences the spirit of lawlessness increased. The Governor himself was threatened with assassination in the public streets and in public meetings, but he set such menaces at defiance and on at least one occasion addressed an assembly with his pistol on a desk before him.

But the repression of the disloyal and the restoration of order by no means included the whole of his duties. Functions not less important remain to be noticed. To the duties of governor and general he added those of quartermaster

[1] Life, Speeches, and Services of Andrew Johnson, pp. 101-104. Philadelphia: T. B. Peterson & Brothers.

and judge. Though thousands of loyal people flocked to him for arms and supplies, he proved equal to every demand, and from their number raised an army that did gallant service in the field. He fed, clothed and sheltered the poor without regard to the army in which their natural protectors were serving. Thus redressing grievances, relieving want and reinstating courts he worked with an intelligent and tireless energy, and when the timid prudence of General Buell would have allowed Nashville to fall into the hands of the enemy " the courage of Governor Johnson," said a panegyrist, " stood a bulwark for its defence." [1] He had been scarcely three months in office when President Lincoln described him as " a true and valuable man, indispensable to us in Tennessee." His zeal, his intense fidelity to the Union, his tremendous energy and undoubted courage peculiarly fitted him to rule in turbulent times. At the outset the only agencies left for the protection of life, liberty and property were force and arbitrary will; these he did not hesitate to employ.

The foregoing account does not notice his activity in another field. His ultimate object, the establishment of civil authority throughout Tennessee, was kept constantly in view. To prepare for this event he addressed in May, 1862, large assemblies at Nashville and Murfreesboro, and in June at Columbia and Shelbyville.[2] This work, however, was brought suddenly to an end later in the summer by General Bragg's raid into Kentucky.

From what has been related it appears, and the opinion will grow stronger with the progress of this narrative, that in appointing a military governor of Tennessee President Lincoln intended no more than to revive an office already known

[1] Memorial Addresses on the Life and Character of Andrew Johnson, pp. 76-80; Memoir by Frank Moore, pp. xxvi-xxvii in Life and Speeches of Andrew Johnson. Boston: Little, Brown & Co.
[2] Life of Andrew Johnson, pp. 98-101; Philadelphia: T. B. Peterson & Brothers.

to the people of the United States; and though Mr. Johnson was expected ultimately to reinaugurate a loyal government throughout the State, his office was regarded primarily as an inexpensive means of holding territory wrested from, and assisting in military operations against, an enemy. Indeed, it is only in this view that his administration of the office can be regarded as a success, and that it was so considered in the North his nomination on the ticket with Mr. Lincoln is undoubted proof.

Besides several colored regiments, the records for 1863 show that 25,000 Tennesseeans were then serving in the Union army, and every succeeding month increased their number.[1] That the political advantage to be gained by restoring a loyal government was not the only or even the principal purpose of the President may be fairly inferred from the following letter:

> I am told you have at least thought of raising a negro military force. In my opinion the country now needs no specific thing so much as some man of your ability and position to go to this work. When I speak of your position, I mean that of an eminent citizen of a slave state and himself a slaveholder. The colored population is the great available and yet unavailed of force for restoring the Union. The bare sight of 50,000 armed and drilled black soldiers upon the banks of the Mississippi would end the rebellion at once; and who doubts that we can present that sight if we but take hold in earnest? If you have been thinking of it, please do not dismiss the thought.[2]

Besides supporting the view of the military governors taken above, this letter also makes it evident that the pressure of events had already convinced Mr. Lincoln that to save the Union it was necessary to possess the untrammeled use of every national resource.

As early as June 8, 1862, the State was included in the department of General Halleck, who ten days later was re-

[1] Ann. Cycl., 1863, p. 828.
[2] Letters and State Papers of Abraham Lincoln, Vol. II. p. 318.

quested by Mr. Lincoln to report any information of value relative thereto. The thought of a movement into East Tennessee was in the mind of the President again on June 30, when he informed the commander that he regarded the possession of the railroad near Cleveland fully as important as the taking of Richmond. Halleck, concurring in this opinion, telegraphed Buell that " the capture of East Tennessee should be the main object of the campaign," the department commander believing its occupation would put an end to guerrilla warfare both in that region and Kentucky.

The inactivity of General Rosecrans for six months after the battle of Murfreesboro left in the interior of the State a strong Confederate force whose presence discouraged all but the most pronounced loyalists; these, by means of meetings and speeches, kept a latent Union feeling alive. A convention, called by Brownlow, Maynard and others, was held at Nashville, July 1, 1863. Delegates were in attendance from forty counties; they took an oath of allegiance to the United States, and in a set of resolutions pronounced the various secession laws and ordinances void. Deeming it vitally important to choose a legislature, they invited Governor Johnson to issue writs of election as soon as expedient; with this request, however, he did not then think it prudent to comply.

Other eyes were observing with interest the progress of events within the State. General Hurlbut, writing from Memphis, August 11, 1863, relative to the political situation in Arkansas, said he was satisfied that Tennessee was " ready, by overwhelming majorities, to repeal the act of secession, establish a fair system of gradual emancipation, and tender herself back to the Union. I have discouraged [he said] any action on this subject here until East Tennessee is delivered. When that is done, so that her powerful voice may be heard, let Governor Johnson call an election for members of the

Legislature, and that Legislature call a Convention, and in sixty days the work will be done." [1]

This desirable event was not long delayed, for by brilliant though bloodless victories both Knoxville and Chattanooga early in the following month were in possession of Federal armies. Then President Lincoln wrote his letter of September 11, which, because of its great importance, deserves to be reproduced in full:

> All Tennessee is now clear of armed insurrectionists. You need not to be reminded that it is the nick of time for reinaugurating a loyal State government. Not a moment should be lost. You and the coöperating friends there can better judge of the ways and means than can be judged by any here. I only offer a few suggestions. The reinauguration must not be such as to give control of the State and its representation in Congress to the enemies of the Union, driving its friends there into political exile. The whole struggle for Tennessee will have been profitless to both State and nation if it so ends that Governor Johnson is put down and Governor Harris is put up. It must not be so. You must have it otherwise. Let the reconstruction be the work of such men only as can be trusted for the Union. Exclude all others, and trust that your government so organized will be recognized here as being the one of republican form to be guaranteed to the State, and to be protected against invasion and domestic violence. It is something on the question of time to remember that it cannot be known who is next to occupy the position I now hold, nor what he will do. I see that you have declared in favor of emancipation in Tennessee, for which may God bless you. Get emancipation into your new State Government—Constitution—and there will be no such word as fail for your case. The raising of colored troops, I think, will greatly help every way. [2]

The reference in this communication to emancipation is explained by the fact that, in deference to the wishes of Andrew Johnson and other Tennessee loyalists, the President in his proclamation of January 1, 1863, had not mentioned that State.[3]

Believing that his commission as military governor did not

[1] Abraham Lincoln, A History by Nicolay & Hay, Vol. VIII. p. 440.
[2] Letters and State Papers of Lincoln, Vol. II. p. 405.
[3] History of Abraham Lincoln, by Isaac N. Arnold, p. 303.

confer upon him powers adequate to every emergency that might arise in the important work of restoring a loyal government Mr. Johnson, to supply this deficiency, prepared a letter which he submitted for the approval of President Lincoln, who amended or modified it to read as follows:

> In addition to the matters contained in the orders and instructions given you by the Secretary of War, you are hereby authorized to exercise such powers as may be necessary and proper to enable the loyal people of Tennessee to present such a republican form of State government as will entitle the State to the guaranty of the United States therefor, and to be protected under such State government by the United States against invasion and domestic violence, all according to the fourth section of the fourth article of the Constitution of the United States.[1]

This supplemental authority is dated September 19, and the private letter enclosing it informs Governor Johnson why his draft was altered.

It was about this time, while the President was thus urging Governor Johnson, that General Rosecrans, surrounded by a victorious enemy, inquired of Mr. Lincoln whether it would not be well "to offer a general amnesty to all officers and soldiers in the Rebellion?" In his reply next day the President, referring first, as was his wont, to the military situation, added, "I intend doing something like what you suggest whenever the case shall appear ripe enough to have it accepted in the true understanding rather than as a confession of weakness and fear."[2] The removal soon after of General Rosecrans from his command and the fortunate appearance at Chattanooga of those great soldiers of the first rank, Grant, Sherman, Thomas and Sheridan, made at Lookout Mountain and Mission Ridge the occasion which the President so much desired, and on December 8, 1863, he issued his famous Proclamation of Amnesty and Reconstruction, a copy of which was transmitted with his third annual

[1] Letters and State Papers of Abraham Lincoln, Vol. II. p. 408.
[2] Ibid. p., 419.

message to Congress. The impression which its candid tone produces on the mind of a student to-day was the impression made at the time of its appearance upon thoughtful and enlightened men everywhere. Nicolay and Hay in an interesting chapter of their valuable history describe the satisfaction, and even enthusiasm, with which it was received by the adherents of all parties in Congress. This proclamation, around which the later controversy raged, was authorized by act of Congress approved July 17, 1862, which, among other provisions, empowered the President "at any time" thereafter "to extend to persons who may have participated in the existing Rebellion in any State or part thereof, pardon and amnesty, with such exceptions and at such time and on such conditions as he may deem expedient for the public welfare." The time for the exercise of this discretion Mr. Lincoln believed had now arrived. Like every measure conceived in his fruitful mind it had been maturely considered and was especially fortunate in being introduced by the concluding paragraphs of the message. The very note of sincerity itself rings in these weighty lines. Perhaps it was the suggestion of unuttered arguments that gave a temporary adherence to the Executive plan, which, we are told, was put forth because "It is now desired by some persons heretofore engaged in said rebellion to resume their allegiance to the United States, and to reinaugurate loyal State governments within and for their respective States." The proclamation informed "all persons who have, directly or by implication, participated in the existing rebellion, except as hereinafter excepted, that a full pardon is hereby granted to them and each of them, with restoration of all rights of property, except as to slaves, and in property cases where rights of third parties shall have intervened, and upon the condition that every such person shall take and subscribe an oath, and thenceforward keep and maintain said oath inviolate; and which oath shall be registered for permanent preservation." This oath bound the subscriber thenceforth to "faithfully support, protect, and defend the Constitution of the United States, and the union of the States thereunder"; to "abide by and faithfully support all acts of Congress passed during the existing rebellion with reference to slaves" unless repealed, modified or held void by Congress, or by decision of the Supreme Court; to support "all proclamations of the President made during the existing rebellion having reference to slaves, so long and so far as not modified or declared void by decision of the Supreme Court."

The classes excepted from the benefits of the amnesty were all persons "who are, or shall have been, civil or diplomatic officers or agents of the so-called Confederate Government; all who have left judicial stations under the United States to aid the rebellion; all who are, or shall have been, military or naval officers of said so-called Confederate Government above the rank of colonel in the army or lieutenant in the navy; all who left seats in the United States Congress to aid the rebellion; all who resigned commissions in the Army or Navy of the United States and afterward aided the rebellion; and all who have engaged in any way in treating colored persons, or white persons in charge of such, otherwise than lawfully as prisoners of war, and which persons may have been found in the United States service, as soldiers, seamen, or in any other capacity." [1]

The proclamation provided further that whenever, in any of the States in rebellion, "a number of persons, not less than one tenth in number of the votes cast in such State at the presidential election" of 1860, "each having taken the oath aforesaid and not having since violated it, and being a qualified voter by the election law of the State existing immediately before the so-called act of secession, and excluding

[1] Letters and State Papers of Lincoln, Vol. II. p. 443.

all others, shall reëstablish a State government which shall be republican, and in nowise contravening said oath, such shall be recognized as the true government of the State and the State shall receive thereunder the benefits of the Constitutional provision which declares that 'The United States shall guaranty to every State in this Union a republican form of Government, and shall protect each of them against invasion; and, on application of the legislature, or of the executive (when the legislature cannot be convened), against domestic violence.'"

Any provision adopted by such State relative to its freed people "which shall recognize and declare their permanent freedom, provide for their education, and which may yet be consistent as a temporary arrangement with their present condition as a laboring, landless, and homeless class, will not be objected to by the national executive." In constructing a loyal government in any State, it was thought not improper to suggest that "the name of the State, the boundary, the subdivisions, the constitution, and the general code of laws, as before the rebellion, be maintained, subject only to the modifications made necessary by the conditions hereinbefore stated, and such others, if any, not contravening said conditions, and which may be deemed expedient by those framing the new State government."

To avoid every occasion of misunderstanding it was expressly stated that the proclamation "has no reference to States wherein loyal State governments have all the while been maintained." The President disclaimed any authority to admit members to seats in Congress, each House being "the judge of the elections, returns, and qualifications of its own members."[1]

In conclusion it was observed that "while the mode presented is the best the executive can suggest, with his present

[1] Art. I. sec. 5, Constitution of the U. S.

impressions, it must not be understood that no other possible mode would be acceptable."[1]

To get an enrollment of those willing to take the oath prescribed in the amnesty proclamation the President, about the middle of January, 1864, sent an agent to Tennessee, as he had already sent one to Louisiana and to Arkansas. About the same time Governor Johnson himself was considering the subject of reconstruction; and on the 21st, to begin proceedings, called a public meeting at Nashville. It was on this occasion that he said: "Treason must be made odious, traitors must be punished and impoverished;" slavery he pronounced dead and declared that reconstruction must leave it out of view. The meeting, which was largely attended, adopted resolutions recommending a constitutional convention and pledged support of only those candidates who favored immediate and universal emancipation. The Governor, however, was cautious, and, January 26, 1864, issued a call for an election, on the first Saturday of March following, for the choice of only county officers.

The ex-Confederate and the loyalist having been placed by the amnesty proclamation on an equal footing, some dissatisfaction was aroused among unconditional Union men. To retain the confidence of this class and to set at rest the hostile feeling thus excited in the State, Governor Johnson framed the oath of allegiance more stringently than Mr. Lincoln had done. This variance occasioned discussion and delay and brought inquiries and protests to the President, who, to prevent confusion, telegraphed, February 20, 1864, Warren Jordan, of Nashville, as follows:

In county elections you had better stand by Governor Johnson's plan; otherwise you will have conflict and confusion. I have seen his plan.[2]

[1] Letters and State Papers of Lincoln, Vol. II. pp. 443-444.
[2] Ibid., p. 486.

A week later he assured the Hon. E. H. East, Secretary of State for Tennessee, that

> There is no conflict between the oath of amnesty in my proclamation of eighth December, 1863, and that prescribed by Governor Johnson in his proclamation of the twenty-sixth ultimo.[1]

While it is perfectly true that no discrepancy existed between the proclamation of the President and that of the military governor, the latter required an additional test. This the communication to Mr. East does not discuss.

To avoid, however, any possible mischief from this source Mr. Lincoln, March 26, issued a supplemental proclamation which explained that the amnesty applied only to "persons who being yet at large and free from any arrest, confinement, or duress, shall voluntarily come forward and take the said oath, with the purpose of restoring peace and establishing the national authority."[2] Prisoners excluded from the amnesty offered in the proclamation of December 8, like all other offenders, might apply to the executive for clemency and have their applications receive due consideration. This oath, it was made known, could be taken before any commissioned officer of the United States, civil, military or naval, or before any officer authorized to administer oaths, in a State or Territory not in insurrection. Such officers were empowered to give certificates thereon to persons by whom the oath was taken and subscribed. The original records, after transmission to the Department of State, were to be there deposited and to remain in the Government archives. The Secretary of State was required to keep a register of such oaths and upon application to issue certificates in proper cases in the customary form.

Meanwhile an election, the returns of which are extremely meagre, had been held on March 5 for the choice of county

[1] Letters and State Papers of Lincoln, Vol. II. p. 487.
[2] Ibid., pp. 504-505.

officers. Though the event was not without influence in confirming the faith of Unionists, it was chiefly of value in attracting the attention of the disloyal to the chances afforded by the proclamation of rehabilitating themselves in their former political rights. The result, however, was not so favorable as was expected by Governor Johnson or the President, and reconstruction in Tennessee once more sank to rest. From this condition it was again revived by the irrepressible Union men of the State. The East Tennessee convention of 1861, by appointing a permanent committee, had kept its organization alive. In April or May, 1864, this body called a convention at Knoxville to discuss reconstruction. Of this gathering one element favored the Crittenden Resolutions; the other, immediate emancipation. Probably it was this antagonism that prevented further action. The next we hear is that Brownlow and others signed a call for a second convention, which was held at Nashville on September 5. In this body forty or fifty counties were represented, some of them irregularly; that is, by volunteer delegates. This assembly recommended the election of a constitutional convention, the abolition of slavery in the State, and provided for taking part in the approaching Presidential election. The programme, however, was only partially carried out. On September 30, Governor Johnson issued a proclamation for holding the election, at which Union voters, so far as the unsettled condition of military operations permitted, cast their ballots for electors of President and Vice-President. It does not appear that in this election any attempt was made to choose a governor, a legislature or a constitutional convention; but that which met in July, 1863, constituted an executive committee, composed of five members from each division of the State, which after the Presidential election issued calls for a State convention at Nashville, December 19, 1864. "The people meet," said the call, "to take such steps as wisdom may direct to restore the State of Tennessee to its once honored status in the great national Union.

. . . . . .

" If you cannot meet in your counties, come upon your own personal responsibility. It is the assembling of Union men for the restoration of their own commonwealth to life and a career of success." [1]

Hood's advance upon Nashville preventing a response to this address, the convention did not meet till January 9, 1865. The enemy had then been dispersed. The State being free from further alarms of war, the convention met and proposed important alterations in the State constitution.

The first article provided: " That slavery and involuntary servitude, except as a punishment for crime, whereof the party shall have been duly convicted, are hereby forever abolished and prohibited throughout the State "; also that " The legislature shall make no law recognizing the right of property in man." The old constitution of Tennessee prohibited the assembly from passing laws to emancipate slaves without the consent of the owner; that prohibition was now removed. " The declaration of independence and ordinance dissolving the federal relations between the State of Tennessee and the United States of America," passed by the Legislature, May 6, 1861, was abrogated and declared " an act of treason and usurpation, unconstitutional, null and void." All laws, ordinances, and resolutions of the usurped State government passed on and after the 6th day of May, 1861, providing for the issuance of State bonds; also all notes of the Bank of Tennessee or any of its branches issued on or after May 6, 1861, and all debts created in the name of the State by said authority were declared unconstitutional, null and void. Future legislatures were restrained from the redemption of said bonds. It was further provided that " The qualification

[1] Misc. Doc. No. 55, p. 5, H. of R., 1 Sess. 39th Cong.

of voters and the limitation of the elective franchise may be determined by the general assembly, which shall first assemble under the amended constitution."

The convention completed its labors on January 26, 1865. The amendatory articles were submitted, February 22, to the people, and ratified by a vote of 21,104 to 40. The schedule provided in the event of ratification that the loyal people of the State should, on the 4th of March next thereafter, proceed by *general ticket* to elect a governor and members to the general assembly to meet in the capitol at Nashville on the first Monday of April, 1865.

A proclamation of Governor Johnson, issued on January 26, referred to the respectable character of the convention and commended its wisdom in submitting for the approval of the electors the result of its deliberations. His executive powers had been employed to enable the people freely to express their judgment on the grave question before them. Provision, he declared, would be made to collect the sentiments of loyal Tennesseeans in the army. The paper concludes with this vigorous exhortation: " Strike down at one blow the institution of slavery, remove the disturbing element from your midst, and by united action restore the State to its ancient moorings again, and you may confidently expect the speedy return of peace, happiness, and prosperity." [1]

About a month later, February 25, he had the happiness to congratulate the people of Tennessee on the favorable result of the election. By their solemn act at the ballot-box the shackles had been stricken from the limbs of more than 275,000 bondmen.

The convention which proposed the constitutional amendments had, in anticipation of its ratification, nominated William G. [" Parson "] Brownlow for Governor, and recommended a full legislative ticket. The nominee of the conven-

[1] Misc. Doc. No. 55, p. 9, H. of R., 1 Sess. 39th Cong.

tion was chosen March 4, almost without opposition, receiving 23,352 votes against 35 scattering. Having been elected on a general ticket the members of both the Senate and House of Representatives received the same support as the Governor. The Legislature met at Nashville, and in a few days thereafter Mr. Brownlow was inaugurated. Civil administration was thus formally begun.

That the successive steps to restoration in Tennessee may be easily traced, the narrative has not been interrupted to relate even matters of undoubted importance. Almost a year before the occurrences described, the Republican national convention had assembled in the city of Baltimore, and on June 6, 1864, unanimously nominated Andrew Johnson for Vice-President on the ticket with Mr. Lincoln. Tidings of the fact aroused great enthusiasm when it became known in Nashville. In addressing an immense meeting called for that occasion Governor Johnson, among other things, said: " While society is in this disordered state, and we are seeking security, let us fix the foundations of our government on principles of eternal justice, which will endure for all time. There are those in our midst who are for perpetuating the institution of slavery. Let me say to you, Tennesseeans, and men from the Northern States, that slavery is dead. It was not murdered by me. I told you long ago what the result would be if you endeavored to go out of the Union to save slavery; and that the result would be bloodshed, rapine, devastated fields, plundered villages and cities; and therefore I urged you to remain in the Union. In trying to save slavery you killed it, and lost your own freedom." [1]

In his letter to Hon. William Dennison, accepting the nomination, he wrote:

> The authority of the Government is supreme, and will admit of no rivalry. No institution can rise above it whether it be slavery or any

[1] Life of Andrew Johnson, pp. 159-160.

organized power. In our happy form of government all must be subordinate to the will of the people, when reflected through the Constitution and the laws made pursuant thereto — State or Federal. This great principle lies at the foundation of every government, and cannot be disregarded without the destruction of the government itself.

In accepting the nomination I might here close, but I cannot forego the opportunity of saying to my old friends of the Democratic party *proper*, with whom I have so long and pleasantly been associated, that the hour has now come when that great party can justly vindicate its devotion to true democratic policy and measures of expediency. The war is a war of great principles. It involves the supremacy and life of the Government itself. If the rebellion triumphs, free government—North and South—fails. If, on the other hand, the Government is successful, as I do not doubt, its destiny is fixed, its basis permanent and enduring, and its career of honor and glory just begun. In a great contest like this, for the existence of free government, the path of duty is patriotism and principle. Minor considerations and questions of administrative policy should give way to the higher duty *of first preserving the Government*, and then there will be time enough to wrangle over the men and measures pertaining to its administration.[1]

For reasons at which Mr. Lincoln hinted in his letter of March 26, 1863, few men in Congress exerted in the beginning of the war so decided an influence upon public opinion in the North as did Mr. Johnson. His conduct as military governor in no way diminished this popularity. His courage in that trying position no less than his devotion to the interests of the Union won him ardent admirers in every loyal State.

Vice-President Hamlin appears to have been the victim of an intrigue which represented him as being no material source of strength to the government and as scarcely loyal to the administration. This injurious suspicion, which seems to have had no substantial basis in truth, happened to coincide with a growing conviction that the Republican party should strengthen itself by placing on the ticket with Lincoln some prominent leader of the opposition. In this connection the names of General Butler, John A. Dix, Daniel S. Dickinson

[1] Life of Andrew Johnson, pp. 160-161. New York: D. Appleton & Co., 1866.

34 LINCOLN'S PLAN OF RECONSTRUCTION

and Andrew Johnson were mentioned. The last named was charged in his administration of the office of military governor with harshness and even with oppression. Investigation proved these rumors to be without foundation, and Mr. Lincoln was not displeased to find them groundless. It does not appear that he was especially favorable to Johnson, but he regarded him as indispensable to the Union cause in Tennessee; Johnson was a slave-holder, was somewhat more outspoken than Butler or Dix, and a more conspicuous representative of the large class known as War Democrats; above all he was an able exponent of Southern Union sentiment and he came from the very heart of the Confederacy. Perhaps no single element of strength made him more acceptable to the majority of the convention than this last consideration. Even these qualifications might not have singled him out for the distinction conferred were it not for the enthusiasm created by a remarkable speech of Horace Maynard, which mentioned Mr. Johnson as a man who "stood in the furnace of treason." His administration as military governor had been distinguished for vigor and ability, and it does not appear that the radical Republicans then regarded his State without the Union. Some of his measures were undoubtedly severe, but the peculiar situation in Tennessee required the employment of methods not adapted to times of peace. Mr. Lincoln could not, of course, show his hand in the Baltimore convention. In fact he repeatedly declined to interfere.[1]

On October 15, 1864, the ten electors on the McClellan ticket presented through Mr. John Lellyett, one of their number, a protest to the President against the proclamation published by Governor Johnson relative to the pending election.

[1] McClure's Lincoln and Men of War Times, pp. 106-108; Blaine's Twenty Years of Congress, Vol. II. p. 7; Hamlin's Life and Times of Hannibal Hamlin, pp. 449-489 and 591-615.

His paper, they asserted, contained provisions for holding elections which differed materially from the mode prescribed by the laws of Tennessee. The proclamation, it was alleged, would admit persons to vote who were not entitled by the State constitution to participate in the election; by another provision which authorized the opening of but one polling-place in each county, many legal voters would be unable to exercise the franchise. The unusual and impracticable test oath proposed, was stated as a further grievance, and they complained generally of military interference with the freedom of elections. To their representations Mr. Lincoln replied orally that General McClellan and his friends could manage their side of the contest in their own way. He could manage his side of it in his way.[1] In a written reply of the 22d, however, the President said that he perceived no military reason for interfering in the matter, and on the same occasion reminded the protestants that the conducting of a Presidential election in Tennessee under the old code had become an impossibility.[2]

In their reply to the written communication of the President, they asserted that an orderly meeting of General McClellan's friends had been broken up by Union soldiers, and a reign of terror inaugurated in Nashville. These acts having been countenanced by Governor Johnson, they announced the withdrawal of the McClellan electoral ticket in Tennessee.[3]

In these circumstances the Union electors were, of course, chosen; but their votes, though offered, were not counted by Congress in the joint convention of February 8, 1865, for the reason that Tennessee was on November 8 preceding in such a state that no free election was held.[4]

[1] McPherson's Pol. Hist., pp. 438-439.
[2] Ibid., p. 425.
[3] Ibid., p. 441.
[4] For a discussion of this subject see Chapter IX.

II

LOUISIANA

THE first movement toward reconstruction in Louisiana, as in the case of Tennessee, was bound up with the war powers of the President, and, no doubt, was made with some expectation of aiding his military plans. The thought of restoring a loyal government there proceeded quite naturally from the peculiar situation in the State. Though not so nearly unanimous for secession as South Carolina, her people acted with energy and promptness when they received tidings of "this last insult and outrage," as the election of Mr. Lincoln was sensationally styled.[1] Three days were deemed sufficient for deliberation, and the convention, January 25, 1861, passed an ordinance of secession. Two weeks before this assembly met at Baton Rouge, the arsenal and the forts, a public building and a revenue cutter had been seized by State troops from New Orleans. In the mint and the custom house of that city more than half a million dollars was secured for the Confederate States, and in accepting these funds the Montgomery Congress expressed its "high sense of the patriotic liberality" of Louisiana.[2] This act of generosity, however, loses much of its merit when it is remembered that both the coin and bullion in the mint, as well as the customs, belonged to the Federal government. Besides, there was then no scarcity of money in the State, for Northern enterprise had found for her cotton and her sugar profit-

---
[1] Ann. Cycl., 1861, p. 427.
[2] McPherson's Pol. Hist., p. 4n.

able markets both at home and abroad. It was benefits of this sort, enjoyed in the Union, that enabled Governor Moore in January, 1861, to report to his Legislature an overflowing treasury.[1] This undoubted prosperity served only to aggravate the war fever. Enthusiasm in New Orleans was only less ardent and general than in Charleston. Business was almost suspended, and by the first of June no less than 16,000 residents of Louisiana were serving in the Confederate army.[2]

President Lincoln's proclamation of April 19 preceding had inaugurated a blockade of every port within the State. The early days of July witnessed the disappearance of Governor Moore's boasted surplus, and during the summer New Orleans became bankrupt;[3] her foreign commerce was destroyed by the blockade, her credit had vanished. Though enlistments continued without interruption, signs of financial distress multiplied with the approach of winter. Rebellion, it was soon discovered, was not attended with unmixed blessings; bad government had produced its usual consequences, and when Governor Taylor, late in the summer of 1862, undertook to raise an army for the defence of his State he was surprised at the universal apathy; neglect and disaster had brought disunionists to a condition little short of hostility to the Richmond government.[4]

Union men in southern Louisiana had not been unobservant of these signs; permanent residents of this portion of the State had, for the most part, maintained their loyalty to the General Government. Indeed, a decided majority of them in the election of 1860 had voted for Bell and Douglas, and though here, as elsewhere in the South, ardent secessionists were found, the proceedings in the convention took the Union

[1] McPherson's Pol. Hist., p. 25; Ann. Cycl., 1861, p. 428.
[2] Ann. Cycl., 1861, p. 432.
[3] Ibid.
[4] Taylor's Destruction and Reconstruction, pp. 102-103.

men by surprise.[1] In the interval they had refrained from violence, but had not become reconciled to oppression.

The importance of New Orleans to their cause had not been overlooked by Confederate authorities, and that city was held firmly in their grasp until the fleet of Captain Farragut, toward the close of April, 1862, steamed up in hostile array before its defences. The occupation by General Butler's army of this strategic position ended in southern Louisiana the activity of the more extreme secessionists, and though some restlessness at the presence of Federal forces was pretended by even Union men, they had not until the surrender made any serious effort to help themselves. Under protection of the army, however, they commenced immediately to form Union associations for the purpose of developing the loyal sentiment in this part of the State. Resolutions recommending an election were passed by these organizations; newspapers discussed the question, and in various ways it was forced upon the attention of the President.[2] The more prudent and intelligent among them began under encouragement of Federal troops to consider measures for relief; the less practical commenced writing complaints to friends in the North.

In a private letter of July 26, 1862, to Hon. Reverdy Johnson, then in New Orleans investigating General Butler's relations with foreign consuls, Mr. Lincoln, noticing a reference to the restlessness of the people under the rule of General Phelps, asks the Maryland Senator to pardon him for believing the complaint "a false pretense." A way to avert the inconveniences arising from military occupation was for the people of Louisiana "simply to take their place in the Union upon the old terms."[3] Writing two days later to

[1] McPherson's Pol. Hist., p. 1.
[2] Ann. Cycl., 1863, p. 589.
[3] Letters and State Papers of Lincoln, Vol. II., pp. 214-215; Ann. Cycl., 1862, p. 650.

Cuthbert Bullett, a Southern gentleman who appears to have enjoyed his personal esteem and confidence, the President, after mentioning difficulties in the way of establishing civil authority in the State, suggested a method of avoiding them: " The people of Louisiana who wish protection to person and property," he wrote, " have but to reach forth their hands and take it. Let them in good faith reinaugurate the national authority, and set up a State government conforming thereto under the Constitution. They know how to do it, and can have the protection of the army while doing it. The army will be withdrawn so soon as such State government can dispense with its presence; and the people of the State can then, upon the old constitutional terms, govern themselves to their own liking." [1] If, however, Union men exerted themselves no further than criticism of the Federal Government, it was more than intimated that there were to be expected greater injuries than military necessity had yet inflicted.

The pressure of events appears even then to have been forcing the President in the direction of emancipation. To August Belmont, of New York, who enclosed the complaints of a New Orleans correspondent, Mr. Lincoln, July 31, 1862, repeated in substance what had already been written to Mr. Bullett, and added: " Those enemies must understand that they cannot experiment for ten years trying to destroy the government, and if they fail still come back into the Union unhurt. If they expect in any contingency to ever have the Union as it was, I join with the writer [Mr. Belmont's correspondent] in saying, ' Now is the time.' " [2]

The appointment in August, 1862, of General George F. Shepley as military governor may be regarded as the first act in the restoration of a loyal government for Louisiana. His selection, though probably intended as a private commendation of the judgment of General Butler, who had

[1] Letters and State Papers of Lincoln, Vol. II., p. 216.
[2] Ibid., pp. 217-218.

already designated him as Mayor of New Orleans, was never considered by that officer adequate atonement for the public censure implied in his removal, December, 1862, from command of the Department of the Gulf.

Upon the Federal occupation of New Orleans and adjacent territory all functions of the disloyal government therein immediately ceased. As controversies were constantly arising the establishment of courts had become a necessity. At first these questions were for the most part adjudicated by General Butler himself, but the pressure of military and other affairs compelled him soon to refer their settlement to civilians or to army officers especially chosen for the purpose. This uncertain system of justice, though immeasurably better than none, led to the institution of courts each of which was known by the name of the officer holding it. Accused persons were brought to trial, and judgments executed by soldiers detailed for such duty. No formal record of proceedings in these tribunals appears to have been kept, though memoranda of judgments rendered were, no doubt, made by an officer who came eventually to be designated as clerk.

For the decision of questions relating exclusively to the force under his command General Butler some time in June, 1862, organized a tribunal known as the Provost Court of the Army of the United States, over which Major Joseph M. Bell presided. Questions in no way connected with the military, especially matters of police and the punishment of crimes, were often submitted for its determination. Aggrieved persons, without reflecting upon the consequence of their acts, naturally appealed for redress to the holder of power. Thus the authority of this institution silently extended, and by the autumn of 1862 it exercised unquestioned jurisdiction over all criminal cases arising in the city of New Orleans.[1] In the absence of courts for adjudicating civil

[1] Ann. Cycl., 1863, p. 586.

questions they, too, were referred to its consideration. All functions of government having been suspended by the capture of the city, it became the duty of the Federal commander, and his right by the laws of war, to provide, among other things, for the administration of justice.

One of the early acts of General Shepley after his appointment as Military Governor was to establish a system of courts for the State. Most of the former officials having fled after the surrender, he was compelled practically to create new tribunals, and this task he greatly simplified by reviving those institutions of justice with which the people of Louisiana were already familiar. John S. Whittaker was accordingly appointed Judge of the Second District Court of the parish of Orleans. Besides possessing in civil matters the ordinary powers of a local court the old tribunal of that name had been a court of probates and successions. The new exercised all the powers of the old court. It should be remembered, however, that the latter derived its authority from the laws of Louisiana, while the former owed its existence to the war powers of the Federal Executive. Its jurisdiction extended to civil cases generally where the defendant resided in the parish of Orleans or was a non-resident of the State.[1]

Judge Hiestand was appointed to the bench of the Fourth District Court of the parish of Orleans. Besides possessing the general authority of other district courts in that parish it entertained appeals from justices' courts; indeed, these constituted a large part of its business.[2]

The Sixth District Court of the parish of Orleans, revived soon after the capture of the city, is, because of the incumbent of that bench, Judge Rufus K. Howell, of greater interest than either of the preceding. Under a commission received from the State of Louisiana before its attempted secession he

[1] Ann. Cycl., 1863, p. 586.
[2] Ibid.

continued to preside over that tribunal while the disunion party ruled New Orleans, and performed his functions up to the very hour of its surrender to the Federal authorities. Having early taken the oath of allegiance to the national Government he was permitted to resume his functions.[1] Like the tribunals mentioned, this court retained and exercised all the powers that it possessed as originally constituted.

These courts, instituted during September and October, 1862, entered upon the discharge of their duties about the 1st of November following. They were the only tribunals of civil jurisdiction in Louisiana, and that jurisdiction was limited, as against defendants resident of the State, to citizens of the parish of Orleans. As to inhabitants beyond the limits of that parish there was no court in which they could be sued. Though the Federal forces held several counties in this condition, their tenure fluctuated with the fortunes of war. A court was therefore needed whose jurisdiction would expand with the advance, and contract with the retreat, of the Union armies. The Provost Court was not deemed adequate, and indeed was never designed to meet such contingencies. To supply this deficiency a tribunal of very extensive powers, designated as "a court of record for the State of Louisiana," was constituted by Executive order on October 20. Of this flexible institution Charles A. Peabody, of New York, a friend of Secretary Seward, was made provisional judge. Besides being empowered to select a prosecuting attorney, a marshal and a clerk, and to make rules for the exercise of his jurisdiction, he was authorized "to hear, try and determine all causes, civil and criminal, including causes in law, equity, revenue and admiralty, and particularly all such powers and jurisdiction as belong to the District and Circuit Courts of the United States, conforming his proceedings, so far as possible, to the course of proceedings and practice

[1] Ann. Cycl., 1863, p. 586.

which has been customary in the Courts of the United States and Louisiana—his judgment to be final and conclusive." These officers were to be paid out of the contingent fund of the War Department, and a copy of the Executive order, certified by the Secretary of War, was "held to be a sufficient commission" for the Judge.

This institution, made up as to its *personnel* in the North, was sent from New York with the great expedition of General Banks constituted and organized for immediate business to Louisiana. Though Judge Peabody, accompanied by Augustus de B. Hughes, Isaac Edward Clarke and George D. Lamont, who had been chosen, respectively, clerk, marshal and prosecuting attorney, arrived in New Orleans December 15, 1862, the opening of court was delayed till the 29th of that month by a change of administration in that Department.[1]

In addition to the tribunals described many other courts were established about this time; of these the Supreme Court of Louisiana is the only one which appears to require especial mention. In former times under the State judicial system appeals had lain to this institution, and it was accordingly held that decisions of the courts now created were subject to its revision. In this manner many of their judgments were stayed and in suspense, so that the new district courts were of little practical benefit. The necessity of a tribunal to remedy this deficiency and adjudicate the accumulated cases of former years soon became apparent, and in April, 1863, Mr. Peabody was appointed Chief Justice of the State Supreme Court; associated with him on this bench were judges chosen from among the people of Louisiana.

Nearly a week before his appointment of Judge Peabody, Mr. Lincoln, by the hand of Hon. John E. Bouligny, who had

[1] Ann. Cycl., 1863, p. 587; Ibid., pp. 770-776. Scott's Reconstruction During the Civil War, pp. 325-326, 328-331, 376.

not left his seat in the House of Representatives when Southern delegations withdrew from Congress, sent to General Butler, Governor Shepley and other Federal officers having authority under the United States in Louisiana a communication requesting each of them to assist Mr. Bouligny in his effort to secure "peace again upon the old terms under the Constitution of the United States."[1] This desirable end was to be attained by the election of "members to the Congress of the United States particularly, and perhaps a legislature, State officers, and United States senators friendly to their object." Federal officers were instructed to give the people a chance to express their wishes at these elections. "Follow forms of law," wrote the President, "as far as convenient, but at all events get the expression of the largest number of the people possible. All see how such action will connect with and affect the proclamation of September 22. Of course the men elected should be gentlemen of character, willing to swear support to the Constitution, as of old, and known to be above reasonable suspicion of duplicity."[2]

Loyal leaders, believing that Northern men holding office under the General Government in Louisiana would be set up as candidates, communicated their fears to the President, who sent to Governor Shepley a fortnight before the election a letter of which the essential portion is as follows:

We do not particularly need members of Congress from there to enable us to get along with legislation here. What we do want is the conclusive evidence that respectable citizens of Louisiana are willing to be members of Congress and to swear support to the Constitution and that other respectable citizens there are willing to vote for them and send them. To send a parcel of Northern men here as representatives, elected, as would be understood (and perhaps really so), at the point of the bayonet, would be disgusting and outrageous; and were I a member of Congress here, I would vote against admitting any such man to a seat.[3]

[1] Letters and State Papers of Lincoln, Vol. II. p. 247.
[2] Ibid.
[3] Ibid., p. 255.

The note of sincerity is unmistakable throughout, and in those Representatives and Senators opposed to Executive policy the concluding sentences especially must have excited strange emotions when they re-read in after years their impassioned attacks in Congress upon that dark spirit who, it was gravely alleged, labored with might unquestioned to subordinate the Legislative branch of Government.

The Union associations referred to appointed committees who waited upon General Shepley and demanded an election. This he hesitated to call until considerable pressure had first been exerted. The sentiments of the President concurring with the local feeling in New Orleans, Shepley finally yielded, and on November 14, 1862, issued a proclamation for an election to be held December 3d following. This election, in the language of his proclamation, was ordered " for the purpose of securing to the loyal electors " of both the First and Second Congressional Districts " their appropriate and lawful representation in the House of Representatives of the United States of America, and of enabling them to avail themselves of the benefits secured by the proclamation of the President of the United States to the people of any State, or part of a State, who shall on the first day of January next be in good faith represented in the Congress of the United States, by members chosen thereto at elections wherein a majority of the qualified voters of such State have participated." [1]

In addition to the qualifications prescribed by the laws of Louisiana, General Shepley required each elector to take an oath of allegiance to the United States, and from among the old and respected citizens of the State appointed sheriffs and commissioners of election, who performed their duties to the entire satisfaction of both candidates and voters. The army, for reasons given above, refrained from all man-

[1] Globe, Part I., 3 Sess. 37th Cong., p. 835.

ner of interference, and no Federal office-holder was a nominee.

For the first time in many years, it was admitted, every qualified elector might freely cast his ballot without fear of intimidation or violence. In a total of 2,643 votes Benjamin F. Flanders was chosen, with little opposition, for the First, and Michael Hahn, by a safe majority, for the Second Congressional District. A larger vote was actually cast for Flanders than had been received by his predecessor, and in both districts 7,760 citizens, or about half the usual number, appeared at the polls. When it is remembered that four thousand soldiers who enlisted in Butler's army from this part of the State did not participate in the contest, that many citizens from this section were serving in the Confederate army and that not a few Union men were exiles in the North or in Europe the vote in this election was by no means light.

With credentials signed by Governor Shepley, Messrs. Hahn and Flanders appeared in Washington as claimants for seats in Congress. After a thorough investigation of the election and several ingenious arguments in opposition both were admitted, February 17, 1863, though not without considerable misgiving, as Representatives for the remainder of the term, which expired March 3 following. For their exclusion the opposition relied mainly upon these grounds:

First. The election, it was asserted, was brought about by a threat of interference with slave property if the State was not represented in Congress by January 1, 1863; this was a measure of coercion, and the compliance of citizens in appearing at the polls was ascribed to selfish motives rather than to loyal and patriotic sentiments.

Second. The existence of any vacancy in a constitutional sense was at least doubtful; and even if vacancies existed in these districts the authority of a military governor to call an election was denied.

Third. It was objected that Governor Shepley had dispensed with the registry required by law and had empowered commissioners of election to decide upon the qualifications of voters; finally, by requiring an oath of allegiance to the United States, he had imposed upon electors a test unknown to the laws of Louisiana.[1]

While the cases of Messrs. Hahn and Flanders were pending the edict of freedom had gone forth, for the President, as announced in his preliminary proclamation of September 22, had declared, January 1, 1863, "as a fit and necessary war measure," that "all persons held as slaves within said designated States and parts of States, are and henceforward shall be free."[2] Louisiana was named as one of the States in rebellion. From the operation of this measure, however, the city of New Orleans and thirteen parishes of the State were excepted.

The admission, February 17, of Hahn and Flanders gave new life to the political reorganization of the State.[3] But with this revival of interest there was discovered among the supporters of the Federal Government a difference of opinion as to the best course to be pursued in the circumstances. This division of sentiment arose concerning the wisdom of retaining slavery in those parishes not included in the President's proclamation. The Union associations, each appointing five delegates, organized what they termed a Free State General Committee with Thomas J. Durant as president. This body, holding anti-slavery views and assuming that rebellion had destroyed the fundamental law, took measures to elect delegates to a general convention for the purpose of framing a new constitution prohibiting slavery.

---

[1] Globe, Part I., 3 Sess. 37th Cong., pp. 831-837, 1030-1036.
[2] McPherson's Pol. Hist., pp. 228-229.
[3] Blaine's Twenty Years of Congress, Vol. II. p. 39; Nicolay and Hay's Lincoln, Vol. VIII. p. 419.

Their plan was approved by General Shepley, who, June 12, 1863, appointed Mr. Durant Attorney-General for the State, with power to act as commissioner of registration.[1] He was ordered on the same day to make an enrollment of all free white male citizens of the United States having resided six months in the State and one month in the parish, who should each take the oath of allegiance and register "as a voter freely and voluntarily for the purpose of organizing a State government in Louisiana, loyal to the Government of the United States."[2]

The conservative element, though less active, was by no means indifferent to these measures, and sent to Washington a committee of planters to consult the President. They represented in a communication to him that they had "been delegated to seek of the General Government a full recognition of all the rights of the State as they existed previous to the passage of an act of secession, upon the principle of the existence of the State constitution unimpaired, and no legal act having transpired that could in any way deprive them of the advantages conferred by that constitution." They further requested him to direct the Military Governor to order an election on the first Monday of November following for all State and Federal officers.[3] To this committee, composed of E. E. Malhiot, Bradish Johnson and Thomas Cottman, Mr. Lincoln, under date of June 19, 1863, replied "that a respectable portion of the Louisiana people desired to amend their State constitution, and contemplated holding a State convention for that object. This fact alone, as it seems to me, is a sufficient reason why the General Government should not give the committal you seek to the existing State constitution.

[1] Ann. Cycl., 1863, p. 589.
[2] N. & H., Vol. VIII. p. 420.
[3] Ann. Cycl., 1863, p. 590; Letters and State Papers of Lincoln, Vol. II. p. 536.

I may add that while I do not perceive how such committal could facilitate our military operations in Louisiana, I really apprehend it might be so used as to embarrass them." [1]

It is evident, when we recall the letter of July 26, 1862, to Reverdy Johnson, that the President, then only contemplating emancipation, had, since his proclamation had gone forth, taken much more advanced ground.[2] The army was still his main reliance, and the wisdom of restoring a loyal government as well as the method of that restoration was regarded favorably or otherwise as it appeared to facilitate or embarrass military operations.

Relative to an election in November he said, " There is abundant time without any order or proclamation from me just now." Though their request was courteously denied, he assured the committee that the people of Louisiana should not lack an opportunity for a fair election for both Federal and State officers by want of anything within his power to give them.[3]

The political reorganization of the State was at this point interrupted by the absence at Port Hudson of General N. P. Banks, then in command of the Department of the Gulf. So energetic and successful was the Confederate General Taylor that by July 10, when he received intelligence of the fall of Port Hudson and the surrender of Vicksburg, his mounted scouts had been pushed to within sixteen miles of New Orleans.[4] The surrender in these strongholds of more than 40,000 men was a crushing blow to the Richmond Government; enough troops were disengaged by these victories to overwhelm the enemy that menaced New Orleans, and General Taylor hurriedly concentrated his army in the valley of the

[1] Letters and State Papers of Lincoln, Vol. II. p. 356.
[2] Ibid., pp. 214-215.
[3] Ibid., p. 356.
[4] Taylor's Destruction and Reconstruction, ch. x; also the general history of military operations in the Red River country.

Red River to observe the movements of the Federal commander. The Union picket line marked at this time the bounds of Governor Shepley's civil jurisdiction; indeed, it was not greatly extended until the surrender of General E. Kirby Smith late in May, 1865, after the engagement at Brazos. Eastern Louisiana, with Alabama and Mississippi, had passed a few weeks earlier under Federal control.

The great numbers withdrawn from production in the South combined with a rigorous enforcement of the blockade had occasioned a cotton famine in the markets of the world. To relieve this condition an outlet was sought for the abundant crops of the Red River country; and this fact was probably, not without considerable influence, in determining the course of the expedition into Texas, which was intended to accomplish a very different though scarcely less important purpose.

Though the vigilance of Mr. Adams, United States Minister to England, was rewarded by the abandonment in that country of any further attempt to build cruisers of the Alabama type, the Confederate naval agent by no means despaired of dealing still severer blows to the commerce of the North, and, attracted by promises which appear to have been authorized by the ruler of France, changed his field of activity from Liverpool to Bordeaux, where a ship-builder was engaged to construct two formidable rams. With the attempts to get these under the Confederate flag this essay is not concerned.[1] French interests in Mexico appeared at that time to require the cultivation of friendly relations with what some European States believed was destined to become a new power among the nations of the world; hence Napoleon's encouragement to the Confederate representatives abroad. This situation was so seriously regarded by the

[1] Bulloch's Secret Service of the Confederate States in Europe, Vol. II. chs. i and ii.

Government at Washington that even at considerable sacrifice it was determined to plant the Union flag somewhere in Texas. To effect this object General Banks had considered and submitted to the War Department plans of his own; these, however, appear to have been reluctantly abandoned because of repeated instructions from General Halleck, and the movement toward Shreveport in the spring and early summer of 1864 was begun. From the protracted and envenomed controversy to which it gave rise among the officers on both sides its disastrous ending is familiar to all.[1]

While this joint land and naval expedition was yet in contemplation Mr. Lincoln found time to inform the Federal commander of his opinions respecting the establishment of a civil government in Louisiana. In his letter of August 5, 1863, to General Banks he wrote:

While I very well know what I would be glad for Louisiana to do, it is quite a different thing for me to assume direction of the matter. I would be glad for her to make a new constitution recognizing the emancipation proclamation, and adopting emancipation in those parts of the State to which the proclamation does not apply. And while she is at it, I think it would not be objectionable for her to adopt some practical system by which the two races could gradually live themselves out of the old relation to each other, and both come out better prepared for the new. Education for young blacks should be included in the plan. After all, the power or element of "contract" may be sufficient for this probationary period; and, by its simplicity and flexibility, may be the better.

As an anti-slavery man, I have a motive to desire emancipation which pro-slavery men do not have; but even they have strong enough reason to thus place themselves again under the shield of the Union; and to thus perpetually hedge against the recurrence of the scenes through which we are now passing.

He expressed his approval of the registry which he supposed Mr. Durant was making with a view to an election for a constitutional convention, the work of which, he hoped,

[1] N. & H., Vol. VIII. pp. 285-286; Conduct of the War, Vol. II. pp. 1-401 (*passim*).

would reach Washington by the meeting of Congress in December. Before concluding this letter he added: "For my own part, I think I shall not, in any event, retract the emancipation proclamation; nor, as executive, ever return to slavery any person who is freed by the terms of that proclamation, or by any of the acts of Congress."[1]

He again invites attention to the fact that if Louisiana should send members to Congress their admission would depend upon the respective Houses and not to any extent upon the wishes of the Executive.

Copies of this communication he intended to send to Hahn, Flanders and Durant. Three months later, when the gentleman last named informed him that nothing had yet been done toward the enrollment, Mr. Lincoln wrote immediately to General Banks a letter which at once reveals both the extent of his interest in this subject and his extreme disappointment on learning that his wishes had been but little regarded. Flanders, then in Washington, confirmed the account of Durant. "This disappoints me bitterly," said the letter of November 5, 1863, and though the President did not blame either General Banks or the Louisiana leaders for this apparent neglect he urged them "to lose no more time." "I wish him [General Shepley], . . ." continued the letter, "without waiting for more territory, to go to work and give me a tangible nucleus which the remainder of the State may rally around as fast as it can, and which I can at once recognize and sustain as the true State government. And in that work I wish you and all under your command to give them a hearty sympathy and support.

"The instruction to Governor Shepley bases the movement (and rightfully, too) upon the loyal element. Time is important. There is danger, even now, that the adverse element seeks insidiously to preoccupy the ground. If a few

[1] Letters and State Papers of Lincoln, Vol. II. p. 380.

professedly loyal men shall draw the disloyal about them, and colorably set up a State government, repudiating the Emancipation Proclamation and reëstablishing slavery, I cannot recognize or sustain their work. I should fall powerless in the attempt. This Government in such an attitude would be a house divided against itself.

"I have said, and say again, that if a new State government, acting in harmony with this government, and consistently with general freedom, shall think best to adopt a reasonable temporary arrangement in relation to the landless and homeless freed people, I do not object; but my word is out to be for and not against them on any question of their permanent freedom. I do not insist upon such temporary arrangement, but only say such would not be objectionable to me."[1]

It should be remembered that Thomas J. Durant, who was authorized to make the enrollment as well as to appoint " registers " to assist him, was spokesman of the wealthy and influential class of planters, or the conservative element whose interests opposed any disturbance of existing conditions. He appears to have drawn for the President a somewhat gloomy picture of the political situation in Louisiana, and finally to have protested against the government organized by the adverse party. The outlook there, however, was not so discouraging as represented; for as early as October 9 Governor Shepley had renewed his order for the registration, modifying the former one so far as to include "all loyal citizens."

Interest was somewhat quickened by the announcement of certain conservative leaders of an intention to hold a voluntary election in conformity with the old constitution and laws of the State. On October 27, 1863, an address signed by the president and vice-president of the Central Executive Com-

[1] Letters and State Papers of Lincoln, Vol. II. p. 436.

mittee was published in the papers of New Orleans. This appeal, directed to the loyal citizens of Louisiana, begins:

> The want of civil government in our State can, by a proper effort on your part, soon be supplied, under laws and a constitution formed and adopted by yourselves in a time of profound peace. It is made your duty, as well as your right, to meet at the usual places, and cast your votes for State and parish officers, members of Congress, and of the State Legislature.
>
> . . . . . .
>
> The day, as fixed by our laws, is Monday, the 2d day of November next, 1863. There is nothing [proceeds the address] to prevent your meeting on the day fixed by law, and selecting your agents to carry on the affairs of government in our own State. The military will not interfere with you in the exercise of your civil rights and duties, and we think we can assure you that your action in this respect will meet the approval of the National Government.

The failure of those citizens addressed to exercise their rights, it was asserted, would subject "the country" to the danger of being thrown as "vacated" territory into the hands of Congress.[1]

The Free State Committee having been invited to coöperate, a correspondence ensued between the rival organizations; but, on the ground that this movement was both illegal and unjust, the Free State men declined to participate in the election. In their reply the latter assert that "There is no law in existence, as stated by you [The Executive Central Committee], directing elections to be held on the first Monday of November.

"The constitution of 1852, as amended by the convention of 1861, was overthrown and destroyed by the rebellion of the people of Louisiana, and the subsequent conquest by the arms of the United States does not restore your political institutions."[2]

The reply then proceeds to discuss the injustice of the

[1] Ann. Cycl., 1863, p. 591.
[2] Ibid.

movement, and upon this subject its reasoning is entitled to more respect. As to the status of the constitution of 1852, it is not easy to comprehend how the secession convention, a body universally regarded as revolutionary, could amend, in the manner attempted, the fundamental law, seeing that this revolution was not yet crowned with success.

Though no general election was held in response to this address, voting took place in two parishes, and certain persons were chosen as Representatives in Congress. Before giving an account of this election of November 2, 1863, it may be proper to notice a petition submitted by the free colored people of New Orleans to Governor Shepley praying to be registered as voters so that they could "assist in establishing in the new Convention a Civil Government" for their "beloved State of Louisiana." This address, prepared at a meeting on November 5, and not without ability, recites in appropriate language the services rendered by free colored men to both the Nation and the State. It is sufficient to observe here that their prayer was not granted. The paper itself will be considered in discussing the successive steps which led to the complete enfranchisement of the race.[1]

The preceding chapter has noticed President Lincoln's Amnesty Proclamation of December 8 as well as that part of the accompanying message to Congress discussing his plan for restoring Union governments in the insurgent States.

The House had not completed its organization for the Thirty-eighth Congress when Thaddeus Stevens, a Representative from Pennsylvania, either from curiosity or an anxiety to oppose, as he conceived, the policy of the President, inquired what names had been omitted in the call of members. At a later stage of its first meeting, December 7, 1863, he again referred to this subject by asking to have read the credentials of persons claiming to be Representatives "from the

[1] Ann. Cycl., 1863, pp. 591-592.

so-called State of Louisiana." The acting clerk facetiously promised compliance, and read a certificate signed by Mr. John Leonard Riddell naming A. P. Field, Thomas Cottman and Joshua Baker as persons elected to represent respectively the First, Second and Fifth Congressional Districts of the State.[1]

On a resolution " That A. P. Field is not entitled to a seat in this House from the State of Louisiana," reported January 29, 1864, from the Committee of Elections, his right to admission was fully discussed.

Under the apportionment of 1850 that State sent four, and by the census of 1860 became entitled to five, Representatives. By an act of Congress approved July 14, 1862, each State entitled to more than one member in the lower House was to be divided into as many districts as it had been allotted Representatives.

But, said Chairman Dawes, as Louisiana had never been so divided no person in that State had been chosen according to Federal law. The election under which Mr. Field claimed a seat occurred in the old First Congressional District, which, with a great portion of the city of New Orleans, included two adjacent parishes, Placquemines and St. Bernard. On November 1, General Shepley issued a military order forbidding the election, and none was held in New Orleans. In the two outlying parishes, however, under the auspices of a citizens' committee, to which returns were made, a few voters appeared at the polls. In the parish of St. Bernard, the only locality in which the House had any proof that electors participated, Mr. Field received one hundred and fifty-six votes, and though no evidence in support of his statement had been offered, about the same number, he alleged, had been cast for him in Placquemines.

The question was, proceeded Mr. Dawes, whether a gentle-

[1] Globe, Part I., 1 Sess. 38th Cong., pp. 5-6.

man with this constituency could be in any sense considered as having been elected. There were in his district over 10,000 qualified voters, and of these the claimant received the support of only one hundred and fifty-six; hence nearly ten thousand electors expressed no opinion, armed interference having prevented 9,844 of them from indicating a preference. There was no evidence that this majority acquiesced in what was done by one hundred and fifty-six men in a corner of St. Bernard parish where an election was permitted. If no other objection existed, the State had not been districted as required by the Act of July, 1862; this consideration of itself appeared to the Committee a reason sufficient for his exclusion. Further, his certificate was signed by one John Leonard Riddell, himself chosen Governor at the same time and in the same parishes. His term, according to the laws of Louisiana, did not commence till January 1, 1864, and it was not easy to comprehend how he came to regard himself as Executive of the State on November 20, 1863, when he signed the certificate presented by the claimant. Mr. Riddell, indeed, had not then been inaugurated.

Had not Congress failed to divide the State, the suppression of this election would have been without justification and have deserved the condemnation of the House. It, however, did not conform to the laws of Louisiana, for the votes were not cast nor were they counted or canvassed as prescribed thereby. This, in substance, was the argument of Mr. Dawes.

By other members attention was invited to the fact that under the same laws and conditions an election had been held in Louisiana a year before, and in consequence two Representatives admitted. To this observation Mr. Stevens replied that Hahn and Flanders, the members referred to, had been seated by the power of the House without, as he then supposed, any law or right. Henry Winter Davis alone among all who spoke on the question approved the action of the Military Governor on the ground that there was no legal right to hold an election, and the attempt of any number of persons to do so was an usurpation of sovereign authority which was properly prevented. Other Representatives, however, strongly condemned this act of Governor Shepley and at least one desired the House to express as an amendment to the resolution its disapproval of his conduct. Though not the question in debate, there could be no mistaking upon this point the sentiments of a majority of the members.

Mr. Field, permitted to address the House, observed that it was the fault of the General Government that Union men in Louisiana had not been aided by the previous administration. If they had been, the blood of Illinois and Massachusetts patriots would not have sprinkled the soil of his State.

To show that some sort of government existed there he caused the clerk to read a list of one hundred and twenty-five officers acting in those parishes included within Federal military lines, and added that though New Orleans since its capture paid annually in taxes, collected through Governor Shepley, two and a half million dollars, besides a considerable sum in internal revenue, her people were represented neither in the local nor the national Government.

The constitution of Louisiana, he said, required that qualified electors should be white males who had attained the age of twenty-one years, and been residents of the State for twelve months immediately preceding the election. The provision was so modified by Governor Shepley that persons of this description were allowed to vote after a residence of six months. Mr. Field did not know whence was derived the authority to amend constitutions.

To secure his coöperation in establishing a loyal government Union men met as early as September 19 in convention at New Orleans, and appointed a committee of nine to present an address to the Military Governor inviting his assistance. He declined, however, after a lengthy interview to order an election for Representatives until the State had first been divided. In fact, until instructions which he had requested, were received from Washington he refused to order any election whatever, though he volunteered to forward to Mr. Lincoln any communication which they desired to address him on that subject. Besides its correspondence with Governor Shepley, the New Orleans convention on September 21 had sent a letter to General Banks, the Department commander, to secure if possible his approval of their movement.

Notice, dated October 20, was given that an election would be held, November 2, at the usual places in the parish of St. Bernard, and the State and Federal offices to be filled, as well as the precise places at which voters could cast their ballots, were mentioned. Since the military authorities had refused to assist them, and had then issued no order against an election, loyal men thought it not improper to express their opinions at the polls. As the Free State people considered Louisiana out of the Union they declined to participate, and though General Banks in obedience to instructions from the President had subsequently ordered an election they maintained the same attitude. The claimant's party did not oppose this order; for if unable to restore their State in the manner most acceptable they were willing to coöperate in any method likely to accomplish that object.

Precisely what number of voters would be called a constituency Mr. Field had not been informed. In the portion of his Congressional District included in St. Bernard and Placquemines parishes there were only 2,400 electors, and the President's plan required only one tenth of the number of votes cast in 1860. Though the election of November 2 preceded the Executive proclamation, that fact should not make it void. The electors in New Orleans were not free to express a choice, and even if it had been otherwise the vote in the First District must have been greatly diminished since 1860, for he was assured by two paymasters that 7,000 men had been recruited there for the Union army.

Some members admitted that the national Government had not given sufficient protection to Union men in Louisiana, and therefore should not now take advantage of that neglect to also deprive them of representation in Congress. These believed that if Mr. Field had received a majority of the votes in his district any informality in the election should be overlooked, for the right to representation in Congress grows out of the Constitution, and regulations governing such elections are matters of mere convenience. The fact that no State organization existed there did not create a legal impediment, and it was no objection that Louisiana had not been redistricted, for the additional member was not imposed as a burden but as a right which she was free to exercise or not; besides, the greater representation includes the less.

Notwithstanding these considerations, and strong, though not universal, testimony to the claimant's loyalty, he was denied admission, February 9, 1864, by a vote of 85 to 48.[1] His case, however, was not exactly similar to that of Messrs. Hahn and Flanders, as stated by one Representative, for they had received, in the circumstances, a comparatively large vote.

To this end came the movement of the planters designed primarily to counteract that inaugurated by the Free State Committee, which also, as we shall see, was soon at variance with the military authorities. Important changes had occurred in the shifting politics of his State before the House had taken final action in the case of Mr. Field; these will be briefly related.

Military necessity had led the President to issue, Decem-

[1] Globe, Part I., 1 Sess. 38th Cong., pp. 411-415, 543-547.

LOUISIANA

ber 8, 1863, his Proclamation of Amnesty and Reconstruction proposing, though not rigidly insisting upon, a plan for reinaugurating State governments wherever there existed such a loyal nucleus as could effectively assist in overthrowing the rebellion. In discussing the affairs of Tennessee that plan has been quoted at such length as to require no further mention in this place.[1]

General Banks on January 8, 1864, announced his intention of ordering an election of State officers. He was urged at this point by the Free State Committee to allow their election to go on, but he refused to yield even under pressure of an immense public meeting favorable to their object.[2] Without his coöperation their plan was doomed to failure, and when entreaties did not avail to move him they promptly inveighed against his methods and his motives in the columns of *The National Intelligencer* at Washington. In a letter dated New Orleans, January 9, 1864, a correspondent writes:

> President Lincoln has started a Missouri case in Louisiana, and has made Banks our master; and Banks is another Schofield, only worse than he. Our mass meeting last evening was a complete success; but its object will be defeated by Banks, who, under orders direct from the President, declares his purpose to order an election for a convention; thus playing into the hands of Cottman, Riddle, and Fields, and their crew. The Union men—the true Union men—are thunderstruck by the course of the President in this matter.
>
> We were not informed of the President's orders to General Banks until the hour of the meeting last night, and the meeting was not informed at all. General Shepley, who is generally liked, and who has done all he could to promote the free State cause, and to organize a free State government, will resign, and the election ordered by Banks will be purely at military dictation, and will be so regarded.

The correspondent does not know the secret springs of all these acts of the President, but thinks he has probably been deceived by base and interested men. " Banks," he believes,

[1] See pp. 24-28 *ante*.
[2] Ann. Cycl., 1863, pp. 592-593.

"has the unchanged confidence of Mr. Lincoln." The writer concludes by asking whether it is not possible to get the President to countermand his orders to Banks immediately, "and let the people manage matters as they have begun to do?"[1] To prove that no line of policy would be acceptable to the Free State Committee Mr. Field, in his remarks before the House, read in full the communication from which these excerpts are taken.

To comprehend clearly the nature of the controversy which so suddenly arose between the Free State General Committee and the Federal commander in Louisiana it may be necessary to explain with some detail the precise attitude of that organization relative to the question at issue between the adverse parties. In discussing the respective merits of the State constitutions of 1852 and 1861 the organ of the Free State men says:

> The question is altogether immaterial; for, in the conflict of arms incident to this rebellion, the predominant ideas of the good people of Louisiana have far preceded either constitution; and to reorganize now the State on the slave basis, which both constitutions and the laws passed under them recognized, has become an utter impossibility. Free soil and free speech have grown up into absolute necessities, directly resulting from the war, which has converted into dust and ashes all the constitutions which Louisiana has ever made, embodying the ideas of property in our fellow-man, and all the baneful results of this system of African slavery. The present war is nothing but the conflict of the ideas of slavery and liberty. . . . We cannot have peace until public opinion is brought quite up to this point. We cannot reorganize the civil government of our city, and still less that of our State, and get rid of the fearful incubus of martial law now pressing down our energies by its arbitrary influence, unless we believe, give utterance to and establish the fundamental principle of our national government: "all men are created free and equal." We know of no better way to effect this than by calling a convention as soon as possible, to declare the simple fact that Louisiana now is and will forever be a free State.[2]

[1] Globe, Part I., 1 Sess. 38th Cong., p. 543.
[2] Ann. Cycl., 1863, p. 590.

The party favoring this method insisted that in August, 1863, when General Shepley was in Washington, their plan in all its parts was adopted in a Cabinet meeting, and that a special order issued from the War Department directing the Military Governor to carry it into execution. The movement for reorganizing the State would thus be placed under control of the steadfast opponents of slavery. They further claimed that Mr. Lincoln then preferred the calling of a convention to an election of State officers under the old constitution. His letter of August 5, 1863, to General Banks certainly leaves no doubt as to his sentiments at that time, for he expressed his approval of the enrollment being taken by Durant with a view to an election for a constitutional convention, the mature work of which, he thought, should reach Washington by the meeting of Congress. The impossibility of so expediting registration outside of New Orleans as to be ready for an election at that early date was explained to the President by the Free State Committee.

Mr. B. F. Flanders returning from Washington in October, 1863, reported the President as saying, in reply to an objection that enough territory and population were not under protection of the Union army to justify an election, that so great was the necessity for immediate action that he would recognize and sustain a State government organized by any part of the population of which the National forces then had control, and that he wished Flanders on his return to Louisiana to say so.[1]

The registration under Governor Shepley, though frequently interrupted, had proceeded, and the Free State Committee, to insure the success of their object, conferred with him for the purpose of holding, about January 25, 1864, an election for delegates to a State convention which, as already

[1] Ann. Cycl., 1863, p. 591.

observed, intended to frame a new constitution abolishing slavery everywhere throughout the State. The announcement, then, on January 8, 1864, by General Banks of his intention to order an election of State officers under the old constitution was regarded by them as a decision for their adversaries. Their objections to the proclamation itself will be noticed in the proper place. It provided not only for an election of State officers on February 22 following, but also for the choice of delegates to a convention to be held in April for a revision of the constitution. The paramount objection of the Free State men was that the election of State officers would, under the course of General Banks, precede that for delegates to the convention, the point at which they desired to begin the work of reëstablishing a civil government for the State.

To Thomas Cottman, who accompanied Mr. Field to Washington claiming a seat in Congress as Representative from the Second Louisiana District, Mr. Lincoln, on December 15, wrote:

> You were so kind as to say this morning that you desire to return to Louisiana, and to be guided by my wishes, to some extent, in the part you may take in bringing that State to resume her rightful relation to the General Government.
>
> My wishes are in a general way expressed, as well as I can express them, in the proclamation issued on the eighth of the present month, and in that part of the annual message which relates to that proclamation. It there appears that I deem the sustaining of the Emancipation Proclamation, where it applies, as indispensable; and I add here that I would esteem it fortunate if the people of Louisiana should themselves place the remainder of the State upon the same footing.[1]

Though this letter expressed as one of Mr. Lincoln's strongest wishes a hope that all Union men in Louisiana would "eschew cliquism," he was destined to be disappointed, for at this very time letters from General Banks, dated December 6 and 16, informed him that Governor Shepley, Mr.

[1] Letters and State Papers of Lincoln, Vol. II. pp. 458-459.

Durant and others had given him to understand that they were charged exclusively with the work of reconstruction in Louisiana and hence he had not felt authorized to interfere. Other officers had set up claims to jurisdiction conflicting and interfering with his own powers of military administration. Annoyed that a misunderstanding was delaying work which he had been urging for a year, the President, on the 24th of December, wrote General Banks as follows:

> I have all the while intended you to be master, as well in regard to reorganizing a State government for Louisiana, as in regard to the military matters of the department; and hence my letters on reconstruction have nearly, if not quite, all been addressed to you. My error has been that it did not occur to me that Governor Shepley or any one else would set up a claim to act independently of you; and hence I said nothing expressly upon the point.
>
> Language has not been guarded at a point where no danger was thought of. I now tell you that in every dispute with whomsoever, you are master.
>
> Governor Shepley was appointed to assist the commander of the department, and not to thwart him or act independently of him. Instructions have been given directly to him, merely to spare you detail labor, and not to supersede your authority. This, in its liability to be misconstrued, it now seems was an error in us. But it is past. I now distinctly tell you that you are master of all, and that I wish you to take the case as you find it, and give us a free State reorganization of Louisiana in the shortest possible time. What I say here is to have a reasonable construction. I do not mean that you are to withdraw from Texas, or abandon any other military measure which you may deem important. Nor do I mean that you are to throw away available work already done for reconstruction; nor that war is to be made upon Governor Shepley, or upon any one else, unless it be found that they will not coöperate with you, in which case, and in all cases, you are master while you remain in command of the department.[1]

This letter making General Banks "master" of the situation in Louisiana the President concluded by thanking him for his successful and valuable operations in Texas. But before receiving this extensive authority and the undoubted assurance of Mr. Lincoln's confidence the commander, on

[1] Letters and State Papers of Lincoln, Vol. II. pp. 465-466.

December 30, submitted to the President a plan of reconstruction based upon the Proclamation and the Message of the 8th of that month. For evident reasons this communication deserves to be reproduced almost entire:

> I would suggest [says General Banks], as the only speedy and certain method of accomplishing your object, that an election be ordered, of a State government, under the constitution and laws of Louisiana, except so much thereof as recognizes and relates to slavery, which should be declared by the authority calling the election, and in the order authorizing it, inoperative and void. The registration of voters to be made in conformity with your Proclamation, and all measures hitherto taken with reference to State organization, not inconsistent with the Proclamation, may be made available. A convention of the people for the revision of the constitution may be ordered as soon as the government is organized, and the election of members might take place on the same or a subsequent day with the general election. The people of Louisiana will accept such a proposition with favor. They will prefer it to any arrangement which leaves the subject to them for an affirmative or negative vote. Strange as this may appear, it is the fact. Of course a government organized upon the basis of immediate and universal freedom, with the general consent of the people, followed by the adaptation of commercial and industrial interests to this order of things, and supported by the army and navy, the influence of the civil officers of the Government, and the Administration at Washington, could not fail by any possible chance to obtain an absolute and permanent recognition of the principle of freedom upon which it would be based. Any other result would be impossible. The same influence would secure with the same certainty the selection of proper men in the election of officers.
>
> Let me assure you that this course will be far more acceptable to the citizens of Louisiana than the submission of the question of slavery to the chances of an election. Their self-respect, their *amour propre* will be appeased if they are not required to vote for or against it. Offer them a government without slavery and they will gladly accept it as a necessity resulting from the war. On all other points, sufficient guarantees of right results can be secured; but the great question, that of immediate emancipation, will be covered *ab initio*, by a conceded and absolute prohibition of slavery.
>
> Upon this plan a government can be established whenever you wish— in thirty or sixty days; a government that will be satisfactory to the South and the North; to the South, because it relieves them from any action in regard to an institution which cannot be restored, and which they cannot condemn; and to the North, because it places the interests

of liberty beyond all possible accident or chance of failure. The result is certain." [1]

Upon receiving this communication the President, who cherished no plan of restoration to which exact conformity was indispensable, expressed, January 13, 1864, in a letter to General Banks his gratitude for the zeal and confidence manifested by him on the question of reinaugurating a free State government in Louisiana. He hoped, because of the authority contained in the letter of December 24, that the Department Commander had already commenced work. "Whether you shall have done so or not," continues the letter, "please, on receiving this, proceed with all possible despatch, using your own absolute discretion in all matters which may not carry you away from the conditions stated in your letters to me, nor from those of the message and proclamation of December 8. Frame orders, and fix times and places for this and that, according to your own judgment." [2]

This letter repeats the idea of subordination to General Banks of all officials in his department holding authority from the President, and stated that the bearer of the communication, Collector Dennison, of New Orleans, understood the views of the commander and was willing to assist in carrying them out. Before Mr. Dennison arrived in New Orleans, however, General Banks had already, in his proclamation of January 11, 1864, fixed a date for the election. This action was determined, said the Department Commander, upon ample assurance "that more than a tenth of the population desire the earliest possible restoration of Louisiana to the Union"; hence he invited "the loyal citizens of the State qualified to vote in public affairs . . . to assemble in the election precincts designated by law, . . . on the 22d of February, 1864, to cast their votes for the election of

[1] N. & H., Vol. VIII. pp. 428-430.
[2] Ibid., p. 469.

State officers herein named, *viz*. Governor, Lieutenant-Governor, Secretary of State, Treasurer, Attorney-General, Superintendent of Public Instruction and Auditor of Public Accounts — who shall, when elected, for the time being, and until others are appointed by competent authority, constitute the civil government of the State, under the constitution and laws of Louisiana, except so much of said constitution and laws as recognize, regulate or relate to slavery, which being inconsistent with the present condition of public affairs, and plainly inapplicable to any class of persons now existing within its limits, must be suspended, and they are therefore and hereby declared to be inoperative and void. This proceeding is not intended to ignore the right of property existing prior to the rebellion, nor to preclude the claim for compensation of loyal citizens for losses sustained by enlistment or other authorized acts of Government."[1]

The qualifications of voters in this election were to be determined by the oath of allegiance prescribed by the President's proclamation together with the condition annexed to the elective franchise by the constitution of Louisiana. Officers elected were to be duly installed on the 4th of March.

So much of the registration effected under direction of Governor Shepley and the several Union Associations as was not inconsistent with the proclamation and other orders of the President was approved. The proclamation further announced that arrangements would be made for the early election of members of Congress for the State, and, that the organic law might be made to conform to the will of the people and harmonize with the spirit of the age, an election of delegates to a convention for the revision of the constitution would be held on the first Monday of April following.

This proclamation declared, among other things, that

[1] Ann. Cycl., 1863, p. 592.

The fundamental law of the State is martial law. . . . The Government is subject to the law of necessity, and must consult the condition of things, rather than the preferences of men, and if so be that its purposes are just and its measures wise, it has the right to demand that questions of personal interest and opinion shall be subordinate to the public good. When the national existence is at stake, and the liberties of the people in peril, faction is treason.

The methods herein proposed submit the whole question of government directly to the people — first, by the election of executive officers, faithful to the Union, to be followed by a loyal representation in both Houses of Congress; and then by a convention which will confirm the action of the people, and recognize the principles of freedom in the organic law. This is the wish of the President.[1]

On February 13, nine days before the election, General Banks issued an order relative to the qualifications of electors. It provided, in addition to the declarations on that subject in his proclamation, that Union voters expelled from their homes by the public enemy might cast their ballots for State officers in the precincts where they temporarily resided and that qualified electors enlisted in the army or navy could vote in those precincts in which they might be found on election day. If without the State, then commissioners would be appointed to receive their ballots wherever stationed, returns to be made to General Shepley.[2]

For governor three candidates were nominated—B. F. Flanders, a representative of the Free State Committee; Michael Hahn, the choice of those who approved the measures of General Banks, and J. Q. A. Fellows, a pro-slavery conservative who favored "the Constitution and the Union with the preservation of the rights of all inviolate." The friends of Hahn would deny to persons of African descent the privileges of citizenship, whereas the supporters of Flanders generally would extend to them such rights and immunities.[3]

[1] Ann. Cycl., 1863, pp. 592-593.
[2] Ann. Cycl., 1864, p. 476.
[3] Ibid.

On Washington's birthday, as announced in the proclamation of General Banks, an election was held in seventeen parishes, Hahn receiving 6,183, Fellows 2,996 and Flanders 2,232 votes, a total of 11,411, of which 107 were cast by Louisiana soldiers stationed at Pensacola, Florida.[1]

Writing February 25 to the President General Banks says:

> The election of the 22d of February was conducted with great spirit and propriety. No complaint is heard from any quarter, so far as I know, of unfairness or undue influence on the part of the officers of the Government. At some of the strictly military posts the entire vote of the Louisiana men was for Mr. Flanders, at others for Mr. Hahn, according to the inclination of the voters. Every voter accepted the oath prescribed by your proclamation of the 8th of December. . . . The ordinary vote of the State has been less than forty thousand. The proportion given on the 22d of February is nearly equal to the territory covered by our arms.[2]

The friends of the Free State General Committee in a protest pronounced the result of the election "the registration of a military edict," and "worthy of no respect from the representatives and Executive of the nation." To the question whether this election had in the meaning of the President reëstablished a State government they promptly answered in the negative, for the commanding general recognized the Louisiana constitution of 1852 and ordered an election under it in which the votes of the people had nothing to do with reëstablishing government; his proclamation, by recognizing the existence of the old constitution, made the reëstablishment beforehand for them. The Governor and Lieutenant-Governor, together with the other executive officers chosen, did not, they argued, constitute a State government; for all the constitutions of Louisiana, including that of 1852, described the government as consisting of three departments: executive, legislative and judicial.

[1] Ann. Cycl., 1864, p. 476.
[2] N. & H., Vol. VIII. pp. 432-433.

Though not avowed, the reason of Banks' failure to order an election for members of the Legislature was plain, for there was not, they claimed, within the Union lines a sufficient number of parishes to elect a majority of that body, and less than a majority was, by the constitution, not a quorum to do business; so that no officer elected could be legally paid, for that could be done by only a legal appropriation. The same constitution, they said further, provided that Justices of the Supreme and District Courts, as well as justices of the peace, should be elected by the people. The present incumbents had been simply appointed by General Shepley. Should Mr. Hahn under pretence of being civil governor undertake to appoint judicial officers, the act would be a mere usurpation.

Not only, they declared, had no State government been established by this election, but still further, the proclamation of the President had not in the matter of electors been complied with; for Article XII. of the constitution of 1852 says: "No soldier, seaman, or marine in the army or navy of the United States . . . shall be entitled to vote at any election in this State." .Yet, continued the protestants, it was a notorious fact that the general commanding permitted soldiers recruited in Louisiana, and otherwise qualified, to vote, and that many availed themselves of the privilege. Again, they went on to say, the Legislature by act of March 20, 1856, provided for the appointment in New Orleans of a register of voters whose office should be closed three days before an election, and no one registered during that period. Now prior to the late election, the register having closed his office according to law, orders were at once given to two other officers, recorders of the city, who had no such powers or functions by law, to register voters, which they did night and day, and persons so registered were allowed to vote.

Referring to the declared intention of General Banks to order an election of delegates to a constitutional convention, and by a subsequent order fix the basis of representation, the number of delegates and the details of the election, they said: " This will put the whole matter under military control, and the experience of the last election shows that only such a convention can be had as the overshadowing influence of the military authority will permit. Under an election thus ordered, and a constitution thus established, a republican form of government cannot be formed. It is simply a fraud to call it the reëstablishment of a State government. In these circumstances, the only course left to the truly loyal citizens of Louisiana is, to protest against the recognition of this pretended Government, and to appeal to the calm judgment of the nation to procure such action from Congress as will forbid military commanders to usurp the powers which belong to Congress alone, or to the loyal people of Louisiana." [1]

But neither the protest nor the criticism of Free State men availed to arrest the march of events, and in the presence of a vast multitude Michael Hahn, who had received a majority of all the votes cast, was inaugurated Governor amidst great enthusiasm on March 4. To the oath prescribed in the amnesty and reconstruction proclamation of December 8, 1863, given above, was added the following:

And I do further solemnly swear, that I am qualified according to the constitution of the State to hold the office to which I have been elected, and that I will faithfully and impartially discharge and perform all the duties incumbent on me as Governor of the State of Louisiana, according to the best of my abilities and understanding, agreeably to the Constitution and Laws of the United States, and in support of and according to the constitution and laws of this State, so far as they are consistent with the necessary military occupation of the State by the troops of the United States for the suppression of the rebellion, and the full restoration of the authority of the United States.[2]

[1] Ann. Cycl., 1863, pp. 593-594.
[2] Ann. Cycl., 1864, p. 477.

This language clearly indicates the legal theory upon which General Banks was proceeding, and citizens understood that Mr. Hahn represented a popular power entirely subordinate to the armed occupation of the State.

On March 13, 1864, the President wrote the following private letter to Governor Hahn:

> I congratulate you on having fixed your name in history as the first free-state governor of Louisiana. Now you are about to have a convention, which, among other things, will probably define the elective franchise. I barely suggest for your private consideration whether some of the colored people may not be let in — as, for instance, the very intelligent, and especially those who have fought gallantly in our ranks. They would probably help, in some trying time to come, to keep the jewel of liberty within the family of freedom. But this is only a suggestion, not to the public, but to you alone.[1]

Speaking of this personal note Mr. Blaine says: "It was perhaps the earliest proposition from any authentic source to endow the negro with the right of suffrage, and was an indirect but most effective answer to those who subsequently attempted to use Mr. Lincoln's name in support of policies which his intimate friends instinctively knew would be abhorrent to his unerring sense of justice."[2]

At the suggestion of General Banks, the President two days later invested Mr. Hahn until further order "with the powers exercised hitherto by the military governor of Louisiana."[3]

From the sentiments of the Free State party it requires little insight into human affairs to foretell that in some manner they would soon be found in opposition. Their candidate, Mr. B. F. Flanders, who received fewer votes than either of his competitors, was a prominent official in the Treasury Department, and from this vantage ground, with-

---
[1] Letters and State Papers of Lincoln, Vol. II. p. 496.
[2] Twenty Years of Congress, Vol. II. p. 40.
[3] Letters and State Papers of Lincoln, Vol. II. p. 498.

out, so far as appears, rebuke from Secretary Chase, began to stir up in Congress a feeling of hostility to the new government in Louisiana. Precisely why Mr. Lincoln decided to take into his own hands the entire subject of reconstruction may be collected without difficulty from what has already been said; but that this determination was confirmed by his knowledge of an alliance between the Free State leaders and the "Radicals" in Congress there can be little doubt.

The Department Commander in a general order gave notice on March 11 that an election would be held on the 28th of that month for the choice of delegates to a State convention to meet in New Orleans "for the revision and amendment of the constitution of Louisiana."[1] Five days later, March 16, Governor Hahn, in a proclamation to the sheriffs and other officers concerned, authorized the election and commanded them to give due notice thereof to the qualified voters of the State and to make prompt returns to the Secretary of State in New Orleans.[2]

Pursuant to these notices the election was held on the 28th, and resulted in the choice of ninety-seven members, two of whom were rejected because of irregular returns. The entire State was entitled to 150 delegates. The parish of Orleans was represented by sixty-three members, leaving to the country parishes but thirty-two. Of the vote, which was exceedingly light, no return appears to have been published. Because of their recent defeat no nominations were made by the Radicals, and this fact, together with heavy rains on election day, was assigned by Governor Hahn in a letter to the President as an explanation of the meagre vote. The Parish of Ascension, which in 1860 had a population of 3,940 whites, elected her delegates by 61 votes; Placquemines, which by the same census had 2,529 white inhabitants, cast 246, while the

[1] Ann. Cycl., 1864, p. 478.
[2] Ibid.

single delegate from Madison was chosen by only twenty-eight electors.[1]

General Banks informed a committee of Congress that all that section of the State as far up as Point Coupée voted; some men from the Red River cast their ballots at Vidalia. In his statement he declared that " The city of New Orleans is really the State of Louisiana "; yet at that time it contained less than half the population of the State.[2]

The constitutional convention, which assembled April 6, 1864, was organized on the 7th with E. H. Durell as president, and after a session of more than two and a half months adjourned July 25. A proclamation of the Governor appointed the 5th of September as the time for taking a vote on the work of the convention. The result was 6,836 for the adoption, and 1,556 for the rejection of the constitution. Besides these there were a number of electors who did not vote on either side of the question.[3]

Of the work of the convention General Banks spoke as follows:

In a State which held 331,726 slaves, one half of its entire population in 1860, more than three fourths of whom had been specially excepted from the Proclamation of Emancipation, and were still held *de jure* in bondage, the convention declared by a majority of all the votes to which the State would have been entitled if every delegate had been present from every district in the State:—

Instantaneous, universal, uncompensated, unconditional emancipation of slaves!

It prohibited forever the recognition of property in man!

It decreed the education of all the children, without distinction of race or color!

It directs all men, white or black, to be enrolled as soldiers for the public defence!

It makes all men equal before the law!

It compels, by its regenerating spirit, the ultimate recognition of all the rights which national authority can confer upon an oppressed race!

[1] Ann. Cycl., 1864, pp. 478-479.
[2] Ibid. [3] Ibid., p. 479.

It wisely recognizes for the first time in constitutional history, the interest of daily labor as an element of power entitled to the protection of the State.[1]

At the same election, that of September 5, the following persons were chosen Representatives in Congress: M. F. Bonzano, A. P. Field, W. D. Mann, T. M. Wells and R. W. Taliaferro. A Legislature was elected at the same time, the members of which were almost entirely in favor of a free State, and by this body seven electors of President and Vice-President were appointed. On October 10th two United States Senators were elected — R. King Cutler for the unexpired term ending March 4, 1867, and Charles Smith for the vacancy created by the resignation of Judah P. Benjamin, and ending March 4, 1865.[2]

It is matter of familiar history that the State government thus organized was never recognized by Congress. The question was presented to that body December 5, 1864, at the opening of the second session of the Thirty-eighth Congress, when the claimants above named appeared in Washington applying for admission to seats, and again in January and February, 1865, upon consideration of a joint resolution declaring certain States not entitled to representation in the Electoral College. As in the case of Tennessee, however, the vote offered by Louisiana was not counted.

The agency of the President in setting up this civil government, and the successive steps in its accomplishment have been related with some degree of minuteness, so that the nature of the controversy between the Executive and the Legislative branches of the Government may be better understood. Whether Mr. Lincoln exceeded his constitutional authority will be considered when an account has been presented of the result of his efforts to restore civil government in the States where Federal authority had been overthrown.

[1] Ann. Cycl., 1864, p. 479.   [2] Ibid.

III

ARKANSAS

THE people of northern Arkansas were strongly attached to the Union, and until December 20, 1860, when a commissioner from Alabama addressed its Legislature, no secession movement took place within the State. Her geographical position classed her with the Western, her productions bound up her interests with the Southern, States.[1] As late as January 5, 1861, resolutions opposing separate action were adopted almost unanimously by the largest meeting ever held at Van Buren. Mr. Lincoln's election was not then deemed a sufficient cause to dissolve the Union. Citizens of every party favored all honorable efforts for its preservation, and demonstrations to the contrary were regarded as the work of only an extreme and inconsiderable faction.[2] So rapid, however, was the succession of events that scarcely two weeks had elapsed when she exhibited signs of resting uneasily in the Union; for on January 16 a bill submitting to popular vote the question of holding a convention passed the Legislature.[3] At the election of delegates to this assembly 23,626 votes were cast for the Union, against 17,927 for the secession, candidates. Though this convention, which assembled March 4, was organized by the choice of Union officers, the proposal to hold it had been carried by a majority of 11,586 in the election of February 18. While secession was strongly urged, a

[1] Ann. Cycl., 1861, p. 22.
[2] Ibid.
[3] McPherson's Pol. Hist., p. 4.

conditional ordinance was defeated by a vote of 39 to 35.[1] At Van Buren and Fort Smith salutes of thirty-nine guns were fired in honor of the loyal members. The inaugural of President Lincoln, received two days after organizing, produced a somewhat unfavorable impression. On the 17th an ordinance, reported by a self-constituted committee of seven secessionists and seven coöperationists, was unanimously adopted.[2] This provided for an election on the first Monday of August, when the qualified voters in the State could cast their ballots either for "secession" or "coöperation." The result, though not wholly satisfactory to either party, afforded time for deliberation.

Tidings of the fall of Sumter, together with the President's proclamation and a requisition for troops from the Secretary of War, interrupted the brief interval of repose following the adjournment of the convention. In these circumstances the State was compelled to make a choice of sides. Governor Rector's reply, April 22, to this requisition shows him to have been ardently in favor of disunion; the president of the convention, concurring in this sentiment, issued a call for that body to reassemble May 6, when an ordinance of secession was promptly passed with but one dissenting vote.[3] By a resolution the convention authorized the Governor to call out, if necessary, 60,000 men, and ordered the issue of $2,000,000 in bonds. Another ordinance confiscated debts due to persons in non-slaveholding States.[4]

The first military movement, after the ordinance of secession had been carried, aimed to secure Federal property within the State, and their value to the South singled out for seizure the arsenals at Fort Smith and Little Rock. The latter city

[1] Ann. Cycl., 1861, p. 22.
[2] Ibid.
[3] Ibid., p. 23.
[4] Ibid., pp. 23-24.

on February 5 was thrown into a great turmoil of confusion and excitement by the unexpected arrival of a body of troops from Helena with the avowed purpose of taking the arsenal; more soldiers arrived during that and the succeeding day until about 400 had assembled. Though the Governor, in response to their inquiry, informed the city council that this force was not there by his order, the troops believed they were acting under his command; at any rate they came to take the arsenal and were not to be diverted from their object. To prevent a collision, which must have followed a refusal of the commanding officer to surrender to a body of men disavowed by their Governor, the latter was easily persuaded to assume the responsibility of the movement and he consented to demand its surrender in the name of the State. This demand Captain Totten asked until three o'clock the next day to consider; then he made known his readiness to evacuate the arsenal, which about noon of the following day was delivered to the State authorities.[1]

The delegates of Arkansas on May 18 took their seats in the Confederate Congress.[2] The convention, it will be observed, assumed at the outset the functions of a law-making body, and, because of further extending its authority by the appointment of a Military Board, soon came into conflict with both the Governor and the Legislature. When the convention empowered the former to call out, if necessary, 60,000 men it divided the State into two districts, an eastern and a western. General Bradley was elected to the command of the former and General Pearce, late of the United States Army, to that of the latter division. Before General McCulloch, stationed in the Indian Territory, could assume any offensive operations the Federal General, Lyon, in pursuit of Jackson, approached the southern boundary of Missouri; upon this

[1] Ann. Cycl., 1861, p. 24.
[2] Ibid.

the Military Board called out ten regiments for defence. On June 21 it despatched to Richmond a messenger who proposed to transfer to the Confederate Government all the State troops with their arms making, however, a condition precedent: they were to be employed for the protection of Arkansas; but as the Secretary of State could make no promise as to their future disposition the transfer was not then effected.[1] On July 4 a second effort was made by a member of the Military Board who visited General Hardee, with whom an arrangement was completed by which a vote should be taken among the troops. If a majority of each company consented, those so consenting were to be turned over as a company. If a majority declined, the company was to be disbanded altogether. One entire company was thus mustered out, and from various motives two or three hundred soldiers returned home. This was from the eastern division. The western was not so easily disposed of. The Military Board after the battle of Springfield directed General Pearce to turn over his force to Hardee, who became angry when the agent proposed to submit the question of transfer, and refused to allow it to be done; this insubordinate conduct he followed up by writing an abusive letter to the Board. Pearce then separated his troops from McCulloch's command and marched them back to Arkansas, where they were informally disbanded and sent home. Fearing such a result, the Board had ordered General Pearce to do nothing further in the matter, but their despatches arrived too late.[2]

Governor Rector's account shows Arkansas troops, claimed to be 22,000 in number, to have been at that time in a state of complete demoralization.[3] The Germans and the Irish, as well as their descendants, showing little inclination to enlist,

[1] Ann. Cycl., 1861, p. 24.
[2] Ibid.
[3] Ibid.

the Governor ascribed their indifference to a want of opportunity for promotion in the service. If this was not the cause, then, he thought, authority should be given to draft a regiment of each race.[1]

More than a third of the voting population was in the field, and as late as October they had received no pay except Arkansas war bonds, the worthlessness of which occasioned much murmuring. This discontent was heightened somewhat by the poor equipment of the regiments, many soldiers being without blankets or shoes.[2] There were other symptoms of unrest within the State. On the charge of attempted insurrection two negro men and a girl were hanged in Monroe County.

All this occasioned much uneasiness, but the chief cause of alarm was the Union sentiment known to exist in the State. In October twenty-seven persons were brought to Little Rock as members of a secret Union organization in Van Buren County and placed in jail to await a civil trial. Many others also were taken about this time, and it was estimated that the "Peace and Constitutional Society" numbered 1 700 members in Arkansas.[3]

The activity of Federal armies in the West excited so much apprehension that Governor Rector on the 18th of February, by proclamation, called into immediate service every man in the State subject to military duty.[4] A Confederate force under Price was driven into Arkansas by General Curtis on the same day, and within a week the commandant at Pocahontas issued an appeal to every man "to turn out promptly, shoulder his musket, and drive the vandals from the State." The Richmond Government being unable to assist Arkansas,

[1] Ann. Cycl., 1861, p. 25.
[2] Ibid.
[3] Ibid.
[4] Ibid., 1862, p. 11.

she was forced to rely upon her own resources and such aid as might be obtained from Missouri, the Indian Territory and Texas.[1]

Disaster and a conviction of neglect led the Governor in May, in an address to the people, to express his indignation and threaten to secede from secession. He said:

> If the arteries of the Confederate heart do not permeate beyond the east bank of the Mississippi, let southern Missourians, Arkansians, Texans and the great West know it and prepare for the future. Arkansas lost, abandoned, subjugated is not Arkansas as she entered the Confederate Government. Nor will she remain Arkansas, a Confederate State, desolated as a wilderness. Her children, fleeing from the wrath to come, will build them a new ark, and launch it on new waters, seeking a haven somewhere of equality, safety and rest.[2]

After the battle of Pea Ridge General Curtis moved to White River, and on May 1 occupied Batesville, where he witnessed many demonstrations of attachment to the Union. Judges of courts, clergymen and other leading citizens came forward and voluntarily took the oath of allegiance to the United States. A threatened advance of the Union forces upon Little Rock created the greatest excitement there, and the Governor by proclamation ordered the militia to repair immediately to its defence; but not finding himself sufficiently supported he fled.[3] The concentration at Corinth of all available Confederate strength was the cause of the weakness of Arkansas at this time. Ten regiments had also been withdrawn from the army of General Curtis to reënforce the Federal troops in Mississippi. This left him in no condition to march upon the State capital, and for the time it was saved. Twelve thousand poorly equipped men had assembled there in response to the appeal of Governor Rector.

After the occupation of Helena by Federal troops Mr. Lincoln appointed John S. Phelps, of Missouri, military govern-

[1] Ann. Cycl., 1862, p. 11.
[2] Ibid.
[3] Ibid.

or.[1] On August 19, 1862, he left St. Louis for Helena; but as the contemplated movement was not then made his office was of little importance. From the Union refugees at that point two regiments of Arkansas men were organized. The fall of Vicksburg in July, 1863, however, enabled the Union army to assume offensive operations, and the summer had not greatly advanced before a strong column was moving on Little Rock, the capture of which, September 10, 1863, was a fatal blow to Confederate authority throughout the State.

Amidst all its distresses the northern section of Arkansas had maintained its loyalty. Recent reverses to Confederate arms encouraged desertion from their ranks, Union sympathizers became active, and movements begun by them were joined by numbers who now regarded the Confederate cause as lost. Many, however, fearing a restoration of that authority, hesitated to identify themselves with the more pronounced loyalists. A newspaper favorable to the General Government was established at the capital. Meetings were held, and resolutions pledging unconditional support of the Union cause adopted. Citizens, both white and black, were organized, and by December, 1863, eight regiments of Arkansas troops had enlisted in the Federal service.[2]

A still more encouraging symptom was the return of eminent persons who now came forward to advocate the Union cause. Prominent among these was Brigadier-General E. W. Gantt, of the Confederate army, recently a prisoner of war and pardoned under the Amnesty Proclamation of the President. Toward the close of 1863 he thus describes the feeling of the people:

> The Union sentiment is manifesting itself on all sides and by every indication — in Union meetings — in desertions from the Confederate army — in taking the oath of allegiance unsolicited — in organizing for home

[1] N. & H., Vol. VI. p. 346.
[2] Ann. Cycl., 1863, p. 15.

defence, and enlisting in the Federal army. Old flags that have been hid in the crevices of rocks, and been worshipped by our mountain people as holy relics, are flung to the breeze, and followed to the Union army with an enthusiasm that beggars all description. The little county of Perry, that votes only about 600, and which has been turned wrong side out in search of conscripts by Hindman and his fellow-murderers and oppressors, with their retinue of salaried gentlemen and negro boys, sent down a company of ninety-four men. Where they came from, and how they kept their old flag during these three years of terror, persecution and plunder, I can't tell. But they were the proudest-looking set of men I ever saw, and full of fight.[1]

The retreat of General Banks from the Red River country changed greatly the aspect of Federal affairs in Arkansas, for it allowed all the Confederate forces in the vicinity to concentrate against the small army of General Steele, compelling him to act on the defensive at Little Rock. The State coming once more to a considerable extent under Confederate control, loyalists became scarce and gradually lost energy and hope.

Local reverses, however, were not allowed to interrupt the comprehensive policy of the President, and early in 1864 preparations were made to reorganize the State government. This movement, like those in Tennessee and Louisiana, was based upon the Amnesty and Reconstruction Proclamation of December 8, 1863. Even before this step had been taken the President was already moulding the diverse elements into a power that would ultimately undermine Confederate influence in the State. In the preceding summer, July 31, 1863, he had written General S. A. Hurlbut:

I understand that Senator Sebastian, of Arkansas, thinks of offering to resume his place in the Senate. Of course the Senate, and not I, would decide whether to admit or reject him. Still I should feel great interest in the question. It may be so presented as to be one of the very greatest national importance; and it may be otherwise so presented as to be of no more than temporary personal consequence to him.

[1] Ann. Cycl., 1863, p. 15.

ARKANSAS

The emancipation proclamation applies to Arkansas. . . . I think I shall not retract or repudiate it. Those who shall have tasted actual freedom I believe can never be slaves or quasi-slaves again. For the rest, I believe some plan substantially being gradual emancipation would be better for both white and black. The Missouri plan, recently adopted, I do not object to on account of the time for ending the institution; but I am sorry the beginning should have been postponed for seven years, leaving all that time to agitate for the repeal of the whole thing. It should begin at once, giving at least the new-born a vested interest in freedom which could not be taken away. If Senator Sebastian could come with something of this sort from Arkansas, I, at least, should take great interest in his case; and I believe a single individual will have scarcely done the world so great a service. See him, if you can, and read this to him; but charge him to not make it public for the present.[1]

Union officers in the West were urged by Mr. Lincoln in October, 1862, to assist and encourage repentant rebel communities to elect both State officers and members of Congress.[2] As this involved a recognition of existing governments it need scarcely be observed that the march of events forced the President later to occupy somewhat different ground; nor is it more necessary to add, that to his main purpose, to undermine secession and restore the Union, he adhered inflexibly. With this fundamental object all his acts harmonize.

At the time of her secession, W. K. Sebastian represented Arkansas in the United States Senate and abandoned his seat; he was now ready to assist in restoring his State to her old status. Of these evidences of disintegration in Confederate interests within the State the President was very exactly informed, and it was because of his conviction that many persons hitherto supporting that cause were either wavering in their allegiance or had become hostile to secession that he wrote, January 5, 1864, to General Steele:

I wish to afford the people of Arkansas an opportunity of taking the oath prescribed in the proclamation of December 8, 1863, preparatory to

[1] Letters and State Papers of Lincoln, Vol. II. p. 379.
[2] Ibid., p. 247.

reorganizing a State Government there. Accordingly I send you by General Kimball some blank books and other blanks, the manner of using which will, in the main, be suggested by an inspection of them; and General Kimball will add some verbal explanations.

Please make a trial of the matter immediately at such points as you may think likely to give success. I suppose Helena and Little Rock are two of them. Detail any officer you may see fit to take charge of the subject at each point; and which officer, it may be assumed, will have authority to administer the oath. These books, of course, are intended to be permanent records. Report to me on the subject.[1]

A week had scarcely elapsed when Mr. Lincoln approved the suggestions of General Banks relative to reinaugurating a civil government for Louisiana, and, doubtless, he knew no reason why similar work might not be going on simultaneously in Arkansas; therefore he repeated to General Steele what in substance he had already communicated to the Federal commander of the Department of the Gulf. His instructions, dated January 20, 1864, and quoted below, are self-explanatory, and in no important particular differ from the Louisiana Plan:

Sundry citizens of the State of Arkansas petition me that an election may be held in that State, at which to elect a governor thereof; . . . that it be assumed at said election and thenceforward that the constitution and laws of the State, as before the rebellion, are in full force, except that the constitution is so modified as to declare that "there shall be neither slavery nor involuntary servitude, except in the punishment for crime whereof the party shall have been duly convicted; but the General Assembly may make such provision for the free people as shall recognize and declare their permanent freedom, provide for their education, and which may yet be consistent, as a temporary arrangement, with their present condition as a laboring, landless, and homeless class;" and also except that all now existing laws in relation to slaves are inoperative and void; that said election to be held on the twenty-eighth day of March next at all the usual voting places of the State, or all such as voters may attend for that purpose; that the voters attending at each place at 8 o'clock in the morning of said day, may choose judges and clerks of election for that place; that all persons qualified by said constitution and laws, and taking the oath prescribed in the President's proclamation of December the

[1] Letters and State Papers of Lincoln, Vol. II. p. 467.

8th, 1863, either before or at the election, and none others, may be voters, provided that persons having the qualifications aforesaid, and being in the volunteer military service of the United States, may vote once wherever they may be at voting places; that each set of judges and clerks may make return directly to you on or before the eleventh day of April next; that in all other respects said election may be conducted according to said modified constitution and laws; that on receipt of said returns, you count said votes, and that if the number shall reach or exceed five thousand four hundred and six, you canvass said votes and ascertain who shall thereby appear to have been elected governor; and that on the eighteenth day of April next, the person so appearing to have been elected, and appearing before you at Little Rock to have, by you, administered to him an oath to support the Constitution of the United States and said modified constitution of the State of Arkansas, and actually taking said oath, be, by you, declared qualified, and be enjoined to immediately enter upon the duties of the office of governor of said State; and that you thereupon declare the constitution of the State of Arkansas to have been modified and amended as aforesaid by the action of the people as aforesaid.

You will please order an election immediately, and perform the other parts assigned you, with necessary incidentals, all according to the foregoing.[1]

By discussion and organization the elements opposed to the Richmond Government aroused so much enthusiasm that Unionists anticipated the wishes of the President by meeting, January 8, 1864, in convention at Little Rock. This assembly, composed of forty-four delegates representing, as they claimed, twenty-two of the fifty-four counties in the State, was made up of members elected at various mass meetings by very meagre votes. This at least was an objection then urged by those who were adverse to the purposes of the convention. They further stated that many of the counties represented were without the Federal military lines. It was admitted that if these counties lay beyond Union lines neither were they occupied by Confederate forces, and that generally the delegates were gentlemen of character and patriotism.[2]

[1] Letters and State Papers of Lincoln, Vol. II. pp. 472-473.
[2] Ann. Cycl., 1864, p. 29; Hough's American Constitutions, Vol. II. p. 81.

In a published address the convention stated frankly:

We found after remaining at Little Rock about a week, under a temporary organization, that delegates were present from twenty-two counties, elected by the people, and that six other counties had held elections, and that their representatives were looked for daily. We then organized the Convention permanently, and determined that while we could not properly claim to be the people of Arkansas in Convention assembled, with full and final authority to adopt a constitution, yet, being the representatives, by election, of a considerable portion of the State, and understanding, as we believed, the sentiment of nearly all our citizens who desire the immediate benefits of a government under the authority of the United States, we also determined to present a constitution and plan of organization, which, if adopted by them, becomes at once their act as effectually as if every county in the State had been represented in the Convention.[1]

An amended constitution was adopted by this convention on January 22. By it the act of secession was declared null and void; slavery was abolished immediately and unconditionally, and the Confederate debt wholly repudiated.[2] These important changes in the fundamental law of the State indicate the sentiments of the delegates. Isaac Murphy was appointed Provisional Governor; C. C. Bliss, Lieutenant-Governor and R. T. J. White, Secretary of State. These officers were inaugurated on the same day that the convention adopted the constitution; this by its schedule was to be submitted to a popular vote at an election to be held March 14, when State officers and Representatives in Congress would also be chosen.[3]

Ignorant that the movement to restore a civil government had proceeded so far, Mr. Lincoln had sent his instructions to General Steele. As these had been carefully considered it was feared the work of the convention would differ in some essential particular from the plan outlined for the Federal

---
[1] Quoted in N. & H., Vol. VIII. p. 414.
[2] Hough's Amer. Cons., Vol. II. p. 81.
[3] Ann. Cycl., 1864, p. 29.

commander. To prevent such a consequence the President wrote General Steele again on January 27 as follows:

> I have addressed a letter to you and put it in the hands of Mr. Gantt and other Arkansas gentlemen, containing a program for an election in that State. This letter will be handed you by some of these gentlemen. Since writing it, I see that a Convention in Arkansas having the same general object, has taken some action, which I am afraid may clash somewhat with my program. I therefore can do no better than to ask you to see Mr. Gantt immediately on his return, and with him do what you and he may deem necessary to harmonize the two plans into one, and then put it through with all possible vigor. Be sure to retain the free-State Constitutional provision in some unquestionable form and you and he can fix the rest. The points I have made in the program have been well considered. Take hold with an honest heart and a strong hand. Do not let any questionable man control or influence you.[1]

The President's interest in the proceedings of the convention and his anxiety about the outcome of its deliberations appear in a letter to General Steele written three days after the above.[2] So favorable were his impressions of the progress reported that he believed the best his subordinate could do " would be to help them on their own plan "; of this, however, General Steele, who was on the ground, was to be the judge. To Governor Murphy he telegraphed, February 6, that his order concerning an election was made in ignorance of any action which the convention might take; also that his subsequent communication to General Steele directed that officer to assist, not to hinder, the delegates.[3] General Thayer also was informed that the apparent conflict between the President and the convention was altogether accidental.[4] On February 17, Mr. Lincoln explained the situation more fully to William M. Fishback:

> When I fixed a plan for an election in Arkansas I did it in ignorance that your convention was doing the same work. Since I learned the

[1] Letters and State Papers of Lincoln, Vol. II. p. 475.
[2] Ibid., p. 476.
[3] Ibid., p. 479.
[4] Ibid., p. 482.

latter fact I have been constantly trying to yield my plan to them. I have sent two letters to General Steele, and three or four despatches to you and others, saying that he, General Steele, must be master, but that it will probably be best for him to merely help the convention on its own plan. Some single mind must be master, else there will be no agreement in anything, and General Steele, commanding the military and being on the ground, is the best man to be that master. Even now citizens are telegraphing me to postpone the election to a later day than either that fixed by the convention or by me. This discord must be silenced.[1]

The President evidently had learned something from his recent experience with his friends and subordinates in Louisiana. General Steele from his headquarters at Little Rock issued on February 29 the following address to the people of Arkansas:

The convention of your citizens, held at Little Rock during the last month [says this proclamation], has adopted a constitution and submitted it to you for your approval or rejection. That constitution is based upon the principles of freedom, and it is for you now to say, by your voluntary and unbiased action, whether it shall be your fundamental law. While it may have defects, in the main it is in accordance with the views of that portion of the people who have been resisting the fratricidal attempts which have been made during the last three years. The convention has fixed the 14th day of March next on which to decide this great question, and the General commanding is only following the instructions of the Government when he says to you that every facility will be offered for the expression of your sentiments, uninfluenced by any considerations save those which affect your own interests and those of your posterity. . . . The election will be held and the return be made in accordance with the schedule adopted by the convention, and no interference from any quarter will be allowed to prevent the free expression of the loyal men of the State on that day.[2]

The election pursuant to this notice began March 14, 1864, the polls remaining open for three days. For the constitution 12,177, and against it 226, votes were cast.[3] Isaac Murphy, against whom there was no opposing candidate, was chosen Governor by 12,430 votes cast by the citizens of more

[1] Letters and State Papers of Lincoln, Vol. II. pp. 483-484.
[2] Ann. Cycl., 1864, pp. 29-30.
[3] Ibid., p. 30.

than forty counties. As early as March 18 the President appears to have received from the Governor-elect some favorable tidings,[1] and on April 27, when more complete returns had reached him from the same source, he expressed in a telegram his gratification at the large vote, more than double that required by the Louisiana Plan, and also at the intelligence that the State government, including the Legislature, was organized and in working order.[2]

Besides a Governor five other officers of the executive and several members of the judicial branch of government together with many county officials were chosen.[3] At the same time three Representatives in Congress, T. M. Jacks, A. A. C. Rogers and J. M. Johnson, were elected from the First, Second and Third Districts respectively. The Legislature, composed of twenty three Senators and fifty-nine members of Assembly, met on the 11th of April, and during the session, which ended June 1 succeeding, appointed William Fishback and Elisha Baxter United States Senators to fill vacancies caused by the secession of the late incumbents, R. W. Johnson and William K. Sebastian. After investigation by a committee of Congress, however, they were declared not entitled to seats; but as each possessed such a title to membership as to justify inquiry they were paid mileage. This consideration they were denied when, without new action, they subsequently presented themselves at a special session of the Senate; on that occasion they were accompanied by William D. Snow, who had been chosen to succeed Fishback. It was agreed, March 9, 1865, to postpone till the next session of Congress consideration of the credentials of Mr. Snow. The House, without admitting as Representatives the three claimants for seats, had consented to allow them mileage. Arkansas, unlike Louisiana

[1] Letters and State Papers of Lincoln, Vol. II. p. 501.
[2] Ibid., p. 515.
[3] Ann. Cycl., 1864, p. 30.

and Tennessee, did not participate in the Presidential election of 1864, because of a feeling that its electoral vote would not be received even if offered. This course appears to have been adopted on the suggestion of their representatives, who returned with such a conviction from a sojourn in Washington.[1]

A succeeding chapter, in tracing the origin and progress of the controversy between the Executive and Legislative branches of Government, will describe more fully the attitude of Congress toward Mr. Lincoln's efforts at reconstruction and afford an opportunity for discussing both the nature of the conventions by which civil government had been restored in Tennessee, Louisiana and Arkansas, and the constitutionality of the various Executive acts by which this reëstablishment was assisted.

[1] See remarks of Senator Pomeroy, February 2, 1865, Congressional Globe, Part II., 2 Sess. 38th Cong., p. 555.

IV

VIRGINIA

THE Federal Government, as already observed, was constrained at an early stage of the Civil War to define its attitude toward loyal citizens of the seceding States. The earliest indications of the policy adopted may be discerned in the case of Virginia, which presents the only instance of a people in any of the insurrectionary States organizing open resistance to revolution. All departments of government in that Commonwealth having gone over to rebellion, the loyal minority were left without any organization for the conduct of domestic affairs. In these circumstances they called a convention which by an original act of sovereignty reconstituted the government. The progress of the conflict was attended in that State by consequences not elsewhere observed, and it is chiefly because of this fact that a slight departure from exact chronological order is believed to be justified. The principles which guided the Administration will be easily comprehended by considering their application to the novel and somewhat embarrassing questions that arose before rebellion was finally crushed within the borders of that once glorious Commonwealth.

" The Convention of Virginia " which, by authority of the Legislature, assembled at Richmond, February 13, 1861, passed on April 17 following an ordinance of secession from the United States.[1] Though the injunction of secrecy was

[1] McPherson's Pol. Hist., p. 7.

never removed from this proceeding, the tally, discovered soon after among the private papers of a member, shows that 88 delegates favored and 55 opposed the measure; one was excused from voting, eight were either absent or silent.[1] This strong opposition is explained in part by the physical characteristics of the State.

The principal chain of the Alleghanies formed in the western portion of the Old Dominion a lofty range which parts the streams finding their way into the Ohio and the Potomac from those that reach the lower waters of Chesapeake Bay or the sounds of North Carolina. The country southeast of this ridge, including the Shenandoah Valley, the Piedmont district, the middle division and the tide-water region, contained about three fourths of the white inhabitants, and something less than three fourths of the area, of Virginia. In this section were found many large tobacco plantations cultivated almost exclusively by negroes. Indeed, it was in the light soil of the tide-water counties of Virginia that English settlers in America first attempted, nearly two and one half centuries before, the memorable experiment of African slave labor. Soon after 1808, when their importation was prohibited by act of Congress, slaves were bred in Virginia to supply the demand of Southern markets, and by 1860 the bondmen in that Commonwealth had become almost two thirds as numerous as the master race.[2] It is sufficiently accurate to say that the triangular district bounded on the north by the winding course of the Potomac, by the parallel of 36° 31' on the south and stretching from the Atlantic to the crest of the Alleghany mountains, comprised all that part of "the good old commonwealth" which was then either historically important or interesting. This prolific soil was the birthplace of many of America's most illustrious sons; its inhabitants for

[1] McPherson's Pol. Hist., p. 7n.
[2] Eighth Census, pp. 516-522.

the most part were proud to trace their descent from the earliest settlers along the James; many were wealthy, and all had long been distinguished for their hospitality.

Beyond this favored region the country, which slopes gradually down to the upper Potomac and the Ohio, is marked by a succession of parallel ranges separated by fertile valleys; but like the large tract which encircled the Adirondacks and a similar one in northern Pennsylvania, the Virginian wilderness remained untouched by the ceaseless tide of immigration which at the close of the Revolution swept westward from the Atlantic seaboard. For this uninviting region the second Federal census indicates less than two inhabitants to the square mile; by 1810 pioneers from the line of the Ohio river encroached on its silent forests. At the next census, however, a portion was still unoccupied, but in the succeeding decennial period it received from various points, chiefly from Pennsylvania, Ohio and New England, many enterprising and thrifty settlers. The sixth census, that of 1840, represents the entire tract as sparsely inhabited.[1] Its abundant resources, then but little developed, subsequently gave rise to a great variety of profitable industries, and it advanced rapidly in population. Extensive plantations, however, were few; the number of slaves, owing somewhat to the facility for escape, had always been small, and in the ten years preceding the outbreak of hostilities had actually diminished by upwards of two thousand.[2] Though it then contained nearly one fourth of the whites, it included no more than one thirtieth of the negroes in the State. Their labor, too, except in other than agricultural occupations, afforded little remuneration. In consequence of its productions as well as its location both the

---

[1] Density maps in Tenth Census (Population), pp. xii-xiii, xiv-xv, xvi-xvii.

[2] Blair in Appendix to Globe, pp. 327-331, 2 Sess. 37th Cong.; Eighth Census, pp. 516-522; Seventh Census, pp. 242-261.

interests and sympathies of the people were with the adjoining States of Ohio and Pennsylvania.

But, apart from geographical considerations, northwestern Virginia had a grievance of long standing: for years its inhabitants had complained that they were not fairly represented in the Legislature, and the immunity from taxation enjoyed by their fellow-citizens east of the mountains was a discrimination too gross to escape attention. The slave oligarchy, they declared, possessed and wielded for its own advantage the political power of the State. The question of its dismemberment had been discussed as early as 1829-30, when the mountain sons of Virginia were on the verge of revolution. The East then yielded a pittance of power, which, though far short of the demands of justice, reconciled western Virginians for the time. In 1850 they were again on the point of insurrection. On this occasion adequate representation was conceded in the lower though withheld in the upper chamber of the General Assembly, the dominant party thus retaining control of that body as well as the benefits of a constitutional provision by which slaves under the age of twelve years were exempt from taxation, and of those liable to assessment none could be valued at more than three hundred dollars even if worth in the market a thousand dollars or upwards.[1] Moreover, much of the public revenue was expended upon internal improvements for the eastern section of the State. The Shenandoah Valley, at one time showing signs of discontent, was bound by the construction of railways, in social as well as in commercial life, more firmly to Richmond. In short, the Alleghanies formed a barrier almost completely cutting off intercourse between the two divisions. Their relations were well expressed by Governor Pierpont, who told Senator Wade that there was no communication whatever between the people except the furnishing a few members to the Legislature

[1] Parker, The Formation of West Virginia, p. 125.

and a few inmates of the penitentiary.[1] Their different interests tended to alienate the sections; the hand of nature had traced the line of separation.

Now, however, that a crisis was impending, the Richmond authorities, to harmonize every element within their Commonwealth, were willing to forego this privilege; to share the burdens of State administration, to meet State liabilities, and generally to place themselves on a footing of equality with their fellow-citizens along the Ohio. This concession, by a majority of 50,000, was actually extorted in an election from the prudence or the fears of disunionists whose magnanimity was duly emphasized by Governor Letcher in an appeal to the people of the northwest.[2] The latter refused, notwithstanding, to acquiesce in the action of the secession convention which, so far as it was able to do so, carried their State, as a political organization, out of the Union.

It may be affirmed generally that the professional politicians and large property owners of this region were disloyal;[3] State officials with surprising unanimity were ardent advocates of secession and active in committing their Commonwealth to its support. An overwhelming proportion of the plain people, however, were devotedly attached to the Union and determined on its preservation. Therefore when the Richmond State government attempted to execute its laws in these parts it encountered the most spirited resistance. Especially was this true in the Pan Handle counties, where opposition was promptly organized.

Probably the first consultation upon the grave questions that had arisen was held at the Court House in Wellsburgh, Brooke County, where a large number of citizens from that and the adjacent county of Hancock assembled to hear the

[1] Globe, 2 Sess. 37th Cong., p. 3038.
[2] Ann. Cycl., 1861, pp. 743-744.
[3] The Formation of West Virginia, p. 36.

report of Mr. Campbell Tarr, their delegate to Richmond. From Harrison came Hon. John S. Carlile, who, like Mr. Tarr, narrowly escaped with his life from that city, where he had represented his county in the convention. They reported the proceedings of that body and urged immediate preparation to resist. As a result of this discussion a committee of four was appointed to procure arms and ammunition in Washington. *En route* thither they had an interview at Harrisburg with Governor Curtin, who not only expressed sympathy with their object, but promised assistance if necessary. On arriving at the national capital they called upon Hon. Edwin M. Stanton, who was a native of Steubenville, Ohio, and a warm personal friend of each member of the committee. They were immediately presented to Mr. Cameron, Secretary of War, who, on learning the purpose of their visit, manifested some hesitation as to his legal right to comply with their request. Upon this Mr. Stanton declared with emphasis that "the law of *necessity* gives the right," and added, "let them have arms and ammunition; we will look for the book law afterwards."[1] Two thousand rifles with suitable ammunition were then furnished, and as security for their proper use Mr. Stanton tendered his own name. From Wellsburgh, where they were temporarily kept in expectation of a rebel attack, these arms were sent for distribution to Wheeling.

United States troops from Ohio and Indiana together with local volunteers soon drove the Confederate forces from this region, and subsequently, though often menaced, it was almost exempt from the ravages of war.[2] Thus encouraged, Union men resolved to form a political organization coextensive with Virginia or to establish a separate and distinct State. Preliminary movements toward that end were promptly inaugurated, and, April 22, 1861, five days after the passage of

[1] The Formation of West Virginia, p. 42.
[2] Ann. Cycl., 1861, pp. 742-743.

the ordinance, nearly 1,200 citizens of Clarksburgh denounced in a public meeting the action of the secession convention and recommended the people of northwestern Virginia to assemble on May 13 at Wheeling. On the 4th a Union mass meeting had been held at Kingwood, near the northern border. The separation of western from eastern Virginia was declared by this body to be essential to the maintenance of their liberties. They also resolved to elect a Representative to Congress. On the following day there convened at Wheeling another assemblage, which considered the question of separating from that portion of the State in rebellion. About the same time other gatherings were held in different localities.

There were thousands of eager and earnest patriots in the city of Wheeling on May 13, when nearly four hundred delegates, mostly appointed by primary meetings, and representing twenty-six counties, assembled to deliberate on the situation. The best method of organizing opposition to treason was the question: how to inaugurate a government which the Federal authorities would recognize and protect?[1] On this important subject there is said to have been considerable diversity of opinion; the decision finally reached was based upon a suggestion by one of the members that since Governor Letcher and other State officers, by adhering to the pretended ordinance of secession, had forfeited their powers, and the existing constitution made no provision for such an emergency, the only way was to ask the people, the source of all political power, to send delegates to a convention authorized to supply their places with loyal men. This proposal was presented to the meeting and adopted with great unanimity.[2] A General State Committee, empowered to appoint sub-committees in all counties where practicable, was then named,

[1] The Formation of West Virginia, p. 43.
[2] Ibid.

and a stirring address put forth. It announced their purpose and urged all loyal citizens to elect representatives to a second convention. Copies of this appeal were sent to influential citizens throughout the State, and it was agreed after a session of three days to choose on May 26 delegates to the proposed convention.

This election having been held at the time appointed, representatives from nearly forty counties assembled at Wheeling on June 11. The convention, numbering 98 members, organized by selecting for its president Hon Arthur I. Boreman. Before proceeding to business the following oath was administered to the delegation from each county: "We solemnly declare that we will support the Constitution of the United States and the laws made in pursuance thereof, as the supreme law of the land, anything in the Ordinance of the Convention that assembled in Richmond on the 13th day of February last to the contrary notwithstanding, so help us God."[1] The State government was reconstituted on the 13th by an ordinance declaring vacant all places, whether legislative, executive or judicial, whose incumbents had espoused the cause of secession. This class, as already observed, included nearly every official in Virginia. These vacancies the convention supplied by the appointment of loyal men. In the constitution they made an important alteration which prescribed the number of delegates necessary to constitute a quorum in the General Assembly. All State, county and town officials were required to take an oath of allegiance which pledged support of both the Federal Constitution and the restored government of Virginia. On June 17 a declaration of independence was adopted without one dissenting voice; it denounced the usurpation of the Richmond convention, which had assumed to place the resources of Virginia at the disposal

[1] Ann. Cycl., 1861, p. 743; The Formation of West Virginia, p. 45, gives the oath in a form slightly different.

of the Confederate Government, to which power it repudiated allegiance. Resolutions expressing a determination never to submit to the ordinance of secession, but to maintain the rights of Virginia in the Union, were then passed. All persons in arms against the national Government were commanded to disband and to return to their allegiance. Though the members seriously endeavored to reorganize their government, it was with an express declaration that a division of the Commonwealth was a paramount object of their labors, and they decided, June 20, by a unanimous vote in favor of ultimate separation.

Under an ordinance previously adopted Hon. Francis H. Pierpont was chosen Governor on the same day; a lieutenant-governor, an attorney-general and an executive council of five were also appointed. Other administrative offices were subsequently filled. The new incumbents were to exercise their functions for six months or until successors should be elected and qualified. The convention on June 25, subject in an emergency to be re-assembled by the Governor and Council, then adjourned to August 6, 1861.

Before concluding this session the convention directed all members willing to swear fealty to the Union, who were elected to the assembly on May 23 preceding, to meet on the 1st of July at Wheeling. At the time of their election these representatives were destined for Richmond. In addition to those regularly chosen under the old law of the Commonwealth, others pursuant to an ordinance of the convention were elected to fill vacancies. All were to qualify themselves by taking an oath or affirmation of allegiance to the United States and to the reorganized government of Virginia. These members, chiefly from the western counties, were to compose the law-making body, which was invested with all the powers and duties pertaining to the General Assembly.

The new Governor was inaugurated on June 20, and, after

taking the oath of office, said: "We have been driven into the position we occupy to-day by the usurpers at the South, who have inaugurated this war upon the soil of Virginia, and have made it the great Crimea of this contest. We, representing the loyal citizens of Virginia, have been bound to assume the position we have assumed to-day for the protection of ourselves, our wives, our children, and our property. We, I repeat, have been driven to assume this position; and now we are but recurring to the great fundamental principle of our fathers, that to the loyal people of a State belongs the law-making power of that State. The loyal people are entitled to the government and governmental authority of the State. And, fellow-citizens, it is the assumption of that authority upon which we are now about to enter."[1]

"It was not the object of the Wheeling convention," he declared on a later occasion, "to set up any new government in the State, or separate, or other government than the one under which they had always lived."[2]

From these utterances his hearers must have concluded that the reorganized government was not for a part but for the whole of Virginia. Indeed, it was to the discernment of Mr. Pierpont that Virginia loyalists were chiefly indebted for a legal solution of the intricate problem that confronted them. While Carlile and others were urging a counter-revolution, Mr. Pierpont was carefully studying the provisions of the Federal Constitution. The clause of that instrument which guarantees a republican form of government was designed, he believed, to meet just such an emergency as had arisen. Though this conservative suggestion was not at first received with much favor, it continued gradually to win adherents until its propriety was universally recognized.[3] By thus proceed-

[1] Ann. Cycl., 1861, p. 743.
[2] Ann. Cycl., 1862, p. 801.
[3] Mr. A. W. Campbell in The Wheeling Daily Intelligencer, April 14, 1897.

ing along constitutional lines a State government in all its branches was soon established in every county not occupied by an armed foe.

The Legislature of the restored State assembled, July 2, at Wheeling and assumed the full exercise of its powers. Two United States Senators, Waitman T. Willey, whose fidelity many considered doubtful, and John S. Carlile, an able, eloquent and then a trusted leader, were elected, July 9; the former to fill the vacancy occasioned by the withdrawal of James M. Mason, the latter to succeed Robert M. T. Hunter, who also had abdicated his seat in Congress. Both were admitted, though not without a vigorous protest from the minority, to seats at the first session of the Thirty-seventh Congress, which met on July 4, 1861.

Their certificates were presented, July 13, by Andrew Johnson. Senator Bayard entered a protest. Their admission, he said, would be a recognition of an organization that was not the regular government of the Commonwealth. Mr. Letcher was still Governor of Virginia, his term not having expired. The Senate had no authority to create a new State out of a part of an existing one. He then moved to refer their credentials to the Committee on the Judiciary. His colleague, Mr. Saulsbury, objected, that Mason and Hunter were not expelled until July 11, whereas the claimants were appointed two days previously, at a time when no vacancies had occurred. To this Senator Johnson replied that the vacancies did in fact exist at the time of their election, July 9, and that the expulsion of Mason and Hunter was not merely a declaration that vacancies existed, but their seats were regarded as filled, and the occupants expelled from the floor of the Senate.

Mr. Bayard denied that, even if Mason and Hunter were guilty of the alleged crimes, there was any power in either the Governor or Legislature to terminate their appointments; they might die, they could be removed by expulsion, but vacancies could not be anticipated by the Legislature of Virginia. The name of Mr. Pierpont could convey no authority to their credentials. On the question of reference five Senators voted in the affirmative, thirty-five in the negative. The oath was therefore administered and they took their seats, July 13, at the special session which began on the 4th.[1]

A resolution was passed by the House of Delegates of the reorganized government instructing the Senators and requesting their Representatives in Congress to vote the necessary appropriation of men and money for a vigorous prosecution of the war, and to oppose all compromise. A stay law was also enacted by the Legislature, and a bill passed which authorized the Governor to organize a patrol in such counties as might require it; two hundred thousand dollars were appropriated for military purposes.

On August 6, 1861, the Wheeling convention reassembled. Hitherto in all its proceedings relative to a reorganization there had been great unanimity, but when the delegates returned they were conscious of a strong popular sentiment in favor of erecting a new State, a subject that had been introduced, though not much discussed, before adjournment. This determination among their constituents seriously troubled many of the members. Political aspirations had been awakened; many of them had enjoyed the benefits of the humbler offices under the mother State; the Union forces, it was confidently expected, would soon crush the insurrection in Virginia, and the reorganized government, with themselves at its head, would be acquiesced in by their recent oppressors. To their ambition this hope was far more flattering than the prospect of administering the affairs of a comparatively small State on the western frontier of the Old Dominion. Then, too, the idea of dismemberment was certain to wound Virginia State pride. Moreover, the movement to form an independent com-

[1] Globe, 1 Sess. 37th Cong., pp. 103-109.

monwealth, when the reorganized government itself had been scarcely recognized, would look premature. Sentiments of this nature had begun to possess the minds of many delegates about the time of their return.

In compliance with what appeared to be a popular demand, however, these considerations were disregarded, and the convention by a vote of 50 to 28 passed an ordinance authorizing the formation out of the Commonwealth of Virginia of a new State to be called Kanawha, which was to embrace thirty-nine counties between the Alleghanies and the Ohio, provided the people thereof, at an election to be held on October 24, should express themselves in favor of such a measure; on certain prescribed conditions other contiguous counties could be annexed. At the election which was to decide this important question delegates to a constitutional convention were also to be chosen, and, if separation was approved by the people, these representatives were to assemble at Wheeling on November 26 and organize themselves into a convention. Any constitution which they might adopt was to be submitted to the qualified electors of the counties concerned. The new commonwealth was to assume a just proportion of Virginia's public debt as it existed prior to January 1, 1861; private rights derived from her laws were to be valid under the proposed State, and were to be determined by the laws then existing in Virginia.[1]

The convention, as previously noted, reassembled on August 6. Three days later one A. F. Ritchie, a member from Marion County, forwarded to Attorney-General Bates at Washington a letter which requested and received an immediate reply. Mr. Ritchie published the response, of which this is the important part:

The formation of a new State out of Western Virginia is an original, independent act of *revolution*. I do not deny the power of revolution (I

[1] The Formation of West Virginia, pp. 47-48.

do not call it right, for it is never prescribed; it exists in force only, and has and can have no law but the will of the revolutionists). Any attempt to carry it out involves a plain breach of *both the constitutions* — of Virginia and of the Nation. And hence it is plain that you cannot take such a course without weakening, if not destroying, your claims upon the sympathy and support of the General Government, and without disconcerting the plan already adopted by both Virginia and the General Government for the reorganization of the revolted States and the restoration of the integrity of the Union.

That plan I understand to be this: When a State, by its perverted functionaries, has declared itself out of the Union, we avail ourselves of all the sound and loyal elements of the State — all who own allegiance to and claim protection of the Constitution — to form a State government as nearly as may be upon the former model, and claiming to be the very State which has been in part overthrown by the successful rebellion. In this way we establish a constitutional nucleus around which all the shattered elements of the commonwealth may meet and combine, and thus restore the old State in its original integrity.

This, I verily thought, was the plan adopted at Wheeling, and recognized and acted upon by the General Government here. Your convention annulled the revolutionary proceedings at Richmond, both in the Convention and the General Assembly, and your new Governor formally demanded of the President the fulfillment of the constitutional guaranty in favor of Virginia — Virginia as known to our fathers and to us. The President admitted the obligation, and promised his best efforts to fulfill it. And the Senate admitted your Senators, not as representing a new and nameless State, now for the first time heard of in our history, but as representing "the good old commonwealth."

Must all this be undone, and a new and hazardous experiment be ventured upon, at the moment when dangers and difficulties are thickening around us? I hope not. . . . I had rejoiced in the movement in Western Virginia, as a legal, constitutional, and safe refuge from revolution and anarchy; as at once an example and fit instrument for the restoration of all the revolted States.

I have not time now to discuss the subject in its various bearings. What I have written is written with a running pen and will need your charitable criticism.

If I had time to think, I could give persuasive reasons for declining the attempt to create a new State at this perilous time. At another time I might be willing to go fully into the question, but now I can say no more.[1]

[1] The Formation of West Virginia, pp. 48-50; also Ann. Cycl., 1861, p. 745.

Mr. Ritchie, who had opposed a dismemberment of the old Commonwealth, was anxious, no doubt, to justify his vote by the endorsement of an eminent public character, and it is not improbable that before finally determining his action in so important a matter he was desirous of the opinion of some member of the Administration. Mr. Bates's communication is dated the 12th; the convention did not adjourn till the 25th of August. At any time prior to January 1, 1862, it was subject to be reassembled by its president or by the Governor.

The election of October 24, by a vote of 18,408 to 781, decided in favor of a division of the Commonwealth.[1] At the same time fifty-three delegates, representing forty-one counties, were chosen to frame a constitution for the proposed State. Of this convention John Hall was elected president and Ellery R. Hall secretary. The task before it, by no means an easy one, was to draft a fundamental law that would secure the approval of the people of western Virginia, of the Legislature of the restored State and of Congress. After a session of nearly three months it adjourned, February 18, 1862. Commissioners to convoke this body, should its work be recognized by Congress, had first been appointed. On December 3 preceding the name of the new State was changed to West Virginia.

In the convention were many members who desired silence on the subject of slavery; others saw clearly that to ignore the cause of their present troubles would ensure a rejection of their work by Congress. This element felt assured that the temper of the national Legislature would not indulge the slave power by giving it two additional Senators besides an increase of strength in the Electoral College. There was also a sentiment which desired a postponement of the disturbing question until all others had first been determined. The friends of gradual emancipation were warned by leading

[1] The Formation of West Virginia, p. 57.

Republicans in Congress that the constitution would not be recognized without a satisfactory provision on this subject. The "peculiar institution," however, still possessed influence enough to defeat such a purpose, and the convention adjourned without inserting any expression concerning slavery. Still, the friends of emancipation did not despair. Mr. Parker, one of these, caused to be printed in Ohio instructions to their assemblymen to make the following provision a part of their constitution if the speedy admission of the new State into the Union should appear to require it: "All children born of slave mothers in this State, after the constitution goes into operation, shall be free, males at the age of twenty-eight years, and females at the age of eighteen years, and the children of such females to be free at birth." [1]

This unauthorized action of Mr. Parker, in connection with appeals through the newspapers, was not without effect. At their county-seat the citizens of Upshur passed, among other resolutions, the following: "That we, the citizens of Upshur County, do endorse and accept the policy recommended by the present Chief Magistrate of the United States, (Abraham Lincoln) in his message of the 6th of March, 1862, to Congress, in regard to the emancipation of the slaves of the border States, as the policy that should be adopted by the people of West Virginia; and we do now pledge ourselves to advocate, defend and carry out the said policy, as the most promotive of our liberty, safety and prosperity in the Union." [2] Another resolution, adopted on this occasion, declared that the meeting expected the convention would have given the people an opportunity of expressing their sentiments on slavery in the proposed State. The convention, they complained, did not reflect the popular will.

The Union men and the loyal press of other counties fol-

[1] The Formation of West Virginia, p. 79.
[2] Ibid., p. 93.

lowed the example of Upshur by approving the measure or copying the "Instructions." Thus at the time of voting on the constitution an informal poll on slavery was obtained in twenty counties.

A faction in the convention proposed to annex the Shenandoah Valley with its large negro population; the success of such a plan, it was well understood, would ensure a rejection of the new State by Congress. To anticipate somewhat the events presently to be narrated it may be remarked at this point that the adversaries of the measure in Washington employed precisely the same tactics to defeat the movement for erecting an independent State.

The new establishment under Pierpont was regarded as representing the old Commonwealth. On December 2, 1861, the reorganized Legislature again assembled. The Governor recommended a repeal of the stay laws and confiscation of the property of secessionists. He congratulated the people that they had contributed their full quota, about 6,000 men, to the Union army.

The adversaries of slavery endeavored to obtain the consent of the restored Legislature to the condition that the gradual emancipation clause should become a part of the constitution as soon as ratified by the people. If Congress at its present session would give its consent and admit the new State on the same condition, the people, they declared, could be trusted to ratify afterward.

An election held April 3, 1862, gave, including the soldiers' vote, 28,321 for and 572 against the constitution, no returns being received from ten counties.[1] The vote for

[1] The Formation of West Virginia, p. 96, says 16,981 for and 441 against the constitution. The Annual Cyclopædia for 1862, p. 801, gives the vote as 18,862 in favor of, and 514 against, the constitution. Poore's Charters and Constitutions, Vol. II. p. 1977, is the authority for the statement in the text.

gradual emancipation, where an expression was had, was almost equal to that given for the constitution, both being nearly unanimous. The former received 6,052 for and 610 against it. How far this informal expression of opinion influenced Congress will presently be noticed.

At an extra session of the Legislature, convoked by Governor Pierpont, an act, in almost the identical language of that assenting to the formation of Kentucky, was passed, May 13, 1862, giving consent to the erection within the jurisdiction of Virginia of a new State to include forty-eight named counties; the second section of this act provided that Berkeley, Jefferson and Frederic counties could be annexed whenever a majority of their votes, at an election to be held for that purpose, should ratify the constitution. The act, together with a certified original of the constitution, was to be transmitted to their Senators and Representatives in Washington, who were requested to use their endeavors to obtain the consent of Congress to the admission of West Virginia into the Union.

On June 23, 1862, Mr. Wade, from the Committee on Territories, reported to the United States Senate a bill for the admission of West Virginia into the Union, and three days later requested its consideration. It stipulated, among other things, that "the convention thereinafter provided for shall, in the constitution to be framed by it, make provision that from and after the fourth day of July, 1863, the children of all slaves born within the limits of the State shall be free"; it also allotted to the new Commonwealth as many Representatives in Congress as her population would justify under the apportionment then existing.

Charles Sumner observed that the former was the imposition of a condition which proposed to recognize the existence of slavery during that generation. " Short as life may be," he declared, " it is too long for slavery." By the admission of West Virginia a new slave State would be added; he moved, therefore, to substitute for this requirement the Jeffersonian interdict that " within the limits of said State there shall be neither slavery nor involuntary servitude, otherwise than in punishment of crime whereof the party shall be duly convicted."

Mr. Hale justly remarked that after consenting to the admission of so many States with pro-slavery constitutions it would be a singular fact if the first that ever applied with a provision for prospective emancipation should be rejected.

Senator Collamer believed that if West Virginia was to enter on a footing of perfect equality with other members of the Union she should, like them, have the right to regulate domestic questions, including slavery, in her own way. The condition imposed by the bill denied her that right.

Mr. Wade disliked the proposition as it stood, because it was very objectionable to him " to say that a man born on the 4th day of July, 1863, shall be free, and one born the day before shall be forever a slave." " I should much prefer," he added, " to have it graduated so that all born after the adoption of this constitution shall be free, and that all between certain ages shall be free at a certain period." At this point Sumner's amendment was lost by a vote of 24 to 11.

Mr. Carlile, of Virginia, who was foremost in organizing resistance to secession, had from the beginning assumed the appearance of a friend, but, after giving direction to the movement for separation, acted as an adversary to the new State; he opposed all conditions on its admission and expressed a preference that it be permitted to enter on the constitution submitted by its people. He would never " consent to have the organic law of a State framed for its people by the Congress of the United States." There were 47,000 voters in the counties to be embraced within the proposed State; of that number only about 19,000 had voted on the constitution. At the last moment he delivered with his usual eloquence a strong argument against admission. An amendment which he submitted would have the effect certainly to postpone, perhaps altogether to defeat, the measure in the Senate. Failing to secure its adoption, he urged a postponement till December following; this motion, however, was voted down.

So surprised were his associates at this unexpected opposition that they inquired pointedly why these belated arguments had not been presented to the Committee on Territories when the measure was before them. Mr. Wade, its chairman, was especially severe in his condemnation of Carlile's extraordinary course, for it was the reasoning of the Virginia Senator that had won their support; he had searched the precedents and submitted cheerfully to all the labors imposed by the Committee. Now by his opposition he brought everything to a stand-still.

His colleague, Mr. Willey, who had been converted in a rather advanced stage of the movement, declared that it was not the desire to be free from that part of the Commonwealth in rebellion that was responsible for the present attitude of western Virginia; the insurrection only precipitated the attempt to settle a controversy which was older than he. To enforce his remarks he added that great numbers of her citizens had determined to fix their abodes elsewhere unless West Virginia became an independent State. During this discussion the Senate had before it the constitution framed by the convention which met November 26, 1861, in the city of Wheeling.

After a vigorous address by Benjamin F. Wade, who had recently investigated the subject, and whose ardor had been aroused by a deputation of West Virginians then in Washington, the bill by a vote of 23 to 17 passed the Senate, July 14, 1862.[1]

By Mr. Brown, of Virginia, a similar measure had already been introduced into the House on June 25. It was read twice and referred to the Committee on Territories.[2] When called up on July 16 succeeding it was agreed to postpone consideration of the bill until the regular session in December,[3] and on the 9th of that month, when Representative Bingham asked that it be put on its passage, discussion of the subject was resumed.

Representative Conway said that if the application of West Virginia came in the proper manner he would be happy to vote for its admission; he regretted, however, that at the beginning of the rebellion a territorial government had not been organized there; Congress could then have passed an enabling act, and the State could be received in a manner to admit of no dispute. The question turned, he declared, on whether the State of Virginia, of which a Mr. Pierpont was Governor, was the lawful State. This he denied. A number of persons without authority met at Wheeling and organized a government. This establishment the President had recognized; one branch of Congress by admitting its Senators had also conceded its legality. These precedents, however, should not be binding on the House. Neither mobs nor mass-meetings, he asserted, make laws under our system, and such bodies had no authority to appoint Mr. Pierpont.

The President intended, Mr. Conway believed, to form similar organizations in all the seceded States. "A policy seems about to be inaugurated," he added, "looking to an assumption of State powers by a few individuals, wherever

[1] Globe, Part III., 2 Sess. 37th Cong., p. 864; Part IV., pp. 2941-2942, 3034-3039, 3134-3135, 3307-3320.
[2] Globe, 2 Sess. 37th Cong., p. 2933.   [3] Ibid., p. 3397.

a military or other encampment can be effected in any of the rebellious districts. The utter and flagrant unconstitutionality of this scheme — I may say, its radically revolutionary character — ought to expose it to the reprobation of every loyal citizen and every member of this House. It aims at an utter subversion of our constitutional system. Its effect would be to consolidate all the powers of the Government in the hands of the Executive. With the admission of this new State, the President will have substantially *created* four Senators — two for Virginia and two for West Virginia." In referring to an extension of this system he declared that the President and a few friends could exercise Federal authority in all those States. " The true policy of this Government, therefore, with regard to the seceded States, is to hold them as common territory wherever and whenever our arms are extended over them. This obviates the terrible dangers which I have alluded to, and is in harmony with the highest considerations of public utility, as well as with sound legal principles." [1]

Mr. Conway directed his criticisms against the President because he believed the Executive was first to recognize the new government. The action of the Senate was based upon this precedent, it being assumed that recognition was an Executive function.

Mr. Brown, who introduced the bill at the preceding session, related concisely the essential facts already placed before the reader. He reminded Representative Conway that, though a State could not commit treason, or any other crime, the officials of government could do so; that the legislative powers, being incapable of annihilation, returned to the people; that the spontaneous assembly at Wheeling merely organized and proposed a plan by which regular elections were to be held to fill vacancies caused by the withdrawal of

[1] Globe, Part I., 3 Sess. 37th Cong., pp. 37-38.

disloyal representatives. A day was fixed, and wherever throughout the State loyal citizens chose to hold an election they could do so. The body thus elected assumed the legislative functions of the people.

In answer to an inquiry he replied that about five counties outside of West Virginia were represented in the Legislature which consented to the erection of the new State, and all the counties in the State were expressly invited to send representatives to the General Assembly. If they were loyal they should have coöperated; if not, they should have no voice in either the State Legislature or Congress. He referred in his remarks to a telegram which he had that morning received from Wheeling. It contained a resolution passed by the Assembly asking the House of Representatives to approve the bill for the admission of West Virginia, which had been favorably acted upon by the Senate at the preceding session.

"It has been asserted," he said in conclusion, "and understood in some quarters, that the organization of the government at Wheeling was for the purpose of forming a new State. I am prepared to say that when the convention originally met in Wheeling, although there were a few radicals there who wanted to form a new State without reinstating the old State of Virginia, we voted them down, and commenced the exercise of our original rights as freemen to build up the loyal government of Virginia; and although we designed eventually to ask for this separation, and it was what we anxiously desired, yet we determined to be a law-abiding people, and ask for what we desired through the forms of law."[1]

Representative Colfax in giving the reasons which should govern his vote stated that the restored government had been recognized by the Senate, by the President as well as

[1] Globe, Part I., 3 Sess. 37th Cong., pp. 38-39, 41-42.

other executive officers, and that the House, by admitting Mr. Segar, elected pursuant to a proclamation of Governor Pierpont, had also recognized the reorganized State. Even the political party in opposition voted for that member's admission. He also remarked that the new State came knocking at the door for admission with the tiara of freedom on her brow.[1]

Mr. Olin, who opposed the bill at the preceding session, said: " I shall vote for it now with reluctance. I shall vote for it mainly upon the ground that the General Government, whether wisely or unwisely I will not undertake to say, has encouraged this movement to create a division of the State of Virginia." [2] The people of West Virginia, with their experience of the evils which slavery brought on them, should not have permitted that institution to exist for an hour in their new government. For this deficiency, however, the bill provided a partial remedy.

Crittenden observed that it was the party applying for admission that gave its consent to a division of the State.[3] To this objection Representative Blair replied that there were counties outside of West Virginia which had assented to dismemberment. Other members, who had hitherto been hostile, now consented to support the measure from a conviction that it would weaken rebellion.

Representative Dawes said that the primary elections which sent delegates to the Wheeling convention discussed not a reorganization of the Virginia government, but the formation of an independent State in western Virginia. To accomplish that, he said, the only way was to restore the government of the entire Commonwealth. That government then had two things to do: to set up a new State within itself and secondly

[1] Globe, Part I., 3 Sess. 37th Cong., pp. 43-45.
[2] Ibid., p. 46.
[3] Ibid., pp. 46-47.

to give its consent thereto. This suggestion, he understood, emanated from Washington.[1]

In reference to the admission, Thaddeus Stevens said:

> I do not desire to be understood as being deluded by the idea that we are admitting this State in pursuance of any provisions of the Constitution. I find no such provision that justifies it, and the argument in favor of the constitutionality of it is one got up by those who either honestly entertain, I think, an erroneous opinion, or who desire to justify, by a forced construction, an act which they have predetermined to do.
>
> . . . .
>
> Now, to say that the Legislature which called this seceding convention was not the Legislature of Virginia, is asserting that the Legislature chosen by a vast majority of the people of a State is not the Legislature of that State. That is a doctrine which I can never assent to. I admit that the Legislature were disloyal, but they were still the disloyal and traitorous Legislature of the State of Virginia; and the State, as a mere State, was bound by their acts. Not so individuals. They are responsible to the General Government, and are responsible whether the State decrees treason or not. That being the Legislature of Virginia, Governor Letcher, elected by a majority of the votes of the people, is the Governor of Virginia — a traitor in rebellion, but a traitorous governor of a traitorous State. Now, then, how has that State ever given its consent to this division? A highly respectable but very small number of the citizens of Virginia — the people of West Virginia — assembled together, disapproved of the acts of the State of Virginia, and with the utmost self-complacency called themselves Virginia.
>
> . . . .
>
> I hold that none of the States now in rebellion are entitled to the protection of the Constitution, and I am grieved when I hear those high in authority sometimes talking of the constitutional difficulties about enforcing measures against this belligerent power, and the next moment disregarding every vestige and semblance of the Constitution by acts which alone are arbitrary. I hope I do not differ with the Executive in the views which I advocate. But I see the Executive one day saying " you shall not take the property of rebels to pay the debts which the rebels have brought upon the Northern States." Why? Because the Constitution is in the way. And the next day I see him appointing a military governor of Virginia, a military governor of Tennessee, and some other places. Where does he find anything in the Constitution to warrant that?

[1] Globe, Part I., 3 Sess. 37th Cong., p. 48.

If he must look there alone for authority, then all these acts are flagrant usurpations, deserving the condemnation of the community. He must agree with me or else his acts are as absurd as they are unlawful; for I see him here and there ordering elections for members of Congress wherever he finds a little collection of three or four consecutive plantations in the rebel States, in order that men may be sent in here to control the proceedings of this Congress, just as we sanctioned the election held by a few people at a little watering place at Fortress Monroe, by which we have here the very respectable and estimable member from that locality with us. It was upon the same principle.

. . . I say, then, that we may admit West Virginia as a new State, not by virtue of any provision of the Constitution, but under our absolute power which the laws of war give us in the circumstances in which we are placed. I shall vote for this bill upon that theory, and upon that alone; for I will not stultify myself by supposing that we have any warrant in the Constitution for this proceeding.

The Union, he declared, could never be restored as it was. His consent would never be given to restore it with a constitutional provision protecting slavery. An additional reason for giving his vote in favor of the bill was that there was a provision which would make West Virginia a free State.[1]

"No right of persons, no right of property," said Mr. Noell, "no social or domestic affairs, could be regulated or controlled by the people of western Virginia, under the circumstances in which they were placed, without recognizing the ordinance of secession, and acting as a State within the Southern Confederacy."[2] This showed both the necessity of reorganizing the government of Virginia and the recognition by Federal authorities of the establishment so constituted.

Mr. Segar declared that eleven of the forty-eight counties to comprise the new State had not participated in its establishment, being represented neither in the reorganized Legislature nor the Wheeling convention; three others were unrepresented both in the House of Delegates and the conventions; ten cast no vote on the constitution and three had in-

---
[1] Globe, Part I., 3 Sess. 37th Cong., pp. 50-51.
[2] Ibid., p. 35.

terests, social and commercial, which bound them up with the East. Then, too, the people of West Virginia made a fundamental law recognizing slavery; an anti-slavery constitution was to be imposed on them as a condition of admission.[1]

An able argument by Representative Bingham, of Ohio, who had charge of the bill, concluded the debate on December 10, 1862, when it passed by 96 yeas to 55 nays.[2]

With the President rested the fate of this important measure; if he vetoed it there would, probably, not be found a two thirds majority in its support. Many members, as will be seen from the preceding abridgment of the debates, yielded only a reluctant support.

On December 23, 1862, Mr. Lincoln sent to his constitutional advisers the following note:

GENTLEMEN OF THE CABINET:

A bill for an act entitled "An act for the admission of the State of West Virginia into the Union and for other purposes" has passed the House of Representatives and the Senate, and has been duly presented to me for my action.

I respectfully ask of each of you an opinion in writing on the following questions, to wit:

1st. Is the said act constitutional?
2d. Is the said act expedient?[3]

To this request six members of the Cabinet responded by submitting their written opinions. Three — Seward, Stanton and Chase — answered both questions in the affirmative. Bates, Blair and Welles replied in the negative; the remaining place in the Cabinet was vacant owing to the resignation of Caleb B. Smith, Secretary of the Interior, who had been raised to the Bench in Indiana. His successor had not yet been appointed.

[1] Globe, Part I., 3 Sess. 37th Cong., pp. 54-55.
[2] Ibid., p. 59.
[3] Letters and State Papers of Lincoln, Vol. II. p. 283.

Upon the constitutional point Mr. Seward said: "It seems to me that the political body which has given consent in this case is really and incontestably the State of Virginia. So long as the United States do not recognize the secession, departure, or separation of one of the States, that State must be deemed as existing and having a constitutional place within the Union, whatever may be at any moment exactly its revolutionary condition. A State thus situated cannot be deemed to be divided into two or more States merely by any revolutionary proceeding which may have occurred, because there cannot be, constitutionally, two or more States of Virginia. . . . The newly organized State of Virginia is therefore, at this moment, by the express consent of the United States, invested with all the rights of the State of Virginia, and charged with all the powers, privileges, and dignity of that State. If the United States allow to that organization any of these rights, powers, and privileges, it must be allowed to possess and enjoy them all. If it be a State competent to be represented in Congress and bound to pay taxes, it is a State competent to give the required consent of the State to the formation and erection of the new State of West Virginia within the jurisdiction of Virginia."

"Upon the question of expediency," he wrote, "I am determined by two considerations. First. The people of Western Virginia will be safer from molestation for their loyalty, because better able to protect and defend themselves as a new and separate State than they would be if left to demoralizing uncertainty upon the question whether, in the progress of the war, they may not be again reabsorbed in the State of Virginia, and subjected to severities as a punishment for their present devotion to the Union. The first duty of the United States is protection to loyalty wherever it is found. Second. I am of opinion that the harmony and peace of the Union will be promoted by allowing the new State to be formed and erected, which will assume jurisdiction over that part of the valley of the Ohio which lies on the south side of the Ohio River, displacing, in a constitutional and lawful manner, the jurisdiction heretofore exercised there by a political power concentrated at the head of the James River." [1]

Mr. Chase, in discussing the constitutional question, said in part: " The Madison Papers clearly show that the consent of the Legislature of the original State was the only consent required to the erection and formation of a new State within its jurisdiction. That consent having been given, the consent of the new State, if required, is proved by her application for admission. . . . The Legislature of Virginia, it may be admitted, did not contain many members from the eastern counties; it contained, however, representatives from all counties whose inhabitants were not either rebels themselves, or dominated by greater numbers of rebels. It was the only Legislature of the State known to the Union. If its consent was not valid, no consent could be. If its consent was not valid, the Constitution, as to the people of West Virginia, has been so suspended by the rebellion that a most important right under it is utterly lost."

Relative to the question of expediency, he writes: " The act is almost universally regarded as of vital importance to their welfare by the loyal people most immediately interested, and it has received the sanction of large majorities in both Houses of Congress. These facts afford strong presumptions of expediency. . . . It may be said, indeed, that the admission of West Virginia will draw after it the necessity of admitting other States under the consent of extemporized legislatures assuming to act for whole States, though really representing no important part of their territory. I think this necessity imaginary. There is no such legislature, nor is there likely to be. No such legislature, if extemporized, is

[1] Quoted in N. & H., Vol. VI. pp. 300-301.

likely to receive the recognition of Congress or the Executive."[1]

Mr. Stanton responded more briefly than either Secretary Seward or Secretary Chase, observing, among other things: " I have been unable to perceive any point on which the act of Congress conflicts with the Constitution. By the erection of the new State, the geographical boundary heretofore existing between the free and slave States will be broken, and the advantage of this upon every point of consideration surpasses all objections which have occurred to me on the question of expediency. Many prophetic dangers and evils might be specified, but it is safe to suppose that those who come after us will be as wise as ourselves, and if what we deem evils be really such, they will be avoided. The present good is real and substantial, the future may safely be left in the care of those whose duty and interest may be involved in any possible future measures of legislation."[2]

One or two excerpts from the opinion of Mr. Welles will indicate the course of his argument in the negative: " Under existing necessities, an organization of the loyal citizens, or of a portion of them, has been recognized, and its Senators and Representatives admitted to seats in Congress. Yet we cannot close our eyes to the fact that the fragment of the State which, in the revolutionary tumult, has instituted the new organization, is not possessed of the records, archives, symbols, traditions, or capital of the Commonwealth. Though calling itself the State of Virginia, it does not assume the debts and obligations contracted prior to the existing difficulties. Is this organization, then, really and in point of fact anything else than a provisional government for the State? It is composed almost entirely of those loyal citizens who reside beyond the mountains, and within the prescribed limits of the

[1] Quoted in N. & H., Vol. VI. pp. 302-303.
[2] Ibid., p. 304.

proposed new State. In this revolutionary period, there being no contestants, we are compelled to recognize the organization as Virginia. Whether that would be the case, and how the question would be met and disposed of, were the insurrection this day abandoned, need not now be discussed. Were Virginia, or those parts of it not included in the proposed new State, invaded and held in temporary subjection by a foreign enemy instead of the insurgents, the fragment of territory and population which should successfully repel the enemy and adhere to the Union would doubtless, during such temporary subjection, be recognized, and properly recognized, as Virginia. When, however, this loyal fragment goes farther, and not only declares itself to be Virginia, but proceeds by its own act to detach itself permanently and forever from the Commonwealth, and to erect itself into a new State within the jurisdiction of the State of Virginia, the question arises whether this proceeding is regular, legal, right, and, in honest good faith, conformable to, and within the letter and spirit of the Constitution. . . . Congress may admit new States into the Union; but any attempt to dismember or divide a State by any forced or unauthorized assumption would be an inexpedient exercise of doubtful power to the injury of such State. Were there no question of doubtful constitutionality in the movement, the time selected for the division of the State is most inopportune. It is a period of civil commotion, when unity and concerted action on the part of all loyal citizens and authorities should be directed to a restoration of the Union, and all tendency towards disintegration and demoralization avoided." [1]

Mr. Blair, likewise in the negative, added little of importance to what Secretary Welles had adduced on that side.

The first and rather hastily formed opinion of Attorney-General Bates has already been given together with an account

[1] Quoted in N. & H., Vol. VI. pp. 304-306.

of the circumstances attending its publication; upon longer reflection he did not greatly change the ground of his original convictions and in an elaborate discussion still reasoned in the negative.[1]

Between these evenly balanced and conflicting opinions of his advisers Mr. Lincoln argued as follows:

> The consent of the legislature of Virginia is constitutionally necessary to the bill for the admission of West Virginia becoming a law. A body claiming to be such legislature has given its consent. We cannot well deny that it is such, unless we do so upon the outside knowledge that the body was chosen at elections in which a majority of the qualified voters of Virginia did not participate. But it is a universal practice in the popular elections in all these States to give no legal consideration whatever to those who do not choose to vote, as against the effect of the votes of those who do choose to vote. Hence it is not the qualified voters, but the qualified voters who choose to vote that constitute the political power of the State. Much less than to non-voters should any consideration be given to those who did not vote in this case, because it is also matter of outside knowledge that they were not merely neglectful of their rights under and duty to this government, but were also engaged in open rebellion against it. Doubtless among these non-voters were some Union men whose voices were smothered by the more numerous secessionists; but we know too little of their number to assign them any appreciable value. Can this government stand, if it indulges constitutional constructions by which men in open rebellion against it are to be accounted, man for man, the equals of those who maintain their loyalty to it? Are they to be accounted even better citizens, and more worthy of consideration, than those who merely neglect to vote? If so, their treason against the Constitution enhances their constitutional value. Without braving these absurd conclusions, we cannot deny that the body which consents to the admission of West Virginia is the legislature of Virginia. I do not think the plural form of the words "legislatures" and "States" in the phrase of the Constitution "without the consent of the legislatures of the States concerned," etc., has any reference to the new State concerned. That plural form sprang from the contemplation of two or more old States contributing to form a new one. The idea that the new State was in danger of being admitted without its own consent was not provided against, because it was not thought of, as I conceive. It is said, the devil takes care of his own. Much more should a good spirit — the spirit of the Constitution and the Union — take care of its own. I think it cannot do less and live.

[1] See pp. 105-106 *ante*.

But is the admission into the Union of West Virginia expedient? This, in my general view, is more a question for Congress than for the Executive. Still I do not evade it. More than on anything else, it depends on whether the admission or rejection of the new State would, under all the circumstances, tend the more strongly to the restoration of the national authority throughout the Union. That which helps most in this direction is the most expedient at this time. Doubtless those in remaining Virginia would return to the Union, so to speak, less reluctantly without the division of the old State than with it; but I think we could not save as much in this quarter by rejecting the new State, as we should lose by it in West Virginia. We can scarcely dispense with the aid of West Virginia in this struggle; much less can we afford to have her against us, in Congress and in the field. Her brave and good men regard her admission into the Union as a matter of life and death. They have been true to the Union under very severe trials. We have so acted as to justify their hopes, and we cannot fully retain their confidence and coöperation if we seem to break faith with them. In fact, they could not do so much for us, if they would. Again, the admission of the new State turns that much slave soil, to free, and thus is a certain and irrevocable encroachment upon the cause of the rebellion. The division of a State is dreaded as a precedent. But a measure made expedient by a war is no precedent for times of peace. It is said that the admission of West Virginia is secession, and tolerated only because it is our secession. Well, if we call it by that name, there is still difference enough between secession against the Constitution and secession in favor of the Constitution. I believe the admission of West Virginia into the Union is expedient.[1]

The bill passed by the House on the 10th was approved by the President on the 31st of December, 1862; after naming the forty-eight counties to constitute the new State the act declares, among other things, that since the convention framed the constitution for West Virginia its people had expressed a wish to change section seven of the eleventh article by inserting the following in its place, *viz.:* " The children of slaves born within the limits of this State after the fourth day of July, eighteen hundred and sixty-three, shall be free; and that all slaves within the said State who shall, at the time aforesaid, be under the age of ten years, shall be free when they arrive at the age of twenty-one years; and all slaves over ten and under twenty-one years, shall be free when they arrive

[1] Letters and State Papers of Lincoln, Vol. II. pp. 285-287.

at the age of twenty-five years; and no slave shall be permitted to come into the State for permanent residence therein." [1]

The constitution thus amended was unanimously ratified by the convention, which on a summons of the commissioners reassembled February 18, 1863, and also by the people, to whom it was submitted at an election held on May 26 following.[2] President Lincoln on April 20 issued a proclamation declaring that the prescribed conditions having been complied with, the constitution would go into force in sixty days from that date; the formation of the new State was complete and it became a member of the Union on the 20th of June, 1863.[3]

Daniel Webster, in an address delivered thirteen years before, at the laying of the corner-stone of an addition to the Federal Capitol, had asked: "And ye men of Western Virginia, . . . what benefit do you propose to yourself by disunion? If you 'secede,' what do you 'secede' from, and what do you 'accede' to? Do you look for the current of the Ohio to change, and to bring you and your commerce to the tide-waters of the eastern rivers? What man in his senses can suppose that you would remain part and parcel of Virginia a month after Virginia should have ceased to be part and parcel of the Union?" [4] The remarkable prediction of the great orator was fulfilled; his inspired vision had pierced the future. The Old Dominion had separated forever along the line of the Alleghanies.

Before relating the subsequent history of the restored government, it is proper to notice a few important events in the early career of the new Commonwealth. On January 31, 1863, an act passed the General Assembly of Virginia giving consent to the transfer of Berkeley County to the

[1] The Formation of West Virginia, p. 152.
[2] Ibid., pp. 192-193.
[3] Letters and State Papers of Lincoln, Vol. II. p. 326.
[4] Webster's Works, Vol. II. pp. 607-608.

State of West Virginia. The preamble of this act affirms that its people desired to be annexed to the proposed State. The question of transfer, however, was to be decided by a majority of voters at an election to be held on the fourth Thursday of May. If, however, the polls could not be safely opened on that day, the Governor was empowered to postpone the election by proclamation. The commissioners who superintended the polling were to certify the results to the Executive. On February 4 succeeding another act made it lawful for voters in certain districts including twenty-three counties to declare, at a general election to be held on the fourth Thursday of May, whether these specified counties should be annexed to West Virginia. The consent of the Legislature of that State was, of course, made a condition of the transfer, after which the jurisdiction of Virginia over such counties was to cease.

West Virginia statutes of August 5 and November 2, 1863, in words, admit Berkeley and Jefferson counties, and they have ever since been under her jurisdiction. When admitted into the Union it was with a provision in her constitution that she might acquire additional territory; therefore Congress gave its consent in advance and it was not afterwards withdrawn. In brief, West Virginia accepted the transfer and it was authorized by the General Assembly of the Commonwealth of Virginia.[1]

---

[1] By a joint resolution, approved March 10, 1866, Congress agreed that both counties formed a part of West Virginia. The parent State, however, by an act of December 5, 1865, had already repealed both the statutes of January 31 and February 4, 1863, as well as section *two* of the act of May 13, 1862; and on December 11, 1866, a bill in equity was filed in the Supreme Court of the United States in which it was contended that it was not the intention of that State to consent to the annexation of Berkeley and Jefferson counties except upon the performance of certain conditions; the state of the county on election day was such as not to permit the opening of all the polls in Berkeley and Jefferson, nor indeed at any considerable part of the usual election places. The voters did not

State officers were elected on May 28, when the following unconditional Union candidates, receiving a vote of about 30,000, were chosen without opposition: Arthur I. Boreman, Governor; J. E. Boyers, Secretary of State; Campbell Tarr, Treasurer; Samuel Crane, Auditor; A. B. Caldwell, Attorney-General; also three judges of a court of appeals.

The inauguration of the new State, which was marked by imposing ceremonies, took place at Wheeling, the capital, on June 20, 1863. Mr. Pierpont, the retiring executive of reorganized Virginia, briefly addressed the assembled citizens and urged them not to forsake the flag; he then introduced his successor, whom he pronounced "true as steel." Governor Boreman in his short speech said that the only terms of peace were that the rebels should lay down their arms and submit to the regularly constituted authority of the United States.

The Legislature of West Virginia convened on the same day. Waitman T. Willey and P. G. Van Winkle were elected United States Senators.[1] In his first message Governor Boreman recommended to the General Assembly the immediate passage of laws effectually to extirpate slavery, and also the enactment of a law that no man should be permitted to vote or to hold office until he had taken the oath of allegiance.

have adequate notice. In short, a great majority of them were then and now, December, 1866, opposed to annexation. Other irregularities are alleged in the complaint of Virginia. A decision, however, has been rendered by the Supreme Court of the United States in favor of the new Commonwealth. [See Virginia *vs.* West Virginia, 11 Wall., p. 39; also Transcripts of Records, Supreme Court U. S., Vol. 152, December Term, 1870.]

[1] Notwithstanding the new State had been organized by a law which passed both Houses of Congress, and was approved by the President, Mr. Davis, of Kentucky, when the members-elect presented themselves before the Senate, opposed their admission on the ground that there was legally and constitutionally no such State in existence as West Virginia. On his motion to administer the customary oath thirty-six Senators voted in the affirmative, five in the negative. [Globe, 1 Sess. 38th Cong., pp. 1-3.]

In the Presidential election of 1864, the first held since the adoption of the Constitution in which any State deliberately neglected to appoint electors, 33,680 votes were polled in West Virginia; of this number the Union ticket received 23,223 and the McClellan electors 10,457.[1] Elections had also been held in Louisiana and Tennessee by authority of the governments established there under Mr. Lincoln's plan of reconstruction; the Republican majority in Congress, however, denied the validity of the organizations in the two States last named and refused to count the votes which they presented. This question will be fully considered when we come to trace the development of the Congressional plan. At the regular State election Governor Boreman was chosen without opposition, receiving 19,098 votes. With the subsequent history of the new Commonwealth the subject of reconstruction is not much concerned.

By the formation of an independent Commonwealth the counties beyond the Alleghanies were withdrawn from the jurisdiction of the restored government, which after the inaugural ceremonies at Wheeling selected for its capital the city of Alexandria, where it continued till May 25, 1865, to exercise its functions in those parts of the Old Dominion within the lines of the Union army. A State government was promptly organized by the election of a legislature and of executive officers. In this establishment the loyal eastern counties participated. Mr. Pierpont was elected Governor for the term of three years beginning January 1, 1864. A Lieutenant-Governor, a Secretary of State, a Treasurer, an Auditor, an Adjutant-General and an Attorney-General were also chosen.

The Governor in his message to the Assembly mentioned slavery as doomed, and recommended the calling of a con-

[1] A History of Presidential Elections, Stanwood, pp. 246-247. Edition of 1884.

vention so to amend the State constitution as to abolish the institution forever. In compliance with this suggestion the Legislature, on December 21, 1863, passed an act directing a convention to be held at Alexandria on the 13th of February succeeding to amend the constitution and prohibit slavery in the counties of Accomac, Northampton, Princess Ann, Elizabeth City and York (including the cities of Norfolk and Portsmouth). These with Berkeley County had been excepted from the operation of the Emancipation Proclamation.

None but loyal citizens who had not assisted the insurgents since January 1, 1863, were allowed to take part, and those whose right to vote might be challenged were required to swear support of the Constitution and to declare that they had not in any way given aid or comfort to the enemy.

The convention, consisting of sixteen members, assembled in the new capital at the appointed time and remained in session till April 11 following, when a constitution was adopted.[1] Various amendments, relating chiefly to the regulation of the elective franchise and to the abolition of slavery, were discussed and agreed upon. The work of this miniature convention was ordered to be proclaimed without a submission to the people. It was not, however, recognized by Congress, though the civil government which authorized its formation was permitted to continue under it, provisionally only, and in all respects subject to the paramount authority of the United States at any time to abolish, modify, or supersede.

Though the bill for the admission of West Virginia passed both Houses, yet Congress was by no means unanimous in giving its consent to that measure. In the debates, of which a synopsis has been given, the hostility of Thaddeus Stevens and other influential members is scarcely concealed. This opposition to executive policy slowly gathered strength, and

[1] Ann. Cycl., 1864, p. 809.

by 1863 had become formidable enough to defeat the admission of Representatives from the Alexandria government. The Senators, however, remained, Lemuel J. Bowden till his death, January 2, 1864, when his successor was refused admission, and John S. Carlile till the expiration of his term in 1865.

On the assembling of the 38th Congress, which commenced its first session December 7, 1863, Joseph E. Segar, Lucius H. Chandler and Benjamin M. Kitchen appeared as Representatives from Virginia. On May 17 succeeding Mr. Dawes from the Committee of Elections reported a resolution to the effect that Joseph E. Segar, from the First District of Virginia, was not entitled to a seat in that Congress. The case of Mr. Chandler, regarded as precisely similar, was considered at the same time.

The district which Mr. Segar claimed to represent was composed of twenty counties; of these, Chairman Dawes asserted, only four participated in the election. Polling places were not opened in any other part of the district, the Confederate authorities being in possession of the remaining counties. As there could be no free exercise of the franchise in this situation Mr. Segar, it was contended, was not properly chosen, and, therefore, was not entitled to a seat. The vote cast, though not accurately ascertained, was estimated at 1,677, of which the claimant received 1,300. Because of his loyalty and the sacrifices he had made, the Committee regretted the necessity of deciding against him.

Mr. Segar, speaking in his own behalf, reminded the House that in a preceding election, when he received 559 out of 1,018 votes polled in three counties, he was admitted after a delay of seven or eight weeks; but when he was sent by a larger constituency and came as the choice of four counties he was informed that he had no right to a seat, and some of his colleagues who favored his admission in 1862 voted to exclude him. The Committee's report, he asserted, admitted the existence of such a State as Virginia. He asked Chairman Dawes a rather embarrassing question when he inquired how a State could have two Senators and no Representative in Congress. In conclusion he pronounced restored State organization and gradual accretion to be the best method of reconstruction.

Concerning the title of Mr. Chandler, from the Second Congressional District, Chairman Dawes stated that of the 779 votes polled in the election 778 were cast for the claimant. For the same reason as in the case of Mr. Segar only a small part of that District was free to participate in the election, and nearly all the votes were polled in the city of Norfolk. The committee reported against his admission on the same ground taken in Mr. Segar's case.

Chandler, who was permitted to state his case to the House, cited a resolution introduced by his former school-mate, Owen Lovejoy, the well-known abolitionist, authorizing the names of the three Virginia claimants to be enrolled as Representatives. That resolution, however, was tabled and their credentials referred to the Committee of Elections.

In 1860 the Union vote in his District was only 6,712; of that number 2,900, he said, were in Norfolk and Portsmouth; the latter city had cast more votes against secession than the remainder of his District. Great numbers of loyal men, however, left there at the beginning of the war. Electors being under no obligation to vote may allow an election to go by default when one citizen could return a member to Congress. Territorially restored Virginia was larger than Delaware and possessed twice the area of Rhode Island.

The case of Benjamin M. Kitchen, on which the Committee had previously made an adverse report, differed from those of the other two claimants in that he had received nearly all of his vote in Berkeley County, which possessed a sort of wandering character, for it was somewhat uncertain whether it was under the jurisdiction of the new or the old State. What action was taken on the Committee's report does not appear, but it may be inferred from a facetious remark of one member who observed that, like Segar and Chandler, Kitchen had been privileged to retire to private life. The two former were refused admission by the decided vote of 94 to 23.

Besides endeavoring to win back the wavering, Governor Pierpont was occupied in taking measures for the relief of the distressed. In the vicinity of Norfolk and Portsmouth there was a large number of destitute persons whose natural supporters were still following the declining fortunes of the Confederacy or had been killed in its service. While it was universally agreed that their necessities should be relieved, the military and civil authorities were in conflict as to the mode of providing for them. The President in his efforts to establish amicable relations between the officers of the army and those of the State invoked the assistance of the Governor. As the restored Commonwealth could not be consistently recognized while its capital was in a state of blockade the President by proclamation, September 24, 1863, declared that the interdiction of trade with the port of Alexandria had ceased.

General Butler with headquarters at Fortress Monroe took command of the Department of Virginia and North Carolina November 2, 1863. His predecessors, he asserted, had endeavored to recruit a regiment of Virginians; but after several months of energetic trial their efforts were abandoned. As eastern Virginia claimed to be a loyal and fully organized State, Butler renewed the attempt, whereupon Governor Pierpont protested vigorously. One and a half companies were all the recruits that the Commonwealth would furnish, and these, Butler asserts, were employed to defend lighthouses and protect Union inhabitants from outrages at the hands of their disloyal neighbors.[1] This experience, it may be supposed, did not tend to raise the Alexandria government in the esteem of the Department Commander. We find accordingly that differences soon sprang up between the civil and military authorities. An attempt to regulate the liquor traffic in Norfolk and vicinity was the occasion of an open rupture. Civil officers continued to collect the payments imposed by law on those engaged in the business; the military power, to keep the traffic under better control, undertook to give to a few firms a monopoly of the importation. In this situation many small retailers refused to pay their licenses and were indicted in the local courts. To foil this purpose, General Shepley issued, June 22, 1864, an order providing that "on the day of the ensuing municipal election in the city of Norfolk a poll will be opened at the several places of voting, and separate ballot-boxes will be kept open during the hours of voting, in which voters may deposit their ballots, 'yes' or 'no,' upon the following question: Those in favor of continuing the present form of municipal government during the existence of military occupation will vote 'yes.' Those opposed to it will vote 'no.'"

Governor Pierpont resented this action and promptly issued a proclamation protesting against it as a revolutionary proceeding in violation of the Federal Constitution, adding, "No loyal citizen, therefore, is expected to vote on the proposed question." In a vigorous pamphlet discussing the "abuses of military power" he repeated his criticism.

Butler at this point took up the cudgels for his subordinate and in a general order, dated June 30, 1864, discussed the incident at some length. Pierpont was alluded to as "a person who calls himself Governor," and as one "pretending to be the head of the restored government of Virginia, which govern-

[1] Butler's Book, p. 618.

ment is unrecognized by the Congress, laws, and Constitution of the United States." The order further recited that as the loyal citizens of Norfolk had voted against the further trial of the experiment of municipal government "therefore it is ordered that all attempts to exercise civil office and power, under any supposed city election, within the city of Norfolk and its environs, must cease, and the persons pretending to be elected to civil offices at the late election, and those heretofore elected to municipal offices since the rebellion, must no longer attempt to exercise such functions; and upon any pretense or attempt so to do, the military commandant at Norfolk will see to it that persons so acting are stayed and quieted."

A memorial to Mr. Lincoln enlisted his sympathy and secured for Pierpont the assistance of Attorney-General Bates, who on July 11 wrote the President a long official letter setting forth his sense of the serious military encroachment by General Butler upon civil law and the authority of Mr. Pierpont as Governor of Virginia. The Department Commander replied in a communication of forty pages in sharp criticism of the Alexandria government, which he characterized as a "useless, expensive, and inefficient thing, unrecognized by Congress, unknown to the Constitution of the United States, and of such character that there is no command in the Decalogue against worshiping it, being the likeness of nothing in the heavens above, the earth beneath, or the waters under the earth."

The Attorney-General, who was accused of a design to create a conflict between the civil and the military power, also came in for a share of rather violent criticism. In this altercation each party accused the other of being assisted by only secessionists and traitors.[1]

It was relative to this controversy that Mr. Lincoln, Decem-

[1] N. & H., Abraham Lincoln, A History, Vol. IX. pp. 439-442.

ber 21, 1864, addressed to General Butler the following communication:

On the 9th of August last, I began to write you a letter, the enclosed being a copy of so much as I then wrote. So far as it goes it embraces the views I then entertained and still entertain.

A little relaxation of the complaints made to me on the subject, occurring about that time, the letter was not finished and sent. I now learn, correctly I suppose, that you have ordered an election, similar to the one mentioned, to take place on the eastern shore of Virginia. Let this be suspended at least until conference with me and obtaining my approval.

[Inclosure.]

EXECUTIVE MANSION, WASHINGTON, *August* 9, 1864.

Major-General Butler:

Your paper of the —— about Norfolk matters, is received, as also was your other, on the same general subject, dated, I believe, some time in February last. This subject has caused considerable trouble, forcing me to give a good deal of time and reflection to it. I regret that crimination and recrimination are mingled in it. I surely need not to assure you that I have no doubt of your loyalty and devoted patriotism; and I must tell you that I have no less confidence in those of Governor Pierpont and the Attorney-General. The former — at first as the loyal governor of all Virginia, including that which is now West Virginia, in organizing and furnishing troops, and in all other proper matters — was as earnest, honest, and efficient to the extent of his means as any other loyal governor.

The inauguration of West Virginia as a new State left to him, as he assumed, the remainder of the old State; and the insignificance of the parts which are outside of the rebel lines, and consequently within his reach, certainly gives a somewhat farcical air to his dominion, and I suppose he, as well as I, has considered that it can be useful for little else than as a nucleus to add to. The Attorney-General needs only to be known to be relieved from all question as to loyalty and thorough devotion to the national cause, constantly restraining as he does my tendency to clemency for rebels and rebel sympathizers. But he is the law-officer of the Government, and a believer in the virtue of adhering to law.

Coming to the question itself, the military occupancy of Norfolk is a necessity with us. If you, as department commander, find the cleansing of the city necessary to prevent pestilence in your army; street-lights and a fire department necessary to prevent assassinations and incendiarism among your men and stores; wharfage necessary to land and ship men and supplies; a large pauperism, badly conducted at a needlessly large expense to the government; and find that all these things, or any of them, are not reasonably well attended to by the civil government, you rightfully may and must take them into your own hands. But you should do so on your own avowed judgment of a military necessity, and not seem to admit that there is no such necessity by taking a vote of the people on the question.

Nothing justifies the suspending of the civil by the military authority but military necessity; and of the existence of that necessity, the military commander, and not a popular vote, is to decide. And whatever is not within such necessity should be left undisturbed.

In your paper of February you fairly notified me that you contemplated taking a popular vote, and, if fault there be, it was my fault that I did not object then, which I probably should have done had I studied the subject as closely as I have since done. I now think you would better place whatever you feel is necessary to be done on this distinct ground of military necessity, openly discarding all reliance for what you do on any election. I also think you should so keep accounts as to show every item of money received and how expended.

The course here indicated does not touch the case when the military commander, finding no friendly civil government existing, may, under sanction or direction of the President, give assistance to the people to inaugurate one.[1]

On the same general subject the President one week later wrote General Butler this brief note:

I think you will find that the provost-marshal on the eastern shore has, as by your authority, issued an order, not for a meeting, but for an election. The order, printed in due form, was shown to me, but as I did not retain it, I cannot give you a copy. If the people, on their own motion, wish to hold a peaceful meeting, I suppose you need not hinder them.[2]

It has elsewhere been observed that a Legislature representing what remained of the restored government was chosen at the time of Mr. Pierpont's election. This body, however, was but the merest shadow of the Assembly of that once proud Commonwealth. Seven Delegates responded to the roll call when the House convened in December, 1863. They adjourned from day to day and on the 9th of that month organized with eight members in the popular branch. Precisely

[1] Letters and State Papers of Lincoln, Vol. II. pp. 619-621.
[2] Ibid., p. 623.

138 LINCOLN'S PLAN OF RECONSTRUCTION

how many Senators composed the upper House does not appear in any notice of their proceedings accessible to the writer; the aggregate number in both chambers, however, is said not to have exceeded 16.[1] This estimate is probably correct; for in the election, February 4, 1864, of a Secretary of State and a Treasurer the total vote on joint ballot was only 14.[2]

It is probable that neither Mr. Lincoln nor Governor Pierpont regarded this organization as anything more than a nucleus around which the loyal elements might rally. Both Congress and the military authorities, however, treated it with scant courtesy. It is not matter of surprise, therefore, that memorials were presented to the United States Senate petitioning for the substitution of a military for this feeble civil government. To offset this movement remonstrances from citizens of Alexandria and from citizens of Loudon County were offered, January 17, 1865, by Senator Willey, of West Virginia. All the memorials of both classes were referred to the Committee on Territories.

By Mr. Willey credentials of Hon. Joseph Segar, Senator-elect from Virginia, were presented, February 17, 1865, to supply the vacancy caused by the death of Lemuel J. Bowden. Mr. Willey moved that the credentials be read and placed on the files, and that the oath of office be administered to Mr. Segar. The credentials were read and immediately after Mr. Sumner moved that the papers be referred to the Committee on the Judiciary. Senator Willey opposed the reference. The credentials, he believed, were proper on their face; they came to the Senate in due form under the seal of the State of Virginia. Mr. Segar was the accredited successor of Mr. Bowden, who died while a member of Congress. If Mr. Bowden was entitled to a seat his successor was likewise entitled if his credentials were regular and correct.

[1] Why The Solid South? p. 222.
[2] Ann. Cycl., 1864, p. 810.

Mr. Cowan also opposed the reference because he did not think it wise to abandon the policy hitherto pursued in dealing with loyal minorities in the rebellious States. He would be sorry, he said, if these States were repulsed when they were desirous to do all they could to achieve the very end for which the present tremendous struggle was taking place. When Mr. Bowden came to take his seat no such objection was made. A question by Senator Hale developed the fact, however, that Mr. Bowden presented himself before the vote was taken on the admission of West Virginia.

Trumbull believed that a reference of the credentials, just as in the Arkansas case, would bring up the question. Senator Howard, who favored a reference, thought that the entire question of the right of Virginia to be represented in Congress should be gone into. He would thank the committee for a concise account of all the proceedings connected with the election of Mr. Segar and his colleague. He asked whether a State like Virginia, in armed rebellion, could have Senators on that floor.

Mr. Saulsbury pointed out the change that had come over the judgment of the Senate. When Messrs. Willey and Carlile appeared there was, he said, but a corporal's guard who opposed their right to seats, because Virginia was in rebellion, and it was then held by the minority that Senators should represent the sovereignty of their States. Those who were then most zealous for the admission of the gentlemen claiming to represent Virginia had become most vehement in their opposition to the admission of Mr. Segar.

Senator McDougall believed that to refer the proposition to the committee would be to bury it, and no resurrection, he said, had been proclaimed for any such thing. He had his impressions and was as well prepared to discuss the question then as at any time. Virginia, according to his understanding of the philosophy of the Constitution, was a State of the

Union. He believed the Senator-elect, by reason of his credentials, could take the oath, though that was not conclusive of his right to a seat in the Senate.

Henry Wilson, of Massachusetts, believed that Congress because of its action for three years was bound to recognize the existence of both the Governor and Legislature of Virginia. He was disposed, however, to support the motion of his colleague, Charles Sumner, as well as the amendment thereto which authorized the committee to inquire into the election, returns and qualifications in the case of the claimant. Certain parts of Virginia, exempted by the President's proclamation, were not in rebellion. Every square mile additional over which Federal authority was restored came by the terms of that proclamation into the same condition.

Mr. Willey asserted that the Legislature sneeringly referred to as "the Common Council of Alexandria" represented 216,000 loyal people. He believed that county after county, as fast as they were relieved from the power of the rebellion, would come to the support of the loyal nucleus at Alexandria. It would place the Senate, he said, in a singular position to repulse the claimant while his State was represented by another Senator [Carlile].

Senator Sherman stated that Mr. Segar's credentials purported to show that he had been elected a member of the Senate on the 8th of December and that they bore date of December 12, 1864. Therefore he had slept for sixty or seventy days on his right to a seat which would, at any rate, expire on the 4th of March. The succeeding Congress, he said, would have ample time to decide the question, for, no doubt, at that time a gentleman claiming to be a Senator from Virginia would present himself. Then it could be deliberately determined. His motion to lay the credentials on the table prevailed by a vote of 29 to 13.[1] When this action was taken Carlile was among the eight absentees.

[1] Globe, Part II., 2 Sess. 38th Cong., pp. 845-849.

Pursuant to a proclamation of the President the Senate assembled at noon of March 4 in executive session. Five days later the question of admitting Senators from Virginia came again before the Senate on presentation by Mr. Doolittle of the credentials of Hon. John C. Underwood as Senator-elect from that State for six years from the 4th of March. His credentials were read and after some discussion it was agreed to postpone their consideration as well as those of Mr. Segar until the following session. Henderson and Doolittle spoke in favor of the early recognition by Congress of the local governments in those States which had been brought partly under Federal power. The account of Virginian affairs will be resumed in the final chapter.

V

ANTI-SLAVERY LEGISLATION

THE efforts of Union minorities in Tennessee, in Louisiana and in Arkansas to establish governments in harmony with the Constitution and laws of the United States, and the agency of President Lincoln in effecting that result, have been somewhat particularly described in the preceding pages. The principal events which marked the progress of secession in those States, the military successes which brought Federal authorities to consider the restoration of loyal governments within their borders, and the operation of those causes which ultimately overthrew rebellion have been more rapidly sketched. To trace the successive steps which led to the emancipation of slaves in the seceding States a somewhat more ample narrative will be required. This subject is not only of intrinsic interest but its culmination in the proclamation of September 22, 1862, marks the introduction into the President's plan of restoration of an element hitherto left out of account.

In December, 1859, when John Brown, for his rash though courageous attempt to liberate slaves, was hanged by the authorities of Virginia a great majority of even Northern people looked on with indifference or with approval. The inhabitants of the free States, however, were rather law-abiding than pitiless and came in time to revere the memory of that stern old Puritan. Ideas in those times matured with amazing rapidity, and fourteen months had scarcely elapsed when James B. McKean, a Representative from New York, introduced into Congress, three days before the Confederate government was organized, the following resolution:

> Whereas the "Gulf States" have assumed to secede from the Union, and it is deemed important to prevent the "border slave States" from following their example; and whereas it is believed that those who are inflexibly opposed to any measure of compromise or concession that involves, or may involve, a sacrifice of principle or the extension of slavery, would nevertheless cheerfully concur in any lawful measure for the emancipation of slaves: Therefore,
> *Resolved,* That the select committee of five be instructed to inquire whether, by the consent of the people, or of the State governments, or by compensating the slaveholders, it be practicable for the General Government to procure the emancipation of the slaves in some, or all, of the "border States"; and if so, to report a bill for that purpose.[1]

Mr. Burnett, of Kentucky, desiring to discuss the proposition, it was laid on the table and received no further consideration. Whether Mr. Lincoln had much reflected upon the principle of this resolution or the reasoning in its preamble, he had not become on March 4 a convert to its essential idea, for in his inaugural address he was content, in expressing his sentiments on the institution of slavery, to re-affirm a declaration which he had formerly made. "I have no purpose," said he, "directly or indirectly, to interfere with the institution of slavery in the States where it exists. I believe I have no lawful right to do so, and I have no inclination to do so."[2] Even if the occasion had not demanded the language of conciliation we might easily credit this solemn assurance. Indeed, for an entire year after this announcement he refrained in his public utterances from taking any attitude hostile to the continuance of slavery. The influences which forced him to adopt other opinions may be briefly related.

On May 22, 1861, General Butler arrived at Fortress Monroe and at once took command of the Department of Virginia; next day he sent a reconnoitering party to Hampton,

[1] McPherson's Pol. Hist., p. 209.
[2] Letters and State Papers of Lincoln, Vol. II. p. 1.

and in the terror and confusion occasioned by the presence of Yankee soldiers three slaves of Colonel Mallory, a Confederate officer, effected their escape; during the afternoon they remained in concealment and at night reached the Union pickets. The following morning they were brought before the Federal commander, whom they informed of their master's purpose to employ them in military operations in North Carolina. On the next day Major John B. Cary, also of the Confederate army, and a former delegate with Butler in the Baltimore Convention, came to the fort with a flag of truce, and as a representative of Colonel Mallory demanded the surrender of these runaways pursuant to the provisions of the Federal Constitution under which the Union commander claimed to act. With characteristic readiness came the reply that the Fugitive Slave Law could not be invoked in this case; Virginia assumed to be a foreign State and she must count it among the disadvantages of her position if, so far at least, she was taken at her word. These negroes further informed General Butler or his officers that if they were not returned others would come next day. On the 26th eight slaves were before him awaiting an audience; one squad of forty-seven came early on the 27th and another lot of a dozen arrived during the same day. Then they came by twenties, thirties and forties both to Fortress Monroe and Newport News.[1]

Thus arose an important question on which the Government had yet developed no policy. As the acts for the rendition of fugitive slaves were not repealed till June, 1864, the views of individual commanders temporarily prevailed. Without precedent or instructions General McDowell by an order entirely excluded them from his lines. Caprice, too, entered into a settlement of the problem, and even a whimsical solution was sometimes attempted. A felicitous invention for deter-

---

[1] Addresses and Papers of Edward L. Pierce, pp. 20-25.

mining these controversies between master and bondman is ascribed to the colonel of a Massachusetts regiment. Both the claimant and the claimed were put outside his tent for a trial of speed; the negro, proving the fleeter, was never heard of again.[1] An institution which had practically determined both the foreign and domestic policy of the United States for an entire generation was suddenly become the sport of a subordinate officer of volunteers! The wise should have heeded these signs.

While the Federal commander in Virginia was exchanging arguments with Confederate officers, General McClellan at his headquarters in Cincinnati was considering a proclamation which on May 26 he issued to the Union men of western Virginia. This document, among other things, says: " All your rights shall be religiously respected, notwithstanding all that has been said by the traitors to induce you to believe our advent among you will be signalized by an interference with your slaves. Understand one thing clearly: not only will we abstain from all such interference, but we will, on the contrary, *with an iron hand crush any attempt at insurrection on their part."* [2]

Scarcely less explicit in its announcement concerning slavery was General Patterson's proclamation of June 3, 1861, to troops of the Department of Pennsylvania. " You must bear in mind," says its concluding paragraph, that " you are going for the good of the whole country, and that, while it is your duty to punish sedition, you must protect the loyal, *and, should the occasion offer, at once suppress servile insurrection."* [3]

Butler's interview with Major Cary had been promptly communicated to the War Department, whose chief, Mr.

[1] Addresses and Papers of E. L. Pierce, p. 26.
[2] McPherson's Pol. Hist. p. 244.
[3] Ibid.

Cameron, expressed in his reply of May 30 approval of the General's action. The Secretary, however, endeavored to distinguish between interference with slave property and the surrender of negroes that came voluntarily within Federal lines. The commander was further directed to "employ such persons in the services to which they may be best adapted, keeping an account of the labor by them performed, of the value of it, and the expenses of their maintenance,"[1] the question of their final disposition to be reserved for future determination.

In defence of his attitude toward masters of fugitives who had been employed in the batteries or on the fortifications of the enemy, international law supplied General Butler with an analogy that he skillfully applied to the novel conditions which had arisen. Articles of assistance in military operations cannot in time of war be imported by neutrals into an enemy's country, and the attempt to introduce such goods renders them liable to seizure as lawful prize. It did not greatly embarrass this versatile lawyer that the term *contraband* applies exclusively to relations between a belligerent and a neutral, or that the decision of a prize court might be necessary to determine whether a particular article had been so designated. No doubt he believed firmly in the doctrine that the wants of war are contraband of war. In his correspondence with General Scott he had observed that "as a military question, it would seem to be a measure of necessity" to deprive disloyal masters of the services of their slaves, and this, on the pretext that they were contraband of war, he proceeded to do by refusing to surrender any negroes coming inside his lines.[2] This method of settling the difficulty was what Secretary Cameron had approved. But this phase presented the question in its extreme simplicity. A refusal to return the slaves

[1] McPherson's Pol. Hist., p. 244.
[2] Ibid., p. 245.

of Confederate officers or of Confederate sympathizers was one thing; similar treatment of loyal slaveholders would not be so readily overlooked by authority. Though such cases were more likely to occur in Maryland, Kentucky or Missouri, that fact did not prevent the subject from assuming very great importance even in Virginia. Whole families escaped from their masters, and General Butler soon had on his hands negroes from three months to almost fourscore years of age.

Attorney-General Bates, writing July 23, 1861, to United States Marshal J. L. McDowell, of Kansas, who had asked whether he should give his official service in executing the fugitive slave law, said in response to the inquiry:

> It is the President's constitutional duty to " take care that the laws be faithfully executed." That means all the laws. He has no right to discriminate, no right to execute the laws he likes, and leave unexecuted those he dislikes. And of course you and I, his subordinates, can have no wider latitude of discretion than he has. Missouri is a State in the Union. The insurrectionary disorders in Missouri are but individual crimes, and do not change the legal status of the State, nor change its rights and obligations as a member of the Union.
> A refusal by a ministerial officer to execute any law which properly belongs to his office, is an official misdemeanor, of which I have no doubt the President would take notice.[1]

The Attorney-General in this instance merely amplified a suggestion contained in the inaugural.

Toward the close of July, 1861, the number of " contrabands " had increased to nine hundred, and the Union commander again requested instructions.[2] Secretary Cameron's reply on the 8th of August following merely authorized, what General Butler had all along been doing, employing them at such labor as they were adapted to and keeping a complete record, so that when peace was restored the essential facts

[1] McPherson's Pol. Hist., p. 235n.
[2] Addresses and Papers of E. L. Pierce, p. 29.

of each case could easily be ascertained.[1] His tact in dealing with this question appears from an act of Congress approved August 6 in which his extension of meaning to the word *contraband* is adopted. This declared that if persons held to labor or service were employed in hostility to the United States, the right to their services should be forfeited and such persons be discharged therefrom.[2]

Exclusion of fugitive slaves from the quarters and camps of troops serving in the Department of Washington was provided by a general order of July 17, 1861, and a few weeks later, August 10, the departure by railway of negroes from the District of Columbia was prevented unless evidence of freedom could be adduced.[3]

Far more important, however, than these prudent regulations of the Adjutant-General was the celebrated proclamation of Fremont, dated St. Louis, August 31, 1861, which declared martial law throughout the entire State of Missouri and expressed a purpose both to confiscate the property and free the negroes of all persons in the State who should take up arms against the United States or who were shown to have taken an active part with their enemy in the field.[4] The President, in a communication of September 2 following, wrote General Fremont expressing anxiety concerning the effects of this proclamation: " I think there is great danger," said Mr. Lincoln, " that the closing paragraph, in relation to the confiscation of property and the liberating slaves of traitorous owners, will alarm our Southern Union friends and turn them against us; perhaps ruin our rather fair prospect for Kentucky.[5]

[1] McPherson's Pol. Hist., p. 245.
[2] Appendix, Globe, 1 Sess. 37th Cong., p. 42.
[3] McPherson's Pol. Hist., p. 245.   [4] Ibid., pp. 245-246.
[5] General Anderson had telegraphed President Lincoln that an entire company of Kentucky soldiers had laid down their arms upon hearing of Fremont's action.

"Allow me therefore to ask that you will, as of your own motion, modify that paragraph so as to conform to the first and fourth sections of the act of Congress entitled, 'An act to confiscate property used for insurrectionary purposes,' approved August 6, 1861, and a copy of which act I herewith send you.

"This letter is written in a spirit of caution, and not of censure."[1]

Though General Fremont had acted wholly on his own responsibility he refused so to modify that portion of his proclamation relative to emancipating slaves as to conform to the act of Congress referred to, and in a letter requested the President "openly to direct" him "to make the correction." Referring to this part of his communication Mr. Lincoln replied on the 11th: "Your answer, just received, expresses the preference on your part that I should make an open order for the modification, which I very cheerfully do. It is therefore ordered that the said clause of said proclamation be so modified, held, and construed, as to conform to, and not to transcend, the provisions on the same subject contained in the act of Congress" approved August 6, 1861.[2]

As late as October 14 the War Department was guided by the principles developed in its correspondence with Butler, the instructions of that date to General T. W. Sherman being based upon this policy.[3] A month later inhabitants of the eastern shore of Virginia were informed by General Dix that "special directions have been given not to interfere with the condition of any person held to domestic service;" to prevent any such occurrence slaves were not permitted to come within his lines.[4]

[1] Letters and State Papers of Lincoln, Vol. II. p. 77.
[2] Ibid., pp. 78-79.
[3] McPherson's Pol. Hist., pp. 247-248.
[4] Ibid., p. 248.

Besides those who favored military emancipation, a large class seriously expected that the war would not only preserve the integrity of the Union, but in some way result in a general liberation of slaves. This feeling, manifested in various ways, was rapidly gathering strength, and as early as November 8 found enthusiastic expression at a public meeting of two thousand citizens held in Cooper Institute, New York city. This assembly, which convened at the suggestion of Mr. Lincoln, was presided over by Hon. George Bancroft and attended by many distinguished persons of both the nation and the State. Besides the remarks of its illustrious chairman addresses were made by William Cullen Bryant, General Ambrose Burnside, Professor Francis Lieber and others. Shortly before the speakers arrived a gentleman arose in the audience, and in a ringing voice proposed " Three cheers for John C. Fremont! " These were given, says a newspaper account, " with electrical effect and without a murmur of dissent." The meeting was evidently not in entire sympathy with the President's order modifying that General's proclamation of the preceding August.

North Carolina, as is well known, was not so ardent for secession as most of her sister States in the South; forced to take sides, however, she imitated the example of her neighbors. Even then all her people did not share the opinions of their leaders, and when Federal troops landed in the vicinity of Hatteras nearly four thousand loyal inhabitants of the coast flocked to their lines and readily took the oath of allegiance to the United States; for this conduct they incurred the extreme hatred of secessionists, who soon reduced them to a condition of distress. To relieve their destitution, by supplies of food and clothing, the meeting was called in Cooper Institute. Resolutions of sympathy were unanimously adopted; a committee of relief was appointed to collect from the city and elsewhere such funds as were necessary for the purchase of supplies, which were to be forwarded and distributed in the most judicious manner.

"If the President," said Mr. Bancroft, "has any doubt under the terrible conflict into which he has been brought, let him hear the words of one of his predecessors. Alien nullification raised itself in South Carolina. Andrew Jackson, in the watches of the night, as he sat alone finishing that proclamation, sent the last words of it to Livingston, his bosom friend and best adviser. He sent it with these words; I have had the letter in my own hands, handed to me by the only surviving child of Mr. Livingston. I know the letter which I now read is a copy: 'I submit the above as the conclusion of the proclamation for your amendment and revision. Let it receive your best flight of eloquence to strike to the heart and speak to the feelings of my deluded countrymen of South Carolina. The Union must be preserved without blood if this be possible; but it must be preserved at all hazards and at any price.'" Mr. Bancroft added: "We send the army into the South to maintain the Union, to restore the validity of the Constitution. If any one presents claims under the Constitution, let him begin by placing the Constitution in power, by respecting it and upholding it."

Francis Lieber referred to slavery as "that great anachronism, out of time, out of place in the nineteenth century," and Rev. Doctor Tyng said, "if slavery is in the way of the Union, then tread slavery down into the dust."[1] These sentiments were received with applause.

Mr. Bancroft a week later wrote to the President:

Following out your suggestion, a very numerous meeting of New-Yorkers assembled last week to take measures for relieving the loyal sufferers of Hatteras. I take the liberty to enclose you some remarks which I made on the occasion. You will find in them a copy of an unpublished letter of one of your most honored predecessors, with which you cannot fail to be pleased.

[1] N. Y. Tribune, November 8, 1861.

152 LINCOLN'S PLAN OF RECONSTRUCTION

> Your administration has fallen upon times which will be remembered as long as human events find a record. I sincerely wish to you the glory of perfect success. Civil War is the instrument of Divine Providence to root out social slavery. Posterity will not be satisfied with the result unless the consequences of the war shall effect an increase of free States. This is the universal expectation and hope of men of all parties.[1]

On the 18th Mr. Lincoln sent this reply:

> I esteem it a high honor to have received a note from Mr. Bancroft inclosing the report of proceedings of a New York meeting taking measures for the relief of Union people of North Carolina. I thank you and all others participating for this benevolent and patriotic movement.
>
> The main thought in the closing paragraph of your letter is one which does not escape my attention, and with which I must deal in all due caution, and with the best judgment I can bring to it.[2]

We have here the key to President Lincoln's treatment of the slavery question down to the hour of his lamented death. As the hostile employment of negroes constituted by act of August 6 a full answer to any claim for service General McClellan was informed by Secretary Seward, December 4, 1861, that the arrest of such persons as fugitives from labor " should be immediately followed by the military arrest of the parties making the seizure." These instructions were called forth by intelligence that Virginia slaves engaged in hostility to the United States frequently escaped from the enemy and took refuge within the lines of the Army of the Potomac. Coming afterward into the District of Columbia, such persons upon the presumption arising from color, were liable to be arrested by the Washington police.[3]

On December 3, 1861, in his first annual message to Congress, Mr. Lincoln discussed without especial emphasis the question of aiding those slaves who had been freed under the act of August 6; he observed that this class was dependent upon the United States; it was believed that, for their own

[1] Letters and State Papers of Abraham Lincoln, Vol. II. p. 90.
[2] Ibid.
[3] Ann. Cycl., 1861, p. 646.

ANTI-SLAVERY LEGISLATION

benefit, many of the States would enact similar laws; he therefore recommended Congress to provide for accepting such persons from the States,

according to some mode of valuation, in lieu, *pro tanto,* of direct taxes, or upon some other plan to be agreed on with such States respectively; that such persons, on such acceptance by the General Government, be at once deemed free; and that, in any event, steps be taken for colonizing both classes (or the one first mentioned, if the other shall not be brought into existence) at some place or places in a climate congenial to them. It might be well to consider, too, whether the free colored people already in the United States could not, so far as individuals may desire, be included in such colonization.

To carry out the plan of colonization may involve the acquiring of territory, and also the appropriation of money beyond that to be expended in the territorial acquisition. Having practiced the acquisition of territory for nearly sixty years, the question of constitutional power to do so is no longer an open one with us. The power was questioned at first by Mr. Jefferson, who, however, in the purchase of Louisiana, yielded his scruples on the plea of great expediency. If it be said that the only legitimate object of acquiring territory is to furnish homes for white men, this measure effects that object; for the emigration of colored men leaves additional room for white men remaining or coming here. Mr. Jefferson, however, placed the importance of procuring Louisiana more on political and commercial grounds than on providing room for population.

On this whole proposition, including the appropriation of money with the acquisition of territory, does not the expediency amount to absolute necessity — that without which the Government itself cannot be perpetuated?

The war continues. In considering the policy to be adopted for suppressing the insurrection, I have been anxious and careful that the inevitable conflict for this purpose shall not degenerate into a violent and remorseless revolutionary struggle. I have, therefore, in every case thought it proper to keep the integrity of the Union prominent as the primary object of the contest on our part, leaving all questions which are not of vital military importance to the more deliberate action of the Legislature.

In the exercise of my best discretion I have adhered to the blockade of the ports held by the insurgents, instead of putting in force, by proclamation, the law of Congress enacted at the last session for closing those ports.

So, also, obeying the dictates of prudence as well as the obligations of law, instead of transcending I have adhered to the act of Congress to confiscate property used for insurrectionary purposes. If a new law upon the same subject shall be proposed, its propriety will be duly considered. The Union must be preserved; and hence all indispensable means must be employed. We should not be in haste to determine that radical and extreme measures, which may reach the loyal as well as the disloyal, are indispensable.[1]

The President's mastery of national affairs is seen in the ability and thoroughness with which he treated a great variety of important public questions; though his message touches with the utmost delicacy the paramount issue of slavery it really marked an advance in his position. However, he was not yet abreast of the aggressive anti-slavery party in the 37th Congress, which had just commenced its first regular session.

The "increase of free States," which Mr. Bancroft hoped would result from the war, and which President Lincoln's reply shows had not escaped his attention, was not to be effected by military emancipation in the field but by the voluntary action of the States themselves. The caution and judgment which he brought to bear on this subject are apparent from even a casual examination of the message, which refers to the number of slaves that had been freed by the incidents of war, and to the extreme probability that still others would be liberated in its progress. It contained also a recommendation of colonization, a topic which had long been familiar to Americans both North and South. To any new law emancipating slaves for the participation of their masters in rebellion, he promised to give due consideration. This part of the message had the additional merit of being easily expanded into a more definite policy. It was this characteristic prudence that led the President to suppress the following remarks in a report which the Secretary of War had prepared for the opening of Congress in December, 1861:

If it shall be found that the men who have been held by the rebels as slaves are capable of bearing arms and performing efficient military serv-

[1] First Annual Message, December 3, 1861. McPherson's Pol. Hist., p. 134; Letters and State Papers of Lincoln, Vol. II. pp. 102-103.

ice, it is the right, and may become the duty, of this government to arm and equip them, and employ their services against the rebels, under proper military regulation, discipline, and command.[1]

Any legislation, or even any extended debate, on these recommendations was prevented by questions deemed more urgent by Congress. Indeed, the President does not appear to have seriously expected favorable action at this time upon his suggestions, for he resumed certain efforts which he had been carefully considering. He believed that by the pressure of war necessities the border States might be induced to take up the idea of voluntary emancipation if the General Government would pay their citizens the full property value of the slaves they were asked to liberate; and this experiment seemed most feasible in the small State of Delaware, which retained only the merest fragment of a property interest in the institution.

Even before the appearance of his message a plan of compensated abolishment had taken definite form in the mind of the President, for about November 26 he had prepared a draft of a bill for gradual emancipation in Delaware.[2] Through Congressman George P. Fisher the proposition was laid before the General Assembly of that State and received favorable consideration in the lower House. By the Senate, which convened November 25, 1861, it was taken up for discussion on February 7 succeeding. Upon the question, 4 voted in favor and 4 against concurring in the action of the more popular branch of the Legislature. The remaining Senator, McFerran, was absent or silent and is not accounted for in the journal of this special session. Therefore the measure was returned non-concurred in to the other chamber. The following preamble and joint resolution relative to the proposed emancipation bill are self-explanatory. The Fed-

[1] McPherson's Pol. Hist., p. 249.
[2] Letters and State Papers of Abraham Lincoln, Vol. II. p. 91.

eral suggestion was repelled as an unwarranted interference in the domestic concerns of that State:

Whereas, There has been circulating among the members of this General Assembly a printed draft for a law to be entitled "An act for the gradual emancipation of slaves in the State of Delaware with just compensation to their owners"; *and whereas* many of the members of this General Assembly have been requested to support it, the said draft being in the following words: [Then follows the title, together with the twenty-one sections composing the bill. To which is added:] *And whereas* it is uncertain that said proposition will be submitted to this General Assembly for its action, nevertheless, viewing it to be unworthy of their support, they desire to place upon record the grounds of their condemnation; therefore

Resolved by the Senate and House of Representatives of the State of Delaware in General Assembly met, That the members of this Legislature were not elected with a view to the passage of any act for the emancipation of slaves, but with the understanding, either expressed or implied, that legislation upon the distracting subject of slavery was hostile to the public peace, and therefore to be avoided; that the passage of the act drafted as aforesaid, inasmuch as it renders Congressional action necessary, would, upon the apparent application of the State of Delaware, introduce the slavery question into Congress, would encourage the abolition element therein, and fortify it in its purpose to destroy entirely all property in slaves, and furthermore, would be injurious to the quiet and harmony that prevail in this State.

Be it further resolved by the authority aforesaid, That it is the opinion of this General Assembly, that Congress has no right to appropriate a dollar for the purchase of slaves, and that such a proposal, coming from the source to which it is traceable, evinces a design on the part of those having control of our national affairs to abolish slavery in the States.

Resolved further, That this General Assembly having in mind the interests of the people of Delaware, are not willing, especially at a time of financial embarrassment, to make the State of Delaware a guarantor of any debt the payment of which depends upon the mere pledge of public faith; that the confidence of the people of this State that nothing would ever be done to promote a disunion of our National system, but that it would remain, as expressed by Webster "one and inseparable, now and forever," having been impaired by the events of the last two years, we are and should be very cautious in resting our obligations on the mere faith of others; that by accepting the terms to be offered by the United States, we should, upon grounds of the plainest equity, be held to have pledged the faith of Delaware for the payment of nine hundred thousand dollars as mentioned in the draft aforesaid; that, keeping in mind the fact that the power of the nation is now put forth to suppress a rebellion prevailing throughout a very large portion of its territory, and that in consequence of such rebellion and the uncertainty of its being speedily quelled, the stocks of the United States, which heretofore brought in the market a sum far beyond the par value thereof, are now selling at a continually increasing rate of discount, we are unwilling to pledge the faith of Delaware (a faith which has never been violated) that the proposed mode of payment is safe and proper.

Resolved further, That when the people of Delaware desire to abolish slavery within her borders, they will do so in their own way, having due regard to strict equity; that any interference from without, and all suggestions of saving expense to the people, or others of like character, are improper to be made to an honorable people, such as we represent, and are hereby repelled — that though the State of Delaware is small, and her people not of the richest, they are beyond the reach of any who would promote an end by improper interference and solicitations.

Resolved further, That a copy of the foregoing resolutions, duly attested, be transmitted to each of our Senators, and to our Representative in Congress, to be laid before their respective houses.[1]

Thus ended, so far as Delaware was concerned, the question of compensated emancipation. Precisely why the offer of Federal assistance was rejected nowhere clearly appears except in the records of the General Assembly. The high ground assumed in the resolutions was, of course, the only one in harmony with public opinion in the State. There are, however, some facts in the history of that Commonwealth which afford a partial explanation of the action of its Legislature. When the Federalist party as a political force had disappeared everywhere outside of New England its principles and traditions still lingered on in Delaware. The same conservative tendency, the same distrust of innovation is seen again in the prudent manner in which the authorities of the State invested and improved her portion of the surplus revenue distributed among the States in 1837. With a half dozen exceptions the shares allotted to other members of the Union

[1] See "Journal of the Senate of the State of Delaware, At a Special Session of the General Assembly, Commenced and held at Dover, on Monday, the 25th day of November, 1861."

have disappeared, in some instances expended patriotically, in others squandered on projects more or less visionary. It has frequently been observed, too, that a community whose population is chiefly agricultural is apt to view with suspicion any financial proposition of great magnitude. Whatever the true explanation of her opposition to the policy of the President, the question at once sank to rest in Delaware; it was soon to be revived elsewhere, however, as will presently be seen.

Meanwhile army officers continued to determine, on their own authority, very important questions relative to the surrender of fugitive slaves. Major-General Halleck declared in a proclamation of February 23, 1862, that " it does not belong to the military to decide upon the relation of master and slave. Such questions must be settled by the civil courts. No fugitive slave will therefore be admitted within our lines or camps, except when specially ordered by the General commanding." [1] General Halleck's order No. 3 of November 20 preceding, as it cut off an opportunity for the escape of thousands, occasioned much bitter discussion both in and out of Congress. By Halleck it was explained in these words: " Unauthorized persons, black or white, free or slaves, must be kept out of our camps, unless we are willing to publish to the enemy everything we do or intend to do." This statement, however, does not altogether harmonize with the spirit of his order.[2]

General Buell up to March 6 appears to have uniformly returned this class of persons, and on the 26th of that month General Hooker permitted nine citizens of Maryland to search for negroes supposed to have taken refuge with some of the regiments in his division. Notwithstanding the commander desired that no obstacles be thrown in their way, trouble occurred when the claimants showed their authority and demanded the surrender of their slaves. They were driven from

[1] McPherson's Pol. Hist., p. 250.   [2] Ibid., p. 248.

ANTI-SLAVERY LEGISLATION

camp because fears for their safety were entertained by some of the officers. The anger of the soldiers appears to have been especially aroused by the fact that when within a few yards of camp the slaveholders fired two pistol shots at a negro who was running past them.[1]

General Doubleday's opinion, as stated April 6, 1862, by the Assistant Adjutant-General, was, "that all negroes coming into the lines of any of the camps or forts under his command, are to be treated as persons and not as chattels.

"Under no circumstances," continues this regulation, "has the commander of a fort or camp the power of surrendering persons claimed as fugitive slaves, as it cannot be done without determining their character.

"The additional article of war recently passed by Congress positively prohibits this." [2]

Notwithstanding the unmistakable tone of the above, General Williams announced two months later from his headquarters at Baton Rouge that commanders of the camps and garrisons in that part of Louisiana were required to turn all fugitives beyond the limits of their guards and sentinels because of "the demoralizing and disorganizing tendencies to the troops of harboring runaway negroes."[3]

Enough has been said to show the divergence of sentiment among Federal commanders on the rendition of fugitive slaves. The party preferences of officers served as a rather reliable index to the treatment of the fugitive in any particular case. This confusion, it is scarcely necessary to add, arose from the failure of Congress to pass a law on the subject, and to a considerable degree from the absence of any clearly expressed policy by the Administration. Of the changing opinions of the President, however, we catch an occasional glimpse. Though the contrabands at Fortress Monroe had, no doubt, brought

[1] McPherson's Pol. Hist., p. 250.   [2] Ibid.
[3] Ibid., p. 251.

before him the entire question of slavery, the sagacity of General Butler had postponed the necessity of any announcement in May, 1861; but the subject could not always be avoided, and the imprudence of Fremont forced a declaration in September following. The events of another year were destined to produce changes which even the wisest could not then foresee.

A new phase of this troublesome question resulted from the capture, November 7, of Hilton Head, South Carolina, and the Federal occupation of the Sea Islands, where the labor of slaves abandoned by their masters was organized under authority of the Treasury Department by Mr. E. L. Pierce. This was, probably, intended as nothing more than an experiment, to be extended if successful. To interest Government officials at Washington in the work among these freedmen, Mr. Pierce, at the suggestion of Secretary Chase, called, February 15, 1862, upon the President, who seemed rather annoyed at the visit, and, after listening a few moments, said somewhat impatiently that he did not think he ought to be troubled with such details; that "there seemed to be an itching to get negroes into our lines." To this Mr. Pierce replied that the negroes were domiciled there when the Union forces took possession. The President then handed his visitor a card by which Mr. Chase was authorized to give what instructions he thought judicious relative to Port Royal contrabands.[1] This impatience Mr. Pierce explains by saying that the President was in expectation of a personal bereavement. This certainly accounts for the anxiety and apparent annoyance of Mr. Lincoln, but his remark that there seemed to be an "itching" to get negroes inside Federal lines shows that he had not yet deliberately considered the novel case of abandoned slaves; abandoned masters had hitherto claimed his attention.

[1] Addresses and Papers of E. L. Pierce, p. 87; also Letters and State Papers of Abraham Lincoln, Vol. II. p. 126.

Though slowly, as it may have appeared to radical members of his own party, the President was surely approaching the great question, and on March 6, 1862, sent to Congress a message which recommended the adoption, and even proposed the form, of a joint resolution declaring:

That the United States ought to coöperate with any State which may adopt gradual abolishment of slavery, giving to such State pecuniary aid, to be used by such State, in its discretion, to compensate for the inconveniences, public and private, produced by such change of system.[1]

As one of the most efficient means of self-preservation it was recommended by the Executive to the coördinate branch of Government; for to deprive the cotton States of the hope of being joined by the border States would, he said, "substantially end the rebellion; and the initiation of emancipation completely deprives them of it as to all the States initiating it. The point is not that all the States tolerating slavery would very soon, if at all, initiate emancipation; but that while the offer is equally made to all, the more Northern shall, by such initiation, make it certain to the more Southern that in no event will the former ever join the latter in their proposed confederacy." Gradual emancipation he believed better for all concerned. The current expenditures of the war would soon purchase, at a fair valuation, all the slaves in any named State. However, it was proposed as a matter of perfectly free choice. "In the annual message, last December," continued the President, "I thought fit to say, 'the Union must be preserved, and hence all indispensable means must be employed.' I said this not hastily, but deliberately. War has been made and continues to be an indispensable means to this end. A practical re-acknowledgment of the national authority would render the war unnecessary, and it would at once cease. If, however, resistance continues, the war must also continue; and it is impossible to foresee all the incidents which may attend and all

[1] Letters and State Papers of Abraham Lincoln, Vol. II. p. 129.

the ruin which may follow it. Such as may seem indispensable, or may obviously promise great efficiency, toward ending the struggle, must and will come."

The message inquired "whether the pecuniary consideration tendered would not be of more value to the States and private persons concerned than are the institution and property in it, in the present aspect of affairs?"[1]

This was really a great step in advance; by many it was regarded as a direct and positive interference with the domestic institutions of the States; it was certainly a preliminary movement to get rid of slavery. The deliberate opinion of the Delaware Legislature has already been noticed.

Easily distinguished in principle from the opposition in Delaware were the sentiments expressed in Virginia when the equitable and generous proposal of the President came up for consideration in the Richmond Legislature. Mr. Collier submitted to that body a preamble and resolution relative to the proposition. In the former it was said that negro slaves having been the property of their masters for two hundred and forty years, by use and custom at first, and subsequently by recognition of the public law, ought not to be, and could not justly be, interfered with in such property relation by the State, by "the people in convention assembled to alter an existing constitution, or to form one for admission into the confederacy, nor by the representatives of the people of the State in the Confederate Legislature, nor by any means or mode which the popular majority might adopt; and that the State, whilst remaining republican in the structure of its government, can lawfully get rid of that species of property, if ever, only by the free consent of the individual owners." For the State to deprive an individual of this species of property would contravene the indispensable principles of free government. This view, as further explained by its author, denied the power of

[1] Letters and State Papers of Lincoln, Vol. II. pp. 129-130.

ANTI-SLAVERY LEGISLATION

even a majority, in making a new State constitution, to disturb a preëxisting and resident property.[1]

Three days after sending his recommendation to Congress, the President wrote privately to Henry J. Raymond, editor of the *New York Times:*

> I am grateful to the New York journals and not less so to the "Times" than to others, for their kind notices of the late special message to Congress.
> Your paper, however, intimates that the proposition, though well intentioned, must fail on the score of expense. I do hope you will reconsider this. Have you noticed the facts that less than one-half day's cost of this war would pay for all the slaves in Delaware at $400 per head — that eighty-seven days' cost of this war would pay for all in Delaware, Maryland, District of Columbia, Kentucky, and Missouri at the same price? Were those States to take the step, do you doubt that it would shorten the war more than eighty-seven days, and thus be an actual saving of expense?
> Please look at these things and consider whether there should not be another article in the "Times."[2]

By his request those Congressmen from the border States then in Washington called, March 10, on Mr. Lincoln, who explained that his recent message was not inimical to the interests they represented. In the progress of the war, slaves would come into camps and continual irritation be thus maintained. In the border States that condition kept alive a feeling of hostility to the Government. He told them further "that emancipation was a subject exclusively under the control of the States, and must be adopted or rejected by each for itself."[3]

Relative to this interview a memorandum of the Hon. John W. Crisfield, one of the Maryland Representatives present, contains the following entry: "He [the President] was constantly annoyed by conflicting and antagonistic complaints; on

---
[1] Ann. Cycl., 1862, pp. 799-800.
[2] Letters and State Papers of Lincoln, Vol. II. p. 132.
[3] McPherson's Pol. Hist., p. 210.

the one side a certain class complained if the slave was not protected by the army; persons were frequently found who, participating in these views, acted in a way unfriendly to the slave-holder; on the other hand, slave-holders complained that their rights were interfered with, their slaves induced to abscond and protected within the lines; these complaints were numerous, loud and deep; were a serious annoyance to him and embarrassing to the progress of the war . . . [they] strengthened the hopes of the Confederates that at some day the border States would unite with them, and thus tend to prolong the war; and he was of opinion, if this resolution should be adopted by Congress and accepted by our [the border slave-holding] States, these causes of irritation and these hopes would be removed, and more would be accomplished toward shortening the war than could be hoped from the greatest victory achieved by Union armies; . . . that he did not claim nor had this Government any right to coerce them " to accept the proposition.

To Mr. Noell's remark that the *New York Tribune* favored the measure and understood it to mean that gradual emancipation must be accepted or the border States would get something worse, the President replied that he must not be expected to quarrel with that journal before the right time; he hoped never to have to do it. The message having said that " all indispensable means must be employed " to preserve the Union, Mr. Crisfield inquired pointedly, what would be the effect of the refusal of a State to accept this proposal. Did the President, he asked, look " to any policy beyond the acceptance or rejection of this scheme." Mr. Lincoln candidly replied that he had " no designs beyond the action of the States on this particular subject," though he should lament their refusal to accept it. Mr. Crisfield said " he did not think the people of Maryland looked upon slavery as a permanent institution; and he did not know that they would be very reluctant to give it up if provision was made to meet the loss and they could be rid of the race; but they did not like to be coerced into emancipation, either by the direct action of the Government or by indirection, as through the emancipation of slaves in this District, or the confiscation of Southern property as now threatened; and he thought before they would consent to consider this proposition they would require to be informed on these points." The President answered that " unless he was expelled by the act of God or the Confederate armies, he should occupy that house for three years; and as long as he remained there Maryland had nothing to fear either for her institutions or her interests on the points referred to." Representative Crisfield immediately added: " Mr. President, if what you now say could be heard by the people of Maryland, they would consider your proposition with a much better feeling than I fear without it they will be inclined to do." To this Mr. Lincoln said that a publication of his sentiments would not do; it would force him before the proper time into a quarrel which was impending with the Greeley faction. This he desired to postpone, or, if possible, altogether to avoid.

To an objection of Governor Wickliffe, of Kentucky, he said that the resolution proposed would be considered rather as the expression of a sentiment than as involving any constitutional question. He did not know how the project was received by the members from the free States; some of them had spoken to him and received it kindly; but for the most part they were as reserved and chary as the border State delegations; he could not tell how they would vote.[1]

To James A. McDougall, of California, who was making some opposition in the Senate, he sent, March 14, this private communication while the resolution was still pending:

[1] Letters and State Papers of Lincoln, Vol. II. pp. 133-135; also Mc-Pherson's Pol. Hist., pp. 210-211.

166 LINCOLN'S PLAN OF RECONSTRUCTION

As to the expensiveness of gradual emancipation with the plan of compensation, proposed in the late message, please allow me one or two brief suggestions.

Less than one half day's cost of this war would pay for all the slaves in Delaware at four hundred dollars per head.

Thus, all the slaves in Delaware by the census of 1860, are...	1,798
	400
Cost of slaves..	$719,200
One day's cost of the war...............................	2,000,000

Again, less than eighty-seven days' cost of this war would, at the same price, pay for all in Delaware, Maryland, District of Columbia, Kentucky, and Missouri.

Thus, slaves in Delaware............................	1,798
Maryland	87,188
District of Columbia.................	3,181
Kentucky	225,490
Missouri	114,965
	432,622
	400
Cost of slaves..$173,048,800
Eighty-seven days' cost of war......................	174,000,000

Do you doubt that taking the initiatory steps on the part of those States and this District would shorten the war more than eighty-seven days, and thus be an actual saving of expense?

A word as to the time and manner of incurring the expense. Suppose, for instance, a State devises and adopts a system by which the institution absolutely ceases therein by a named day — say January 1, 1882. Then let the sum to be paid to such a State by the United States be ascertained by taking from the census of 1860 the number of slaves within the State, and multiplying the number by four hundred — the United States to pay such sums to the State in twenty equal annual installments, in six per cent. bonds of the United States.

The sum thus given, as to time and manner, I think, would not be half as onerous as would be an equal sum raised now for the indefinite prosecution of the war; but of this you can judge as well as I. I enclose a census table for your convenience.[1]

[1] Letters and State Papers of Lincoln, Vol. II. pp. 137-138.

ANTI-SLAVERY LEGISLATION

On the same day of the conference with the border State delegations, March 10, the resolution, in precisely the language suggested by the President, was introduced by Roscoe Conkling, and on the following day by a vote of 89 to 31 passed the House.[1] The Senate by 32 yeas to 10 nays took favorable action upon it on the 2d of April succeeding.[2]

It is important to notice that at this time, March, 1862, the Government set up no claim of a right by Federal authority to interfere with slavery within the limits of a State; also that public opinion in the North had advanced to the position occupied by Representative McKean more than a year before, when he introduced into Congress his resolution for compensated emancipation.[3]

At a session, May 28, 1862, of the Union Convention of Baltimore its Business Committee reported a series of resolutions which were adopted unanimously, among them one approving the wise and conservative policy proposed by the President in his message of March 6; that it was not only the duty but the interest of the loyal people of Maryland to accept the offer of pecuniary aid tendered by the Government to inaugurate an equitable plan of emancipation and colonization.[4] This was the dawn of emancipation in Maryland.

The President approved, April 16, six days after the passage of his cherished measure, an act prohibiting slavery and liberating slaves in the District of Columbia. It included both compensation to owners and the principle of colonization.[5]

---

[1] Ann. Cycl., 1862, pp. 346-347.
[2] Globe, Part II., 2 Sess. 37th Cong., p. 1496.
[3] See p. 143, *ante*.
[4] McPherson's Pol. Hist., pp. 226-227.
[5] The question of colonizing free blacks out of the United States engaged the attention of Thomas Jefferson and James Monroe, who had some correspondence on the subject at the beginning of the nineteenth century. Late in the year 1816 there was organized in the city of Washington the "National Colonization Society," of which the expressed purpose was to encourage emancipation by procuring a place outside the

Shortly before its passage, April 17, a resolution was favorably considered by the House to appoint a committee of nine empowered to report whether any plan could be proposed and recommended for the gradual emancipation of all African slaves and the extinction of slavery in Delaware, Maryland, Virginia, Kentucky, Tennessee and Missouri by the people or local authorities thereof, and how far and in what way the United States could and ought equitably to aid in facilitating either of the above objects. This measure was adopted by a vote of 67 to 52, and one week later a committee was appointed by the Speaker.

General Hunter by an order of April 25 had extended martial law over South Carolina, Georgia and Florida. Two weeks later he proclaimed persons in those States heretofore held as slaves forever free. "Slavery and martial law in a free country" he declared "altogether incompatible." The President in his proclamation of May 19, 1862, rescinding this order once more reveals his sentiments on the slavery question. The act of the Department commander, he said, was wholly unauthorized. The document continues: "I further make known that, whether it be competent for me, as Commander-in-Chief of the army and navy, to declare the slaves of any State or States free, and whether, at any time, in any

---

United States, preferably in Africa, to which free negroes could be aided in emigrating. This, it was believed, would rid the South of its free colored population which had already become a nuisance. Until 1830 it was warmly supported everywhere, and branches of the society were established in nearly every State. In the South its purposes were furthered by James Madison, by Charles Carroll and by Henry Clay. Bushrod Washington became president of the association. Rufus King and President Harrison were among its friends in the North.

Though Texas and Mexico were looked upon as favorable places for locating a colony of free blacks, they were sent to the British possession of Sierra Leone. In 1821 a permanent location was purchased in Liberia. This settlement, with Monrovia as its capital, became independent in 1847. The American Colonization Society attracted little notice after the rise, about 1829-30, of those known as immediate abolitionists.

case, it shall have become a necessity indispensable to the maintenance of the Government to exercise such supposed power, are questions which, under my responsibility, I reserve to myself, and which I cannot feel justified in leaving to the decision of commanders in the field." [1]

Mr. Lincoln took this opportunity to point out to those most nearly concerned the unmistakable signs of the times, and earnestly appealed to them to embrace the offer of compensated abolishment, quoting upon that subject the joint resolution of Congress. The order of General Hunter, so far as it concerned the President, could have been dismissed by its disavowal; but he went farther: he not only took advantage of this occasion earnestly to urge upon the border States very serious consideration of the principle of compensated emancipation, but he raised, without pausing to discuss it, the question of his right as Commander-in-Chief of the army and navy to declare the freedom of slaves within the limits of a State should such a measure become indispensable to the maintenance of the Union.

For refusing to employ his regiment in returning fugitive slaves of disloyal masters, Colonel Paine, of the Fourth Wisconsin Volunteers, was placed under arrest in the summer of 1862; about the same time Lieutenant-Colonel Anthony was similarly disciplined both for refusing permission to search his camp and for ordering the arrest of those hunting for slaves.[2]

Instructions from the War Department, dated July 22, and applying to all the States in rebellion except South Carolina and Tennessee, authorized the employment as laborers of so many persons of African descent as the military and naval commanders could use to advantage, and the payment of reasonable wages for their labor.[3]

[1] Letters and State Papers of Abraham Lincoln, Vol. II. p. 155.
[2] McPherson's Pol. Hist., p. 251.   [3] Ibid., p. 252.

On May 12, 1862, Representative Lovejoy proposed a bill, a substitute for one previously reported by him and introduced by Mr. Isaac N. Arnold:

To the end that freedom may be and remain forever the fundamental law of the land in all places whatsoever, so far as it lies within the powers or depends upon the action of the Government of the United States to make it so: Therefore,

Be it enacted by the Senate and House of Representatives of the United States of America in Congress assembled, That slavery or involuntary servitude, in all cases whatsoever (other than in the punishment of crime, whereof the party shall have been duly convicted) shall henceforth cease, and be prohibited forever in all the Territories of the United States, now existing, or hereafter to be formed or acquired in any way.[1]

This measure passed by 85 yeas to 50 nays. In the Senate, June 9, it was reported amended by inserting this substitute: "That from and after the passage of this act there shall be neither slavery nor involuntary servitude in any of the Territories of the United States now existing, or which may at any time hereafter be formed or acquired by the United States, otherwise than in punishment of crimes whereof the party shall have been duly convicted." In this form it passed by a vote of 28 to 10 and the House concurred by 72 yeas to 38 nays.[2]

Charles Sumner, writing June 5, 1862, to a correspondent who was impatient at what seemed the short-comings of the President, says:

Your criticism of the President is hasty. I am confident that, if you knew him as I do, you would not make it.

Of course, the President cannot be held responsible for all the misfeasances of subordinates, unless adopted or at least tolerated by him. And I am sure that nothing unjust or ungenerous will be tolerated, much less adopted, by him.

I am happy to let you know that he has no sympathy with Stanly in his absurd wickedness, closing the schools, nor again in his other act of

[1] Globe, Part III., 2 Sess. 37th Cong., p. 2068.
[2] Ibid., p. 2618. Ibid., p. 2769.

turning our camp into a hunting ground for slaves. He repudiates both — positively. The latter point has occupied much of his thought; and the newspapers have not gone too far in recording his repeated declarations, which I have often heard from his own lips, that slaves finding their way into the national lines are never to be re-enslaved. This is his conviction, expressed without reserve.

Could you have seen the President — as it was my privilege often — while he was considering the great questions on which he has already acted — the invitation to emancipation in the States, emancipation in the District of Columbia, and the acknowledgment of the independence of Hayti and Liberia — even your zeal would have been satisfied, for you would have felt the sincerity of his purpose to do what he could to carry forward the principles of the Declaration of Independence. His whole soul was occupied, especially by the first proposition, which was peculiarly his own. In familiar intercourse with him, I remember nothing more touching than the earnestness and completeness with which he embraced this idea. To his mind, it was just and beneficent while it promised the sure end of slavery. Of course, to me who had already proposed a bridge of gold for the retreating fiend, it was most welcome. Proceeding from the President, it must take its place among the great events of history.

. . . .

I wish that you really knew the President, and had heard the artless expression of his convictions on these questions which concern you so deeply. You might, perhaps, wish that he were less cautious, but you would be grateful that he is so true to all that you have at heart. Believe me, therefore, you are wrong, and I regret it the more because of my desire to see all our friends stand firmly together.[1]

The President requested and obtained, July 12, 1862, an interview with the border State delegations. The near adjournment of Congress would deprive him of an opportunity of seeing them for several months. He believed they held more power for good than any other equal number of members, and felt that the duty of making an appeal to them could not be waived. This he did by reading a carefully prepared paper.

The Confederate States, he said, would cling to the hope of an ultimate union with the border States as long as they per-

[1] McPherson's Pol. Hist., p. 233.

petuated the institution of slavery. If the members had supported his plan of gradual emancipation in the preceding March the rebellion would now, 1862, be substantially ended.

Looking to the stern facts in the case he inquired whether they could do better for their States than to follow the course which he urged. If the war continued long, the institution "will be extinguished by mere friction and abrasion,"— by the incidents of war much of its value was already gone. He did not speak of immediate emancipation, "but of a decision at once to emancipate gradually." Room for colonization could be procured in South America ample and cheap enough. When their numbers increased sufficiently to be company for one another the freed people would not be so reluctant to go. His repudiation of General Hunter's proclamation had given offence to some whose support the Government could not afford to lose. The pressure from such persons was still upon him and the Congressmen from the border slave States could relieve him and the country. He begged them to re-examine his message of March 6, and commend it to the consideration of their constituents. The peril of their common country demanded the loftiest views and the boldest action if they desired to perpetuate popular government.[1]

It was represented to him, in a conversation which followed this appeal, that the resolution of Congress, being no more than an expression of sentiment, could not be regarded by them as a basis for substantial action. Mr. Lincoln admitted that, as a condition of taking into consideration a proposition so nearly affecting their social system, the border slave States were entitled to expect a substantial pledge of pecuniary aid.

It was further represented at this conference that the people of the border States were interested in knowing the great importance which Mr. Lincoln attached to the policy in ques-

[1] Letters and State Papers of Lincoln, Vol. II. pp. 204-205.

ANTI-SLAVERY LEGISLATION

tion, while it was equally due to the country, to the President and to themselves that they should publicly announce the motives under which they were called to act, and the considerations of public policy urged upon them and their constituents. With a view to such a statement of their position the members met in council to deliberate on the reply they should make, and two days later the majority sent the following paper to the President:

"The undersigned . . . have listened to your address with the profound sensibility naturally inspired by the high source from which it emanates, the earnestness which marked its delivery, and the overwhelming importance of the subject of which it treats. We have given it our most repectful consideration, and now lay before you our response. . . .

" . . . Repudiating the dangerous heresies of the secessionists, we believed, with you, that the war on their part is aggressive and wicked, and the objects for which it was to be prosecuted on ours, defined by your message at the opening of the present Congress, to be such as all good men should approve. We have not hesitated to vote all supplies necessary to carry it on vigorously. . . . "

This support, continues the response, was yielded " in the face of measures most distasteful to us and injurious to the interests we represent, and in the hearing of doctrines, avowed by those who claim to be your friends, [which] must be abhorrent to us and our constituents."

The greater number of them did not, however, vote for the measure recommended in his message of March 6, and they proceeded to state the principal reasons which influenced their action. First, it proposed a radical change in their social system; it was hurried through both Houses with undue haste; and was passed without any opportunity whatever for consultation with their constituents, whose interests it deeply involved. "It seemed," said the majority, "like an interference by this Government with a question which peculiarly and exclusively belonged to our respective States, on which they had not sought advice or solicited aid. Many of us doubted the constitutional power of this Government to make appropriations of money for the object designated, and all of us thought our finances were in no condition to bear the immense outlay which its adoption and faithful execution would impose upon the national Treasury. If we pause but a moment to think of the debt its acceptance would have entailed, we are appalled by its magnitude. The proposition was addressed to all the States and embraced the whole number of slaves."

The census of 1860 showed a slave population of nearly 4,000,000; from natural increase the number in 1862 exceeded that. "At even the low average of $300, the price fixed by the emancipation act for the slaves of this District, and greatly below their real worth, their value runs up to the enormous sum of $1,200,000,000; and if to that we add the cost of deportation and colonization, at $100 each, which is but a fraction more than is actually paid by the Maryland Colonization Society, we have $400,000,000 more. They were not willing nor could the country bear a tax sufficient to pay the interest on that sum in addition to the vast and daily increasing debt already fixed upon them by the exigencies of the war. The proposition is nothing less than the deportation from the country of $1,600,000,000 worth of producing labor and the substitution of an interest-bearing debt of the same amount. Even if it were expected that only the border States would accept the proposition, that involved a sum too great for the financial ability of the Government at this time. The total number of slaves in those States according to the late census was 1,196,112. The same rate of valuation with expenses of deportation and colonization gives the enormous sum of $478,038,133.

" We did not feel that we should be justified in voting for a measure which, if carried out, would add this vast amount to our public debt at a moment when the Treasury was reeling under the enormous expenditure of the war."

To them the resolution seemed no more than the enunciation of a sentiment. " No movement was then made to provide and appropriate the funds required to carry it into effect; and we were not encouraged to believe that funds would be provided. And our belief has been fully justified by subsequent events. Not to mention other circumstances, it is quite sufficient for our purpose to bring to your notice the fact that, while this resolution was under consideration in the Senate our colleague, the Senator from Kentucky, moved an amendment appropriating $500,000 to the object therein designated, and it was voted down with great unanimity. What confidence, then, could we reasonably feel that if we committed ourselves to the policy it proposed, our constituents would reap the fruits of the promise held out; and on what ground could we, as fair men, approach them and challenge their support?"

They denied that if, as the President alleged, they had supported the resolution of March 6, the war would be substantially ended, and they added, " The resolution has passed and if there be virtue in it, it will be quite as efficacious as if we had voted for it."

The war, they asserted, was prolonged not by reason of their conduct, but because of the union of all classes in the South. Those who wished to break down national independence and set up State domination, the State-rights party, could not be reconciled; but the large class who believed their domestic interests had been assailed by the Government might be if only they were convinced " that no harm is intended to them and their institutions," but that the Government was simply defending its legitimate authority.

" Twelve months ago," adds this response, " both Houses of Congress, adopting the spirit of your message, then but recently sent in, declared with singular unanimity the objects of the war, and the country instantly bounded to your side to assist you in carrying it on. If the spirit of that resolution had been adhered to, we are confident that we should before now have seen the end of this deplorable conflict. But what have we seen?

"In both Houses of Congress we have heard doctrines subversive of the principles of the Constitution, and seen measure after measure founded in substance on those doctrines proposed and carried through which can have no other effect than to distract and divide loyal men, and exasperate and drive still further from us and their duty the people of the rebellious States. Military officers, following these bad examples, have stepped beyond the just limits of their authority in the same direction, until in several instances you have felt the necessity of interfering to arrest them. . . . The effect of these measures was foretold, and may now be seen in the indurated state of Southern feeling."

To these causes, and not to the failure of the border delegations to support the measure, they attributed the terrible earnestness of those in arms against the Government. Nor was the institution of slavery the source of insurgent strength, but rather the apprehension that the powers of a common Government would be wielded against the institutions of the Southern States.

The reply concludes: "If Congress, by proper and necessary legislation, shall provide sufficient funds and place them at your disposal, to be applied by you to the payment of any of our States or the citizens thereof who shall adopt the abolishment of slavery, either gradual or immediate, as they may determine, and the expense of deportation and colonization of the liberated slaves, then will our State[s] and people take this proposition into careful consideration, for such decision as in their judgment is demanded by their interest, their honor, and their duty to the whole country." [1]

The minority, seven in number, in their reply of the 15th declared themselves ready to make any sacrifice to save the Government and the institutions of their fathers, and promised to ask the people of their States calmly, deliberately and fairly to consider the recommendations of the President; they were encouraged to assume this position because the leaders of the rebellion had offered to abolish slavery among them as a condition of foreign intervention in favor of their independence as a nation.[2]

Horace Maynard, though not representing a border State proper, expressed his approval of the President's policy and stated the physical impossibility of submitting to the consideration of his people that or any other proposition until Tennessee had first been freed from hostile arms.[3]

A fourth paper submitted to the President was that of Senator J. B. Henderson, of Missouri, who had cheerfully supported the measure at the time of its introduction; he believed the proposition would have received the approbation of a large majority of the border State delegations if they could have foreseen that the war would have been protracted a twelvemonth and had felt assured that the dominant party in Congress would, like the President, be as prompt in practical action as they had been in the expression of a sentiment. "In this period of the nation's distress," says Senator Henderson, "I know of no human institution too sacred for discussion; no material interest belonging to the citizen that he should not willingly place upon the altar of his country, if demanded by the public good."[4]

Mr. Henderson did not agree with the opinion of the Presi-

[1] McPherson's Pol. Hist., pp. 214-217.   [2] Ibid., pp. 217-218.
[3] Ibid., p. 218.   [4] Ibid., pp. 218-220.

dent that "the war would now be substantially ended" had the members from the border States supported the measure in the preceding March. Personally he was favorable to the proposition, but remembered that he was the servant not the master of the people of Missouri.

To the sudden and unexpected collapse of McClellan's Richmond campaign has been ascribed the determination of President Lincoln to adopt general military emancipation so much sooner than he otherwise would have done. The great and decisive element of military strength in the slave population which he saw so clearly a little later could not even then, June and July, 1862, have been altogether concealed from his keen insight into affairs. His personal appeal to the border Congressmen was made July 12; the result of that conference he easily anticipated. Nor was the receipt of their written replies necessary to inform him that his offer would be rejected. So much he could readily collect from their oral objections and verbal criticisms. The decision to give notice of his intention to issue a proclamation concerning slavery was probably made within a few hours after he had assured Mr. Crisfield that the emancipation policy extended no farther than to a refusal of the border States to accept his tender of pecuniary aid to any commonwealth voluntarily adopting the plan of gradual abolishment. However this may be, he confided on the following day, July 13, 1862, to Secretaries Seward and Welles his intention to emancipate slaves by proclamation if their masters did not cease to make war on the Government. From the diary of the latter, we learn under what circumstances this important communication was made.

> President Lincoln [writes Mr. Welles] invited me to accompany him in his carriage to the funeral of an infant child of Mr. Stanton. Secretary Seward and Mrs. Frederick Seward were also in the carriage. Mr. Stanton occupied at that time, for a summer residence, the house of a naval officer, some two or three miles west or northwesterly of Georgetown. It was on this occasion and on this ride that he first mentioned

to Mr. Seward and myself the subject of emancipating the slaves by proclamation in case the rebels did not cease to persist in their war on the Government and the Union, of which he saw no evidence. He dwelt earnestly on the gravity, importance, and delicacy of the movement; said he had given it much thought, and had about come to the conclusion that it was a military necessity, absolutely essential for the salvation of the nation, that we must free the slaves or be ourselves subdued, etc., etc. This was, he said, the first occasion where he had mentioned the subject to any one, and wished us to frankly state how the proposition struck us. Mr. Seward said the subject involved consequences so vast and momentous that he should wish to bestow on it mature reflection before giving a decisive answer; but his present opinion inclined to the measure as justifiable, and perhaps he might say expedient and necessary. These were also my views. Two or three times on that ride the subject, which was of course an absorbing one for each and all, was adverted to, and before separating, the President desired us to give the subject special and deliberate attention, for he was earnest in the conviction that something must be done. It was a new departure for the President, for until this time, in all our previous interviews, whenever the question of emancipation or the mitigation of slavery had been in any way alluded to, he had been prompt and emphatic in denouncing any interference by the General Government with the subject. This was, I think, the sentiment of every member of the Cabinet, all of whom, including the President, considered it a local domestic question appertaining to the States respectively, who had never parted with their authority over it. But the reverses before Richmond, and the formidable power and dimensions of the insurrection, which extended through all the slave States and had combined most of them in a confederacy to destroy the Union, impelled the Administration to adopt extraordinary measures to preserve the national existence. The slaves, if not armed and disciplined, were in the service of those who were, not only as field laborers and producers, but thousands of them were in attendance upon the armies in the field, employed as waiters and teamsters, and the fortifications and intrenchments were constructed by them.[1]

The session of Congress was drawing to a close, but before adjournment the Confiscation Act, passed July 17, 1862, was approved by the President. This with kindred laws increased the number of forfeitures of title to slaves for the crimes of

[1] Quoted in Nicolay and Hay's Abraham Lincoln, A History. Vol. VI. p. 121 *et seq.*

treason and rebellion. These penalties were by him considered just and their imposition constitutional.

Within five days after the adjournment of Congress the President, July 21, 1862, reached his final conclusions on the subject of emancipation. The diary of Secretary Chase contains the following record:

[Having received notice of a Cabinet meeting, Mr. Chase says:] I went to the President's at the appointed hour and found that he was profoundly concerned at the present aspect of affairs, and had determined to take some definite steps in respect to military action and slavery. He had prepared several orders, the first of which contemplated authority to commanders to subsist their troops in the hostile territory; the second, authority to employ negroes as laborers; the third, requiring that both in case of property taken and negroes employed, accounts should be kept with such degree of certainty as would enable compensation to be made in proper cases. Another provided for the colonization of negroes in some tropical country.

A good deal of discussion took place upon these points. The first order was unanimously approved. The second was also unanimously approved; and the third by all except myself. I doubted the expediency of attempting to keep accounts for the benefit of inhabitants of rebel States. The colonization project was not much discussed.

The Secretary of War presented some letters from General Hunter, in which General Hunter advised the Department that the withdrawal of a large proportion of his troops to reënforce General McClellan rendered it highly important that he should be immediately authorized to enlist all loyal persons without reference to complexion. Mr. Stanton, Mr. Seward, and myself expressed ourselves in favor of this plan, and no one expressed himself against it. Mr. Blair was not present. The President was not prepared to decide the question, but expressed himself as averse to arming negroes.[1]

This Cabinet meeting came to no final conclusion, and, as we learn from the same source, the discussion was resumed on the following day, July 22, when the question of arming the slaves was brought up.

I advocated it warmly [writes Secretary Chase].[2] The President was unwilling to adopt this measure, but proposed to issue a proclamation

[1] Schuckers' Life of Salmon Portland Chase, pp. 439-440.
[2] Ibid., p. 440.

on the basis of the Confiscation Bill, calling upon the States to return to their allegiance — warning rebels that the provisions of the act would have full force at the expiration of sixty days — adding, on his own part, a declaration of his intention to renew, at the next session of Congress, his recommendation of compensation to States adopting gradual abolishment of slavery — and proclaiming the emancipation of all slaves within States remaining in insurrection on the first day of January, 1863.[1]

Mr. Chase promised the measure his cordial support, but preferred that no new expression on the subject of compensation be made at that time. Secretary Chase, in the diary mentioned, says: " The impression left upon my mind by the whole discussion was, that, while the President thought that the organization, equipment, and arming of negroes, like other soldiers, would be productive of more evil than good, he was not unwilling that commanders should, at their discretion, arm for purely defensive purposes, slaves coming within their lines."[2] On the kindred policy of emancipation, however, the President had reached a definite conclusion which was in advance of the opinions entertained by even the most radical members of his Cabinet. When, therefore, he read to them, on July 22, his draft of an emancipation proclamation they were for the most part taken completely by surprise. This momentous document deserves to be reproduced entire.

In pursuance of the sixth section of the act of Congress entitled " An act to suppress insurrection and to punish treason and rebellion, to seize and confiscate property of rebels, and for other purposes," approved July 17, 1862, and which act and the joint resolution explanatory thereof are herewith published, I, Abraham Lincoln, President of the United States, do hereby proclaim to and warn all persons within the contemplation of said sixth section to cease participating in, aiding, countenancing, or abetting the existing rebellion, or any rebellion, against the Government of the United States, and to return to their proper allegiance to the United States, on pain of the forfeitures and seizures as within and by said sixth section provided.

And I hereby make known that it is my purpose, upon the next meeting of Congress, to again recommend the adoption of a practical

[1] Shuckers' Life of Chase, pp. 440-441. [2] Ibid., p. 441.

measure for tendering pecuniary aid to the free choice or rejection of any and all States which may then be recognizing and practically sustaining the authority of the United States, and which may then have voluntarily adopted, or thereafter may voluntarily adopt, gradual abolishment of slavery within such State or States; that the object is to practically restore, thenceforward to be maintained, the constitutional relation between the General Government and each and all the States wherein that relation is now suspended or disturbed; and that for this object the war, as it has been, will be prosecuted. And as a fit and necessary military measure for effecting this object, I as Commander-in-Chief of the army and navy of the United States, do order and declare that on the first day of January, in the year of our Lord one thousand eight hundred and sixty-three, all persons held as slaves within any State or States wherein the constitutional authority of the United States shall not then be practically recognized, submitted to, and maintained, shall then, thenceforward, and forever be free.[1]

The diary of Secretary Chase, as well as the President's endorsement on his draft, shows the emancipation proclamation to have been read to the Cabinet July 22, 1862. Various suggestions were offered; but except an objection of Secretary Seward they had all been fully anticipated by Mr. Lincoln and settled in his own mind. Secretary Seward said: " Mr. President, I approve of the proclamation, but I question the expediency of its issue at this juncture. The depression of the public mind, consequent upon our repeated reverses, is so great that I fear the effect of so important a step. It may be viewed as the last measure of an exhausted Government, a cry for help; the Government stretching forth its hands to Ethiopia, instead of Ethiopia stretching forth her hands to the Government."

Speaking afterwards of this incident, Mr. Lincoln said: " Seward's idea was ' that it would be considered our last *shriek* on the retreat. Now,' added Mr. Seward, ' while I approve the measure, I suggest, sir, that you postpone its issue, until you can give it to the country supported by military success, instead of issuing it, as would be the case now, upon the

[1] Letters and State Papers of Lincoln, Vol. II. p. 213.

greatest disasters of the war!' The wisdom of this view," said Mr. Lincoln in recalling the occasion, " struck me with very great force. It was an aspect of the case that, in all my thought upon the subject, I had entirely overlooked. The result was that I put the draft of the proclamation aside, as you do your sketch for a picture, waiting for a victory."[1]

Instead of the proclamation so carefully discussed, a short one was published three days later, of which the most important part is as follows:

In pursuance of the sixth section of the act of Congress entitled " An act to suppress insurrection and to punish treason and rebellion, to seize and confiscate the property of rebels, and for other purposes," approved July 17, 1862, and which act, and the joint resolution explanatory thereof, are herewith published, I, Abraham Lincoln, President of the United States, do hereby proclaim to and warn all persons within the contemplation of said sixth section to cease participating in, aiding, countenancing, or abetting the existing rebellion, or any rebellion, against the Government of the United States, and to return to their proper allegiance to the United States, on pain of the forfeitures and seizures as within and by said sixth section provided.[2]

This warning was required by the sixth section of the act mentioned.

During the following month President Lincoln waited patiently for tidings of some unquestioned success that would justify the publication of his proclamation, but when instead he received in the closing days of August intelligence of the second disaster at Manassas his anxiety must have become intense. This victory, together with the succession of others recently attending Confederate arms, encouraged General Lee's invasion of Maryland. An army, notwithstanding its late reverses, still formidable in numbers and once more thoroughly reorganized marched leisurely from the vicinity of Washington to locate and destroy him. When, where or how the

[1] Carpenter's Six Months at the White House, pp. 21-22.
[2] Letters and State Papers of Lincoln, Vol. II. p. 214.

battle-cloud would break was uncertain. All eyes were turned on McClellan, again in command of the Union forces and strengthened by every soldier that could be spared from the defences of the Federal capital. It was in this state of suspense, and on the very day, September 13, that Lee's victorious legions entered Frederick City that the President gave audience to a deputation from the religious denominations of Chicago, presenting a memorial for the immediate issue of an emancipation proclamation, which was enforced by some remarks from the chairman. The President replied that he had for weeks past, even for months, thought much upon the subject of their memorial.

"I am approached," said he, "with the most opposite opinions and advice, and that by religious men, who are equally certain that they represent the Divine will. I am sure that either the one or the other class is mistaken in that belief, and perhaps, in some respect, both. I hope it will not be irreverent for me to say that if it is probable that God would reveal His will to others, on a point so connected with my duty, it might be supposed He would reveal it directly to me; for, unless I am more deceived in myself than I often am, it is my earnest desire to know the will of Providence in this matter. And if I can learn what it is I will do it! These are not, however, the days of miracles, and I suppose it will be granted that I am not to expect a direct revelation. I must study the plain physical facts of the case, ascertain what is possible, and learn what appears to be wise and right."

The difficulties of the subject and the impossibility of even anti-slavery men, in or out of Congress, agreeing upon any measure of emancipation were then referred to. However, he would discuss the merits of the case and asked pointedly:

"What good would a proclamation of emancipation from me do, especially as we are now situated? I do not want to issue a document that the whole world will see must necessarily be inoperative. . . . Would my word free the slaves, when I cannot even enforce the Constitution in the rebel States? Is there a single court, or magistrate, or individual that would be influenced by it there?"

He admitted to his visitors, however, that he raised no objections to such a proclamation as they desired on legal or on constitutional grounds; for, continued he, "as Commander-in-Chief of the Army and Navy, in time of war I suppose I have a right to take any measure which may best subdue the enemy, nor do I urge objections of a moral nature, in view of possible consequences of insurrection and massacre at the South. I view this matter as a practical war measure, to be decided on according to the advantages or disadvantages it may offer to the suppression of the rebellion."

The committee replied, and the President added, "I admit that slavery is at the root of the rebellion. . . . I will also concede that emancipation would help us in Europe, and convince them that we are incited by something more than ambition. I grant, further, that it would help somewhat at the North, though not so much, I fear, as you and those you represent imagine. . . . Unquestionably, it would weaken the rebels by drawing off their laborers, which is of great importance; but I am not so sure we could do much with the blacks."[1] The President, too, called attention to the fact that the border slave States had 50,000 bayonets in the Union army. It would be a serious matter if in consequence of such a proclamation they should go over to the South. In conclusion he said that he had not decided against a proclamation of liberty to the slaves, but held the matter under advisement and assured them that the subject was on his mind by day and by night more than any other.

It was currently reported among anti-slavery men in Illinois that the emancipation proclamation was extorted from

[1] McPherson's Pol. Hist., pp. 231-232.

the President by the pressure of such delegations as this from the Christian Convention.[1] To determine how little foundation there is for this opinion it is only necessary to recall what had occurred in the Cabinet on July 22 preceding.

The repulse of Lee's veterans at Antietam, September 17, 1862, raised somewhat the hopes of the President. On the 19th General McClellan telegraphed an account of his victory, and Mr. Lincoln three days later announced his intention to issue the postponed proclamation.

All the Cabinet members, having been summoned by messenger from the State Department, were in attendance at the White House on September 22, 1862. After some talk of a general nature, and the reading by Mr. Lincoln of a humorous chapter from a book by Artemus Ward, the conversation assumed a more serious tone. What subsequently transpired on that eventful occasion we learn from the following record in the diary of Secretary Chase:

"Gentlemen, [said the President] I have, as you are aware, thought a great deal about the relation of this war to slavery, and you all remember that, several weeks ago, I read to you an order I had prepared upon the subject, which, on account of objections made by some of you, was not issued. Ever since then my mind has been much occupied with this subject, and I have thought all along that the time for acting on it might probably come. I think the time has come now. I wish it was a better time. I wish that we were in a better condition. The action of the army against the rebels has not been quite what I should have best liked. But they have been driven out of Maryland, and Pennsylvania is no longer in danger of invasion. When the rebel army was at Frederick I determined, as soon as it should be driven out of Maryland, to issue a proclamation of emancipation, such as I thought most likely to be useful. I said nothing to any one, but I made a promise to myself and [hesitating a little] to my Maker. The rebel army is now driven out, and I am going to fulfill that promise. I have got you together to hear what I have written down. I do not wish your advice about the main matter, for that I have determined for myself. This I say without intending anything but respect for any one of you. But I already know the views of each on this question. They have been

[1] McPherson's Pol. Hist., p. 233.

heretofore expressed, and I have considered them as thoroughly and as carefully as I can. What I have written is that which my reflections have determined me to say. If there is anything in the expressions I use or in any minor matter which any one of you thinks had best be changed, I shall be glad to receive your suggestions. One other observation I will make. I know very well that many others might, in this matter as in others, do better than I can; and if I was satisfied that the public confidence was more fully possessed by any one of them than by me, and knew of any constitutional way in which he could be put in my place, he should have it. I would gladly yield it to him. But though I believe that I have not so much of the confidence of the people as I had some time since, I do not know that, all things considered, any other person has more; and, however this may be, there is no way in which I can have any other man put where I am. I am here. I must do the best I can, and bear the responsibility of taking the course which I feel I ought to take."

The President then proceeded to read his Emancipation Proclamation, making remarks on the several parts as he went on, and showing that he had fully considered the subject in all the lights under which it had been presented to him.

After he had closed, Governor Seward said: "The general question having been decided, nothing can be said further about that. Would it not, however, make the proclamation more clear and decided to leave out all reference to the act being sustained during the incumbency of the present President; and not merely say that the Government *recognizes,* but that it will maintain the freedom it proclaims?"

I followed, saying: "What you have said, Mr. President, fully satisfies me that you have given to every proposition which has been made a kind and candid consideration. And you have now expressed the conclusion to which you have arrived clearly and distinctly. This it was your right, and, under your oath of office, your duty to do. The proclamation does not, indeed, mark out the course I would myself prefer; but I am ready to take it just as it is written and to stand by it with all my heart. I think, however, the suggestions of Governor Seward very judicious, and shall be glad to have them adopted."

The President then asked us severally our opinions as to the modifications proposed, saying that he did not care much about the phrases he had used. Every one favored the modification, and it was adopted. Governor Seward then proposed that in the passage relating to colonization some language should be introduced to show that the colonization proposed was to be only with the consent of the colonists, and the consent of the states in which the colonies might be attempted. This, too, was agreed to, and no other modification was proposed. Mr. Blair then said that the question having been decided, he would make no objection to issuing the proclamation; but he would ask to have his paper, presented some days since, against the policy, filed with the proclamation. The President consented to this readily. And then Mr. Blair went on to say that he was afraid of the influence of the proclamation on the border States and on the army, and stated, at some length, the grounds of his apprehensions. He disclaimed most expressly, however, all objections to emancipation *per se,* saying he had always been personally in favor of it — always ready for immediate emancipation in the midst of slave States, rather than submit to the perpetuation of the system.[1]

The foregoing account from the diary of Secretary Chase is fully corroborated by a narrative of Mr. Welles describing the same event.[2] Mr. Blair, as already observed, believed the time inopportune for issuing the proclamation and feared as a result that the border States would go over to secession. The President, however, thought the difficulty not to act as great as to act. There were two sides, he said, to that question. For months he had labored to get those States to move in this matter, convinced in his own mind that it was their true interest to do so, but his labors were vain. "We must take the forward movement," he declared. "They would acquiesce, if not immediately, soon; for they must be satisfied that slavery had received its death-blow from slave-owners — it could not survive the rebellion."[3]

When the Cabinet had concluded its deliberations the document was duly attested, the seal affixed and the President's signature added. On the following morning, September 23, 1862, the proclamation was published in full by all the leading newspapers of the loyal States, where it excited the most profound surprise. Indicating, as it does, the progress of opinion, it was the first great landmark of the war; behind it lay the old, before it the new order of things. The successive steps by which Mr. Lincoln reached this position have been

[1] Quoted in Schuckers' Life of Chase, pp. 453-455.
[2] The Galaxy, December, 1872, pp. 846-847.
[3] Ibid., p. 847.

sketched in the present chapter with fullness and, it is believed, with accuracy. It has been shown how fugitive slaves escaping to the Federal lines were at first surrendered to their masters; how soon afterward, as in the case of General Butler's command, they were protected by the army and employed as laborers; how in a later stage, certain Union commanders who proposed to confiscate slave property or to arm negroes as soldiers were gently rebuked and their acts disavowed by the President. This forbearance, however, was without effect on the Southern people, whose hatred was quite as likely to ascribe it to Yankee cowardice as to Yankee magnanimity.

With this account of the introduction into the problem of reconstruction of a novel and very perplexing element we are prepared to examine the various theories of State status held by those whose position and ability made them leaders of public opinion. That subject will be more properly discussed in a separate chapter.

VI

THEORIES AND PLANS OF RECONSTRUCTION

IN considering the different plans of reconstruction it is not deemed necessary to discuss further than has been done in the preceding pages the President's theory of State status. There, in his effort to establish loyal governments in three of the rebellious States, as well as in the protection and encouragement extended to reorganized Virginia, we have seen practical applications of that theory. In his first inaugural Mr. Lincoln said: " It is safe to assert that no government proper ever had a provision in its organic law for its own termination," and on the same occasion he added, " No State, upon its own mere motion, can lawfully get out of the Union; that *resolves* and *ordinances* to that effect are legally void." [1] From the principles of March 4, 1861, was logically deduced the central idea of the plan announced in December, 1863, and maintained by the President till the last hour of his life. In his first message to Congress, submitted at the special session beginning July 4, 1861, he again attempted to remove the fears of those whose prejudice ascribed to the dominant political party a purpose to interfere in the domestic concerns of the slaveholding States. As will be seen by the following quotation he little more than reiterated on that occasion what he had solemnly declared four months earlier:

> Lest there be some uneasiness in the minds of candid men as to what is to be the course of the Government towards the Southern States *after* the rebellion shall have been suppressed, the Executive

[1] McPherson's Pol. Hist., p. 106.

deems it proper to say, it will be his purpose then, as ever, to be guided by the Constitution and the laws; and that he probably will have no different understanding of the powers and duties of the Federal Government relatively to the rights of the States and the people, under the Constitution, than that expressed in the inaugural address.

He desires to preserve the Government, that it may be administered for all, as it was administered by the men who made it. Loyal citizens everywhere have the right to claim this of their Government, and the Government has no right to withhold or neglect it. It is not perceived that, in giving it, there is any coercion, any conquest, or any subjugation, in any just sense of those terms.[1]

The first paragraph quoted expresses his perfect confidence in a successful conclusion of the war, and in this respect suggests the faith of Charles Sumner, in whose private correspondence the same thought constantly occurs. In his message the President observed also that Virginia had allowed "this giant insurrection to make its nest within her borders; and this Government has no choice left but to deal with it *where* it finds it. And it has the less regret, as the loyal citizens have, in due form, claimed its protection. Those loyal citizens this Government is bound to recognize, and protect, as being Virginia."[2]

As early as June, 1861, Mr. Lincoln, on application of Governor Pierpont, recognized the restored State of Virginia by promising assistance to repel invasion and to suppress domestic violence; his example was followed by both Houses of Congress: first, in the prompt admission of Senators and Representatives from that Commonwealth, and long afterward, when there was ample time for reflection, by consenting to admit the new State of West Virginia, to whose separate and independent existence the reorganized Legislature had formally assented. The recognition of Pierpont's government, however, involved on the constitutional question little difference of opinion between the President and Congress. Thus far

[1] McPherson's Pol. Hist., p. 129.
[2] Ibid., p. 125.

the political departments, if not in complete harmony, were at any rate not in conflict. This act, though it marked no distinct Executive policy, was the occasion of some discordant notes which will be referred to in their proper relation.

It may not be unnecessary to observe that underlying the early policy of the President was a conviction that the rebellion was effected by a small but treasonable faction; indeed, in the message of July 4 he expressed his belief that, with the probable exception of South Carolina, the disloyal were in a minority in all the seceding States. The great mass of Southern people, it was assumed, opposed disunion, and with Federal assistance would soon right themselves. Peaceful citizens of that section, being regarded as still under protection of the Constitution, were, therefore, not to be molested. The conflict waged by the General Government was a personal war against insurgents. Leaders who encouraged sedition and committed acts of hostility against the United States could be tried precisely as in a consolidated state like Great Britain, and upon conviction punished for their treason. This attitude was not only wise, but had the additional merit of greatly simplifying the method of restoration. It asserted further that the rebellious States were still in the Union, and under the existing compact could not lawfully withdraw from it; being in the Union, they were entitled to all the rights accorded to other members of the confederation. In brief, its essential idea was the indestructibility of a State, and it denied that the integrity of the national domain had been impaired or the number of States diminished by the ordinances of secession. The General Government could properly aid the people of a State to express their will, but, beyond what was demanded by the exigencies of the war, could not legally exercise those powers constitutionally reserved to the States. By the treasonable act of levying war against the Republic the rights and franchises incident to

United States citizenship were forfeited. The power of Congress extended no further than to a guaranty of preëxisting republican forms of government.

To the correctness of these principles Democrats and Republicans alike gave almost universal assent. But the war was increasing in magnitude, and the measures adequate to the suppression of a gigantic rebellion proved to be very different from those adapted to a local insurrection. The President's original intention was to overcome armed resistance to Federal power and as speedily as possible restore the States to their former relations. This task, however, was more easily conceived than accomplished, and in the terrible conflict that ensued political parties as well as individual statesmen were swept onward from point to point to very different resting-places. From this condition resulted the great number of theories of reconstruction presented before the end of the rebellion.

The President early in the war adopted principles that found little favor with conservative Democrats. His readiness to recognize the restored State of Virginia was equivalent to a declaration that if a majority of the people in one of the seceded States voluntarily transferred their obedience and support to a hostile power the loyal minority constituted the State and should govern it. In this connection will be remembered the objections of Bayard and Saulsbury to receiving Senators Willey and Carlile from the reorganized government of Virginia. A further advance is indicated by Mr. Lincoln's appointment, early in 1862, of military governors for those States that had been brought partly within Federal military lines. After the proclamation of September 22, 1862, and that of January 1 succeeding, the question of restoration was left permanently out of view. If the erring States were ever to resume their places they must first recognize the anti-slavery legislation summarized in the preceding chapter. Hitherto the paramount consideration with the President was a speedy restoration of former relations; thenceforth "the Union as it was" became impossible, because slaves liberated in the progress of the war could never be returned to a condition of servitude. The introduction of this element greatly increased the difficulties of a problem already sufficiently intricate. But neither this nor any other consequence of his proclamation appears to have been overlooked by the Executive.

The message of December 8, 1863, together with the accompanying proclamation sketched in outline the only plan which Mr. Lincoln ever published on the subject of reconstruction, and even to this mode of reinstatement he did not require exact conformity, recognizing that its modification might be demanded by inherent differences in situation among the returning States. By its terms all persons who participated in the rebellion, except certain described classes, were promised amnesty with restoration of property (excluding slaves and those cases of property in which rights of third parties intervened) upon taking an oath which pledged support of the Constitution and the Union; of the slavery legislation enacted during the war (unless such acts were repealed by Congress, or were modified or annulled by the Supreme Court), and adherence to all Executive proclamations on that subject so long and so far as not modified or declared void by the Judiciary. Whenever in any of the rebellious States a number of persons equal to one tenth of the voters participating in the Presidential election of 1860, who were qualified electors under the laws existing immediately before the ordinance of secession, should reëstablish a State government republican in form, and not contravening this oath, it would be recognized as the true government of that State and should receive the benefits of the constitutional guaranty. To the emancipated race renewed assurance of permanent freedom was given. It was also suggested that in reorganization the political framework of the States be maintained. The admission of members elected to Congress was a matter for the determination of its respective Houses.

It is proper to notice in this method of reorganization, known afterward as "the Louisiana Plan," the absence of any provision for conferring on the freedmen the elective franchise. In a private letter to Governor Hahn the President had, it is true, expressed his personal preference for including among the electors such of the colored race as had fought gallantly in the Union ranks and also the very intelligent among them.[1] This, however, was only an unofficial suggestion. Nor were securities of any sort required for the future as a condition of reinstatement.

Under this plan, which was presented as only a rallying point, Union governments had been inaugurated in Tennessee, Louisiana and Arkansas; the first two participated in the Presidential election of 1864, and before the close of the war they had all elected members to Congress. The legality of these governments Mr. Lincoln always maintained. How Congress regarded them will be related in succeeding chapters.

Long before the announcement of any mode of reorganization by the Executive, members of the Legislative branch of Government had made some efforts in this field; these, however, were for the most part tentative and hesitant. The question had not yet been brought fairly before Congress; indeed, it was in discussing the results and tendencies of Presidential reconstruction that the Congressional plan, destined ultimately to prevail, slowly assumed definitive form.

As early as December, 1861, Mr. Harlan, of Iowa, introduced into the Senate a bill for the establishment of provisional governments for the territory embraced by the States of Georgia, Alabama, Mississippi, Louisiana, Texas, Arkan-

[1] See p. 73,*ante*.

sas and Tennessee. It was referred to the Committee on Territories, but was never reported.

More important, however, than this proposed enactment, both because of the acknowledged position of their author and the influence which they exerted upon the mode of reconstruction finally adopted, were the nine resolutions offered, February 11, 1862, by Charles Sumner. These were "declaratory of the relations between the United States and the territory once occupied by certain States, and now usurped by pretended governments, without constitutional or legal right." A preamble in the characteristic style of this celebrated statesman introduced his famous propositions, which were as follows:

> Whereas certain States, rightfully belonging to the Union of the United States, have through their respective governments wickedly undertaken to abjure all those duties by which their connection with the Union was maintained; to renounce all allegiance to the Constitution; to levy war upon the national Government; and, for the consummation of this treason, have unconstitutionally and unlawfully confederated together, with the declared purpose of putting an end by force to the supremacy of the Constitution within their respective limits; and whereas this condition of insurrection, organized by pretended governments, openly exists in South Carolina, Georgia, Florida, Alabama, Mississippi, Louisiana, Texas, Arkansas, Tennessee, and Virginia, except in Eastern Tennessee and Western Virginia, and has been declared by the President of the United States, in a proclamation duly made in conformity with an act of Congress, to exist throughout this territory, with the exceptions already named; and whereas the extensive territory thus usurped by these pretended governments and organized into a hostile confederation, belongs to the United States, as an inseparable part thereof, under the sanctions of the Constitution, to be held in trust for the inhabitants in the present and future generations, and is so completely interlinked with the Union that it is forever dependent thereupon; and whereas the Constitution, which is the supreme law of the land, cannot be displaced in its rightful operation within this territory, but must ever continue the supreme law thereof, notwithstanding the doings of any pretended governments acting singly or in confederation, in order to put an end to its supremacy: Therefore:
>
> 1. *Resolved,* That any vote of secession or other act by which any State may undertake to put an end to the supremacy of the Constitution

within its territory is inoperative and void against the Constitution, and when sustained by force it becomes a practical *abdication* by the State of all rights under the Constitution, while the treason which it involves still further works an instant *forfeiture* of all those functions and powers essential to the continued existence of the State as a body politic, so that from that time forward the territory falls under the exclusive jurisdiction of Congress as other territory, and the State being, according to the language of the law, *felo-de-se,* ceases to exist.

2. That any combination of men assuming to act in the place of such State, attempting to insnare or coerce the inhabitants thereof into a confederation hostile to the Union, is rebellious, treasonable, and destitute of all moral authority; and that such combination is a usurpation incapable of any constitutional existence and utterly lawless, so that everything dependent upon it is without constitutional or legal support.

3. That the termination of a State under the Constitution necessarily causes the termination of those peculiar local institutions which, having no origin in the Constitution or in those natural rights which exist independent of the Constitution, are upheld by the sole and exclusive authority of the State.

4. That slavery, being a peculiar local institution, derived from local laws, without any origin in the Constitution or in natural rights, is upheld by the sole and exclusive authority of the State, and must therefore cease to exist legally or constitutionally when the State on which it depends no longer exists; for the incident cannot survive the principal.

5. That in the exercise of its exclusive jurisdiction over the territory once occupied by the States, it is the duty of Congress to see that the supremacy of the Constitution is maintained in its essential principles, so that everywhere in this extensive territory slavery shall cease to exist practically, as it has already ceased to exist constitutionally or legally.

6. That any recognition of slavery in such territory, or any surrender of slaves under the pretended laws of the extinct States by any officer of the United States, civil or military, is a recognition of the pretended governments, to the exclusion of the jurisdiction of Congress under the Constitution, and is in the nature of aid and comfort to the rebellion that has been organized.

7. That any such recognition of slavery or surrender of pretended slaves, besides being a recognition of the pretended governments, giving them aid and comfort, is a denial of the rights of persons who, by the extinction of the States, have become free, so that, under the Constitution, they cannot again be enslaved.

8. That allegiance from the inhabitant and protection from the Government are corresponding obligations, dependent upon each other,

so that while the allegiance of every inhabitant of this territory, without distinction of color or class, is due to the United States, and cannot in any way be defeated by the action of any pretended Government, or by any pretence of property or claim to service, the corresponding obligation of protection is at the same time due by the United States to every such inhabitant, without distinction of color or class; and it follows that inhabitants held as slaves, whose paramount allegiance is due to the United States, may justly look to the national Government for protection.

9. That the duty directly cast upon Congress by the extinction of the States is reinforced by the positive prohibition of the Constitution that "no State shall enter into any Confederation," or "without the consent of Congress keep troops or ships-of-war in time of peace, or enter into any agreement or compact with another State," or "grant letters of marque and reprisal," or "coin money," or "emit bills ot credit," or "without the consent of Congress lay any duties on imports or exports," all of which have been done by these pretended Governments, and also by the positive injunction of the Constitution, addressed to the nation, that "the United States shall guaranty to every State in this Union a republican form of government," and that in pursuance of this duty cast upon Congress, and further enjoined by the Constitution, Congress will assume complete jurisdiction of such vacated territory where such unconstitutional and illegal things have been attempted, and will proceed to establish therein republican forms of government under the Constitution; and in the execution of this trust will provide carefully for the protection of all the inhabitants thereof; for the security of families, the organization of labor, the encouragement of industry, and the welfare of society, and will in every way discharge the duties of a just, merciful and paternal Government.[1]

Sumner, as already noticed, having confidence in the ultimate triumph of the national cause, began early in the war to reflect on the subject of reorganization. As might have been expected from his previous career, his opinion of the changes that would result from rebellion inclined him at the outset to adopt the views of the less extreme anti-slavery men. Notwithstanding this fact, however, his scheme of reconstruction, because of its radical and comprehensive character, caused something of a sensation when introduced in the Senate, and disturbed the repose of many conservative

[1] McPherson's Pol. Hist., pp. 322-323.

patriots outside. By leading Republicans it was promptly disavowed as the policy of their party. These resolutions, though never adopted or even formally discussed by Congress, colored somewhat the final work of reconstruction. An account of the extent and the manner in which they influenced the legislative plan belongs properly to a consideration of the acts of March, 1867. What appeared to be a public necessity had by that time brought many members of his party fully abreast of Mr. Sumner.

The interval had been employed in various ways to keep his peculiar theory before the public. A private letter to Francis Lieber, dated March 29, 1862, shows that Sumner's view of the measures essential to restoration had not been modified by the discussions of a month. "Assuming," he says, " that our military success is complete, and that the rebel armies are scattered, what next? Unless I am mistaken, the most difficult thing of all, — namely, the reorganization. How shall it be done, — by what process? What power shall set a-going the old governments? Will the people coöperate enough to constitute self-government? I have positive opinions here. If successful in war, we shall have then before us the alternative: (1) Separation; or (2) subjugation of these States with emancipation. I do not see any escape. Diplomatists here and abroad think it will be separation. I think the latter, under my resolutions or something like."[1]

By a distinguished Confederate officer Sumner has been described as a statesman who seemed over-educated, and who had retained without having digested his learning;[2] by an admirer of his own party as wanting in tact and practical wisdom as a legislator.[3] Though it must be admitted that a grain of truth forms the basis of these criticisms, yet the letter to his

[1] Memoir of Charles Sumner by E. L. Pierce, Vol. IV. pp. 74-75.
[2] General Richard Taylor in Destruction and Reconstruction, p. 245.
[3] Blaine, Twenty Years of Congress, Vol. II. p. 114.

friend Dr. Lieber shows no lack of insight into the events and tendencies of the times. Without anticipating a subsequent portion of this narrative it may be observed here that if his vision did not pierce the remote future, his knowledge and experience enabled him to see as much of coming events as the most gifted of his contemporaries. Writing a year later, July 21, 1863, to Hon. John Bright, one of our few friends in England, he remarked that " so great a revolution cannot come to a close at once." [1] The defeat of General Lee at Gettysburg a few weeks earlier suggested the thought that the destruction of the Army of Northern Virginia would have precipitated on Congress the entire question of reconstruction, and time was an essential element in the development of Sumner's most cherished plans.

Not only in his private correspondence and in the discussion of every conceivable measure before Congress did he endeavor to enforce his theory of State status, but he also published in a leading periodical an elaboration and defence of his opinions. For many reasons the undelivered speech forming the basis of his article in the *Atlantic Monthly* for October, 1863, is of remarkable interest. It reveals the mental habits of one of the most useful and influential characters then in public life; the statesman is really thinking aloud. He appears, for instance, to have been much impressed by the fact that, under the Commonwealth, Cromwell partitioned his country into military districts of which Sumner remarked that there were precisely *eleven,* just the number of States in rebellion. One view is enforced by an appropriate passage from Cicero, while of Edmund Burke it is asserted that had he lived during the Civil War his eloquence would have blasted Southern leaders for their folly and madness in entering upon a career of rebellion. All who are familiar with the debates of that period must have observed that Sumner

[1] Memoir of Sumner by E. L. Pierce, Vol. IV. p. 143.

was considerably influenced by the authority of great names, and in consequence sometimes exposed himself to rebuke from men who, though in many respects inferior, had studied the questions of the day in the light of their own times.

It is not intended, however, to trace the origin of the doctrine of State suicide or even to suggest all the arguments upon which he relied for its support, the purpose of these remarks being rather to show on what principles its essential propositions were based. This, it is believed, cannot be better done than by explaining the resolutions in his own language.

In the *Atlantic Monthly* he wrote: "It is sometimes said that the States themselves committed *suicide,* so that as States they ceased to exist, leaving their whole jurisdiction open to the occupation of the United States under the Constitution. This assumption is founded on the fact that, whatever may be the existing governments in these States, they are in no respect constitutional, and since the State itself is known by the government, with which its life is intertwined, it must cease to exist constitutionally when its government no longer exists constitutionally."

He acknowledges the difficulty of defining the entity which we call a State. "Among us," says Mr. Sumner, "the term is most known as the technical name for one of the political societies which compose our Union. . . . Nobody has suggested, I presume, that any 'State' of our Union has, through rebellion, ceased to exist as a *civil society,* or even as a *political community.* It is only as a *State of the Union,* armed with State rights, or at least as a *local government,* which annually renews itself, as the snake its skin, that it can be called in question. But it is vain to challenge for the technical 'State," or for the annual government, that immortality which belongs to civil society. The one is an artificial body, the other is a natural body; and while the first, overwhelmed by insurrection or war, may change or die, the latter can change or die only with the extinction of the community itself, whatever may be its name or its form."

Phillimore is quoted in support of the proposition that a "State," even in a broader signification, may lose its life. That author says: "A state, like an individual, may die," and, among the various ways in which this may occur, adds, "by its submission and the donation of itself to another country." "But in the case of our Rebel States," resumes Mr. Sumner, "there has been a plain submission and donation of themselves,— *effective, at least, to break the continuity of government,* if not to destroy that immortality which has been claimed. Nor can it make any difference, in breaking this continuity, that the submission and donation, constituting a species of attornment, were to enemies at home rather than to enemies abroad,— to Jefferson Davis rather than to Louis Napoleon. The thread is snapped in one case as much as in the other.

"But a *change of form* in the actual government may be equally effective. Cicero speaks of a change so complete as 'to leave no image of a state behind.' But this is precisely what has been done throughout the whole Rebel region: there is no image of a *constitutional* State left behind."

The first resolution of the series quoted declares "That any vote of secession or other act by which any State may undertake to put an end to the supremacy of the Constitution within its territory is inoperative and void against the Constitution, and when sustained by force it becomes a practical *abdication* by the State of all its rights under the Constitution." Perhaps Mr. Sumner in the essay failed to strengthen his original statement of this proposition, which he believed was "upheld by the historic example of England, at the Revolution of 1688, when, on the flight of James II. and the abandonment of his kingly duties, the two Houses of Parliament voted that the monarch, 'having violated the fundamental laws, and having withdrawn himself out of the kingdom, *had abdicated the government,* and that the throne had thereby become vacant.'" This precedent, which Senator Sumner thought applicable, was by no means so formidable an argument against the rebellious States as he chose to regard it. If the term *abdicate* is equivalent to a species of informal resignation it did not apply strictly to the case of James II., for that unfortunate ruler presented to Englishmen the unusual spectacle of withdrawing from his kingdom under an escort of Dutch troops. Doubtless he remembered the saying of his father, who proved the truth of the adage in his own person, that the distance is short between the prison and the grave of a king. The expectation of recovering his throne was a motive with James scarcely less powerful than that of taking precaution for his personal safety. This intention appears from the unsuccessful campaign in Ireland, which he had selected as a rallying point. That monarch's real offence was his violation of the laws of England. Many of his predecessors, as well as some of his successors, were as unreasonable and as obstinate as he. The charge of abdication was scarcely a decent pretext for declaring the throne vacant, and Mr. Sumner appears to have forgotten for the moment that the Federal Government is one of limited while Parliament is clothed with absolute powers. In reality James was coerced by the Prince of Orange into "withdrawing" from the Kingdom. It is not intended here to call in question the accepted vindication of the Revolution of 1688, but merely to show that the Massachusetts statesman was at times not above supporting an argument by a legal or an historical fiction.

The same resolution continues: "The treason which it [the attempt by force to terminate the supremacy of the Constitution] involves still further works an instant *for-*

feiture of all those functions and powers essential to the continued existence of the State as a body politic."

On the idea of State forfeiture his reasoning is entitled to more respect. He argues: "But again it is sometimes said that the States, by their flagrant treason, have *forfeited* their rights as States, so as to be civilly dead. It is a patent and indisputable fact, that this gigantic treason was inaugurated with all the forms of law known to the State; that it was carried forward not only by individuals, but also by States, so far as States can perpetrate treason; that the States pretended to withdraw bodily in their corporate capacities; — that the Rebellion, as it showed itself, was *by* States as well as *in* States; that it was by the governments of States as well as by the people of States; and that, to the common observer, the crime was consummated by the several corporations as well as by the individuals of whom they were composed. From this fact, obvious to all, it is argued that, since, according to Blackstone, ' a traitor hath abandoned his connection with society, and hath no longer any right to the advantages which before belonged to him purely as a member of the community,' by the same principle the traitor State is no longer to be regarded as a member of the Union. But it is not necessary, on the present occasion, to insist on the application of any such principle to States."

Discarding as not essential to his defence the theories of State forfeiture, State abdication, or even State suicide, the article adds: "It is enough, that, for the time being, and *in the absence of a loyal government,* they can take no part and perform no function in the Union, *so that they cannot be recognized by the National Government.* The reason is plain. There are in these States no local functionaries bound by constitutional oaths, so that, in fact, there are no constitutional functionaries; and since the State government is necessarily composed of such functionaries, there can be no State government. Thus, for instance, in South Carolina, Pickens and his associates may call themselves the governor and legislature; and in Virginia, Letcher and his associates may call themselves governor and legislature; but we cannot recognize them as such. Therefore to all pretensions in behalf of State governments in the Rebel States I oppose the simple FACT, that for the time being no such governments exist. The broad spaces once occupied by those governments are now abandoned and vacated."

Discussing the question of transition to rightful government he says: " And here the question occurs, How shall this rightful jurisdiction be established in the vacated States? Some there are, so impassioned for State rights, and so anxious for forms even at the expense of substance, that they insist upon the instant restoration of the old State governments in all their parts, through the agency of loyal citizens, who meanwhile must be protected in this work of restoration. But assuming that all this is practicable, as it clearly is not, it attributes to the loyal citizens of a Rebel State, however few in numbers, — it may be an insignificant minority, — a power clearly inconsistent with the received principle of popular government, that the majority must rule, . . . but the argument for State Rights assumes that all these rights may be lodged in voters as few in number as ever controlled a rotten borough of England.

" Pray admitting that a minority may organize the new government, how shall it be done? and by whom shall it be set in motion? . . . It is not easy to see how the new government can be set in motion without a resort to some revolutionary proceeding, instituted either by the citizens or by the military power, — unless Congress, in the exercise of its plenary powers, should undertake to organize the new jurisdiction.

" But every revolutionary proceeding is to be avoided. It

will be within the recollection of all familiar with our history, that our fathers, while regulating the separation of the Colonies from the parent country, were careful that all should be done according to the forms of law, so that the thread of *legality* should continue unbroken. To this end the Continental Congress interfered by a supervising direction. But the Tory argument in that day denied the power of Congress as earnestly as it denies this power now." . . .

"But, happily," he says, "we are not constrained to any such revolutionary proceeding. The new governments can all be organized by Congress, which is the natural guardian of people without any immediate government, and within the jurisdiction of the Constitution of the United States. Indeed, with the State governments already *vacated* by rebellion, the Constitution becomes, for the time, the supreme and only law, binding alike on President and Congress, so that neither can establish any law or institution incompatible with it. And the whole Rebel region, deprived of all local government, lapses under the exclusive jurisdiction of Congress, precisely as any other territory; or, in other words, the lifting of the local governments leaves the whole vast region without any other government than Congress, unless the President should undertake to govern it by military power." . . .

This part of the essay concludes with a declaration that its author had no pride of opinion, but would cheerfully abandon his views when convinced of their error. He next proceeds to an examination of the sources of Congressional power. These, he asserts, are derived from the necessity of the case, for Congress must have jurisdiction over every portion of the United States *where there is no other government;* and from the *Rights of War*, which he deemed not less abundant for Congress than for the President. "It is Congress," he contended, "that conquers; and the same authority that conquers must govern." A third source of authority, common alike to Congress and the President, was the constitutional provision imposing on the United States the duty of guarantying republican forms of government. These ample powers were confirmed by an additional grant in the clause concerning the admission of new States "into this Union." The latter left it with Congress to prescribe the time and manner of the return of the rebel States, assuming that they were no longer *de facto* States of the Union.

Among the "unanswerable reasons for Congressional governments" the article says: "Slavery is so odious that it can exist only by virtue of positive law, plain and unequivocal; but no such words can be found in the Constitution. Therefore Slavery is impossible within the exclusive jurisdiction of the National Government. . . . I am glad to believe that it is implied, if not expressed, in the Chicago Platform; . . . but if the rebel territory falls under the exclusive jurisdiction of the National Government, then Slavery will be impossible there. . . . The moment that the States fell, Slavery fell also; so that, even without any Proclamation of the President, Slavery had ceased to have a legal and constitutional existence in every rebel State."[1]

"Let it be established in advance," declared Mr. Sumner, "as an inseparable incident to every Act of Secession, that it is not only impotent against the Constitution of the United States, but that, on its occurrence, both soil and inhabitants will lapse beneath the jurisdiction of Congress, and no State will ever again pretend to secede."

The argument of which an epitome has been given was regarded by the Postmaster-General, Montgomery Blair, as formidable enough to merit attention, and he accordingly

[1] Mr. Sumner, notwithstanding this view, proposed to enact the Emancipation Proclamation into a law. See pp. 272-273 *infra*.

replied in a speech at Rockville, Maryland, in which Sumner, for arraying himself directly against the President on a question of fundamental policy in the conduct of the war, was mentioned with sharp censure. This brought upon the Cabinet member, and upon Mr. Lincoln over his shoulders, much vehement criticism. It was in relation to this address that the President said:

> The controversy between the two sets of men represented by Blair and by Sumner is one of mere form and little else. I do not think Mr. Blair would agree that the States in rebellion are to be permitted to come at once into the political family and renew their performances, which have already so bedeviled us, and I do not think Mr. Sumner would insist that when the loyal people of a State obtain supremacy in their councils and are ready to assume the direction of their own affairs they should be excluded. I do not understand Mr. Blair to admit that Jefferson Davis may take his seat in Congress again as a representative of his people. I do not understand Mr. Sumner to assert that John Minor Botts may not. So far as I understand Mr. Sumner, he seems in favor of Congress taking from the Executive the power it at present exercises over insurrectionary districts and assuming it to itself; but when the vital question arises as to the right and privilege of the people of these States to govern themselves, I apprehend there will be little difference among loyal men. The question at once is presented, In whom is this power vested? and the practical matter for discussion is how to keep the rebellious population from overwhelming and outvoting the loyal minority.[1]

Concisely expressed, the theory of State suicide based reconstruction upon the right of Congress to legislate for Federal territories and to admit new States into this Union. In one view it rested on a provision in the Constitution which makes it obligatory on the States to have republican governments. This side of the doctrine shaded into the conservative view, according to which it is the duty of the States to be represented in Congress; but Sumner, as will subsequently appear, maintained that the Confederate States should not be counted when numbers were to be estimated in the

[1] N. and H., Vol. IX. pp. 335-336.

adoption of constitutional amendments; also that Congress had power to prescribe the qualifications of voters for conventions in those States. This view regarded the war as a conflict of ideas; it assumed to find authority in the individual conscience discerning the will of God, was inclined to disallow objective standards, and to consider all law as matter of subjective determination. From a careful perusal of his speeches Mr. Sumner appears to have insisted that a republican form of government could be such a one only as conformed to his subjective ideas. Except his own State, whose constitution of 1780 was held to have abolished slavery in that Commonwealth, no one of the States in 1789 possessed, according to his notions, a republican form of government. His touchstone of republicanism was the Declaration of Independence. In short, the requirements of the Constitution appear to have been found, not in the written instrument, but in his individual conceptions of political justice, equality and liberty whereby he constituted himself a new source of law. In the matter of a subjective standard of natural justice and the like, the "radicals" generally agreed with Sumner.[1]

The position that the object of the war from the beginning, on the part of the Federal authorities, was to fulfill the guaranty of a republican form of government is untenable. It may well be doubted whether the community so guaranteed can be restricted to any particular government; indeed, it is difficult to see how a government not voluntarily instituted by the people of a State can be called republican. By having a government imposed by Congress they would resemble the people of a Territory, and the result would be an inequality among the States composing the Union.

[1] In his Theory of our National Existence *(passim)* and in the American Law Review for January, 1865, Mr. John C. Hurd has much keen criticism of the reconstruction theories of Sumner and others.

Though it has been commended as well written, there is some crude thinking and even cruder phraseology in the preamble as well as in the resolutions themselves. Mr. Sumner appears to have been much influenced by feudal and other historical analogies. It will be seen later how he recoiled somewhat from accepting fully the consequences of his own principles.[1] The famous theory of State suicide, as tersely stated by an able advocate of the doctrine, was in effect that "a Territory by coming into the Union becomes a State; a State by going out of the Union becomes a Territory."[2]

To offset the resolutions of Sumner, Hon. Garrett Davis, of Kentucky, introduced two days later a series of eight propositions. Of these the first asserts that the rights, privileges and liberties which the Constitution assures to the people of the United States "are fixed, permanent, and immutable through all the phases of peace and war, until changed by the power and in the mode prescribed by the Constitution itself."

In the light of subsequent events, however, the last is the most interesting of the series. This declares "That the United States Government should march their armies into all the insurgent States, and promptly put down the military power which they have arrayed against it, and give protection and security to the loyal men thereof, to enable them to reconstruct their legitimate State governments, and bring them and the people back to the Union and to obedience and duty under the Constitution and the laws of the United States, bearing the sword in one hand and the olive branch in the other, and whilst inflicting on the guilty leaders condign and exemplary punishment, granting amnesty and oblivion to the comparatively innocent masses; and if the people of any State cannot, or will not reconstruct their State gov-

---

[1] Colloquy with Senator Doolittle, December 19, 1866, Cong. Globe, p. 192.   [2] Brownson's American Republic, p. 308.

ernment and return to loyalty and duty, Congress should provide a government for such State as a Territory of the United States, securing to the people thereof their appropriate constitutional rights."[1]

These propositions, like the resolutions of Sumner, were never taken up for discussion, and they are referred to as containing a clear expression, by a Southern Democrat,[2] of extra-constitutional powers in treating incorrigible States as Territories.

Sumner was not alone in maintaining novel opinions concerning the relation of the seceded States to the Federal Government. A theory destined to exert even greater influence in shaping the plan of reconstruction finally adopted was announced at the very commencement of hostilities by Thaddeus Stevens, of Pennsylvania, then one of the foremost members of the Republican party and a few years later its acknowledged leader in the House. Unlike the Massachusetts Senator, Mr. Stevens never formulated his views of State status; but as he urged them on almost every conceivable occasion the essential principles of his system may be easily collected from his numerous speeches in Congress. Subjects of legislation only remotely related to his favorite topic appear to have been regarded by him as important chiefly because of the opportunity afforded to express his sentiments on the measures necessary to reorganization. These opinions, he declared, had been deliberately formed; we know that to the end they were persistently urged and ably defended. Because of their radical nature and the frequency with which they were reiterated Stevens was by many regarded as a sort of fanatic; this estimate was confirmed, no doubt, by his bodily deformity as well as by an apparent want of amiability and a certain bluntness of expression. Even by keen observers he

[1] McPherson's Pol. Hist., p. 323.
[2] Mr. Davis is sometimes classed as a Unionist.

was at first considered a man of mediocre ability. But, though not to be compared with the giant race of an earlier generation, he was a statesman far above the common-place. Among the multitude of plans and theories offered in Congress his system was distinguished for the harmony of its parts; and enemies who hated, no less than followers who feared, him were forced to admit the consistency of his principles.

The limitations of Stevens in the field of constructive statesmanship cannot now be discussed; for their consideration belongs properly to an examination of the first reconstruction act, which was no more than a modification of his theory. Long before Sumner's plan had agitated timid conservatives the Pennsylvania leader by his extreme opinions had astonished Congress. When the question of discharging from labor or service those slaves employed in hostility to the United States came before the House at the special session beginning July 4, 1861, Stevens said:

Mr. Speaker, I thought the time had come when the laws of war were to govern our action; when constitutions, if they stood in the way of the laws of war in dealing with the enemy, had no right to intervene. Who pleads the Constitution against our proposed action? Who says the Constitution must come in, in bar of our action? It is the advocates of rebels, of rebels who have sought to overthrow the Constitution and trample it in the dust — who repudiate the Constitution. Sir, these rebels, who have disregarded and set at defiance that instrument, are, by every rule of municipal and international law, estopped from pleading it against our action. Who, then, is it that comes to us and says, "You cannot do this thing, because your Constitution does not permit it?" The Constitution! Our Constitution, which you repudiate and trample under foot, forbids it! Sir, it is an absurdity. There must be a party in court to plead it, and that party, to be entitled to plead it in court, must first acknowledge its supremacy, or he has no business to be in court at all. I repeat, then, that those who bring in this plea here, in bar of our action, are the advocates of rebels. They are nothing else, whatever they intend. I mean it, of course, in a legal sense. I mean they are acting in the capacity of counsellors-at-law for the rebels; they are speaking for them, and not for us — who are the plaintiffs in this transaction. I deny that they have any right to plead at all. I deny that they have any standing in court. I deny that they have any right to invoke this Constitution, which they deny has authority over them, which they set at defiance and trample under foot. I deny that they can be permitted to come here and tell us we must be loyal to the Constitution.[1]

The expectation almost universally cherished at this time was that when the insurrection should have been suppressed, as it was confidently believed it speedily would be, the erring States, without the interposition of Federal authority, would resume their normal relations to the General Government. With this state of public opinion in mind it will readily be perceived how great an interval separated Mr. Stevens from both parties in Congress. The opening sentence of the remarks quoted contains the essential idea of his theory of the change resulting from rebellion. Armed secession had unlocked the war powers, and the Constitution, where it conflicted with these powers, had ceased to be a restraint upon government. The military had risen superior to the civil authority. The principle was boldly and emphatically announced that those who repudiated and defied the supreme law could not at the same time plead its provisions.

On January 8, 1863, the appropriation bill being under consideration, an amendment was offered to add to the clause " for compensation of thirty-three commissioners, at $3,000 each, and eleven clerks, at $1,200 each, $112,200," the following:

Provided, A sufficient sum shall be collected in the insurrectionary States to pay said salaries: *And provided further,* That no greater sum shall at any time be paid to said commissioners, or to any of them, than shall have been collected from the taxes in the insurrectionary States, and paid into the Treasury of the United States.[2]

The discussion which ensued brought out an expression of views relative to the position of the seceded States under the Federal Government. Stevens in the course of his remarks

[1] Globe, 1 Sess. 37th Cong., p. 414.
[2] Globe, Part I., 3 Sess. 37th Cong., p. 238.

said: "I did say, sir, that I find no warrant in the Constitution for the admission, under the Constitution, of West Virginia. I do not know whether the gentleman from Kentucky voted for that bill or not." Mr. Dunlap, the member referred to, stated that he had voted against the bill, because he deemed it unconstitutional. After this explanation the Pennsylvania leader proceeded as follows:

> Then the gentleman voted against it upon the same opinion I expressed, that it was unconstitutional. But I went further and voted for it because I did not believe that the Constitution embraced a State now in arms against the Government of this Union and I hold that doctrine now. It was not said upon the spur of the occasion. It is a deliberate opinion, formed upon a careful examination of the law of the United States and the laws of nations.
>
> Though it may be out of place just now, I will give one or two reasons for my opinion. The establishment of our blockade admitted the Southern States, the Confederates, to be a belligerent power. Foreign nations have all admitted them as a belligerent power. Whenever that came to be admitted by us and by foreign nations, it placed the rebellious States precisely in the condition of an alien enemy with regard to duties and obligations. Now, I think there is nothing more plainly written in the law of nations than that whenever a war, which is admitted to be a national war, springs up between nation and nation, ally and ally, confederate and confederate, every obligation which previously existed between them, whether treaty, compact, contract, or anything else, is wholly abrogated, and from that moment the belligerents act toward each other, not according to any municipal obligations, not according to any compacts or treaties, but simply according to the laws of war. And I hold and maintain that with regard to all the Southern States in rebellion. I do not speak of Kentucky, but of those States which have gone out under an act of legislation or convention — the Constitution has no binding influence and no application.

In answer to a question by Representative Dunlap he stated further that the seceded States, in his opinion, were not members of the Union. "The ordinances of secession," he added, "backed by the armed power which made them a belligerent nation, did take them, so far as present operations are concerned, from under the laws of the nation." When asked how, as Chairman of the Committee of Ways and

Means, he proposed to pass an appropriation to pay officers to collect revenue in States which did not belong to the Union, he said:

> I propose to levy that tax, and collect it as a war measure. I would levy a tax wherever I can upon these conquered provinces, just as all nations levy them upon provinces and nations they conquer. If my views and principles are right, I would not only collect that tax, but I would, as a necessary war measure, take every particle of property, real and personal, life estate and reversion, of every disloyal man, and sell it for the benefit of the nation in carrying on this war. We have such power and we are to treat them simply as provinces to be conquered, and as a nation fighting in hostility to us until we do conquer them. To me it is a great absurdity to say that men, by millions, in arms, shall claim the protection of the provisions of the Constitution and laws made for loyal men, while they do not obey one of those laws, but repudiate their binding effect. There never was a principle more clear than that every obligation, whether in a national or civil point of view, in order to be binding, must be reciprocal; and that the moment the duty ceases upon the one part, the obligation ceases upon the other; and that, in my judgment, is precisely the condition of the rebel States now.

The secession ordinance of South Carolina he characterized in response to an inquiry as an act of treason and rebellion, and when asked whether the backing up of these ordinances by armed force imparted to them any validity, he replied: "I hold that so long as they remain in force against us as a belligerent power, and until they are conquered, it is in fact an existing operation. I will not say anything about its legality. [Laughter.] I hold that it is an existing *fact,* and that so far from enforcing any laws, you have not the power."

To Mr. Yeaman, who asked whether those people were then citizens of the United States, or whether they formed an independent nation, and if the latter whence was derived the right or the authority to wage war against them, and to tax them for the support of that war, Stevens answered: "I hold that the Constitution, in the first place, so far operated that when they went into secession and armed rebellion they committed treason; and that when they so combined themselves as to make themselves admitted as belligerents — not merely as men in insurrection, but as belligerents — they did acquire the right to be treated as prisoners of war, and all the other rights which pertain to belligerents under the laws of nations."

Some members held in utter abhorrence the principles of the Pennsylvania leader; others were astonished at their boldness. It was in the course of this discussion, participated in by many Representatives, that Stevens defined his existing as well as his past relations to his party, and referred, not without a touch of pride, to the fact that hitherto he had pointed out the way for the Republican majority — in short, that he had been the political prophet of his party. He declared:

I know perfectly well, as I said before, I do not speak the sentiments of this side of the House as a party. I know more than that: that for the last fifteen years I have always been a step ahead of the party I have acted with in these matters; but I have never been so far ahead with the exception of the principles I now enunciate, but that the members of the party have overtaken me and gone ahead; and they, together with the gentleman from New York, [Mr. Olin] will again overtake me and go with me, before this infamous and bloody rebellion is ended. They will find that they cannot execute the Constitution in the seceding States; that it is a total nullity there; and that this war must be carried on upon principles wholly independent of it. They will come to the conclusion that the adoption of the measures I advocated at the outset of the war, the arming of the negroes, the slaves of the rebels, is the only way left on earth in which these rebels can be exterminated. They will find that they must treat those States now outside of the Union as conquered provinces and settle them with new men, and drive the present rebels as exiles from this country; for I tell you they have the pluck and endurance for which I gave them credit a year and a half ago in a speech which I made, but which was not relished on this side of the House, nor by the people in the free States. They have such determination, energy, and endurance, that nothing but actual extermination or exile or starvation will ever induce them to surrender to this Government. I do not ask gentlemen to indorse my views, nor do I speak for anybody but myself; but in order that I may have some credit for sagacity, I ask that gentlemen will write this down in their memories. It will not be two years before they will call it up, or before they will adopt my views, or adopt the other alternative of a disgraceful submission by this side of the country.[1]

For himself, for the Administration and for the Republican party even so radical an anti-slavery man as Owen Lovejoy made haste to repudiate these extreme opinions.

In debate, January 22, 1864, Stevens enunciated still more clearly the fundamental principles of his system. "I mean to say," he declared on that occasion, "that if a State, as a State, makes war upon the Government and becomes a belligerent power, we treat it as a foreign nation, and when we conquer it we treat it just as we do any other foreign nation." "There can be no neutrals," he added, "in a hostile State." If loyal people domiciled in the South desired to avoid punishment or the hardships of public enemies, they should change their place of residence.

Relative to discerning the State in the Union minority he observed: "If ten men fit to save Sodom can elect a Governor and other State officers for and against the eleven hundred thousand Sodomites in Virginia, then the democratic doctrine that the majority shall rule is discarded and dangerously ignored. When the doctrine that the *quality* and not the *number* of voters is to decide the right to govern, then we are no longer a republic, but the worst form of despotism." It was a mere mockery, he affirmed, to say that a tithe of the residents, because they were holier or more loyal than others, could change the form and administer the government of an organized State. The people who took a State out of the Union were subject to the laws of the commonwealth, and, so far as the General Government is concerned, subject to the laws of war and of nations, both while the war continued and when it ended.[2]

Northern Democrats, from the beginning to the end of

[1] Globe, Part I., 1 Sess. 37th Cong., pp. 239-243.
[2] Globe, Part I., 1 Sess. 38th Cong., p. 317.

reconstruction, were consistent advocates of a doctrine which involved no contradictions like the system of Sumner and no element of vindictiveness like the "conquered province" theory of Stevens. Ordinances of secession they held to be null and void; these measures in no way impaired the vitality or contracted the scope of the Constitution because the power by which they were temporarily maintained, however near to attaining its object, had not been crowned with success. The result of the conflict could alone determine whether the bond of union between the seceding and the loyal States had been severed. Armed resistance to the supreme law was treason in those so engaged, even though such resistance was decreed by States. *Ante-bellum* relations would continue unimpaired if the General Government succeeded in suppressing the rebellion. This doctrine, once a State in the Union always a State, was, so far, in harmony with the policy adopted by the Administration at the commencement of hostilities.

With all the following propositions, however, the policy of the Government was not in entire accord, nor, indeed, was it in exact conformity with the principles above ascribed to the President. The people of a State, the Democratic leaders asserted, are the State, in the widest sense of that term, and they make its fundamental law; to be their constitution it must be their unrestrained and voluntary act, not a result of coercion or intimidation. When they have freely acted, then the only essential conditions of a State constitution, in its Federal relations, are that it should be republican in form and not conflict with the Constitution of the United States. South Carolina, for example, was made a member of the Union by the Constitution and the consent of her people; except successful revolution no other power could unmake her. That revolution being unsuccessful she was still in the Union. The idea that a State was partly out of and partly in the Union, Democratic doctrine regarded as an absurdity. State officers, indeed, could commit suicide; a majority of its people could commit suicide; but the State did not, therefore, cease to exist, for the idea of a State involved the fourfold notion of a defined territory, people occupying it, functions constituting a system of government and officers to administer it.

Representative Joseph K. Edgerton, of Indiana, in an able speech delivered February 20, 1865, said that he accepted the principle of President Lincoln's inaugural and only regretted that after so clear and sound a statement of constitutional law and good intentions the President had subsequently come to the same conclusion as Mr. Stevens. The theory then announced was the only one consistent with the true constitutional idea that the Federal Union is a perpetual union of States, and that each State, as an individual member of the Union, has in itself the same element of perpetuity that belongs to the aggregate Republic formed by the Federal union of States. The Union can be held to be perpetual only on the principle that the States composing it are perpetual corporations or bodies politic, and indestructible by any act of the aggregate body or by their own act. The States united cannot destroy a single commonwealth; power to do that is power to consolidate the States into one. A single member cannot destroy the Union; power to do that is power to secede, and neither consolidation nor secession is a principle of the Union. Here we have in amplified form the celebrated declaration of Chief Justice Chase, that the Constitution in all its provisions contemplates " an indestructible union of indestructible States." [1] For a different though a very able presentation of Democratic theory the reader is referred to the address of Mr. Pendleton on the bill to guarantee republican forms of government to the rebellious States.[2]

[1] Texas vs. White, 7 Wall., p. 725.   [2] See Chapter VII., pp. 257-261, *infra.*

Though this theory of a perpetual Union was the one almost universally held at the beginning of the war, it came during the progress of the conflict to be little regarded by the dominant party in Congress; by Republican leaders it was soon cast aside with indignation or contempt; it remained unaltered when their views of State status were adapted to changed conditions, and the Democratic organization, so far at least as reconstruction was concerned, settled down into little more than a party of protest.

The silence in which Sumner's propositions were received may be regarded as a negative testimony to the conservative sentiments of Senators even after war had existed for nearly a year; the House, however, just twelve months before the Massachusetts Senator offered his plan, February 11, 1861, made a positive declaration of its opinion relative to the limitations of Federal authority by passing unanimously the following resolution: "That neither Congress, nor the people or the governments of the non-slaveholding States, have the right to legislate upon or interfere with slavery in any of the slaveholding States in the Union." [1] This deliberate expression establishes beyond question the fact that the Constitution, as then understood, gave no authority to the Federal Government to interfere with, control or regulate relations between master and slave in any State which recognized the right of property in man. On this subject the people were practically unanimous, their Representatives entirely so. Even three months of war, with all the antagonisms and all the bitterness excited, failed to shake this conviction.

On July 22, 1861, the day after the disaster at Bull Run, Representative Crittenden, of Kentucky, introduced the following resolution:

That the present deplorable civil war has been forced upon the country by the disunionists of the Southern States, now in arms against

[1] Globe, Part I., 2 Sess. 36th Cong., p. 857.

the constitutional Government, and in arms around the capital; that in this national emergency, Congress, banishing all feelings of mere passion or resentment, will recollect only its duty to the whole country; that this war is not waged on their part in any spirit of oppression, or for any purpose of conquest or subjugation, or purpose of overthrowing or interfering with the rights or established institutions of those States, but to defend and maintain the *supremacy* of the Constitution, and to preserve the Union with all the dignity, equality, and rights of the several States unimpaired; and that as soon as these objects are accomplished the war ought to cease.

Only two votes were recorded against it.[1] Four days later Andrew Johnson offered in the upper House a resolution in nearly the same language, and it was opposed by only five Senators. There is little doubt that this practical unanimity in Congress reflected the sentiment of almost the entire North. This conspicuous landmark, so frequently referred to before the reunion was completed, will be useful to show how far the warring factions drifted during the progress of the conflict.

Senator Trumbull, of Illinois, who disliked certain expressions in the form in which it was proposed, said, relative to the object of the war as declared by the resolution:

I trust this war is prosecuted for the purpose of subjugating all rebels and traitors who are in arms against the Government. What do you mean by "subjugation"? I know that persons in the Southern States have sought to make this a controversy between States and the Federal Government, and have talked about coercing States and subjugating States; but, sir, it has never been proposed, so far as I know, on the part of the Union people of the United States, to subjugate States or coerce States. It is proposed, however, to subjugate citizens who are standing out in defiance of the laws of the Union, and to coerce them into obedience to the laws of the Union. I dislike that word in this connection. In its broadest sense I am opposed to it. If it means the war is not for the purpose of the subjugation of traitors and rebels into obedience to the laws, then I am opposed to it. I trust the war is prosecuted for that very purpose. I move to strike out the words "and in arms around the capital," and also the words "or subjugation."[2]

[1] Globe, 1 Sess. 37th Cong., pp. 222-223.
[2] Ibid., p. 258.

Mr. Harris, of New York, said: "If slavery shall be abolished, shall be overthrown as a consequence of this war, I shall not shed a tear over that result; but, sir, it is not the purpose of the Government to prosecute this war for the purpose of overthrowing slavery. If it comes as a consequence, let it come; but it is not an end of the war."[1]

In the succeeding chapter will be traced with some degree of fullness the sentiments on reconstruction, in July, 1864, not only of the majority but of every important element composing Congress. The position then attained by the average Republican member, it must be repeated, was not reached at a single bound. Its progress has been described in the preceding pages. The vote on the Crittenden resolution marks the starting point. There was then, though war had existed for three months, no diversity of opinion worthy of notice. The successive advances from the declaration, February 11, 1861, that neither Congress nor the governments of the free States had a constitutional right to interfere with slavery in any slaveholding State of the Union to the passage by both Houses, July 2, 1864, of the Wade-Davis bill, which proposed by Federal law to regulate the franchise in the rebellious States, to appoint provisional governors (empowered to dissolve State conventions), and to prescribe provisions for their local constitutions, form one of the most instructive commentaries on the importance of necessity as a principle of constitutional interpretation.

A resolution introduced December 4, 1861, by Mr. Holman, of Indiana, for the purpose of getting the House to reaffirm the Crittenden propositions of July 22 preceding, was tabled by a vote of 71 to 65.[2]

A discussion of the various theories of reconstruction might seem to require in this place, by way of anticipation, at least

[1] Globe, 1 Sess. 37th Cong., p. 259.
[2] Ann. Cycl., 1862, p. 277.

a summary of the Congressional plan; but as this was the mode of reorganization which was finally imposed on the South it is preferred to present its development chronologically and to consider it apart. Several of the remaining chapters will be devoted to an account of its successive modifications until the subject was taken, in December, 1865, altogether out of Executive hands.

VII

RISE OF THE CONGRESSIONAL PLAN

A PREVIOUS chapter, in relating the military events which succeeded the disaster at Chickamauga, noticed a suggestion of the defeated Federal commander as well as Mr. Lincoln's reply relative to the publication at that time of a declaration of amnesty to those in arms against the Government.[1] The double victory of Mission Ridge and Lookout Mountain, following the removal of Rosecrans, confirmed the President in his purpose of offering a general pardon to those who would lay down their arms and return to their obedience to the laws. The Proclamation of December 8, 1863, followed promptly and brought the subject of reconstruction before the Thirty-eighth Congress at its first session. The preceding pages have alluded to the universal favor with which that announcement was received. Though opposition to Executive measures was hushed for the time, it appears only to have gathered strength in this brief interval of silence. One short week introduced into the House of Representatives a resolution the subsequent progress of which brought the dominant party in Congress to the support of a measure hostile to that submitted by the President. Its interesting history may be collected from the pages of the *Congressional Globe*.

On December 15, from the Committee of Ways and Means, Thaddeus Stevens reported among other resolutions one to refer so much of the President's message as was contained in

[1] See p. 23, *ante*.

the Proclamation, and as related to the condition and treatment of rebellious States, to a special committee of nine to be appointed by the Speaker. Henry Winter Davis inquired whether Mr. Stevens would accept for that resolution an amendment pointing more directly to the purpose in view. This substitute read as follows:

That so much of the President's message as relates to the duty of the United States to guarantee a republican form of government to the States in which the governments recognized by the United States have been abrogated or overthrown, be referred to a select committee of nine, to be named by the Speaker, which shall report the bills necessary and proper for carrying into execution the foregoing guaranty.[1]

Stevens offering no objection, Representative Davis remarked that the language of the resolution was general, and, he believed, would cover the whole war; the committee, he supposed, intended to point to what, in the very inaccurate phraseology of the day, was known as the question of reconstruction; but believing there had been no destruction, he carefully avoided the use of that term.

The Government of the United States, continued Mr. Davis, was engaged in two operations: the suppression of armed resistance to the supreme authority of the nation and a very delicate, and perhaps as high a duty — to see, when armed resistance should be overcome, that governments republican in form should be restored in all those States. His substitute directed the investigations of the committee to that one point. It was not intended as a peremptory instruction to the committee to report any particular measure, but to take such action as their wisdom should recommend.

Democratic feeling on this subject appears in an inquiry by Representative Brooks, of New York, as to whether republican governments had not been abrogated and overturned

[1] Globe, Part I., 1 Sess. 38th Cong., p. 33.

north as well as south of the Potomac since the revolution began.[1]

The amendment of Mr. Davis prevailed, and of the special committee appointed he was made chairman. On January 18, 1864, he asked unanimous consent to report a bill to guarantee certain States a republican form of government. Objection having been made, he moved a suspension of the rules; but failing to receive the necessary two thirds vote his motion was lost. On February 15 succeeding, when he brought the measure before the House again and requested a postponement of its consideration for two weeks, it encountered Democratic opposition. The bill was then read a first and second time, ordered to be printed, and returned to the committee.

On March 22 the bill came before the House on the question of ordering it to be engrossed and read a third time. In its support Mr. Davis made an able address in which he analyzed the plan proposed by the Executive and emphasized its deficiencies. He said:

> The bill which I am directed by the Committee on the Rebellious States to report is one which provides for the restoration of civil government in States whose governments have been overthrown. It prescribes such conditions as will secure not merely civil government to the people of the rebellious States, but will also secure to the people of the United States permanent peace after the suppression of the rebellion.
> The bill challenges the support of all who consider slavery the cause of the rebellion, and that in it the embers of rebellion will always smoulder; of those who think that freedom and permanent peace are inseparable, and who are determined, so far as their constitutional authority will allow them, to secure these fruits by adequate legislation.
> . . . It is entitled to the support of all gentlemen upon this side of the House, whatever their views may be of the nature of the rebellion; and the relation in which it has placed the people and States in rebellion toward the United States, not less of those who think that the rebellion has placed the citizens of the rebel States beyond the protection of the Constitution, and that Congress, therefore, has supreme power over them as conquered enemies, than of that

[1] Globe, Part I., 1 Sess. 38th Cong., p. 34.

other class who think that they have not ceased to be citizens and States of the United States, though incapable of exercising political privileges under the Constitution, but that Congress is charged with a high political power by the Constitution to guarantee republican governments in the States, and that this is the proper time and the proper mode of exercising it. It is also entitled to the favorable consideration of gentlemen upon the other side of the House, who honestly and deliberately express their judgment that slavery is dead. To them it puts the question whether it is not advisable to bury it out of our sight, that its ghost may no longer stalk abroad to frighten us from our propriety.

It does not address itself to that class of gentlemen upon the other side of the House, if there be any, nor to that class of the people of the country who look for political alliance to the men who head the rebellion in the South. . . . .

It purports, sir, not to exercise a revolutionary authority, but to be an execution of the Constitution of the United States, of the fourth section of the fourth article of that Constitution, which not merely confers the power upon Congress, but imposes upon Congress the duty of guaranteeing to every State in this Union a republican form of government. That clause vests in the Congress of the United States a plenary, supreme, unlimited political jurisdiction, paramount over courts, subject only to the judgment of the people of the United States, embracing within its scope every legislative measure necessary and proper to make it effectual; and what is necessary and proper the Constitution refers, in the first place, to our judgment, subject to no revision but that of the people. It recognizes no other tribunal. It recognizes the judgment of no court. It refers to no authority except the judgment and will of the majority of Congress, and of the people on that judgment, if any appeal from it.

[Secession he described as] the act of the people of the States, carrying with it all the consequences of such an act. And therefore it must be either a legal revolution which makes them independent, and makes of the United States a foreign country, or it is a usurpation against the authority of the United States, the erection of governments which do not recognize the Constitution of the United States, which the Constitution does not recognize, and, therefore, not republican governments of the States in rebellion. The latter is the view which all parties take of it. I do not understand that any gentleman on the other side of the House says that any rebel government which does not recognize the Constitution of the United States, and which is not recognized by Congress, is a State government within the meaning of the Constitution. Still less can it be said that there is a State government, republican or unrepublican, in the State of Tennessee, where there is no government of any kind, no civil authority, no organized form of administration except that represented by the flag of the United States, obeying the will, and under the orders of the military officer in command. It is the language of the President of the United States in every proclamation, of Congress in every law on the statute-book, of both Houses in their forms of proceeding, and of the Courts of the United States in their administration of the law. It is the result of every principle of law, of every suggestion of political philosophy, that there can be no republican government within the limits of the United States that does not recognize, but does repudiate, the Constitution, and which the President and the Congress of the United States do not, on their part, recognize. Those that are here represented are the only governments existing within the limits of the United States. Those that are not here represented are not governments of the States, republican under the Constitution. And if they be not, then they are military usurpations, inaugurated as the permanent governments of the States, contrary to the supreme law of the land, arrayed in arms against the Government of the United States; and it is the duty, the first and highest duty, of the Government to suppress and expel them. Congress must either expel, or recognize and support them. If it do not guarantee them, it is bound to expel them; and they who are not ready to suppress them are bound to recognize them.

"In the famous Rhode Island cases," he continued, the Supreme Court of the United States by the mouth of Chief Justice Taney, declared "that a military government, established as the permanent government of a State, is not a republican government in the meaning of the Constitution, and that it is the duty of Congress to suppress it. That duty Congress is now executing by its armies. He [Justice Taney] further said in that case that it is the exclusive prerogative of Congress — of Congress, and not of the President — to determine what is and what is not the established government of the State; and, to come to that conclusion, it must judge of what is and what is not a republican government, and its judgment is conclusive on the Supreme Court, which cannot judge of the fact for itself, but accepts the fact declared by the political department of the Government."

Mr. Davis resumed:

We are now engaged in suppressing a military usurpation of the authority of the State government. When that shall have been accomplished, there will be no form of State authority in existence which Congress can recognize. Our success will be the overthrow of *all* semblance of government in the rebel States. The Government of the United States is then, in fact, the *only* Government existing in those States, and it is there charged to guarantee them republican governments.

. . . The duty of guaranteeing carries with it the right to pass all laws necessary and proper to guaranty. . . . It places in the hands of Congress the right to say what is and what is not, with all the light of experience and all the lessons of the past, inconsistent, in its judgment, with the permanent continuance of republican government; and if, in its judgment, any form of policy is radically and inherently inconsistent with the permanent and enduring peace of the country, with the permanent supremacy of republican government, and it have the manliness to say so, there is no power, judicial or executive, in the United States, that can even question this judgment but the PEOPLE; and they can do it only by sending other representatives here to undo our work. The very language of the Constitution and the necessary logic of the case involve that consequence. The denial of the right of secession means that all the territory of the United States shall remain under the jurisdiction of the Constitution. If there can be no State government which does not recognize the Constitution, and which the authorities of the United States do not recognize, then there are these alternatives, and these only: the rebel States must be governed by Congress till they submit and form a State government under the Constitution; or Congress must recognize State governments which do not recognize either Congress or the Constitution of the United States; or there must be an entire absence of *all* government in the rebel States; and that is anarchy. To recognize a government which does not recognize the Constitution is absurd, for a government is not a constitution; and the recognition of a State government means the acknowledgment of men as governors, and legislators, and judges, actually invested with power to make laws, to judge of crimes, to convict the citizens of other States, to demand the surrender of fugitives from justice, to arm and command the militia, to require the United States to repress all opposition to its authority, and to protect it from invasion — against our own armies; whose Senators and Representatives are *entitled* to seats in Congress, and whose electoral votes must be counted in the election of the President of a Government which they disown and defy!! To accept the alternative of anarchy as the constitutional condition of a State is to assert the failure of the Constitution and the end of republican government. Until, therefore, Congress recognize a State government, organized under its auspices, there is no government in the rebel States except the authority of Congress. In the absence of all State government, the duty is imposed on Congress . . . to administer civil government until the people shall, under its guidance, submit to the Constitution of the United States, and, under the laws which it shall impose, and on the conditions Congress may require, reorganize a republican government for themselves, and Congress shall recognize that government.

. . . Is it yet time to reorganize the State governments? or is there not an intermediate period in which sound legislative wisdom requires that the authority of Congress shall take possession of and temporarily control the States now in rebellion until peace shall be restored and republican government can be established deliberately, undisturbed by the sound or fear of arms, and under the guidance of law?

After referring to the condition of the rebellion, Mr. Davis declared: "We have occupied a vast area wrested from its power, but to this day we have not expelled the rebels from *any State* they ever held." In no portion of those States could military power "be withdrawn for a moment without instant insurrection"; and he added, "There is no rebel State held now by the United States enough of whose population adheres to the Union to be intrusted with the government of the State. One tenth cannot control nine tenths. Five tenths are nowhere willing to undertake the control of the other five tenths." In West Virginia, he said, such a condition existed and had been recognized. "In no other State — the only one in respect to which a doubt can exist is Tennessee — in no other State is there such a portion of territory held, or any such portion of population under our control, or any such portion of it which is in our control inspired by such sentiments toward the Government of the United States, so free from fear of the returning wave of rebel invasion, so assured of the continued supremacy of the United States, that we ought to be willing to trust them with this power. You can get a handful of men in the several States who would be glad to take the offices if protected by the troops of the United States, but you have nowhere a body of independent, loyal partisans of the United States, ready to meet the rebels in arms, ready to die for the Republic, who claim the Constitution as their birthright, count all other privileges light in comparison, and resolve at every hazard to maintain it."

Concerning the loyal masses of the South, of whom so much was heard at the beginning of the war, he remarked:

> It is the most astounding spectacle in history that in the Southern States, with more than half of the population opposed to it, a great revolution was effected against their wishes and against their votes, without a battle, a riot, or a protest in behalf of the beneficent Government of their fathers — a revolution whose opponents hastened to lead it, without a martyr to the cause they deserted except the nameless heroes of the mountains of Tennessee, or a confessor of the faith they had avowed save the illustrious Petigru of South Carolina!
>
> . . . There is no fact that any one has stated on authority at all reliable that any respectable proportion of the people of the Southern States now in rebellion are willing to accept any terms that even our opponents on the other side of the House are willing to offer them.
>
> . . . .
>
> What, then, are we to do with the population in these States? To make "confusion worse confounded" by erecting by the side of the hostile State government a new State government on the shifting sands of that whirlpool, to be supported by us while we are there and to turn its power against us when we are driven out? That would be to erect a new throne where
>
> > "Chaos umpire sits,
> > And by decision more embroils the fray
> > By which he reigns."
>
> In my judgment, it is not safe to confide the vast authority of State governments to the doubtful loyalty of the rebel States until armed rebellion shall have been trampled into the dust, until every armed rebel shall have vanished from the State, until there shall be in the South no hope of independence and no fear of subjection, until the United States is bearded by no military power and the laws can be executed by courts and sheriffs without the ever-present menace of military authority. Until we have reached that point, this bill proposes that the President shall appoint a civil governor to administer the government under the laws of the United States in force in the States respectively at the outbreak of the rebellion, subject, of course, to the necessities of military occupation.

When military opposition shall have been suppressed, continued Mr. Davis, then call upon the people to reorganize their governments in their own way, "subject to the conditions that we think essential to our permanent peace, and to prevent the revival hereafter of the rebellion. . . ."

To establish republican forms of government that the people of the United States would agree to, three modes were indicated: "One is to remove the cause of the war by an alteration of the Constitution of the United States prohibiting slavery everywhere within its limits. That, sir, goes to the root of the matter, and should consecrate the nation's triumph. But there are thirty-four States — three fourths of them would be twenty-six. I believe there are twenty-five States represented in this Congress, so that we, on that basis, cannot change the Constitution. It is, therefore, a condition precedent in that view of the case, that more States shall have governments organized within them."

He next noticed the calculation based on three fourths of the States then represented in Congress, a construction held by Thaddeus Stevens, but even that view was not without its difficulties. The States of New Jersey, Kentucky, Maryland and Delaware were named as doubtful. If such an amendment were adopted it still left "the whole field of the civil administration of the States prior to the recognition of State governments, all laws necessary to the ascertainment of the will of the people, and all restrictions on the return to power of the leaders of the rebellion, wholly unprovided for." The constitutional amendment met his hearty approval, but it was not a complete remedy.

Relative to the Administration policy, he observed:

The next plan is that inaugurated by the President of the United States in the proclamation of the 8th of December, called the amnesty proclamation. That proposes no guardianship of the United States over the reorganization of the governments, no law to prescribe who shall vote, no civil functionaries to see that the law is faithfully executed, no supervising authority to control and judge of the election. But if, in any manner, by the toleration of martial law, lately proclaimed the fundamental law, under the dictation of any military authority, or under the prescriptions of a provost marshal, something in the form of a government shall be presented, represented to rest on the votes of one tenth of the population, the President will recognize that, provided it does not *contravene* the proclamation of freedom and the laws of Congress; and, to secure that, an oath is exacted.

Now you will observe that there is no guarantee of law to watch over the organization of that government. It may combine all the population of a State; it may combine one tenth only; or ten governments may come competing for recognition at the door of the Executive mansion. The executive authority is pledged; Congress is not pledged. It may be recognized by the military power and may not be recognized by the civil power, so that it would have a doubtful existence, half civil and half military, neither a temporary government by law of Congress nor a State government, something as unknown to the Constitution as the rebel government that refuses to recognize it.

In examining the operation of the Executive proclamation on the existence of slavery, Mr. Davis asked, how does it accomplish the reorganization of the government on the basis of universal freedom? and added:

The only prescription is that the government shall not *contravene* the provisions of that proclamation. Sir, if that proclamation be valid, then we are relieved from all trouble on that score; but if that proclamation be not valid, then the oath to support it is without legal sanction, for the President can ask no man to bind himself by an oath to support an unfounded proclamation or an unconstitutional law even for a moment, still less till it shall have been declared void by the Supreme Court of the United States. . . . If, therefore, he shall have taken the oath, he can, in good conscience as well as in good law, disregard it the next moment; so that, in point of fact, the law leaves us where the proclamation does; it adds nothing to its legality, nothing to its force.

But what is the proclamation which the new governments must not contravene? That certain negroes shall be free, and that certain other negroes shall remain slaves. The proclamation therefore recognizes the existence of slavery. It does just exactly what all the constitutions of the rebel States prior to the rebellion did; . . . and, therefore, the old constitutions might be restored to-morrow without *contravening* the proclamation of freedom. Those constitutions do not say that the President shall not have the right, in the exercise of his military authority, to emancipate slaves within the States. . . . They do not even establish slavery. . . . They merely recognize it just as the proclamation recognizes its existence in parts of Virginia and in parts of

Louisiana. So that the one tenth of the population at whose hands the President proposes to accept and guarantee a State government, can elect officers under the old constitution of their State in exactly the same terms and with exactly the same powers existing at the time of the rebellion, and may, under his proclamation, demand a recognition. . . . So soon as the State government is recognized, the operation of the proclamation becomes merely a judicial question. The right of a negro to his freedom is a legal right divesting a right of property, and is to be enforced in the courts; and then the question is what the courts will say about the proclamation. Is it valid or invalid? Does it of itself confer a legal right to freedom on negroes who were slaves? Is it within the authority of the Executive? . . . How local State courts, created by the Southern people, will decide such a question *no one* can doubt. . . . It is, therefore, under the scheme of the President, merely a judicial question, to be adjudged by judicial rules, and to be determined by the courts. . . . I do not desire to argue the legality of the proclamation of freedom. I think it safer to *make it law.* . . . Under the act of 1862 the President is authorized to use the negro population for the suppression of the rebellion; while the rebellion lasts, his proclamation in law exempts the slave from the duty of obeying his master, but after the rebellion is extinguished, the master's rights are in his own hands, subject only to the opinion of the courts on the legal effect of the proclamation, without a single precedent to sanction it, and opposed by the solemn assertions of our Government against the principle worked to authorize it. Gentlemen are less prudent or less in earnest than I am if they will risk the great issues involved in this question on such authorities before the courts of justice.

By the bill we propose to preclude the judicial question by the solution of a political question. How so? By the paramount power of Congress to reorganize governments in those States, to impose such conditions as it thinks necessary to secure the permanence of republican government, to refuse to recognize any governments there which do not prohibit slavery forever. Ay, gentlemen take the responsibility to say, in the face of those who clamor for speedy recognition of governments tolerating slavery, that the safety of the people of the United States is the supreme law; that their will is the supreme rule of law, and that we are authorized to pronounce their will on this subject — take the responsibility to say that we will revise the judgments of our ancestors; that we have experience written in blood which they had not; that we find now, what they darkly doubted, that slavery is really, radically inconsistent with the permanence of republican governments; and that, being charged by the supreme law of the land, on our conscience and judgment, to guarantee, that is, to continue, maintain, and enforce, if it exist, to institute and restore when overthrown, republican governments throughout the broad limits of the republic, we will weed out every element of their policy which we think incompatible with its permanence and endurance. . . . It [the bill] adds to the authority of the proclamation the sanction of Congress. . . .

Gentlemen must deny the jurisdiction of Congress over the States where there are no recognized governments, or place a bound or limit to the discretion of Congress. . . .

And if the sentiments of State pride and State rights be touched by the assertion of this wide discretion, which men may deny but cannot expunge, I would admonish those who dislike it that it is a jurisdiction which nothing but the dereliction of the States can wake into activity, and they who wish to exclude it from their limits have only not to give occasion for its exercise by renouncing obedience to the Constitution and pulling down their own State governments. But now the jurisdiction has attached in all the rebel States. Until Congress has assented, there is no State government in any rebel State, and none will be recognized except such as recognize the power of the United States; so that we come down to this: whether we — and when I say we, I mean we upon this side of the House, who are firmly, thoroughly, and honestly convinced that the time has come not merely to strike the arms from the hands of the rebels, but to strike the fetters from the arms of the slaves, and remove that domineering and cohesive power without which we could have had no rebellion, and which now is its animating spirit, and which will die when it dies — . . .

And if it be time [for Congress to assert its authority] then all I ask in conclusion is, that gentlemen will go and read that great argument of Daniel Webster in the Rhode Island case . . . where he met this semi-revolutionary attempt to count heads and call that the people, and maintained — and so the Supreme Court judged when it refused to take jurisdiction of the question — that the great political law of America is that every change of government shall be conducted under the supervising authority of some existing legislative body throwing the protection of law around the polls, defining the rights of voters, protecting them in the exercise of the elective franchise, guarding against fraud, repelling violence, and appointing arbiters to pronounce the result and declare the persons chosen by the people. . . . He [Webster] maintained it to be the great fundamental principle of the American government that legislation shall guide every political change, and that it assumes that somewhere within the United States there is always a permanent, organized legal authority which shall guide the tottering footsteps of those who seek to restore governments which are disorganized and broken down.

The bill, he asserted in conclusion, was an effort to apply this great principle of American law.[1]

Representative Scofield, of Pennsylvania, said, April 29, 1864, when the subject was again before the House, that the continuity of constitutional government in the seceded States had been broken, the regular transmission of political power interrupted. How, he inquired, should the severed thread be joined? By the unconstrained action of the people themselves, say the gentlemen in opposition. He indorsed that sentiment, and added that when the people of those States should ground the arms of their rebellion, and uncoerced take upon themselves the easy yoke and light burden of the ever gentle Federal Government it would mark a glad day in those uncheerful years of our history.

For those States from which hostile armies had been excluded Congress should legislate or leave the people in the rough hand of military law. The bill designed to discharge that duty was generally acceptable to any one who conceded the propriety of Congressional action, its three prohibitions being probably the only debatable points,— that is the assumption of Confederate debts, the prevention of Confederate officers from voting and the prohibition of involuntary servitude.

To assume the rebel debt, he asserted, would be to offer a high bounty for future rebellions; if rebel officers were permitted to vote, upon what principle of comparative justice could the privilege be denied to ordinary criminals? These officers were guilty of the highest crime against government. As to the third prohibition he had more to say.

"If God shall give us victory," continued Mr. Scofield, "and enable us to subdue or scatter the army of the enemy,

[1] Appendix, Part IV., Globe, 1 Sess. 38th Cong., pp. 82-85; also Speeches and Addresses of Henry Winter Davis. New York: Harper & Brothers, 1867, pp. 368-383.

is a voluntary reunion of the States possible? I say *voluntary* because I suppose nobody desires a Union always to be maintained by force; and I use the word *reunion* because nobody proposes a form of government different from our present system of State brotherhood. I am not now speaking of the several plans of reconstruction, for they are designed only as temporary devices, looking to a reunion. . . . My question looks beyond the battle and beyond reconstruction. When the victory is won, if won it shall be, and the transition over, will the insurgent States *willingly stay* where they have been *forcibly put* in their old places in the old Union? . . . Our own liberties could not survive their permanent subjugation. When the Federal Government becomes strong enough to hold eleven States as colonies, it will be too strong, I fear, for the people's liberties." All motives for those States ever to depart should be removed.

Similarity of ideas he characterized as the bond of nationality, and named Ireland, Hungary and Poland to show the opposite. In the United States slavery was the one subject of estrangement. Could North and South be brought to think alike on that subject? The theory that each side could hold its own opinions on slavery and no evil consequences follow was somewhat to blame. That theory failed in practice and for that failure each side blamed the other.

The fathers, he said, lived under that theory, that slavery and freedom could coexist, but they expected that the institution would soon become extinct. Hence they only tolerated it. Slavery was to recede slowly and freedom to follow steadily. Upon *that* basis they got along very well and so could their descendants. Instead of consenting to go, slavery demanded expansion and perpetuity. This was reversing the compromise of the fathers; this change had to be discussed, the slave power took umbrage and secession followed. If one sentiment must prevail, then slavery, which could not stand discussion, must yield if there was to be a reunion. To live in peace together the North must embrace slavery or the South must abandon it.

To adopt slavery would mean the adoption by 20,000,000 people of sentiments favorable thereto, whereas the institution never had any friends in the North. Those in that section so considered were only its apologists. If, three years ago, slavery had no real friends in the North, who would advocate it when it had attempted to destroy the most beneficent of governments? To reconcile the free States would necessitate a change of opinion — to adopt freedom as the dominant idea would require simply a change of *investment* in the sections. For the present extinguish the conflagration, for the future remove the inflammable material from which it was kindled. For the present seize the mad revolutionists of the South, for the future destroy the virus that poisoned their blood.

All who favored emancipation he favored as co-workers for a voluntary and peaceful reunion of the States; slavery was presented merely as an element of discord and disunion and as such he asked for its removal.[1]

Mr. Williams said that the war was inaugurated on the theory that the States were *in,* whereas the great fact of war was a proclamation that they were *out*. Northern Democrats were willing to accept the fact that they were *out, without war* — to adopt the principle of the *laissez nous faire* of the rebel authorities and to treat with them upon the idea of a *reconstruction;* peaceful secession with *reconstruction by treaty*. The severance of the States was complete, though the hope of recovery remained. By releasing the crews of their privateers, by blockading their ports the Federal authorities had recognized them as a *de facto* government; Federal legislation had put them under the ban as alien enemies. In the

[1] Globe, Part III., 1 Sess. 38th Cong., pp. 1970-1972.

minds of the framers of the Constitution the theory of an indissoluble Union referred to *the right,* to its organic law. They did not mean that it could not be ruptured by violence. If the governments of the States were dissolved " they must, of course, be reconstructed under the auspices of the conquering power, and that not by the Executive, but by the Legislature of the Union, whose sword he bears, and which only, consistently with the genius of our institutions, the past practice of the Government, and the letter as well as spirit of the Constitution, can venture to determine what use shall be made of the territories conquered by it, and when and upon what terms they shall be readmitted into full communion as members of this Government. . . . To permit any executive officer to declare its law, and set it in motion, and place it under the control of a minority — a mere tithe of its citizens — with power to send delegates to Congress with representation unimpaired and unaffected — even though he should reenact a part of its abrogated Constitution — would be, as I think, a monstrous anomaly, a violation of fundamental principles, and a precedent fraught with great danger to republican liberty. . . . To come back into the Union, it must either be born anew or come back with all its rights unimpaired, except those material ones which have been destroyed in the progress of the war. There is, I think, no middle ground, as there is no power either here or elsewhere to prescribe terms which shall abridge the rights or privileges of a State that has *not* been out of the Union, or returns to it in virtue of its original title." The rebellious States, he declared, " are in the Union for correction, not for *heirship.*" In point of fact they were out.

Replying to an observation of Fernando Wood, Mr. Williams said: " We are in favor, at all events, of preserving all that is left of it [the Union], and intend, with the blessing of God, to win back the residue, and pass it through the fire until it shall come out purged of the malignant element that has unfitted it for freedom.

" . . . Say that they [the rebellious States] are in the Union as before, and all your sacrifices have been idle, and all the blood spilled by you has sunk into the earth in vain."

The confiscation and distribution of the great baronial possessions of rebel leaders were in his judgment an essential element in any feasible plan of reconstruction. He deduced from passages in Bynkershoek and Barbeyrac that "everything belonging to the offending party is confiscated. . . . *Indemnity, security,* and *punishment* are all, therefore, means of self-defense which may be legitimately used."

Is the forfeiture, he asked, of the estates and property of traitors, whether they consist of lands or slaves, required for these purposes? "*Vae Victis*" is not the maxim of a humane conqueror. Though he would not exclude the idea of mercy, he was not clear as to "the wisdom of a proclamation of amnesty in advance as a measure of pacification, without limits as to time, and where submission after conquest, and when it is no longer a virtue but a necessity, is to be rewarded with the same impunity as a voluntary return to duty before that time."

Speaking of the nature, cause and fury of the war, he continued: "Its suppression has become impossible without removing the cause of the strife, and disabling our enemy by liberating his slaves, and arming them against him."

No reparation was adequate for the injury inflicted; for, said he, "there can be no punishment, except in the divestiture of the rights and the seizure of the estates of the guilty leaders. There is no security except in the distribution of the latter." From these he would carve out inheritances for the widow and the helpless offspring of the Northern soldier.

For eighteen months, he observed in conclusion, the war

was conducted upon the principle of inflicting as little injury as possible upon the enemy.[1]

The speech of Mr. Williams was marked by considerable fluency as well as great elegance of diction; it was the effort of a scholar, though not confined strictly to the question before the House. He introduced with directness and vigor the ideas of indemnity, security and punishment; these, it may be remarked, became important elements in determining the mode of reinstatement that finally emerged from the chaos of resolutions and plans submitted to Congress.

Representative Baldwin, of Michigan, believed the bill "to be an utter subversion of the Constitution"; even a latitudinarian construction of that instrument would not justify it. It embraced a plan that could be enforced by only the military arm. It was the precursor of the establishment of a despotism. That measure, as well as the President's plan, was fraught with danger.

He lamented interference with the elective franchise and the denial of the privileges of the writ of *habeas corpus.* For eighteen months the war had been waged for the destruction of the South, not for the restoration of the Union. Did not wisdom, he asked, suggest that all plans of reconstruction which tended only to intensify hate and postpone the day of peace be abandoned? Speaking of the effect of Mr. Lincoln's policy he observed: "That it was intended that the amnesty proclamation of last December would hasten the end of this strife, I do not believe. We are told that nearly every Southern paper published it, and it only nerved them to the performance of more earnest deeds." The President's plan as well as that of Congress, he believed, were designed to perpetuate the present dominant party by the vote of reconstructed States. A considerable portion of his remarks was devoted to criticism of the Administration.[2]

[1] Globe, Part III., 1 Sess. 38th Cong., pp. 1974-1981.   [2] Ibid., pp. 1981-1983.

Mr. Thayer, of Pennsylvania, believed that the powers delegated by the people of the United States to the national Government were sufficient for the great work of reconstruction, and added: "That the time has come in which Congress, in the exercise of the great powers conferred upon it, should settle and authoritatively declare the terms and conditions upon which the people of the rebellious districts should be restored to their State privileges and resume their just relations to the national Government, does not admit of doubt." People occupying territory wrested from the rebellion should be restored with the least possible delay to the privileges of representative government. "Congress alone can enact the laws which are to reconstruct the political societies in which the fundamental principle of loyalty to the national Government and obedience to its laws and respect for its authority have been obliterated by the violence of rebellion. The President of the United States cannot enact these laws, and it is in my opinion a reproach to Congress that by its inaction up to the present time it has rendered it necessary that the national Executive should be obliged by a sense of obligation to the public welfare to resort to temporary expedients for the preservation of public order and the assertion of national supremacy in those districts and States which the valor of our soldiers has redeemed from the insulting domination of the rebel army."

Executive action, he asserted, was suggested by necessity. "What has been done in that respect by the President I believe to have been well done, wisely done, and patriotically done, and to have been demanded alike by the necessity of the case and for the welfare of the Republic." The exclusive right over the subject, however, belonged to Congress, which should relieve the President of all responsibility therein.

Safeguards against the recurrence of similar outbreaks in the future should be required. He would support the measure before the House because of these safeguards or pledges. Unconditional and perpetual loyalty in the new governments in the rebellious States to that of the United States, extirpation and perpetual prohibition of slavery and compulsory repudiation of the rebel debt were the chief among these.

"The safety of the country," said he, "its future repose, the continuance of the Union, and the firm establishment of our political system imperatively demand that in the reorganization of local governments in the rebel States the foundations of such governments must rest upon the principle of submission to the Constitution and laws of the United States.

" . . . It is also necessary to guard the elective franchise and the privilege of holding office in those States against the intrusion and treachery of all who have in any sense been leaders in the present rebellion. For this purpose prudence requires that all who have held office under the pretended rebel government should be excluded from these privileges."

The seventh section of the bill he would like to see so modified as to declare that no debt of the pretended Confederate States, and no debt contracted by the State for the purpose of prosecuting the war against the United States or of giving aid to its enemies, should be recognized or paid by the State.

It was a singular doctrine, he remarked in conclusion, that those who had thrown off all restraints of the Constitution and who for years had waged war for the purpose of overthrowing it should be entitled to demand its protection while engaged in armed hostility to it.[1]

Mr. Yeaman did not believe Congress had a right to legislate away the laws and institutions of these States. The American people, he said, would come out of the contest with a better political education, an education having for its basis the idea that *they are a nation,* and he added, "a war to

[1] Globe, Part III., 1 Sess. 38th Cong., pp. 2002-2006.

enforce the theory of secession will end in an increased consolidated nationality." The theory expressed in the Virginia and Kentucky Resolutions was the fatal blow in our political history. His address was in the nature of an essay in political science and not altogether germane to the measure under consideration.[1]

"Pass a judicious enabling act," urged Mr. Longyear, "with proper safeguards, of which the people may avail themselves to organize civil governments at the very earliest opportunity, and it will afford a rallying point for the Union sentiment remaining there, and tend to foster it and nourish it into a healthful and vigorous existence. It will prevent perplexing and complicated irregularities and diversities of action, and tend largely to harmony and strength in our future deliberations. No stronger illustration of the necessity and propriety of immediate action need be given than the case of Tennessee, Louisiana, and Arkansas.

"The President's proclamation does not solve the difficulty. As a proclamation of amnesty, as a general outline or plan for organizing new State governments, as a prescription of safeguards and conditions precedent to such organization, it will ever stand as a bright and glorious page in the history of the present Administration. But it is incomplete for lack of constitutional power. That can be conferred by Congress alone, under the power to admit new States.

. . . .

"If we succeed [in the war] we make no conquest of territory, because that is already ours. We simply succeed, in that respect, in bringing that which is our own again under our control." Because of rebellion the constitutions and laws of those States had ceased to exist, and as slavery was established solely in State laws that also ceased to exist. The only object of a constitutional amendment was to prohibit its es-

[1] Globe, Part III., 1 Sess. 38th Cong., p. 2008.

tablishment forever. Freedom, he added, was being substituted for slavery. In respect to slavery and the slave power we were in the midst of a revolution. They proved themselves inimical to civil liberty, to the Constitution and to republican institutions.[1]

To the remark of Fernando Wood, of New York, that the South could not be subdued, Ignatius Donnelly replied, "We are doing it!" and he added, if the system of the President is deficient in the machinery that will ensure safety "it is our duty to supply that defect. The plan of the President, unsupported by any action on our part, hangs upon too many contingencies. It may be repealed by his successor; it may be resisted by Congress; it may be annulled by the Supreme Court. It rests the welfare of the nation upon the mind of one man; it rests the whole structure of social order upon the unstable foundation of individual oaths." Upon this subject Mr. Donnelly observed that General Jefferson Thompson, C. S. A., noted in passing through those regions that men consulted their memorandum books to see what oath they had taken last. Thousands of rebel dead had been found on the battle field with oaths of allegiance, sworn to and subscribed, in their pockets. Mr. Donnelly favored the bill, and if any measure of greater security could be found he would support that. He desired, as soon as it could be attained, an amendment of the Constitution that would prohibit slavery.

"I am aware, Mr. Speaker," he continued, "of the great claims which Mr. Lincoln has upon the people of the United States. I recognize that popularity which accompanies him, and which, considering the ordeal through which he has passed, is little less than miraculous. I recognize that unquestioning faith in his honesty and ability which pervades all classes, and the sincere affection with which almost the

[1] Globe, Part III., 1 Sess. 38th Cong., pp. 2011-2014.

entire population regard him. We must not underrate him even in our praises. He is a great man. Great not after the old models of the world, but with a homely and original greatness. He will stand out to future ages in the history of these crowded and confused times with wonderful distinctness. He has carried a vast and discordant population safely and peacefully through the greatest of political revolutions with such consummate sagacity and skill that while he led he appeared to follow; while he innovated beyond all precedent he has been denounced as tardy; while he struck the shackles from the limbs of three million slaves he has been hailed as a conservative! If to adapt, persistently and continuously, just and righteous principles to all the perplexed windings and changes of human events, and to secure in the end the complete triumph of those principles, be statesmanship, then Abraham Lincoln is the first of statesmen.

" If the end of the war is to be a restoration *of the appearance* of the old Government; a patching together of the broken shreds and fragments; a propping up of the fabric in such style that the next Administration may possibly get out from under it before it falls, then that proclamation may be found all-sufficient. But for all other purposes it will be utterly unavailing. It does not reach the heart of the distemper. . . .

" We owe more than this to ourselves; we owe more than this to the South. We must regenerate the South." [1]

This discriminating tribute to the character and genius of Mr. Lincoln was paid by no servile flatterer; it was not the eulogy of even a supporter of the Presidential plan of reconstruction; nor was it designed as a discharge of, or uttered in expectation of compelling, Executive favors, but appears rather to have been the spontaneous testimony of a keen interpreter of men and measures not less creditable to the insight of the

[1] Globe, Part III., 1 Sess. 38th Cong., p. 2038.

speaker than to the subject of his remarks. Others, it is true, refrained from misrepresenting the President's attitude and cheerfully ascribed to him patriotic and enlightened motives in his public conduct. Mr. Donnelly alone condensed into a paragraph a panegyric with which the judgment of posterity is in complete accord. This portion of his speech is quoted both to show that there were men in Congress who fully appreciated the greatness of the President, and that criticism of his measures was not in many instances suggested by feelings of personal hostility.

Very different were the remarks of Mr. Dennison, who declared that "The passage of this law will be the final gathering up of the reserved rights of States, and the last vestige of protection of the citizen under State constitutions will be taken away, and all power centralized in the General Government." He opposed the bill for the additional reason that it was intended to legalize and perpetuate the unconstitutional acts of the President. "There does not exist on the earth a more despotic government than that of Abraham Lincoln. He is a despot in fact if not in name."[1] These excerpts sufficiently indicate the character of his invective.

"I have offered a substitute to the bill of the committee," said Thaddeus Stevens, "because that does not, in my judgment, meet the evil. It partially acknowledges the rebel States to have rights under the Constitution, which I deny, as war has abrogated them all. I do not inquire what rights we have under it, but they have none. The bill takes for granted that the President may partially interfere in their civil administration, not as conqueror but as President of the United States. It adopts in some measure the idea that less than a majority may regulate to some extent the affairs of a republic."[2] The chief objection of Mr. Stevens, however,

[1] Globe, Part III., 1 Sess. 38th Cong., pp. 2039-2041.
[2] Ibid. p. 2041.

was that it removed the opportunity of confiscating the property of the disloyal.

Representative Wadsworth, of Kentucky, he said, agreed with him that the people of the South could plead none of the constitutional provisions in their defence. Whatever rights they possessed were those of belligerents engaged in war. "When we come to enforce the rights of conquest," continued the Pennsylvania member, "we should be justified in insisting upon the *extreme rights* of war, without yielding to the mitigations dictated by modern usage with regard to belligerents originally composed of foreign nations engaged in war which they deemed just." Explaining former recommendations which in many quarters had called forth severe criticism, he said: "I thought that the women and children, the non-combatants, and those who were forced by the laws of their State into the armies, should be spared; and the property of the guilty, morally as well as politically guilty, only should be taken. And yet we hear a howl of horror from conservative gentlemen at the inhumanity of the proposition." He still further explained his sentiments on this occasion. After stating that the people of the Confederate States were sovereign and acted through their representatives, he asserted that they had commenced and were continuing to wage an unjust war and therefore their private property was liable to confiscation. The right to take their property existed, but no one, he said, "advises the execution of the extreme right. But the right exists and ought to be enforced against the most guilty. To allow them to return with their estates untouched, on the theory that they have never gone out of the Union, seems to me rank injustice to loyal men." Of those who denied that the Confederate States had gone out of the Union he inquired, "What are we making war upon them for? For seceding; for going out of the Union against law. The law forbids a man to rob or murder, and yet robbery and murder exist *de facto* but not *de jure*." Hence the Constitution does not allow the States to go out of the Union. He referred also in his speech to a resolution introduced by Mr. Schenck, of Ohio, which passed the House without a division and declared the Confederate States a public enemy, engaged in a public war.[1]

On the same day, May 2, Representative Strouse remarked that immediately after the disaster of Bull Run the House almost unanimously passed the Crittenden Resolutions, which declared that " This war is not waged in any spirit of oppression, or for any purpose of conquest or subjugation, or purpose of overthrowing or interfering with the rights or established institutions of these States." This announcement, he asserted, brought volunteers, whereas now, 1864, county, State and Federal bounties combined could not induce men to enlist, and the cause of the apathy was that the war had been perverted from the purpose announced in the resolutions referred to. The entire speech had little reference to the bill of Mr. Davis, but seemed rather designed, by an attack on the Administration, to please his Democratic constituents.[2]

Mr. Cravens said that the dominant party did not distinguish between loyalty to the Administration and loyalty to the Government. The time for compromise had passed when the Republican party refused to accept the Crittenden Resolutions. That organization was in all essentials an abolition party. If there ever was a distinction it no longer existed. He cited a rather complete list of all the measures acted upon by Congress showing their concern for the negro; he charged neglect of the white soldier, his widow and orphans; quoted from the speech of Thaddeus Stevens on the admission of West Virginia, and named Representative Julian as uttering sentiments little behind the Pennsylvania member

[1] Globe, Part III., 1 Sess. 38th Cong., pp. 2041-2042.
[2] Ibid., p. 2043.

in boldness and exhibiting no more reverence for the Constitution. The incapacity and dire wickedness of the President and his "courtiers" came in for a share of criticism.

Mr. Gooch on the following day, May 3, remarked that the rebellion was but the military phase of the conflict of ideas which began with the adoption of the Constitution. "When we shall have crushed the rebellion and restored peace to all parts of the country we shall hold this territory, not by a new title, but by the old, not as territory acquired by conquest, but territory defended and maintained against revolt. . . . I can see no reason why the President, as Commander-in-Chief, should not, in the meantime, so use the military power as to aid and assist the loyal people of any one of these States in the organization of a loyal State government. . . . All these acts by the President, or the military power under him, in thus aiding and assisting the loyal people in these States, impose no obligation upon Congress to recognize them until such time as it shall deem proper to do so, and any recognition the military power may see fit to give to these governments can never fix their status in the Union. Congress alone has the power to determine what government is the legitimate one in a State, and its decision is binding on the other departments of the Government."[1]

Mr. Perry, of New Jersey, spoke of the duration of the war, predicted the general bankruptcy which its great expense would bring about, and calculated that in eleven years the cost of the war would equal the assessed value of property.

Speaking of the Executive plan he said: "And here the President's design is perfectly evident, to secure a majority of the delegates to the nominating convention of his party, and to provide for his own election by the House of Representatives in the event of there not being an election by the

[1] Globe, Part III., 1 Sess. 38th Cong., p. 2071.

people. By this plan the narrow foothold maintained by our armies in North Carolina, Louisiana, Texas, Alabama, Florida, Arkansas, and elsewhere may send the pretended full delegations of those States to this House. Mr. Speaker, I denominate the whole plan a political trick worthy of the most adroit and unscrupulous wire-puller of our ward primary meetings." The State governments had not been destroyed, he added, "nor can they be destroyed unless the rebels are finally victorious, and establish their independence."[1]

Fernando Wood said that Mexico had a republican form of government, and that Texas came into the Union without changing the character of her government except to substitute a governor for President and to change the titles of some officials. Every Southern State possessed the same form of government which it did before secession. If, he asserted, they were then republican in form, " they are so now." The Confederate constitution had all the elements of republicanism. The bill provided that hereafter none of the States in rebellion should hold slaves. It did not leave to the people the right to regulate their domestic institutions. Is it republicanism to take from the people this privilege? " To impose upon them a form of government of your own making, under the pretext of this bill, would be the worst kind of tyranny, whatever the provisions of your constitution might be."[2]

He defended himself against serious charges of General Schenck, whom he criticised severely. These accusations, however, were reiterated by Hon. William D. Kelley, of Pennsylvania, who at this point rose to speak on the merits of the bill.

The proposed measure did not meet his unqualified approval. It lacked some of the amendments suggested by Mr. Stevens. " I should like to see his distinct declaration," said Congress-

[1] Globe, Part III., 1 Sess. 38th Cong., p. 2073.
[2] Ibid., p. 2074.

man Kelley, "that 'The Confederate States are a public enemy, waging an unjust war, whose injustice is so glaring that they have no right to claim the mitigation of the extreme rights of war which are accorded by modern usage to an enemy who has the right to consider the war a just one.'" He would like to see the bill of Mr. Davis provide also for the exclusion from Congress of all those States that seceded, and every part of them.

As more immediately important, however, he would prefer to see included in the measure the proposition of Mr. Stevens respecting amendments of the Constitution; he denied the immortality of a State. It has its beginning, its transitions and may have its end. "A State may be killed, a State may commit suicide. An act of God, by destroying its inhabitants, might extinguish a State. A State could be conquered and held by some strong and hostile power. The political people of each of those States have overthrown the State. Through its corporate power each State destroyed its corporate life, and no one of them exists." He also denied that a State could transfer to any foreign power territory within the jurisdiction of the United States. The Supreme Court had decided that the Southern States were alien enemies and entitled to only the rights of such.[1]

The message of the President, Representative S. S. Cox believed, "should be welcomed, not so much for what it is as for what it pretends to be. It is his first adventure beyond the line of force into the field of conciliation. . . .

"To test the genuineness of this amnesty: five months have gone, but we see no signs of thousands of Southern citizens rushing to embrace this amnesty. Indeed, it is conceded that the rebellion is now more formidable than ever." There was no genuine movement toward the restoration of the seceded States. He would not take the oath of allegiance and swear

[1] Globe, Part III., 1 Sess 38th Cong., p. 2078.

support of the negro policies. How could Southern men be expected to take the oath? Its terms provoked or irritated them still more. The structure, he declared, was built on the Emancipation Proclamation.

The bill of Mr. Davis had the same defects. That, too, was based upon the one tenth system and the policy of forced emancipation. "In some of its features," he said, "it is an improvement upon the rickety establishment proposed by the President.

" . . . The emancipation act of the gentleman [Lincoln] can never be reconciled with the normal control of the States over their domestic institutions, so all oaths to sustain the same are oaths to subvert the old governments, Federal and State. . . . The President's plan, therefore, whether intended or not, is an oath to encourage treason, and the plan of the gentleman from Maryland is a plan to consummate revolution.

" . . . If his [the President's] plan of making one tenth rule in the States should succeed, then he will have ready at hand the electoral votes of Florida, Arkansas, Louisiana, Tennessee, North Carolina, and other States. He began this business in Florida the other day, and the blood which flowed at Olustee is the result of this scheme of personal ambition!

. . . .

"There is a sort of *odium historicum*," proceeded Mr. Cox, "attached to all political test oaths. . . . They have been the bane and foil of good government ever since bigotry began and revenge ruled. You cannot make eight million people, nearly all in revolt at what they regard as the detestable usurpations of abolition, forswear their hatred to abolition. You force by this oath the freed negro into the very nostrils of the Southern man, whose submission to law you seek.

"The conditions of pardon only inflame but do not quench rebellion. . . .

"We may yet change the war from the diabolical purposes of those in power, by changing that power to other hands, and we are not ready to sever our Union while that hope remains."

Precedents and analogies from both ancient and contemporary history were cited to demonstrate the folly of attempting to hold the South in her place by force. These together with censure of the Administration and criticism of the dominant party in Congress made up a great part of Mr. Cox's very long speech.[1]

Representative Boutwell, of Massachusetts, referring, May 4, to the remarks of his colleague, Mr. Ashley, of the committee which reported the bill, observed that "since this rebellion opened the Thirty-seventh Congress commenced its existence and ceased to exist; that this Congress is now closing the fifth month of its First Session, and that up to this time no efficient, indeed no legislative steps whatever have been taken by which the Executive is to be guided in the affairs of the people occupying the territory that has been reclaimed from rebel domination. Under these circumstances I think it due to the country that this House, at least, should do nothing which conveys any reflection upon his policy unless that policy be clearly and manifestly in contravention of the Constitution or of the well-ascertained and admitted principles of the Government."

When the populous parts of Louisiana were torn from rebel domination, and the State of Arkansas indicated in various ways the growth of a sentiment of loyalty and returning allegiance to the General Government, the Executive had but one of three courses before him: either to be silent, to govern by military authority alone, or else to establish a civil government or at least to take initiatory steps toward such establish-

[1] Globe, Part III., 1 Sess. 38th Cong., pp. 2095-2102.

ment. "It was unquestionably his right and duty, in the absence of all legislative action, to govern these territories as fast and as far as they were reclaimed by military power."

He defended both the President and General Banks, who had for years been consistent advocates of liberty. He then announced himself in favor of the bill of Mr. Davis.

"The gentleman from Pennsylvania [Mr. Stevens]," continued Mr. Boutwell, "maintains, as I understand, that these States are out of the Union; that their territory is alien territory, and that we are making war against alien enemies. I do not admit either of these positions to be true. I feel quite sure that these eleven once-existing States are no longer States of the Union. The evidence on which I rely in support of this position is found first in the declaration made by the authorities of those States that they no longer exist as States of the American Union. Next, we find that for three years and more they have been resisting the authority of the Government and have been carrying on a war against it. It is absurd to say that States or people are a part of the Government under the Constitution, and entitled to constitutional rights and privileges, when they have been carrying on war against the Government.

. . . .

"Nor do I admit that the people in the rebellious States are aliens. They are not of any other country, they are not of any other legal jurisdiction, they are within the jurisdiction of the Union. Three years ago they were a portion of this Union, and although they have been carrying on a war, that war has not thus far been successful, their independence has not been acknowledged by us, nor has it been recognized by any other nation. They, therefore, are not aliens. They are, to be sure, public enemies, but they are not alien enemies.

" . . . These States as political organizations have by their own will ceased to exist. . . . The existence of a State is a fact within the control of the people themselves, and cannot be influenced by any extraneous power whatever, and therefore these States have by the will of the people thereof as political organizations ceased to exist."

Admitting that the Government of the United States had legal jurisdiction over this territory and over the people who occupied it, it was an absurdity, he declared, "to say that these States still exist and that the people there may without our consent elect officers and send Representatives to this body and Senators to the other branch of Congress."

To the taunt of the Democrats that the war had been changed from a war to restore the Union to one for the purpose of emancipating the slave, Mr. Boutwell replied by a denial of the fact, but added that even if it were so, it was not the first instance of the sort in human history. Up to 1774 every American expected to preserve the old relations with England, yet within two years Independence was declared. The pending measure, he asserted, had not elicited marked attention in Congress nor any great interest throughout the country, yet in it lay the germ of a new civilization for half a continent.

The limitation of the elective franchise to white males did not meet his approval; for though the suffrage is not a natural, it is the highest political, right. Where the suffrage is denied to any large number of men, that community is never free from the danger of intestine commotion.

As South Carolina and Georgia were responsible for breathing into slavery the breath of life after it had everywhere been condemned, he would not have them again reappear in the Union. Florida did not deserve a place in the Union and, by giving the colored men local suffrage in that district, South Carolina, Georgia and Florida, he would invite the blacks thither as fast as they could be spared from the industries in which they were elsewhere engaged. He would not ask to

RISE OF THE CONGRESSIONAL PLAN

extend this principle to loyal Northern or to border States with a negro population.[1]

Mr. Pendleton, of Ohio, made by far the ablest Democratic argument against the proposed enactment. Its details as well as its general policy, he said, required examination. After stating quite fully the provisions of the bill, he continued:

> The gentleman from Maryland [Mr. Davis] facetiously entitles it "a bill to guaranty to certain States whose governments have been usurped or overthrown a republican form of government."
> At last the mask has been thrown off. At last the pretenses have all been laid aside. Three years of war have done their work, and the purposes and objects of the Republican party have been at last acknowledged. This bill is the consummation of its statesmanship the fruit of its experience, the demonstration of its purposes. The gentleman from Maryland introduced it; it is understood to be distasteful to some of his party friends; but it is a party measure; it will be voted for by every member of the Republican organization; it marks their policy of restoration; it defines their ideas of Union; it interprets their construction of the Constitution. As such I accept it. We have had double-dealing, hypocrisy and fraud for the last three years. We have had false professions, false names, and double-faced measures. We have had armies raised, taxes collected, battles fought, under the pretense that the war was for the Union, the old Union, the Union of the Constitution. These were the catchwords for the patriotic people. In the secret council-chambers of the party they were sneered at as devices with which to ensnare the innocent, to deceive the ignorant, to coax the obstinate. They were to be discarded as soon as, in the heat of war, in the exasperation of passion, in the exultation of victory, or in the bitterness of defeat and disaster and oppression, it would be safe to divulge the great conspiracy against the Union, the constitutional confederation, the principles of free government.
> That time has come. The veil is drawn aside. We see clearly. The party in possession of the powers of the Government is revolutionary. It seeks to use those powers to destroy the Government, to change its form, to change its spirit. It seeks under the forms of law to make a new Government, a new Union, to ingraft upon it new principles, new theories, and to use the powers of the law against all who will not be persuaded. It is in rebellion against the Constitution; it is in treasonable conspiracy against the Government. It differs in nothing from the

[1] Globe, Part III., 1 Sess. 38th Cong., pp. 2102-2105.

armed enemies except in the weapons of its warfare. They fight to overthrow its authority over them, while it seeks to destroy that authority at home. They would curtail the limits of the jurisdiction of the Federal Government; it would extend those limits, but change the basis and principles upon which it rests. If revolt against constituted authority be a crime, if patriotism consist in upholding in form and spirit the Government our fathers made, those in power here to-day are as guilty as those who in the seceded States marshal armed men for the contest.

"Revolutions move onward." That is true. But call things by their true names. Admit you are in revolution; admit you are revolutionists; admit that you do not desire to restore the old order; admit that you do not fight to restore the Union. Take the responsibility of that position. Avow that you exercise the powers of the Government because you control them; that you are not bound by the Constitution, but by your own sense of right. Avow that resistance to your schemes is not treason, but war. Dissolve the spell which you have woven around the hearts of our people by the cunning use of the words conservatism, patriotism, Union. And we will cease all criminations, we will hush all reproaches for oaths violated, pledges falsified, faith betrayed. We will meet you on your own ground, we will fight you with your weapons, and by the issue of that contest, whether of argument or of arms, we will abide.

Am I to be told that I misrepresent the Republican party? The gentleman who has just taken his seat [Mr. Boutwell], an able and honored member of that party, has said in your hearing, "If I could direct the force of public sentiment and the policy of this Government, South Carolina as a State and with a name should never re-appear in this Union. Georgia deserves a like fate. Florida does not deserve a name in this Union."

The gentleman from Maryland felt that this charge could be truthfully made. He sought to answer it in advance. He denied that the provisions of the bill contravened any clause of the Constitution. Where is the authority for it? Where is the authority to declare State governments overthrown? Where is the authority to reconstruct them? Where is the authority to appoint a governor; to call a convention to remodel their constitutions; to fix the qualifications of its members; to prescribe the conditions of their organic law; and until a *new* constitution shall be made, to administer by Federal officers such parts of the old constitution and laws as the governor, or the President, or Congress may select? . . .

At this point he quoted Madison on the guaranty clause, a subject elaborated in the Senate by Carlile, of Virginia. Mr. Pendleton observed that if slavery, which, with one possible exception, existed in all the States at the time of the adoption of the Constitution, was not inconsistent with a republican form of government then it was not inconsistent with it in 1864.

And yet the advocates of this bill [continued Mr. Pendleton] propose to deprive the States of power over the question of slavery, power over their own indebtedness, power to regulate the elective franchise, and the right to hold office, under the pretense that they thereby execute the provision that the United States must guaranty a republican form of government to the States.

The gentleman from Massachusetts [Mr. Boutwell] has shown how he would execute it. South Carolina, Georgia, and Florida should never again appear as State[s] or in name in this Confederation. Is their exclusion a guarantee to them of a republican government?

. . . If Congress may insist upon the three fundamental conditions prescribed in this bill, . . . by a parity of reasoning it ought to insist upon their incorporation into the constitution of the States remaining steadfast by the Union. If they are essential to republicanism in the one class of States they are equally so in all.

. . . .

. . . Gentlemen must not palter in a double sense. These acts of secession are either valid or they are invalid. If they are valid, they separated the State from the Union. If they are invalid, they are void; they have no effect; the State officers who act upon them are rebels to the Federal Government; the States are not destroyed; their constitutions are not abrogated; their officers are committing illegal acts, for which they are liable to punishment; the States have never left the Union, but so soon as their officers shall perform their duties or other officers shall assume their places, will again perform the duties imposed and enjoy the privileges conferred by the Federal compact, and this not by virtue of a new ratification of the Constitution, nor a new admission by the Federal Government, but by virtue of the original ratification, and the constant, uninterrupted maintenance of position in the Federal Union since that date.

Acts of secession are not invalid to destroy the Union, and valid to destroy the State governments and the political privileges of their citizens. We have heard much of the two-fold relation which citizens of the seceded States may hold to the Federal Government — that they may be at once belligerents and rebellious citizens. I believe there are some judicial decisions to that effect. Sir, it is impossible. The Federal Government may possibly have the right to elect in which relation it will deal with them; it cannot deal with them at one and the same time in inconsistent relations. Belligerents being captured are entitled to be treated as prisoners of war; rebellious citizens are liable to be hanged. The private property of belligerents, according to the rules of modern war, shall not be taken without compensation; the property of rebellious citizens is liable to confiscation. Belligerents are not amenable to the local criminal law, nor to the jurisdiction of courts which administer it; rebellious citizens are, and the officers are bound to enforce the law, and to exact the penalty of its infraction. The seceded States are either in the Union or out of it. If in the Union, their constitutions are untouched, their State governments are maintained; their citizens are entitled to all political rights, except so far as they may be deprived of them by the criminal law which they may have infracted. This seems incomprehensible to the gentleman from Maryland. In his view the whole State government centers in the men who administer it; so that when they administer it unwisely, or put it in antagonism to the Federal Government, the State government is dissolved, the State constitution is abrogated, and the State is left, in fact and in form, *de jure* and *de facto*, in anarchy, except so far as the Federal Government may rightfully intervene. This seems to be substantially the view of the gentleman from Massachusetts [Mr. Boutwell]. He enforces the same position, but he does not use the same language.

. . . If by a plague or other visitation of God every officer of a State government should at the same moment die, so that not a single person clothed with official power should remain, would the State government be destroyed? Not at all. For the moment it would not be administered, but as soon as officers were elected and assumed their respective duties it would be instantly in full force and vigor. If these States are out of the Union their State governments are still in force unless otherwise changed. And their citizens are to the Federal Government as foreigners, and it has in relation to them the same rights, and none other, as it had in relation to British subjects in the war of 1812, or to the Mexicans in 1846. Whatever may be the true relation of the seceded States, the Federal Government derives no power in relation to them or their citizens from the provision of the Constitution now under consideration, but in the one case derives all its power from the duty of enforcing the " Supreme law of the land; " and in the other from the power " to declare war."

. . . .

The gentleman [Mr. Davis] states his case too strongly. The duty imposed on Congress is doubtless important, but Congress has no right to use a means of performing it forbidden by the Constitution, no matter how necessary or proper it might be thought to be. But, sir, this doctrine is monstrous. It has no foundation in the Constitution. It subjects all the States to the will of Congress; it places their institutions at the feet of Congress. It creates in Congress an absolute unqualified despotism. It asserts the power of Congress in changing the State governments to be "plenary, supreme and unlimited" — "subject only to revision by the people of the whole United States." The rights of the people of the State are nothing, their will is nothing. Congress first decides, the people of the whole Union revise. My own State of Ohio is liable at any moment to be called in question for her constitution. She does not permit negroes to vote. . . . From that decision of the Congress there is no appeal to the people of Ohio, but only to the people of Massachusetts, and New York, and Wisconsin, at the election of Representatives; and if a majority cannot be elected to reverse the decision, the people of Ohio must submit. Woe be to the day when that doctrine shall be established, for from its centralized despotism we will appeal to the sword!

The rights of the States, he said in conclusion, had reconciled liberty with empire, the freedom of the individual with increase of the public domain; by the proposed measure these were all swept instantly away. It substituted "despotism for self-government; despotism the more severe because vested in a numerous Congress elected by a people who may not feel the exercise of its power. . . . It maintains integrity of territory but destroys the rights of the citizen." Finally he declared that he preferred separation to the unity which the bill would create.[1]

Debate was concluded by Henry Winter Davis, who rose for the purpose of perfecting the pending measure by moving as a substitute a bill essentially the same as that under consideration in the House; from that plan, however, it differed in two not unimportant particulars. First, it excluded what his friend Mr. Cox had objected to, the rule of one tenth, and required a majority to concur in forming a government. The other softened the operation of the clause excluding officers of the State and Confederate government, by saving merely ministerial officers and the inferior military officers; so that the exclusion merely affected persons of dangerous political influence. By an arrangement with Thaddeus Stevens, in-

[1] Globe, Part III., 1 Sess. 38th Cong., pp. 2105-2107.

stead of having a direct vote on his substitute, a portion of it was proposed as a preamble to this bill, which, of course, would be voted on separately and take whatever fate the House might assign to it. With these observations Mr. Davis said, " I offer this as a substitute, and move the previous question upon it." The substitute was agreed to, and the amendment to the preamble adopted, the preamble itself being rejected. By 73 yeas to 59 nays, the bill passed the House, May 4, 1864.[1]

This important measure authorized the President, by and with the advice and consent of the Senate, to appoint for each of the States declared in rebellion a provisional governor, with pay and emoluments not to exceed that of a brigadier-general of volunteers, and who was to be charged with the civil administration of such State until a government was recognized as existing therein. As soon as military resistance to Federal authority had been suppressed, and the people had sufficiently returned to their obedience to the Constitution and the laws, it was made the duty of the governor to direct the United States marshal to enroll all white male citizens of the United States, resident in the State, in their respective counties; and wherever a majority of them took the oath of allegiance, the loyal people of the States were, by proclamation, to be invited by the governor to elect delegates to a convention to act upon the reëstablishment of a State government, the proclamation to prescribe the details of the election. Qualified electors in the army could vote at the headquarters of their respective commands. No person who had held or exercised any civil, military, State or Confederate office under the rebel occupation, and who had voluntarily borne arms against the United States, could either vote or be eligible as a delegate. The convention was required to insert in the constitution the following provisions:

[1] Globe, Part III., 1 Sess. 38th Cong., p. 2108.

First. No person who has held or exercised any office, civil or military, except offices merely ministerial and military offices below colonel, State or Confederate, under the usurping power, shall vote for or be a member of the Legislature, or Governor.

Second. Involuntary servitude is forever prohibited, and the freedom of all persons is guaranteed in said State.

Third. No debt, State or Confederate, created by or under the sanction of the usurping power, shall be recognized or paid by the State.

Upon the adoption of such a constitution by the convention and its ratification by the voters of the State the provisional governor should so certify to the President, who, after obtaining the assent of Congress, was empowered by proclamation to recognize the government so established, and none other, as the constitutional government of the State; from the date of such recognition, and not before, Senators and Representatives as well as electors for President and Vice-President could be legally chosen in such State. Until reorganization the provisional governor was to enforce the laws of the Union, and of the State before rebellion.

The remaining provisions were as follows:

Section 12 declared that "all persons held to involuntary servitude or labor in the States referred to, are emancipated and discharged therefrom, and they and their posterity are declared to be forever free. And if any such persons or their posterity shall be restrained of liberty, under pretense of any claim to such service or labor, the courts of the United States shall, on *habeas corpus,* discharge them."

Section 13 provided that "if any person declared free by this or any law of the United States, or any proclamation of the President, be restrained of liberty, with intent to be held in or reduced to involuntary servitude or labor, the person convicted before a court of competent jurisdiction of such act shall be punished by a fine of not less than $1,500, and be imprisoned not less than five nor more than twenty years."

By section 14 it was declared that "every person who shall

hereafter hold or exercise any office, civil or military, except offices merely ministerial, and military offices below the grade of colonel, in the rebel service, State or Confederate, is declared not to be a citizen of the United States." [1]

On the following day the proposed measure came up in the Senate, was read twice by its title and referred to the Committee on Territories. On May 27 Mr. Wade reported the bill with amendments, and on June 30 succeeding moved to postpone all prior orders and proceed to its consideration. His motion, however, was not agreed to, and it was not till July 1, when the session was drawing rapidly to a close, that its discussion began. To save time the amendments proposed by the committee were voted down. Senator Brown, of Missouri, believed that the subject of reconstruction could and should be postponed to a later day, and offered for the bill, by way of amendment, a substitute which declared incapable of voting " for electors of President or Vice-President of the United States, or of electing Senators or Representatives in Congress," until the rebellion was abandoned, the inhabitants of all those States hitherto proclaimed in a state of insurrection. That question he regarded as the necessity of the hour.[2]

Mr. Wade hoped this amendment would not prevail; there was nothing, he asserted, in the argument that sufficient time did not remain for its careful consideration, because it was early and thoroughly debated in the House and had been fully discussed by the Senate Committee. It was five months on their desks and the attention of Senators had often been called to it. On Republicans at least its consideration had frequently been urged by himself. More than ordinary care had been taken in this matter, and if the bill was not then understood it never would be.

The question would arise in the ensuing campaign. Sen-

[1] Globe, Part IV., 1 Sess. 38th Cong., pp. 3448-3449.
[2] Ibid., p. 3449.

ators, he said, had been refused admission to Congress, and the principles on which they would be received should be declared. They were announced in the bill which had passed the House. It protected the Government against Confederate sympathizers and guarded the interests of loyal Southerners during the period of transition.

The status of the seceded States was a question upon which men differed widely. It was a question to be ascertained and declared by Congress, " for the Executive ought not to be permitted to handle this great question to his own liking. It does not belong, under the Constitution, to the President to prescribe the rule, and it is a base abandonment of our own powers and our own duties to cast this great principle upon the decision of the executive branch of the Government. . . . I know very well that the President from the best motives undertook to fix a rule upon which he would admit these States back into the Union. It was not upon any principle of republicanism; it would not have guarantied to the States a republican form of government, because he prescribed the rule to be that when one tenth of the population would take a certain oath and agree to come back into the Union they might come in as States. When we consider that in the light of American principle, to say the least of it, it was absurd. The idea that a State shall take upon itself the great privilege of self-government when there are only one tenth of the people that can stand by the principle is most anti-republican, anomalous, and entirely subversive of the great principles that underlie all our State governments and the General Government. Majorities must rule, and until majorities be found loyal and trustworthy for State government, they must be governed by a stronger hand. . . .

" . . . I hold that once a State of this Union, always a State; that you cannot by wrong and violence displace the rights of anybody or disorganize the State." It was marvellous to him how gentlemen could fancy that States forfeited their rights because more or less of the people had gone off into rebellion, and he added, " This bill proceeds upon that idea and discards absolutely the notion that States may lose their rights and that they may be abrogated and may be reduced to the condition of Territories. It denies any such thing as that. No sound principle can be adopted that warrants any such thing."

Noticing the imposition of conditions on the admission or on the readmission of a State, he remarked that this feature of the bill would probably receive more criticism than any other, and declared, " that the great Union party of the country are altogether convinced that slavery mixed up in a Government is so unsafe, so liable to overthrow that it cannot be admitted as an element in a State government. . . . Therefore this bill has taken special pains to say that the new government shall, in its constitution, proclaim emancipation as a condition upon which it shall be permitted to come into the Union." There was a time, he admitted, when it would have been deemed unconstitutional in Congress to prescribe any particular principle for a constitution when a State was seeking to come into the Union. " We have done so, however," he asserted, " in every State that we have ever admitted," and yet perhaps the question was never entirely settled. " Would it be wise for us," he asked, " in admitting States back into this Union to permit them to come with the very element that carried them out, with the very seeds of destruction which had destroyed them already? The framers of this bill," he continued, " have sedulously shut it out, and made it a condition on which the seceded States shall come back that it shall be a fundamental principle of their constitution that slavery is excluded."

The amendment of Senator Brown he characterized as a bare negative; it did not inform the people of the seceded

States upon what principle they were to be again admitted into the Union.[1]

Mr. Carlile, of Virginia, observed on entering into the discussion that everything the bill proposed to do in the way of remedying existing evils would be accomplished by adopting the amendment offered by the Senator from Missouri. The provisions of the bill were not to be enforced and were not to have any life until after the suppression of the rebellion, and, therefore, there could be no pressing necessity for action at that time, when a large majority of Senators expected in three or four days to leave Washington for their homes. Senator Wade interrupted him to point out that there was provided a military governor whose duties could be performed in any stage of the rebellion, from the time Federal forces obtained a foothold in any State until it was in the Union again. The Virginia Senator agreed with Mr. Wade as to the extent of the President's power in the matter, and in the belief that once a State in the Union always a State; but the bill, he said, not only maintained that State governments were overthrown, but so far as it could do so, recognized and assumed the right to overthrow the State governments if that work was not already accomplished. If the President had not the right to prescribe rules for the return of rebellious States, where was the constitutional provision which authorized Congress to do so? The title of the bill was an insult, he declared, to the understanding of every enlightened man in the nation and the bill itself one of the most revolutionary that ever was proposed in a deliberative body claiming to be the representatives of a free people.

The question mooted in Congress forty years before, he continued, was insignificant compared to the present. That was a proposition to impose upon the inhabitants of a Territory seeking admission into the Union a restriction upon their

[1] Globe, Part IV., 1 Sess. 38th Cong., pp. 3448-3450.

right of self-government when they became a State. After one of the most exhaustive and learned debates that ever graced the Capitol of the nation that assumption for Congress was abandoned. It was permitted to rest as the settled law of the land that Congress had no power to impose limitations affecting the right of the people of a State to regulate their own domestic affairs, even when sought to be applied to the inhabitants of a Territory seeking admission to the Union. This continued the settled action of Congress until reversed at the preceding session by assuming to create an independent State out of a portion of the Commonwealth which he represented.

"No State can have a Republican form of government," he declared, "no State has a republican government, when that government, no matter what are its provisions, is prescribed to them by another outside of their limits. A republican form of government must emanate and emanate alone from the people that are to be governed. It belongs not to the Congress of the United States; it belongs not to the thirty-three States of this Union to prescribe for the smallest State within its folds a constitution or form of government. If you have a right to impose a limitation upon this power as to one subject of domestic legislation you have a right to impose it upon every subject. If you have a right to make one provision of a constitution for a people you have the right to make the entire instrument itself."

An interruption of his argument by Mr. Wade drew from the Virginia Senator a query rather embarrassing to the Ohio statesman. "Where," asked Carlile, "does the Senator derive the power to appoint a governor for a State, a State which he acknowledges to be in existence, a State government that he acknowledges to be in existence, a State government that he acknowledges it to be his duty to protect and maintain? By what provision of the Constitution does the Senator derive the authority to appoint for such a State an executive head?" Mr. Wade replied that when the Constitution imposed the duty of guaranteeing a republican form of government it conferred the power to do so, and he in turn inquired, "Is not that good law?" "No, sir," answered Carlile, who proceeded: "Now, Mr. President, I will satisfy the Senator himself, I think; and really it is not necessary for me to attempt to satisfy him, for he is too good a lawyer not to know the meaning of the word 'guaranty.' What is it? Does the authority to 'guaranty to each State in this Union a republican form of government' authorize this Union to set up a government, to create a government, or to make a government? Is the maker of a note the man who guaranties its payment? There is no man in the Senate who knows better the definition and legal significance of the word 'guaranty' than the Senator from Ohio, and none, I am sure, is more familiar, too, with the power that was intended to be conferred by this provision of the Constitution." After admitting that he would bring the power of the Government to bear on a faction who undertook to establish a monarchical form of government, Mr. Wade put this hypothetical case: "Suppose now that we have conquered them and the people are still bent on their monarchy, shall we not guaranty a republican government to them by putting one over them?" "If the Senator be right," answered Carlile, "Mr. Madison, the author of the Constitution, was wrong." He then quoted from the forty-third number of the Federalist:

"To guaranty to every State in the Union a republican form of government; to protect each of them against invasion; and on application of the Legislature, or of the Executive (when the Legislature cannot be convened), against domestic violence."

In a confederacy founded on republican principles and composed of republican members, the superintending government ought clearly to possess authority to defend the system against aristocratic or monarchical innovations.

"The very case put by Senator Wade," observed Carlile; "and how it is to be done is stated: "

> The more intimate the nature of such a Union may be, the greater interest have the members in the political institutions of each other; and the greater right to insist that the forms of government under which the compact was entered into should be *substantially* maintained. . . . It may possibly be asked, what need there could be of such a precaution, and whether it may not become a pretext for alterations in the State governments, without the concurrence of the States themselves. These questions admit of ready answers. If the interposition of the General Government should not be needed, the provision for such an event will be a harmless superfluity only in the Constitution. But who can say what experiments can be produced by the caprice of particular States, by the ambition of enterprising leaders, or by the intrigues and influence of foreign powers? To the second question it may be answered that if the General Government should interpose by virtue of this constitutional authority, it will be, of course, bound to pursue the authority. But the authority extends no further than to a *guaranty* of a republican form of government, which supposes a *preëxisting government* of the form which is to be guaranted.

Sustained in his position by Madison's commentary Carlile resumed: "Now, sir, is the Senator answered? . . . It is not claimed or pretended, I suppose, by the Senator from Ohio, or by any advocate of this bill, that under any other provision of the Constitution can a pretext be afforded for the assertion of such a power as this bill proposes to assert." To Senator Wilkinson's inquiry, what would the Government of the United States do if the people of South Carolina determined that they would not have a republican form of government in that State, the Virginia Senator answered:

"I would have the Government of the United States do nothing that it has not the power under the Constitution to do, because I believe that the Government of the United States is a Government of limited powers. I believe it to be its duty under the grant of power in the Constitution to guaranty the existence of a preëxisting republican government. That government existed in South Carolina; the people have not determined, at least before this war they had not determined, to have any other than a republican form of government. We had recognized that government as a republican form of government by the recognition of the State in all its departments and the admission of all its national representatives. It is made the duty of the Government of the United States, not of Congress; and I desire to call the attention of the Senator to that, because it bears upon his assumption for Congress of power which does not belong to the Executive. It is not alone the duty of Congress to guaranty a republican form of government to the people of the several States; the extent of that guarantee is not limited alone to the means which Congress may employ; but the words of the Constitution are 'the United States shall guaranty.' Hence every department of the Government is equally bound; and Congress being the legislative branch of course participates to a greater extent in the discharge of that duty."

After a discussion with Mr. Clark, Carlile proceeded in his argument: "But, sir, the Senator from Ohio says the Union is to be preserved. So say I. Upon what principle are these States to come back into the Union? The people, says the Senator from Ohio, will meet you with that inquiry. Sir, when was ever such an inquiry suggested to the brain of any loyal man in this Union? When was such an inquiry ever put? Never until after a policy different from that which characterized the commencement of this struggle was entered upon by the party in power. All said the Union was to be restored; all accepted the struggle as the use of the military power of the Government in the restoration of the Union. What Union? The Union of the Constitution. The Union into which new States are to be admitted. It is not into 'a Union' but into 'this Union' that the States are admitted. What Union? The Union of the Constitution, none other; and he who seeks to preserve the Union can only do it by an observance of the Constitution and of the constitutional means to restore it, not reconstruct it.

" . . . In this Union, created by this Constitution, of limited and delegated powers, all prescribed and written in the instrument, you propose to exercise your legislative power by usurping the rights and liberties of the people, a power which all the people you represent could not use or could not exert without the destruction of the Union which the Constitution formed. There is no power in this Government, there is no power in the parties to this Government, there is no power in all the States of this Union to prescribe a constitution for the little State of Rhode Island. If every other State in the Union, the adhering as well as the rebellious States, if every man, woman, and child in them were to meet and prescribe a constitution for the people of Rhode Island, they would have no power or authority to do so under the Union; and tell me where the people's representatives derive the power to do that which all the people in their collective capacity, save the small minority which constitutes that State, cannot do?" [1]

Mr. Carlile emphasized the fact that the bill under consideration was not a war measure. In a running argument with several Senators he showed both a ready and comprehensive knowledge of the Constitution and made some telling points against the bill as well as against the radical tendencies in Congress. His speech was, perhaps, the very ablest delivered by any Senator in opposition to the proposed measure. At its conclusion Mr. Brown's amendment was agreed to.

An amendment offered by Charles Sumner to enact the Emancipation Proclamation into a law was rejected by a vote of 21 to 11. The Massachusetts statesman did not wish, he said, to see the edict of freedom " left to float on a Presidential proclamation." [2]

[1] Globe, Part IV., 1 Sess. 38th Cong., pp. 3451-3453.
[2] Ibid., p. 3460.

RISE OF THE CONGRESSIONAL PLAN

The bill concerning States in insurrection against the United States then passed the Senate by 26 yeas to 3 nays.[1] When the vote was taken 20 Senators were absent. On the succeeding day, July 2, 1864, a message announced the disagreement of the House to the Senate amendment and requested a committee of conference. A subsequent motion of Mr. Wade that the Senate recede from its amendment and agree to the bill of the House was carried after some discussion by a vote of 18 to 14, thus passing the bill on the same day.[2] The names of Doolittle, Henderson, Ten Eyck and Trumbull voting with the Democrats in opposition foreshadowed that division in the Republican ranks which afterwards occurred.

The history of this famous bill from the moment of its passage by Congress until the publication a week later of the President's proclamation concerning it is best related in the Life of Mr. Lincoln by his private secretaries, Messrs. Nicolay and Hay. These writers possessed an unusual opportunity for ascertaining the sentiments of the President upon nearly every question of public interest.

"Congress," says the diary of Mr. Hay, "was to adjourn at noon on the Fourth of July; the President was in his room at the Capitol signing bills, which were laid before him as they were brought from the two Houses. When this important bill was placed before him he laid it aside and went on with the other work of the moment. Several prominent members entered in a state of intense anxiety over the fate of the bill. Mr. Sumner and Mr. Boutwell, while their nervousness was evident, refrained from any comment. Zachariah Chandler, who was unabashed in any mortal presence, roundly asked the President if he intended to sign the bill. The President replied: ' This bill has been placed before me

[1] Globe, Part IV., 1 Sess. 38th Cong., p. 3461.
[2] Ibid., p. 3491.

a few moments before Congress adjourns. It is a matter of too much importance to be swallowed in that way.' 'If it is vetoed,' cried Mr. Chandler, 'it will damage us fearfully in the Northwest. The important point is that one prohibiting slavery in the reconstructed States.' Mr. Lincoln said: 'That is the point on which I doubt the authority of Congress to act.' 'It is no more than you have done yourself,' said the Senator. The President answered: 'I conceive that I may in an emergency do things on military grounds which cannot be done constitutionally by Congress.' Mr. Chandler, expressing his deep chagrin, went out, and the President, addressing the members of the Cabinet who were seated with him, said: 'I do not see how any of us now can deny and contradict what we have always said, that Congress has no constitutional power over slavery in the States.' Mr. Fessenden expressed his entire agreement with this view. 'I have even had my doubts,' he said, 'as to the constitutional efficacy of your own decree of emancipation, in those cases where it has not been carried into effect by the actual advance of the army.'

"The President said: 'This bill and the position of these gentlemen seem to me, in asserting that the insurrectionary States are no longer in the Union, to make the fatal admission that States, whenever they please, may of their own motion dissolve their connection with the Union. Now we cannot survive that admission, I am convinced. If that be true, I am not President; these gentlemen are not Congress. I have laboriously endeavored to avoid that question ever since it first began to be mooted, and thus to avoid confusion and disturbance in our own councils. It was to obviate this question that I earnestly favored the movement for an amendment to the Constitution abolishing slavery, which passed the Senate and failed in the House. I thought it much better, if it were possible, to restore the Union without the necessity of a violent quarrel among its friends as to whether certain States have been in or out of the Union during the war — a merely metaphysical question, and one unnecessary to be forced into discussion.'

"Although every member of the Cabinet agreed with the President, when, a few minutes later, he entered his carriage to go home, he foresaw the importance of the step he had resolved to take and its possibly disastrous consequences to himself. When some one said to him that the threats made by the extreme radicals had no foundation, and that people would not bolt their ticket on a question of metaphysics, he answered: 'If they choose to make a point upon this, I do not doubt that they can do harm. They have never been friendly to me. At all events, I must keep some consciousness of being somewhere near right. I must keep some standard or principle fixed within myself.'"[1]

A perusal of the preceding abridgment of debates shows clearly that the bill was designed by Congress as a measure of reconstruction and intended by many of its leading advocates as a rebuke of the President. He was not, however, a statesman whom even the deliberate censure of a coördinate branch of Government could hurry into an act of rashness; he had never been precipitate; indeed, the burden of radical criticism was that Mr. Lincoln was provokingly slow. This was the opinion which Charles Sumner expressed in confidential correspondence with his English friends[2] and which Secretary Chase entered in the pages of his diary.[3] The President was, it is true, the most cautious of men, and the fact goes far to explain the absence during his eventful administration of even a single serious blunder; the dis-

[1] Diary of John Hay, quoted in Abraham Lincoln, A History, Vol. IX. pp. 120-122.
[2] Pierce's Memoir of Sumner, Vol. IV. pp. 57, 60, 83, 84, 106, 108, 130, etc.
[3] Shuckers' Life of Chase, pp. 440n, 442, 453, 495.

covery of a gross error of judgment seldom or never rewarded the researches of his ablest critics. Though his modesty was scarcely less than his prudence, he entertained a just conception of the dignity of his office; long reflection upon constitutional questions, which made him familiar with the extent of executive power, taught him likewise to recognize those limitations which the fundamental law had imposed upon legislative action. Another characteristic which made him a formidable adversary in every controversy was a constant purpose to be always, as he expressed it himself, " somewhere near right."

The measure had been so long under consideration that none of its provisions could have taken him by surprise, and we are justified in concluding that when the bill was presented for his approval he had already determined on his course of action. Indeed there is evidence that some of his supporters in Congress had written to their friends in Louisiana predicting the very fate that afterward befell the bill. Their outline of the President's course admits of no other explanation than that he had communicated to them his intentions respecting it. The progress of the measure in the Senate was to be so retarded that the adjournment of Congress would relieve him of the necessity of exercising the veto, and that is precisely what happened. In the very last hour of the session it was submitted for his approval; his disposal of the bill on that occasion has already been noticed; his approval was withheld and Congress rose before the expiration of the ten days which would enact the bill into a law without his signature. Though an interested view had not been overlooked, he disregarded in discharge of his duty every personal consequence of the important step which he purposed to take. His hostility to the measure had long been suspected, but when knowledge of his failure to approve it had become a certainty the anger of the more radical members of his party became extreme. They had clearly been outwitted by the President and many of them, eager for retaliation, returned to their homes meditating schemes of revenge.

For the present, at least, anything like adequate discipline of Mr. Lincoln was not within their power, for the Baltimore convention, which renominated him for the Presidency, had adjourned nearly a month before. This at least was secure. His election, though not entirely a foregone conclusion, was reasonably assured; few of the discomfited members even imagined the thought of injuring their party to embarrass the President. It is easy to believe, however, that they intended such criticism of his policy as would be consistent with party success. But even here he resolved to dispute with them a field of operations which they believed entirely their own. The President, it is true, could not, even if so inclined, justify his conduct in person before the voters of every State in the Union; he could, however, and did forestall expected criticism from Congressmen by publishing a proclamation vindicating his "pocket" veto, thus destroying whatever hope remained to radical Republicans of diminishing his popularity by ascribing to him base or selfish motives for opposing the sense of the Legislative department of Government. As on other critical occasions so on this he found no precedent to guide him, but with characteristic firmness proceeded deliberately to establish one. When some of the Congressmen reached their States they found their constituents already pondering the proclamation of July 8, 1864. Its importance requires that it be quoted in full:

Whereas, at the late session, Congress passed a bill to "guarantee to certain States, whose governments have been usurped or overthrown, a republican form of government," a copy of which is hereunto annexed;

And whereas the said bill was presented to the President of the United States for his approval less than one hour before the *sine die* adjournment of said session, and was not signed by him;

And whereas the said bill contains, among other things, a plan for restoring the States in rebellion to their proper practical relation in the Union, which plan expresses the sense of Congress upon that subject, and which plan it is now thought fit to lay before the people for their consideration:

Now, therefore, I, Abraham Lincoln, President of the United States, do proclaim, declare, and make known, that, while I am (as I was in December last, when by proclamation I propounded a plan for restoration) unprepared, by a formal approval of this bill, to be inflexibly committed to any single plan of restoration; and, while I am also unprepared to declare that the free-State constitutions and governments already adopted and installed in Arkansas and Louisiana shall be set aside and held for naught, thereby repelling and discouraging the loyal citizens who have set up the same as to further effort, or to declare a constitutional competency in Congress to abolish slavery in States, but am at the same time sincerely hoping and expecting that a constitutional amendment abolishing slavery throughout the nation may be adopted, nevertheless I am fully satisfied with the system for restoration contained in the bill as one very proper plan for the loyal people of any State choosing to adopt it, and that I am, and at all times shall be, prepared to give the Executive aid and assistance to such people, so soon as the military resistance to the United States shall have been suppressed in any such State, and the people thereof shall have sufficiently returned to their obedience to the Constitution and laws of the United States, in which cases Military Governors will be appointed, with directions to proceed according to the bill.[1]

This unexpected publication was very differently received by the various elements composing the Republican party; a large majority of those acting with that organization still confided in Mr. Lincoln; by the radical wing, however, he was sharply censured. Notwithstanding the necessity for harmony in the approaching campaign two of the boldest leaders, disregarding every consideration of prudence, arraigned the President in language which for severity was never surpassed by the invectives of his ablest political opponents. In the entire experience of the Republic no Executive had ever assumed to reject those provisions in a legislative measure which he disliked and adopt those that were acceptable. This is precisely what Mr. Lincoln did, and the reasons for his action he

[1] Letters and State Papers of Abraham Lincoln, Vol. II. p. 545; McPherson's Pol. Hist., pp. 318-319.

declared to the people with a confidence which forcibly recalls the direction of Andrew Jackson to the editor of his official organ: "Speak out to the people, sir, and tell them that instead of supporting me and my policy Congress is engaged in President-making." There was, however, this difference: Abraham Lincoln addressed the people directly and ventured no criticism of their representatives. Like his more impulsive though not less popular predecessor he was not deceived in the reliance which he placed in the patriotic instincts of the multitude, which cared little for nice metaphysical distinctions; by the masses of the people he was trusted to the end.

By Henry Winter Davis and Benjamin F. Wade, chief authors of the bill, its progress had been watched with feverish anxiety; when convinced that their labor was lost they became greatly agitated and made no effort to conceal their indignation at the conduct of the President. Their joint protest, printed in the *New York Tribune* of August 5, was, perhaps, the most bitter attack made upon Mr. Lincoln during his Presidential career. Their fierce manifesto, addressed "To the supporters of the Government," declares that the writers had "read without surprise, but not without indignation, the proclamation of the President of the 8th of July, 1864.

"The supporters of the Administration are responsible to the country for its conduct; and it is their right and duty to check the encroachments of the Executive on the authority of Congress, and to require it to confine itself to its proper sphere."

The paper then related the history of the bill. Its treatment by the President, they declared, indicated a persistent though unavowed purpose to defeat the will of the people by the Executive perversion of the Constitution. They insinuated that only the lowest personal motives could have dictated this action. "The President," they said, "by preventing this bill from becoming a law, holds the electoral votes of the rebel States at the dictation of his personal ambition.

"If those votes turn the balance in his favor, is it to be supposed that his competitor, defeated by such means, will acquiesce?

"If the rebel majority assert their supremacy in those States, and send votes which elect an enemy of the Government, will we not repel his claims?

"And is not that civil war for the Presidency inaugurated by the votes of the rebel States?

"Seriously impressed with these dangers, Congress, '*the proper constitutional authority*,' formally declared that there are no State governments in the rebel States, and provided for their erection at a proper time; and both the Senate and the House of Representatives rejected the Senators and Representatives chosen under the authority of what the President calls the free constitution and government of Arkansas.

"The President's proclamation 'holds for naught' this judgment, and discards the authority of the Supreme Court, and strides headlong toward the anarchy his proclamation of the 8th of December inaugurated.

"If electors for President be allowed to be chosen in either of those States, a sinister light will be cast on the motives which induced the President to 'hold for naught' the will of Congress rather than his government in Louisiana and Arkansas.

"The judgment of Congress which the President defies was the exercise of an authority exclusively vested in Congress by the Constitution, to determine what is the established government in a State, and in its own nature and by the highest judicial authority binding on all other departments of the Government."

They ridiculed the President's expressed hope that the constitutional amendment abolishing slavery might be adopted. "We curiously inquire," continue Messrs. Wade and Davis, "on what his expectation rests, after the vote of the House of Representatives at the recent session, and in the face of the political complexion of more than enough of the States to prevent the possibility of its adoption within any reasonable time; and why he did not indulge his sincere hopes with so large an installment of the blessing as his approval of the bill would have secured?

. . . .

"A more studied outrage on the legislative authority of the people has never been perpetrated.

"Congress passed a bill; the President refused to approve it, and then by proclamation puts as much of it in force as he sees fit, and proposes to execute those parts by officers unknown to the laws of the United States, and not subject to the confirmation of the Senate.

"The bill directed the appointment of provisional governors by and with the advice and consent of the Senate.

"The President, after defeating the law, proposes to appoint, without law and without the advice and consent of the Senate, military governors for the rebel States!

"He has already exercised this dictatorial usurpation in Louisiana, and defeated the bill to prevent its limitation."

Scarcely an expression of the proclamation, which was examined in detail, escaped its share of censure or of ridicule. To suppose that the President was ignorant of the contents of the bill was out of the question, for it had been discussed, they asserted, during more than a month in the House of Representatives, by which it was passed as early as the 4th of May. It passed the Senate in absolutely the form in which it came from the House. Indeed, at the President's request, a draft of a bill substantially the same in material points, and almost identical in those features objected to by the proclamation, was submitted for his consideration during the winter of 1862-1863.

The "Protest" included also a sharp contrast between the Executive plan of December 8, 1863, and that embodied in the bill which had passed Congress. That measure, said Messrs. Wade and Davis, required a majority of the voters to establish a State government, the proclamation was satisfied with one tenth; "the bill requires one oath, the proclamation another; the bill ascertains voters by registering, the proclamation by guess; the bill exacts adherence to existing territorial limits, the proclamation admits of others; the bill governs the rebel States *by law,* equalizing all before it, the proclamation commits them to the lawless discretion of military governors and provost marshals; the bill forbids electors for President (in the rebel States), the proclamation and defeat of the bill threaten us with civil war for the admission or exclusion of such votes. . . ."

This arraignment of the President's course concluded with the language of admonition, if not indeed of absolute menace: "The President has greatly presumed on the forbearance which the supporters of his Administration have so long practised, in view of the arduous conflict in which we are engaged, and the reckless ferocity of our political opponents.

"But he must understand that our support is of a cause, and not of a man; that the authority of Congress is paramount and must be respected; that the whole body of the Union men of Congress will not submit to be impeached by him of rash and unconstitutional legislation; and if he wishes our support, he must confine himself to his Executive duties, — to obey and execute, not make the laws,— to suppress by arms armed rebellion, and leave political reorganization to Congress.

"If the supporters of the Government fail to insist on this, they become responsible for the usurpations which they fail to rebuke, and are justly liable to the indignation of the people whose rights and security, committed to their keeping, they sacrifice.

" Let them consider the remedy for these usurpations, and, having found it, fearlessly execute it." [1]

The authors of this remarkable paper were eminent in the councils of their party and stood high in the estimation of Union men everywhere. Senator Wade was distinguished no less for his physical than for his moral courage — qualities impaired somewhat, it is true, by a temper fierce and vindictive. Henry Winter Davis, whose zeal for civil liberty will constitute his best claim to the gratitude of posterity, possessed literary gifts scarcely surpassed by any statesman then in public life. Though treated with extreme fairness, not to say generosity, by the President, he pursued toward the Administration a course of consistent hostility. This opposition, which even Mr. Lincoln's tact could never disarm, has been ascribed to disappointment at his failure to obtain a place in the Cabinet. While the selection of Montgomery Blair from his own State of Maryland may have been a cause of estrangement, a sense of what Mr. Davis regarded as public duty contributed, doubtless, to intensify this feeling, which led him ultimately to think the President scarcely entitled to courteous treatment. With the Ohio Senator the pitiless maxim, *vae victis*, had an undoubted influence. Both were gentlemen of wide experience and acknowledged ability, and yet their vigorous and fearless arraignment of the President revealed an astonishing lack of political sagacity. They inquired, for example, on what foundation he rested his expectation of an adoption of the constitutional amendment abolishing slavery. The incorporation, soon after, of such a provision in the fundamental law shows their want of insight into the tendencies of the times. The fire of the

[1] Ann. Cycl., 1864, pp. 307-310n.

prophet, indeed, was present in the protest; his inspiration was altogether wanting. Their absurd assertion that the electoral votes of Louisiana, Arkansas and Tennessee were the prime consideration with the President must be attributed to the passion rather than to the reason of his critics, for few men of that generation were more familiar with the Constitution in all its relations. Better than most of their readers they knew that the duty of counting such votes was entrusted not to a possibly interested Executive, but to a joint convention of both Houses. If the Maryland member believed the President had committed the misdemeanors charged and insinuated it was his duty to bring before the House the question of impeachment. Far less than was expressed in the protest would have been ground for investigation. If tenderness to Lincoln, a weakness of which Mr. Davis at least was never suspected, or a concern for party welfare prevented such a step, then he was himself guilty of a gross neglect of duty. Doubtless this consideration, together with the want of moderation shown in the manifesto, subjected its authors to a suspicion of insincerity. Indeed, one does not read a dozen lines of their arraignment without discovering the chief if not the sole cause of its publication. "The President," they say, "did not sign the bill 'to guarantee to certain States whose governments have been usurped, a republican form of government'—passed by the supporters of his Administration in both Houses of Congress after mature deliberation." In brief, the political departments of Government had entered upon a struggle for power; Congress had been defeated, and its discomfited leaders sought to relieve their feelings by railing at the President.

Except that it probably defeated the renomination of Mr. Davis for Congress, their protest was followed by no political result of moment.[1] In it the mass of Republicans perceived

[1] Twenty Years of Congress, Vol. II. p. 44.

only the seeds of dissension within their ranks. In this view it was a source of delight to Democrats, though they felt little sympathy with either the defeated bill or the purposes of its chief authors.

VIII

AN ATTEMPT TO COMPROMISE

WHEN Congress met in December, 1864, Mr. Lincoln, who received the electoral votes of twenty-two of the twenty-five States participating in the contest, had again been chosen President. In the struggle for power he had refrained with his usual prudence from improving his advantage over the Legislative department. The annual message omitted all reference to the controversy occasioned by his failure to sign, and his proclamation concerning, the bill of Messrs. Wade and Davis; the question of reconstruction was noticed in only the most casual manner. A statement of the satisfactory condition of foreign relations introduced the Executive communication; the subject of finance received the consideration that its importance required. The vast proportions and the efficient state of the navy were mentioned as matter of congratulation. General Sherman's projected march of three hundred miles through hostile regions was characterized as the most remarkable feature in the military operations of the year. This with other evidences of approaching disruption in the Confederacy led logically to a summary of what had been accomplished toward reorganization in those States already wrested from insurgent armies. On this subject the message observed: " Important movements have also occurred during the year to the effect of molding society for durability in the Union. Although short of complete success, it is much in the right direction that twelve thousand citizens in each of the States of Arkansas and Louisiana have organized loyal State governments, with free constitutions, and are earnestly struggling to maintain and administer them."[1] Movements in the same direction, he said, more extensive though less definite, were in progress elsewhere and should not be overlooked. No plan of reconstruction was proposed, or even alluded to in the message.

Among questions beyond Executive authority to adjust was specified the admission of members to Congress. In disclaiming power over this subject he anticipated the criticism of those Senators and Representatives who later in the session ascribed to him a design to usurp important functions of the Legislative branch of Government.

From its concluding paragraphs we are enabled to collect the sentiments of the President relative to his offer, a year before, of a general pardon to designated classes upon specified terms. In this connection he said: "But the time may come — probably will come — when public duty shall demand that it [the door open to repentant rebels] be closed; and that, in lieu, more rigorous measures than heretofore shall be adopted." This seems to establish beyond question the fact that Mr. Lincoln feared some measures more stringent than he had been hitherto pursuing might be rendered necessary by the failure of a policy of clemency to recall any large number of insurgents to their obedience to the Constitution and the laws.

He ventured to recommend a reconsideration of the proposed constitutional amendment abolishing slavery throughout the United States, which at the preceding session had passed the Senate, but failed to receive in the House the requisite two thirds vote. Though the present, he reminded them, was the same Congress and composed of nearly the same members, their judgments were, no doubt, influenced by an inter-

[1] McPherson's Pol. Hist., p. 557.

vening election, which, though it imposed on them no obligation to change their views, made it reasonably certain that if they did not submit the amendment to the States the succeeding Congress would. He inquired, since its passage was merely a question of time, whether they would not agree that the sooner the better? The voice of the people, he added, had for the first time been heard on that question.[1]

As the President believed, the House had been so far converted to his views that a joint resolution adopting the amendment was passed early in the session by a vote of 119 to 56.[2]

When Congress assembled the public was occupied chiefly in watching the progress of naval and military operations. The sinking of the *Alabama* and the capture of the *Florida* practically ended Confederate privateering, for any expectations based upon the escape of the *Albemarle* were frustrated by the enterprise and daring of Lieutenant Cushing. One army had been destroyed by Sheridan, another crippled by Thomas. Tidings of telling blows inflicted by General Sherman gave something like assurance of his safety. Though not without heavy loss, Grant had forced Lee within the defences of Richmond and Petersburg. Some of the lesser Union advantages had, it is true, been offset by Southern victories; signs of disintegration within the Confederacy, however, were multiplying, and this condition forced upon Congress the inevitable question of reconstruction.

By unanimous consent of the House Thaddeus Stevens, on December 8, offered resolutions distributing the President's message. To the Committee on the Rebellious States was referred so much of it as was alleged to relate " to the duty of the United States to guaranty a republican form of gov-

[1] McPherson's Pol. Hist., pp. 555-558.
[2] Rise and Fall of the Slave Power in America, Vol. III. p. 452.

AN ATTEMPT TO COMPROMISE 289

ernment to the States in which the governments recognized by the United States have been abrogated or overthrown."[1]

Nothing whatever in the message or the accompanying documents related to any such duty on the part of the United States, and the resolution assumed such a recommendation, no doubt, for the purpose of bringing the subject before Congress. One week later, Mr. Ashley, of Ohio, reported a bill, on the subject of Stevens's resolution, which was read twice, ordered to be printed and returned to the Committee. On January 12 succeeding Representative Eliot, of Massachusetts, gave notice of his intention to offer at the proper time an amendment to the bill in charge of Mr. Ashley. No objection having been made, it was ordered to be printed. This was, in fact, a substitute for the bill reported by the Ohio member, and provided "that no State engaged in rebellion against the Government of the United States shall be allowed to resume its political relations with the Government of the United States until by the action of the loyal citizens within the limits of the same a State constitution shall be ordained and established, republican in form, forever prohibiting involuntary servitude within the State, and guarantying to all persons freedom and equality of rights before the law." Its second section provided "that the State of Louisiana shall be permitted to renew its political relations with the Government of the United States under the constitution adopted by the convention assembled at New Orleans on the 6th of April, 1864."[2]

That some of the more influential among the radical members desired to avoid, if possible, a controversy with the President may be fairly inferred from a letter of Charles Sumner, written December 27, 1864, to Doctor Lieber. Among other

[1] Globe, Part I., 2 Sess. 38th Cong., pp. 12-13.
[2] Ibid., p. 234.

things the Senator says: " I have presented to the President the duty of harmony between Congress and the Executive. He is agreed. It is proposed to admit Louisiana (which ought not to be done), and at the same time pass the reconstruction bill for all the other States, giving the electoral franchise to 'all citizens' without distinction of color. If this arrangement is carried out, it will be an immense political act."[1] A communication to John Bright, written a few days after the above, January 1, 1865, confirms this view. On that occasion Mr. Sumner said: " The President is exerting every force to bring Congress to receive Louisiana under the Banks government. I do not believe Louisiana is strong enough in loyalty and freedom for an independent State. The evidence on this point seems overwhelming. I have discussed it with the President, and have tried to impress on him the necessity of having no break between him and Congress on such questions. Much as I am against the premature recognition of Louisiana, I will hold my peace if I can secure a rule for other States, so that we may be saved from daily anxiety with regard to their condition."[2] These passages explain the amendment to the revived bill. Sumner was willing to remain a neutral spectator of the debates on the recognition of Louisiana provided the reorganization of the remaining States should be made on the lines indicated by Congress.

On January 16, Ashley's bill was reached in the regular order of business; by direction of the Committee on the Rebellious States, it was offered as a substitute for the original measure, from which it differed in one very important particular. It expressly recognized the loyal governments of both Louisiana and Arkansas. By unanimous consent the proposed enactment, considered as an original bill, was offered for the

[1] Pierce, Memoir of Charles Sumner, Vol. IV. p. 205.
[2] Ibid., p. 221.

AN ATTEMPT TO COMPROMISE

plan submitted by Henry Winter Davis at the preceding session. Representative William D. Kelley, of Pennsylvania, would amend the clause providing for the enrollment of "all the white male citizens of the United States" by inserting the words "and all other male citizens of the United States who may be able to read the Constitution thereof." Mr. Eliot then introduced the amendment of which he had previously given notice. By Representative Arnold another amendment was offered to that of Eliot.

Judge Kelley opened the debate by declaring that indemnity for the past the victors in the war could not hope to obtain; they could, however, demand security for the future. In a very long speech he discussed the status of the negro in the early days of the Republic; this portion of his address was concluded with the remark that his amendment did not contemplate that the entire mass of people of African descent, degraded and brutalized by laws and customs, be immediately clothed with all the rights of citizenship, but only those so far fitted by education for its judicious exercise as were able to read the Constitution and the laws of the United States. This, indeed, he admitted, was only an entering wedge and was to be regarded as an aid to their improvement; when sufficiently advanced they were to be endowed with every right necessary to their protection. A strong plea was made to confer the suffrage on the colored man; otherwise, asked the Pennsylvania member, how will it be possible to prevent his subjugation? He would not rely on men's abstract sense of justice, for that had not prevented outrages in the past. Justice should be embodied in laws and constitutions while it was in the power of Congress to do so. That body was to determine who should select delegates to the conventions that were to frame governments for the insurgent States.

The Union minorities in the South required the political support of every loyal man in their communities. It was the power, he reminded Representatives, not the spirit of the rebellion that Federal armies were overthrowing. In conclusion he declared himself in favor of conferring the suffrage on "every man who fights or pays," a doctrine which he ascribed to Jefferson, in whose party he said he had been trained.[1]

Mr. Eliot, who spoke on January 17, regretted that he had not been able to support the amended bill reported from the select committee. Partly because of the interest, he said, which his friend Henry Winter Davis took in the subject he came to its consideration prepossessed in its favor. The provisions of the measure passed at the preceding session, however, were not then discussed. There were strong reasons for action at that time which no longer existed to the same extent. There was time enough on the present occasion, January, 1865, to make it more perfect and more practicable than the plan offered by the committee.

Entering upon an examination of the bill he declared that its terms were peremptory; eleven States were in rebellion, and by the first section the President was called upon to appoint for each of them a provisional governor. Such appointments were to be made when the measure became a law. Except in Louisiana, Arkansas and Tennessee these appointments would be not only useless but a needless source of expense, and though section *fifteen* recognized the governments established in the two former, the machinery of the bill would be applied to all the States in rebellion.

It imposed upon the several governors proposed to be appointed executive duties which they could not assume until the power of the United States had vindicated itself within those States; there were other duties which they should not

[1] Globe, Part I., 2 Sess. 38th Cong., pp. 281-291.

AN ATTEMPT TO COMPROMISE

be required to perform. They were to see that the laws which were in force in that section in 1860 should be faithfully executed, with no knowledge on the part of the House of the import of those laws. Why should Congress assume responsibility for enforcing the black code? Why demand the enforcement, he asked, of minute police regulations in States where complexion appointed or reduced punishment? Other laws were specified, such as those punishing the circulation of books or writings advocating human rights, laws requiring the removal from those States of free persons of color, prohibiting them from engaging in business, and punishing by the lash upon suspicion of false testimony and before conviction. There was a law, he said, in one of those States requiring the imprisonment of free colored sailors in her ports.[1] These provisions and many others of the same tenor were contained in the statute books of those States in 1860 and had been enforced. The penalty differed according to color; offences when committed by a white man were punished in one way, and when committed by colored men in another way. The provisional governor was charged with the faithful execution of such laws.

The provision for the assessment and collection of taxes he characterized as a remarkable proposition; they were to be imposed without representation, without any persons at the national capital to enlighten Congress on the subject; they were to be laid without the knowledge of the parties concerned or the parties to be affected.

The sixth section, he continued, provided that every person who should thereafter hold certain offices in the Confederacy was "declared not to be a citizen of the United States." That, Mr. Eliot contended, was applying the pun-

[1] An interesting account of the imprisonment of colored seamen in the ports of South Carolina is given in The Rise and Fall of the Slave Power in America, Vol. I. pp. 576-586.

ishment before the offence had been committed. If Congress declared that a man should for a certain offence be deprived of citizenship, could he, then, be indicted for treason subsequently committed?

The question of electing delegates to constitutional conventions presented a practical difficulty. Colored soldiers and sailors in the service were made voters by the bill; but they were not enrolled, they were not registered or credited to any county or parish; they were aggregated. They had no legal local habitation. They may have belonged to men owning plantations in several districts. The bill did not designate. With the white soldier the case was different, for he was known to belong to a certain district. If colored men entitled, because of military or naval service, to participate in the choice of delegates should be out of the service before the election occurred, and others should have taken their places, which class could vote, those in the service of the Government when the election for delegates took place, or those serving when the bill passed Congress?

Whether the difficulties pointed out were inseparable from any bill on the subject, he would not undertake to say. But in his judgment it would be unsafe for Congress to permit a measure containing such provisions to become a law. "Why," he asked, "is it not more wise to take the States as they shall present themselves for admission?" Arkansas had acted in one way, Louisiana in another, and Tennessee was proceeding in still a different manner.

Notwithstanding his objections to some features of the Louisiana constitution, he favored her recognition. From information derived from the highest sources, he had no doubt that her Legislature would supply such deficiencies. There were influences bearing on that body which he believed could not be resisted.

Thaddeus Stevens inquired, "If Louisiana and those other

States are in the Union, by what authority do we legislate for their internal police?" This provoked laughter on the Democratic side of the House. "If they are in the Union," answered Mr. Eliot, "just as Pennsylvania is, we ought not to; but the difficulty is that they are not in the Union in that sense, to that extent, thus fully. They are not out of the Union territorially, and yet rebellion has overthrown their governments for a time, and it is needful that the Congress of the United States should intervene and should legislate." To this the Pennsylvania leader further observed, "I understand the gentleman to say that they are partly in the Union, and partly out. About how much are they in the Union and about how much out?" This keen thrust was greeted by more laughter from the Democratic members.[1]

On his motion to postpone further consideration for two weeks Mr. Wilson demanded the previous question. Henry Winter Davis appealed to him to withdraw the motion. This Mr. Wilson declined to do, upon which the Maryland member observed, "a vote to postpone is equivalent to a vote to kill the bill." By 103 yeas to 34 nays, however, further debate was postponed till the 1st of February succeeding.[2]

Though Representative Washburne, of Illinois, moved on February 7 a further postponement of two weeks, the subject was before the House again on the following day, when it went over informally. Debate was not resumed till the 20th, when Mr. Dawes, of Massachusetts, took the floor.

The Thirty-eighth Congress, he said, was in the last days of its last session; a bill containing the main features of the measure under consideration, though it passed both Houses, failed at the preceding session to become a law; this circumstance led him to make a careful examination of the subject. The proposed enactment was not designed to invigorate the

[1] Globe, Part I., 2 Sess. 38th Cong., pp. 298-301.
[2] Ibid.

army, the navy or the Executive; it was intended rather to follow the army. It was intended to be applied to the condition in which the army left the State. "It is an attempt," he said, " to gather up the ' *disjecta membra* ' of those States, the broken and torn fragments of those communities, and out of the chaos, as well as the ruins and *debris* that are left in the march of those armies, to create a State capable of discharging the functions, exercising the authority, and invoking the recognition of this Government, and of the people under which it lives. . . .

" . . . The bill proceeds upon the supposition not only that there are States still existing, but that their old constitutions and laws are still in full force and operation "; for it imposed upon the provisional governor the faithful execution of those laws in force when rebellion overthrew their State governments, with the single exception of the provision touching the enforcement of laws against slavery and the mode of trial and punishment of colored people. Two remarkable features of the bill, he asserted, were those empowering the Executive in Washington, by and with the advice and consent of the Senate, to appoint governors in every one of those States; then, no matter what provisions for their election existed in the State law, the President was authorized to appoint just as many and just as few officers as he pleased. It might be a judge of the highest court of judicature in the State; or it might be the humblest roadmaster; it might be any one or all of the countless corps between them. There was no provision in the bill that they should be even residents of the State. "An army of officers," he continued, "in one paragraph of four lines, is here created, subject to the sole authority and control of the President of the United States." In a Confederate report Mr. Dawes noticed that there were 13,000 of them in a single State.

"What," he asked, "is the effect to be on the people over whom, from every quarter of this Union, broken-down politicians, men without place, foot-loose, are to be placed? Sir, it is a reproach to our Government at this hour that there are, about this capital and in the Northern States, men who have been appointed to the judgeships of district and other courts of the rebel States and Territories, drawing quarterly the salaries of those offices, although they have never been able, from the hour they received their commissions to the present moment to set foot in the States over whose courts they have been appointed. They could not go one rod into the State, positions in whose highest courts they have held for more than a year, without being hung on the first tree. . . . But my friend [Mr. Ashley] has reported a bill here which authorizes an army of thousands of these officeholders to go into those States, with commissions from this capital in their pockets, to lord it over the poor, miserable inhabitants left behind the army there. These rebel States may be thus converted into asylums for broken-down politicians."

In the language of indignation he entered into a criticism of that policy which proposed to levy on the house-less and homeless wanderers in the South, even then only saved from starvation by the charity of the North, precisely the same amount of taxes raised in 1860 when, by comparison, the people were in a princely state. "Sir," he declared, "there is not an army, great as our army is, that has power enough to accomplish that one single feat provided for in this bill, for the very plain reason that there is not money enough left in any one of these States outside the Government with which to pay that round sum for one single year. . . . This wise, efficacious policy is resorted to in this bill to hasten on, I suppose, that other day mentioned in it, when a majority of these people, molded by this process, won by its benignity 'shall voluntarily take the oath of allegiance.'"

He asserted, as Eliot had done, that the committee were calling upon Congress to sanction all the black codes of those States, save only that part which held men in bondage, and that was allowed to enforce itself.

The omissions, he asserted, were not less remarkable than the provisions of the bill. The state of things established by it was of indefinite duration. There was no provision for the peculiar conditions existing there. "There is no attempt at any adaptation of these laws to the new state of things consequent upon the rebellion, and consequent upon our constitutional action here. Not only is there no provision for the new wants and necessities of this wasted and wretched people who have been involved in the rebellion, but for that other people who have now passed into freedom by our legislation, and by the military consequences of this rebellion, who are now without food, without subsistence, without knowledge, and without opportunity to support and maintain themselves; yes, sir, without homes, literally without where to lay their heads." There were 3,000,000 of these people, he added, whose very existence was ignored by the bill; there was no provision for schools; no provision for even a poorhouse; no provision to teach them the arts of civilization, no provision for kindling in them hope, for holding up before them incentives to industry or securing to them its reward. Under the operations of the bill they were the objects of free plunder; they were to go forth to be hunted, despoiled and persecuted: outcasts in the land.

By the bill it was left in the discretion of the provisional governor, he asserted, to terminate the system set over them. He, as well as the army of officeholders under him, would be

AN ATTEMPT TO COMPROMISE

interested in prolonging the period until the people had *sufficiently* returned to their obedience. Before the initiatory steps could be taken, even if the provisional governor were willing, a majority of the people in each State must of their own choice signify their loyalty by taking the oath of allegiance. This made the matter dependent not upon the wish of the loyal, but of the disloyal persons who constituted the majority in those States.

The plan, he further stated, ignored the principle that the American people have the right to shape and alter for themselves the rules by which they are to be governed. If the matter was left in the hands of the disloyal, the time would be far distant when Union governments would be instituted in those States. The only wise policy was to establish a government among the loyal; even though it might be weak and inefficient at first, it would finally win back those who desired to be reconciled. The other numerous class, those who deserved to be hanged, were not provided for in the bill. He was opposed to the provision which would turn over to insurgents the loyal minorities in those States, and was not less opposed to prescribing a fixed iron rule by conformity to which alone out of chaos and anarchy might be made a loyal government.

Further, the bill proceeded upon the assumption that there was no power in these people, except what was conferred on them by Federal legislation, to establish State governments. This he denied, and the authors of the proposed measure, by offering to recognize the establishments otherwise organized in Arkansas and Louisiana had conceded as much. In the people, he said, and in them alone, existed the authority to form an organic law subject to the constitutional provision that the government should be republican in form. He favored a recognition of the Louisiana government not because it was formed under the guidance of General Banks, but because it was made by the loyal people of that State, was acquiesced in by them, and because under it they were building up a loyal government.

Governors Hahn and Murphy and the officials chosen in Louisiana and Arkansas who had been exercising their functions for a year would be dispossessed by foreigners sent amongst them by the President, who was empowered to do so by the bill; bickerings, heartburnings and discontent would follow any attempt to enforce this policy. Sooner or later the people of those States must be allowed to form governments for themselves, protected by the parental care of the central authority.[1]

Fernando Wood declared that he had listened with interest and pleasure to words of conciliation for the South; little but subjugation, devastation and annihilation had thus far been heard from the party, the Administration and the people represented by Mr. Dawes.

The seceding States, Mr. Wood contended, had republican forms of government which the treason of individuals did not affect. Nor did individual crimes destroy the rights of the people to regulate their domestic institutions. The forms of government were the same as those that existed in the rebellious States six years before. Even admitting that they had not such governments in existence among them, the bill did not provide a *republican* form of government for those States.[2]

He was followed in opposition to the proposed enactment by Mr. LeBlond, of Ohio, who discussed both the status of the rebellious States and their form of government. His speech on the former question added nothing of value to what Representative Pendleton had said at the preceding session,

[1] Globe, Part II., 2 Sess. 38th Cong., pp. 934-937.
[2] Ibid., pp. 937-939.

AN ATTEMPT TO COMPROMISE 301

nor did he enter upon so able an examination of the clause guaranteeing a republican form of government as did Senator Carlile on that occasion.

Henry T. Blow, of Missouri, made an appeal for the admission of Arkansas and Louisiana to prevent destructive military raids into those States as well as his own. He would support any measure that would restore them and strengthen their loyal population. However, he did not favor negro suffrage. His remarks scarcely touched the measure before the House.[1]

Joseph K. Edgerton, of Indiana, who followed in a lengthy speech in opposition, said:

> The forerunner of this measure of legislation, so far as this House is concerned, may be found in the territorial bill reported by the gentleman from Ohio [Mr. Ashley] from the Committee on Territories in the Thirty-seventh Congress, in March, 1862. It was aptly termed at the time by the gentleman's colleague from the Cincinnati district of Ohio [Mr. Pendleton] "A bill to dissolve the Union and abolish the Constitution of the United States." The bill was summarily, if not indignantly, rejected by the House without a second reading. But, sir, men and events have since changed, if the Constitution of the United States has not changed, and the stone of revolutionary reconstruction then rejected by the masterbuilders in this House bids fair to become the head of the corner. Then the Constitution was not altogether repudiated as the foundation of our legislation; now revolutionary opinions and plans override it as a thing of the past. Not many are there in this Congress, and fewer there will be in the next, I fear, to do reverence to the Constitution and obey its commands.

The President's proclamation of December 8, 1863, was then noticed, and his usurpation of authority denounced; the subject of the Louisiana government was also entered upon and fully discussed. He next referred to the introduction early in the preceding session of a resolution by Henry Winter Davis providing for the appointment of a special committee authorized to report a bill guaranteeing a republican form of government to the rebellious States. The fate of that bill,

[1] Appendix to Globe, Part II., 2 Sess. 38th Cong., pp. 73-75.

President Lincoln's proclamation concerning it, and the protest of Wade and Davis were successively dwelt upon.

The question between the President and his two Congressional friends, Wade and Davis, was to Mr. Edgerton's mind " one between two usurping powers, the Executive and the Legislative "; but, he continued, " I am free to say my sympathies were with the legislators and not with the President. Executive edicts have done more than acts of Congress during the last four years to sap the foundations and remove the landmarks of the Constitution." The majority in Congress, he asserted, by consenting to recognize the governments of Louisiana and Arkansas, kissed the hand that smote them.

He opposed a recognition of the Louisiana government because of its unconstitutional origin; Arkansas, he said, differed from it in no material respect. After stating the provisions of the bill he gave the following summary of its effects:

1. To take from the people of the State all power to initiate proceedings to reorganize their own State government in harmony with the Constitution of the United States, or even to prescribe the qualifications of suffrage. The bill ignores the idea that there is any vital power in the people to restore their State government — not only taken from them by rebellion but kept from them by Federal power — . . .

2. The effect is to exclude from the reorganization the entire white population of the State who shall have held office or voluntarily borne arms against the United States, or who shall not take the oath of July 2, 1862.

3. To confine the right of suffrage and power of reorganization to enrolled men and Federal soldiers taking the oath; and the law affords no guaranty that even the enrollment shall embrace a majority of males over twenty-one years of age. The majority required as a basis of action is so many of enrolled persons taking the oath as, with the soldiers, shall constitute a majority of the persons enrolled; that majority, through defect or fraud in enrollment, may be not even one tenth of the males of the State over twenty-one years of age.

4. The effect is the absolute disfranchisement of eleven States and their continuance in a state of war until they accept " the abandonment of

AN ATTEMPT TO COMPROMISE 303

slavery," as dictated to them by the United States, and until by organic law they declare that all persons shall have "equality of civil rights before the law" of the State; a well-seeming phrase of broad import; the precise meaning of which I do not understand. A woman is a person, a negro is a person, an alien is a person, and the right of suffrage is a civil right. Does this high-sounding phrase of the bill mean that women, negroes, and aliens shall have equal right to vote in a regenerated State with white male citizens? What does "equality of civil rights before the law for all persons" mean?

. . . .

In fact and in purpose, then, the bill before the House is one to abolish slavery in the United States, and to enfranchise and elevate negroes, and to disfranchise and degrade white men; a bill to change the social and industrial systems and internal policy of eleven States; a bill to take from those States their inherent reserved constitutional right to regulate in their own way their internal policy, not inconsistent with the Constitution of the United States. It is a bill to punish treason without trial or conviction; a bill to confiscate private property without adequate compensation; in short, a bill to reconstruct States and make State constitutions, when in truth no States or their constitutions have been destroyed, or need reconstruction, unless by the voluntary action of their own people.

. . . .

If this is a revolutionary Congress, you have a revolutionary power to pass this bill; but if it be, as I am bound by my oath of office to believe and assert, a Congress sitting under the Constitution of the United States, and having no powers outside of or unknown to it, then you cannot constitutionally pass this bill.

He stated further that the bill "embodies a spirit and purpose toward the Southern people which, if impolitic and vindictive one year ago, when the bill first came before the House, and when our enemy was far stronger and more defiant than now, is still more impolitic and vindictive at this time, when the minds of all good men are searching diligently for ways of reconciliation and peace."

In conclusion he declared: "The Congress of the United States, the legislative power of the Union, and the Constitution, is asked by this bill to be the minister and executioner of the great revenge of section upon section, States

North upon States South. For one, sir, I wash my hands of the deed."[1]

The passages quoted convey no adequate idea of the able and comprehensive character of Mr. Edgerton's speech. It was concerned not only with the subject under discussion, but extended to a rather searching examination of Republican professions in 1861 and the revolutionary practices of a later time. It was marked throughout by perfect temper, but was not on that account less effective. Any extension of time, however, even twenty minutes, was denied him by the majority.

At this point, February 21, Ashley withdrew a motion he had previously made to recommit the bill, and by authority of his committee withdrew the measure which was the original text and, in lieu thereof, introduced another. With this substitution the pending amendments fell. Representative Wilson desired his substitute to hold its original place. Messrs. Wilson, Kelley and Eliot then modified their amendments to the measure hitherto under discussion, and Ashley explained his action in a brief address.

He referred to the bill which at the preceding session failed to receive the President's approval. Since then he had labored earnestly to conciliate members on his side of the House who had scruples about the measure as it originally passed, and, if possible, obtain a united vote in its favor. For that purpose he consented to a compromise in providing for the recognition of Louisiana, Arkansas and Tennessee. The conditions were not such as he would prescribe if those States stood alone. But in order to secure what he thought of paramount importance — universal suffrage to the liberated black men of the South — he consented to insert in the bill which he had proposed a few days previously, a conditional recognition of existing governments in the States of Louisiana

[1] Appendix to Globe, Part II., 2 Sess. 38th Cong., pp. 75-83.

and Arkansas, and the government then being organized in Tennessee.

Disappointed in his efforts to win the coöperation of Representatives who entertained practically the same opinions which he did in favor of universal suffrage for the colored man, and in favor of the early recognition of every Confederate State with a population sufficient to maintain a government, he now declined to offer his substitute. At the request and with the concurrence of his committee the bill of the preceding session was offered with some modifications. These alterations were to strike out all that the bill contained to which gentlemen had raised objection, in that it seemingly authorized the execution of State laws as they existed at the commencement of the rebellion. To make it perfectly clear what the committee intended, they had inserted a provision that the governor should execute only such laws as related to the protection of persons and property; that all laws inconsistent with the proposed enactment, and all laws recognizing the relation of master and slave, should not be enforced. The section which authorized the collection of taxes had been omitted. He preferred not to commit himself to a recognition of the Louisiana and Arkansas governments, unless he could secure what he thought of paramount importance in reorganizing the other States.

"It is very clear to my mind," he asserted, "that no bill providing for the reorganization of loyal State governments in the rebel States can pass this Congress. I am pretty sure that this bill and all the amendments and substitutes offered will fail to command a majority of this House."

The course of debate had shown on the Republican side, he said, so strong an individuality that no compromise could bring them together on the great question of reconstruction. Many on his side were capital leaders in the minority; they were good at pulling down, but not so good at leading majorities and building up. He admitted their utter inability to agree on the subject, and had consented to a conditional recognition of certain State governments because he knew they could be upheld by military power until the rebellion should be crushed. Republicans were so nearly unanimous at the preceding session, he said, that he felt the concessions embodied in his substitute would enable them to agree without much discussion or without consuming the valuable time of the House so late in the session. His remarks not only showed disappointment at the attitude of his party, but clearly revealed the existence of a schism in its ranks.[1]

Henry Winter Davis then rose to state the case for the House. The bill, he said, to which amendments were pending was the same as that which at the preceding session received the assent of both Houses of Congress, with some modifications to suit the tender susceptibilities of gentlemen from Massachusetts: " first, the sixth section, declaring rebel officers not citizens of the United States, has been stricken out; second, the taxation clause has been stricken out; third, the word ' government ' has been inserted before ' trial and punishment,' to meet the refined criticisms of the two gentlemen from Massachusetts who suppose that penal laws would be in force and operative when the penalties were forbidden to be enforced; that discriminating laws could survive the declaration that there should be no discrimination between different persons in trial or punishment. There has been one section added to meet the present aspect of public affairs; that section authorizes the President, instead of pursuing the method prescribed in the bill in reference to the States where military resistance shall have been suppressed, in the event of the legislative authority under the rebellion in any rebel State taking the oath to support the Constitution of the United States, annulling their confiscation laws and ratifying

[1] Globe, Part II., 2 Sess. 38th Cong., pp. 968-969.

AN ATTEMPT TO COMPROMISE

the amendment proposed by this Congress to the Constitution of the United States, before military resistance shall be suppressed in such State, to recognize them as constituting the legal authority of the State, and directing him to report those facts to Congress for its assent and ratification. With these modifications, the bill which is now the test for amendment is the bill which was adopted by this House at the last session."

He need not be at the trouble, he said, to answer the arguments of gentlemen who at the preceding session voted for the bill, and who, in the repose of the intervening period, had criticised in detail the language and, not stopping there, had found in its substance that it violated the principles of republican government and sanctioned the enormities of those laws with which slavery had covered and defiled the statutes of every Southern State.

With increasing severity Mr. Davis proceeded:

That these discoveries should have been made since the vote of last session is quite as remarkable as that they should have been overlooked before that vote. But they were neither overlooked before nor discovered since. The vote was before a pending election. It is the will of the President which has been discovered since.

It is not at all surprising, Mr. Speaker, that the President, having failed to sign the bill passed by the whole body of his supporters by both Houses at the last session of Congress, and having assigned, under pressure of events, but without the authority of law, reasons, good or bad, first for refusing to allow the bill to become a law, and therefore usurping power to execute parts of it as law, while he discarded other parts which interfered with possible electoral votes, those arguments should be found satisfactory to some minds prone to act upon the winking of authority.

The weight of that species of argument I am not able to estimate. It bids defiance to every species of reply. It is that subtle, pervading epidemic of the time that penetrates the closest argument as spirit penetrates matter that diffuses itself with the atmosphere of authority, relaxing the energy of the strong, bending down the upright, diverting just men from the path of rectitude, and substituting the will and favor of power for the will and interest of the people as the rule of legislative action.

. . . .

All I desire now to do is to state the case and predict results from one course or the other. The course of military events seems to indicate that possibly by the 4th of next July, probably by next December, organized, armed rebellion will cease to lift its brazen front in the land. Disasters may intervene; errors or weaknesses may prolong the conflict; the proverbial chances of war may interpose their caprices to defer the national triumph; but events now point to the near approach of the end. But whether sooner or later, whenever it comes, there is one thing that will assuredly accompany it. If this bill do not become a law, when Congress again meets, at our doors, clamorous and dictatorial, will be sixty-five Representatives from the States now in rebellion, and twenty-two Senators, *claiming* admission, and, upon the theory of the honorable gentleman, *entitled* to admission beyond the power of argument to resist it; for peace will have been restored, there will be no armed power but that of the United States; there will be quiet, and votes will be polled under the existing laws of the State, in the gentleman's view. Are you ready to accept that consequence? For if they come to the door of the House they will cross the threshold of the House, and any gentleman who does not know that, or who is so weak or so wild as to suppose that any declaratory resolution adopted by both Houses as a condition precedent can stop that flood, had better put his puny hands across the flood of the flowing Mississippi and say that it shall not enter the Gulf of Mexico.

There are things, gentlemen, that are possible at one time and not possible at another. You can now prevent the rise of the flood, but when it is up you can not stop it. If gentlemen are in favor of meeting that state of things, then do as has been already so distinctly intimated in the course of this debate, vote against this bill in all its aspects; leave the door wide open; let "our brethren of the South," whose bayonets are now pointed at our brothers' hearts, drop their arms, put on the seemly garb of peace, go through the forms of an election, and assert the triumph of their beaten faction under the forms of political authority after the sword has decided against them. I am no prophet, but that is the history of next December if this bill be defeated; and I expect it not to become a law.

But suppose the other course to be pursued; suppose the President sees fit to do what there is not the least reason to suppose that he desires to do; suppose that after he has destroyed the armies in the field he should go further, and do, as I think he ought to do, what the judgment of this country dictates, treat those who hold power in the South as rebels and not as governors or legislators; disperse them from the halls of legislation; expel them from executive mansions, strip them of the emblems of authority, and set to work to hunt out the pliant and supple "Union men," so-called, who have cringed before the storm, but who will be willing to govern their fellow-citizens under the protection of United States bayonets; suppose that the fruitful example of Louisiana shall spread like a mist over all the rest of the southern country, and that Representatives like what Louisiana has sent here, with such a backing of votes as she has given, shall appear here at the doors of this Hall; whose representatives are they? I do not mean to speak of the gentlemen now here from Louisiana in their individual character, but in their political relations to their constituency. Whose representatives are they? In Louisiana they are the representatives of the bayonets of General Banks and the will of the President, as expressed in his secret letter to General Banks. If you admit such representatives, you must admit, on the same basis and under the same influences, Representatives from every State from Texas to Virginia; the common council at Alexandria — which has just sent two Senators to the other House and has ratified the amendment to the Constitution abolishing slavery in all the rest of Virginia, where none of them dare put his portly person — would be entitled to send ten Representatives here and two Senators to speak for the indomitable "Old Dominion." If the rebel Representatives are not here in December next you will have here servile tools of the Executive who will embarrass your legislation, humble your Congress, degrade the name of republican government for two years, and then the natural majority of the South, rising indignantly against that humiliating insult, will swamp you here with rebel Representatives and be your masters. These are their alternatives and there is no middle ground.

To Mr. Eliot's objection the Maryland member replied that provisional governors " are appointed *now without law*, and all we propose is that they shall be *under the responsibility of law and subject to the control and confirmation of the Senate.*" Having in mind this condition and the Executive appointments to judicial places in Louisiana, Mr. Davis added:

Sir, when I came into Congress ten years ago, this was a Government of law. I have lived to see it a Government of personal will. Congress has dwindled from a power to dictate law and the policy of the Government to a commission to audit accounts and to appropriate moneys to enable the Executive to execute his will and not ours. I would stop at the boundaries of law. When I look around for them I seem to be in a waste; they are as clean gone as the division fences of Virginia estates from here to the Rapidan.

After explaining the efforts of Mr. Ashley and himself to remove the objectionable features of the bill as pointed out by the two members from Massachusetts [Messrs. Dawes and Eliot] he again criticised both with some severity, and continued:

Sir, my successor may vote as he pleases. But when I leave this Hall there shall be no vote from the third congressional district of Maryland that recognizes anything but the body and mass of the people of any State as entitled to govern them, and to govern the people that I represent. And they who may wish to substitute one tenth, or any other fractional minority, for that great power of the people to govern, may take, and shall take, the odium. Ay! I shall brand it upon them that in the middle of the nineteenth century, in the only free Republic that the world knows, where alone the principles of popular government are the rules of authority, they have gone to the dark ages for their models, reviving the wretched examples of the most odious governments that the world has ever seen, and propose to stain the national triumph by creating a wretched, low, vulgar, corrupt, and cowardly oligarchy to govern the freemen of the United States — the national arms to guaranty and enforce their oppressions. Not by my vote, sir; not by my vote!

If the majority of the people will not recognize the authority of the Constitution of the United States, what does the gentleman say who proposes these declaratory resolutions? That they shall come here without it? No, sir; but I would govern them for a thousand years first by the supreme authority of the Constitution which they have defied and will not acknowledge. And govern them how? Not by the uncontrolled will of this or any other President that ever lived, George Washington included. I would govern them by the laws that in the hours of their sanity they enacted, unaltered excepting so far as the progress of events require that they should be altered; to the extent that we have proposed to alter them in our bill, and no further. I leave their own rules for their government, make the President appoint, under his official and public responsibility, the officers who are to execute them; and if they do not like to be governed in that way, let us trust that the prodigal will come one day to his senses, and humbly kneeling before the Constitution that he has vainly defied, swear before Almighty God that he will again be true to it.

That is my remedy for the grievance. That is what we propose. . . .[1]

[1] Globe, Part II., 2 Sess. 38th Cong., pp. 969-970.

AN ATTEMPT TO COMPROMISE 311

Though not his last word on the subject of reconstruction, this was the last great speech of Mr. Davis in Congress on the question of restoring political power to the rebellious States. His alliance with Stevens, a somewhat unnatural union, had brought him only disaster. As noticed in the preceding chapter, he had been defeated for renomination in his district. It is thought that disappointment hastened somewhat his early death, which occurred toward the close of the year, December 30, 1865. Though a touch of pathos may be discerned in his concluding remarks, his was not the craven spirit that was ready, in the words of Edgerton, to kiss the hand that smote him.

Representative Mallory, of Kentucky, on his motion to lay the bill and amendments on the table, called for the yeas and nays. The question being taken was decided in the affirmative; 91 voting to lay the bill and amendments on the table; 64 were opposed, and 27 did not vote.[1] The Democratic members were a unit against the measure, and in a body voted to lay it on the table.

The defeat of Davis now appeared complete, but the struggle was not to be abandoned without another effort. On the following day, February 22, 1865, Mr. Wilson from the Committee on the Judiciary reported House Bill No. 740, to establish the supremacy of the Constitution in the insurrectionary States, with a substitute which provided that neither the people nor the legislature of any rebellious State should elect Representatives or Senators to Congress until the President had proclaimed that armed hostility to the United States within such State had ceased; nor until the people of such State had adopted a constitution not repugnant to the Constitution and laws of the United States; nor until by law of Congress such State had been declared entitled to representation in the Congress of the United States.

[1] Globe, Part II., 2 Sess. 38th Cong., pp. 970-971.

The authority for this bill he professed to find in the fourth section of Article I. of the Constitution, which reads as follows:

> The Times, Places and Manner of holding elections for Senators and Representatives shall be prescribed in each State by the Legislature thereof; but the Congress may, at any time, by law, make or alter such regulations, except as to the Places of choosing Senators.

Mr. Wilson was somewhat embarrassed in defending his bill. Dawes and Mallory exposed its weakness, and Representative Kernan, of New York, believed it would put it in the power of the Executive to say whether States should be represented in Congress. Fernando Wood observed that neither by that bill nor any other could either House of Congress be deprived of the right to pass upon the election, returns and qualifications of members.[1]

Mr. Ashley at this point moved to amend the substitute offered by the Committee on the Judiciary by striking out all after the enacting clause and inserting the reconstruction bill that was tabled the day before. When a point of order was raised against its introduction the Speaker said that there was an important amendment; the word "white" having been inserted before the expression "male citizen," thus restricting the class to be enrolled by the United States marshal. Mr. Kelley would amend it by striking out the word "white." To this the Ohio member had no personal objection; indeed, he was abreast of Mr. Kelley in the matter of the suffrage: the only restriction he would impose being that of intelligence. Ashley appears, however, to have regarded himself as but the mouthpiece of his committee by whose authority he had only a few months before inserted a provision in his reconstruction bill to recognize the Louisiana and Arkansas governments, though he expressly declared on a subsequent occasion that he was opposed to such recognition.

[1] Globe, Part II., 2 Sess. 38th Cong., pp. 997-1001.

By a vote of 80 to 65 the bill and its amendments was again laid on the table. Thirty-seven members abstained from voting; fourteen Republicans voted with the Democrats.[1] This action was taken on the 22d of February, 1865; the session closed on the 4th of March following without any further attempt to pass the bill. Before the vote was taken Ashley stated his sentiments candidly. He wanted a record made on the question. " I do not expect," said he, " to pass this bill now. At the next session, when a new Congress fresh from the people shall have assembled, with the nation and its Representatives far in advance of the present Congress, I hope to pass even a better bill. Sir, I know that our loyal people will never be guilty of the infamy of inviting the blacks to unite with them in fighting our battles, and after our triumph — a triumph which we never could have achieved but for their generous coöperation and aid — deny those loyal blacks political rights while consenting that pardoned but unrepentant white rebels shall again be clothed with the entire political power of these States."[2] The desire to obtain negro suffrage explains the inconsistent course of Representative Ashley throughout these debates.

By a singular method of abridging history Mr. Blaine in his *Twenty Years of Congress* passes without observation the attempt to revive the " pocketed " bill, though it was during its discussion that there was for the first time unmistakably revealed the existence of a schism in the Republican party.

[1] Globe, Part II., 2 Sess. 38th Cong., p. 1002.
[2] Ibid.

IX

THE ELECTORAL VOTE OF LOUISIANA

A PRECEDING chapter has noticed the result of the Presidential election of 1864. It was thought proper, however, to reserve for separate treatment the various questions presented by the participation in that contest of Louisiana and Tennessee, two States reorganized under Executive auspices. On the introduction by Mr. Wilson of a joint resolution declaring certain named States not entitled to representation in the Electoral College, the entire subject came before the House soon after the meeting of Congress in December.

The proposed resolution was read twice and referred to the Committee on the Judiciary. On the following day, December 20, 1864, it was reported, ordered to be printed and recommitted. Under the operation of the previous question it passed the House on January 30 succeeding. Its preamble, which was favorably considered at the same time, declared that "the inhabitants and local authorities of the States of Virginia, North Carolina, South Carolina, Georgia, Florida, Alabama, Mississippi, Louisiana, Texas, Arkansas, and Tennessee rebelled against the Government of the United States, and have continued in a state of armed rebellion for more than three years, and were in a state of armed rebellion on the 8th of November, 1864."

The joint resolution provided that these States were not entitled to representation in the Electoral College for the choice of President and Vice-President for the term of office

THE ELECTORAL VOTE OF LOUISIANA 315

beginning March 4, 1865, and that no electoral votes from them, relative to the choice of said officers for that term, should be received or counted.[1]

In a modified form the measure subsequently passed the Senate, which proposed that there be stricken from the preamble the words " and were in such condition of armed rebellion for more than three years," and that there be inserted in lieu thereof, " and were in such condition on the 8th day of November, 1864, that no valid election for electors of President and Vice-President, according to the Constitution and laws thereof, was held therein on said day." In this amendment the House promptly concurred, February 6, 1865.

In the Senate, February 1, Mr. Trumbull asked consideration of the measure inasmuch as the electoral votes were to be counted a week later. When the amendment was under discussion, Senator Ten Eyck, of New Jersey, moved to strike out the word "Louisiana" in the preamble, and added that it was a matter of history that the State had reorganized, or at least attempted to do so, and in the opinion of many, and perhaps most, of her loyal citizens had reorganized as a State. It was matter of history that they had elected State officers and a State Legislature; that they had elected members to a constitutional convention and framed a new constitution for that State; that the Legislature passed a law authorizing the choice of electors for President and Vice-President of the United States in the last Presidential election, and that such electors had met and cast their votes. "Under these circumstances," said Mr. Ten Eyck, " I think there is a striking distinction between the State of Virginia and the State of Louisiana." The object of his amendment, he stated, was to afford opportunity to a loyal people who had suffered all the horrors of the rebellion, who had got the better of it, and put it under foot, of coming back and resuming their place in the

[1] Globe, Part I., 2 Sess. 38th Cong., p. 505.

councils of the nation. He did not then desire to make any further remarks.[1]

Senator Trumbull then took up the discussion of Ten Eyck's amendment to the amendment. The electoral votes, he said, were to be opened and canvassed a week later, and it was known to all that no rules for action had ever been adopted in that joint convention. He recalled the fact that in 1856 there arose a question over the counting of the electoral vote of Wisconsin. A severe snow storm had prevented the electors from meeting at their State capital on the day fixed by law, and it was not until the day following that they were able to cast their votes for President and Vice-President. The question was not then decided, for Buchanan and Breckenridge were the successful candidates in either event, and were so declared.

He believed a similar question was likely to arise when the electoral votes would be counted on February 8. It was a matter of public notoriety, he continued, that several of the States included in the President's proclamation of 1861, Arkansas, Tennessee and Louisiana, had cast electoral votes. There was a question as to their authority to do so in consequence of the insurrection which prevailed there on the 8th of November, when the election took place, and the House of Representatives had passed the joint resolution declaring that the votes of certain named States should not be counted. The motion of the Senator from New Jersey would have the effect of counting the vote of Louisiana. " If we decide to receive the vote from Louisiana," declared Mr. Trumbull, " it will be a decision by the Congress of the United States that the State of Louisiana was in such a condition as to vote for President and Vice-President on the 8th of November last."

The alteration proposed by the Committee on the Judiciary, said he, was for the purpose of avoiding any such committal

[1] Globe, Part I., 2 Sess. 38th Cong., p. 533.

on the subject as the motion of the Senator from New Jersey brought up. If the preamble " is adopted and the resolution passed, Congress will not have decided whether Louisiana is in the Union or out of the Union, whether she is a State or not a State." It would be time enough, he believed, to decide that question when it was presented to the Senate. No statement of facts, he asserted in reply to Senator Howe, accompanied the joint resolution from the Committee on the Judiciary; it was a House resolution, and no report accompanied it from the House Committee.

A large part of Louisiana, he added, was on the 8th of November preceding in the possession of a hostile force. In a very considerable portion of the State there was no opportunity to vote for President or Vice-President, and it might be a very serious question whether, when half a State or the third of a State was overrun by an enemy, an election held under such circumstances and under the auspices of Federal guns would be an election which would authorize the Congress of the United States, when in joint convention it came to canvass the votes for President and Vice-President, to count ballots cast under such circumstances.

In acting upon the resolution he did not mean to commit the Senate one way or another relative to the organization which had been formed in Louisiana. A decision to strike out Louisiana would be to decide that her electoral vote would be received and that on November 8th there was a State government there. That he did not believe. No evidence, he asserted, had been submitted to show how many votes were cast.

Pursuant to an act of Congress the President had declared the inhabitants of Louisiana in insurrection against the United States. That proclamation had not been recalled. " Sir," concluded Mr. Trumbull, " until there shall be some action by Congress recognizing the organization which has been set up in Louisiana, we ought not in my judgment to count electoral votes from the State." Whether Congress would recognize it, he could not say; that had not yet been done, and, until it had been, the electoral vote ought not to be counted. He hoped, therefore, that Ten Eyck's amendment would not prevail.[1]

Mr. Ten Eyck said it was with great diffidence that he undertook to propose an amendment to the resolution; but he held the doctrine that these commonwealths having taken up their lot and part with their sister States when admitted into the Union were not legally out of it; their governments had been in abeyance; they had been overrun by the feet of hostile armies, and many of their citizens, by usurpation and in violation of their duty to their fellow-men and to their God, had attempted to carry these States out of the Union.

That being his opinion, whenever these States, by the aid of the General Government, or by the efforts of their own people, or by the act of both combined, reëstablished themselves, or set their State governments in action anew, and had commenced again to revolve in their old orbits, he should feel it his duty, so far as he was concerned, to extend to them all the privileges and all the rights to which the loyal people of a loyal State were entitled at the hands of their sister States, whether upon the floor of the Senate or anywhere else. It was to exclude Louisiana from the operation of the resolution that he made his motion. As to those States manifestly in the condition described in the preamble there was propriety in passing the resolution.

In reply to an observation of the chairman of the Judiciary Committee, that the majority desired to avoid a committal on this subject, Mr. Ten Eyck suggested that it would not, perhaps, be amiss to insist that a committal should not be had

[1] Globe, Part I., 2 Sess. 38th Cong., pp. 534-535.

against the interest of the State any more than in its favor, and if his amendment involved the question whether Louisiana was in a condition to perform all the functions of a State government and to appoint State officers and Senators and members of the national House of Representatives, the same question was involved in the resolution and it would be determined against her if the joint resolution passed as it stood; for that would decide that Louisiana was in a state of rebellion such as to deprive her of all the powers, rights and privileges of a member of the Union. He was not prepared to go to that extent.

From various memorials, papers and documents that had come into possession of the Senate, he continued, and were published by its order, as well as from information derived from other sources, it appeared that nearly, if not quite, a year before an election for State officers was held in Louisiana and a very large number of votes cast, about two thirds or approximating two thirds of the largest number that had been cast at any former election for State officers. Trumbull interrupted to remark that no such statements had been received by the committee. In those localities which voted, perhaps two thirds of the former vote had been cast, but not two thirds of that cast in the entire State. Ten Eyck replied that the vote was 11,414; it was alleged that a large number of former voters had entered the rebel army and a great many had been killed. He might be in error concerning the whole vote of the State. All these elections were free and uninterrupted and without the interference of any military power whatever. A person on the ground had declared that "no effort whatever was made on the part of the military authorities to influence the citizens of the State, either in the selection of candidates or in the election of officers, and that the direct influence of the Government of the United States was less in Louisiana than in the elections probably of any State of the Union; that the officers representing the Government, both civil and military, were divided, so far as they entertained or expressed opinions, on the question of candidates and upon the policy pursued in the organization of the government." If any military interference was exerted it was in aid of the loyal people, and the civil authority was not at all in subordination to the military.

In view of the invitation that had been held out by the Government to all the loyal people of those States to come back and to endeavor to organize themselves anew and, when they had gained sufficient strength, to present themselves civilly and quietly at the ballot-box to choose their own State officers and to choose delegates to form a new State constitution, and when they claim the rights of other States, are they to be met by the plea that upon certain out-bounds of the State there may still be heard the tread of rebel feet? It appeared by all the testimony that the population, the business and the property of Louisiana were confined to the cities and regions of country immediately bordering upon the river, and that the residue of the State was very sparsely settled indeed. That portion not submerged was used for planting purposes. The wealth and population of the State were confined within a small space and this contracted area was chiefly under control of the United States. The Presidential electors were chosen by the State Legislature, and he did not think that method legal. That is why the vote cast in the election did not appear in the testimony submitted to the Committee on the Judiciary.

As to the withdrawal by the President of his proclamation declaring the inhabitants of Louisiana in a state of insurrection, if that were the test either the present incumbent or his successor could keep the loyal people of those States from returning to the Union during the remainder of his administration, and, if reëlected, for the following term. This

THE ELECTORAL VOTE OF LOUISIANA

even if every soul within the State were loyal and anxious to return.[1]

Mr. Howe announced his intention of voting for the amendment of Ten Eyck, though for reasons very different from those which influenced the New Jersey Senator. His support would not be controlled by the number of citizens who participated in the choice of electors. " I am governed," said he, " by the single fact that a statute of your own, existing at the time of that election, declared that the people of that State had the right to choose electors, and that certain of them did participate in making that choice. The Senator from Illinois [Trumbull] says but a small portion of the people of the State participated in that choice. Your statute said that all might. Does the refusal of a large portion or a small portion of the people of a State to participate in an election deprive the minority, if you please, no matter how small, of their right under your statute?" Besides Louisiana he understood that two other States had made choice of electors. He would vote for an amendment to strike them out of the resolution also. [2]

Trumbull argued that a mere refusal to count the electoral vote of Louisiana did not settle the question against the existing organization. Wisconsin had a right to vote in 1856, and nobody supposed otherwise; but many opposed the counting of that vote. The State organization may be perfect and yet its electoral vote rejected. If the Senate had refused to count Wisconsin's vote, it would not therefore have decided that there was no such State. Ten Eyck promptly indicated the weakness of this reasoning by pointing out that the preamble of the pending resolution declared Louisiana in such a condition of rebellion that no election could be had. Senator Trumbull then put the case of a foreign enemy having such

[1] Globe, Part I., 2 Sess. 38th Cong., pp. 535-536.
[2] Ibid., p. 536.

possession of Louisiana that no election could be held throughout the State, and asked whether the Senator from New Jersey would count the electoral vote of Louisiana when not twenty men could have assembled in the State and voted for President and Vice-President. If the Senate refused to count her vote under such circumstances, would it decide that the organization of the State of Louisiana was not to be recognized, and was repudiated? Whether the organization established in Louisiana was a valid one was a question which would come before the Senate when they inquired into the right to seats of those gentlemen who had presented themselves as Senators.

Replying to an assertion of Senator Howe, who was not in his seat, Mr. Trumbull said he would like to see the statute which gave Louisiana a right to vote in the Presidential election of 1864. If any such existed it would be repealed by the act of Congress which empowered the President to declare the people of certain commonwealths in a state of insurrection.

In referring to the objection of Mr. Ten Eyck that the President, if he desired, could keep a State out during his entire administration, Senator Trumbull observed that it was only necessary for Congress to repeal the act upon which the proclamation was based and then the proclamation itself would fall.

The refusal of a State to vote when she had an opportunity to do so, said Mr. Trumbull, would be no reason for excluding her electoral vote; but the people of Louisiana did not have an opportunity unawed by hostile armies and unrestrained by military authority to vote for President and Vice-President. This, he said, was not the real point at issue; the question for the Senate to consider and determine was whether the Legislature of Louisiana was a lawful assembly, for it was by that body that electors of President and Vice-President were chosen in the election of 1864.

Mr. Trumbull believed that on November 8 about three fourths of the area of Louisiana was in possession of the Confederates. No person could have voted within that jurisdiction. Eleven or twelve thousand was the largest vote ever cast under these organizations; while the vote of the State, when all her legal voters had the privilege of going to the polls, was more than 60,000.

Mr. Ten Eyck stated that 51,000 was the highest vote ever cast, and that the average was but 34,000. Trumbull believed the Senate should concur in the House resolution and that it need not commit itself one way or the other on the Louisiana organization. The counting of the electoral vote, which pressed for settlement, should soon be determined.[1]

Mr. Harris thought the question of counting the votes could be disposed of without committing the Senate or deciding the matter of admitting Senators, as was done in the case of Wisconsin in 1856. "If we count the votes of these States," said he, "the number of votes for Mr. Lincoln and Mr. Johnson will be so many; if we reject these votes the number of votes will be so many; and in either case these candidates are elected." By this or a similar declaration, the phraseology of which was suggested by the precedent of 1856, the question could be passed over. He asked the chairman of the Committee on the Judiciary why Congress had not the power to declare that New York should not vote. He opposed the preamble because he did not believe it true, and he denied that the local authorities in Louisiana, Arkansas and Tennessee were in rebellion on the 8th of November preceding.

When, on February 2, Senator Harris resumed his remarks he observed that the question as to the power of Congress to legislate in relation to the counting of votes for President and Vice-President was not considered by the committee.

[1] Globe, Part I., 2 Sess. 38th Cong., pp. 535-537.

Reflection had led him to doubt the competence of Congress to legislate on the subject. That body could fix the time for choosing electors and specify the time when they should perform the functions of their office. That, he contended, was the extent of the power of Congress over the subject. He could find no authority in the Constitution, however, which empowered Congress to pass a law, for the resolution amounted to that, excluding any votes returned to the Vice-President. Even if Congress had the authority it was inexpedient to exercise it. Why should such extreme power be exercised when the necessity did not exist? The result, it was conceded, would be the same whether Congress counted the votes of Louisiana, Tennessee and Arkansas or not. The power was not contained in the Constitution. Those States specified in the preamble did certainly rebel, but that Louisiana, Arkansas and Tennessee were in that condition on November 8 was at least open to question.[1]

Senator Doolittle believed that Congress by legislation could provide in advance for the manner of counting electoral votes; but that, he insisted, was very different from passing a law which declared certain votes null and void after they had been cast. That would be retroactive legislation. He doubted the power of Congress over the subject of counting the electoral votes, beyond that contained in the Constitution.

"The Congress," he continued, quoting the fourth clause of section one of the second article, "may determine the time of choosing the electors, and the day on which they shall give their votes; which day shall be the same throughout the United States." Pursuant to this provision Congress passed the act of January 23, 1845. It was not for the president of the Senate to open such as Congress told him to open, but he should "open all the certificates" which were sent to him, "and the votes shall then be counted." Here, said the Sena-

[1] Globe, Part I., 2 Sess. 38th Cong., pp. 537, 548.

tor, arose the grave question whether the president of the joint convention was made the sole judge as to what votes should be counted. The question practically came up in 1856, but it was not then necessary to decide it, and it was waived as not being essential to the result. On the present occasion, 1865, it was the same, the result of the election would not be affected by the matter of counting or not counting the votes of Tennessee and Louisiana; but it was not necessary for Congress to assert a doctrine which in some future time might be the very destruction of the Government, namely, " That a political party in Congress can decide that certain votes of certain States shall be canceled and others shall be received. It will never do to set that precedent." It would be time enough, he said in conclusion, to meet the question when it came up in the joint convention.[1]

Mr. Hale said that he had foreseen the difficulty and at the preceding session had introduced a joint resolution directing in advance what should be done; but the pressure of other business, certainly not more important, prevented action thereon. If the result of the Presidential election had depended upon the votes of Louisiana, Tennessee and Arkansas would the party have submitted against which their votes had been cast? The rebellion then existing was caused, he believed, by nothing at all in comparison with such a question.

He denied the assertion of Senator Doolittle that Congress had no power over the counting of the electoral votes. Suppose, he argued, that, contrary to the constitutional provision, a member of Congress or any officer of the Federal Government holding an office of profit or trust happened to be an elector, would not Congress have power to say that such vote of Federal officer should not be counted?

The framers of the Constitution, he declared, made the most ample provision for just such a case. That instrument

[1] Globe, Part I., 2 Sess. 38th Cong., pp. 548-549.

confers on Congress the power " to make all laws which shall be necessary and proper for carrying into execution the foregoing powers, and all other powers vested by this Constitution in the Government of the United States." Was not the power to choose a President one vested in the Government of the United States?

Mr. Hale contended that then, when action by Congress would not affect the result of the election, was the time to settle the principle, and the precedent could be pointed to showing the action and sentiment of Congress at a time when there was no inducement to anything but an honest and straightforward decision of the case.

Suppose, he went on, that Nevada while in the territorial condition had grown restless under her provincial state and had sent certificates signed by her electors, would Congress have no authority to say whether they should be counted? In Washington's first election the vote of New York State was not counted. Now her Senator, Mr. Harris, doubted the competence of Congress either to exclude, or refuse to count, the votes of a State.[1]

Mr. Doolittle objected to being quoted quite so strongly as to say that Congress had no power over this subject. Congress had power over the subject, but that power was limited. When the Constitution says that the States shall do certain things, such as directing the appointment of electors, that is a limitation on the power of Congress over the matter. What he maintained was that after the ballots had been cast there was no power in Congress as a legislative body to declare certain votes valid or invalid. The tribunal to which the question was referred was the president of the Senate presiding over the joint convention of both Houses. The power in the first instance was with that officer to count or not to

[1] Globe, Part I., 2 Sess. 38th Cong., pp. 549-550.

count the votes. He was to decide whether they were from States or from Territories.[1]

Senator Trumbull maintained that so far from being empowered to decide disputes, the president of the joint convention was not authorized to even count the votes. In the practice of the Government the Vice-President had never since the days of Washington counted the votes. The Constitution says that he shall " open all the certificates and the votes shall then be counted." It does not state by whom, but it does state that Congress has power to pass all laws necessary to carry the instrument into effect. Congress, he said, had exercised such power from the beginning.

There was no legal difference, he asserted, between South Carolina and Louisiana. An individual trading in the latter State, except under a particular license, could be taken up and tried as a felon, and yet " we are told that we cannot determine by act of Congress that they cannot elect a President for us!"

Mr. Trumbull contended that if a question arose upon the counting of the vote of any State, the joint convention could not decide upon it. The bodies would have to separate and, by passing a concurrent resolution, each act independently. There was no popular election, he said, in the State of Louisiana, but a body assuming to be its Legislature had appointed electors of President and Vice-President. He did not know whether the new constitution of Louisiana authorized that method.

The purpose of the Senate, he continued, in amending the joint resolution of the House was to avoid declaring that the people of Louisiana were on the 8th of November in a state of armed insurrection. The preamble, even as it was amended, did not wholly satisfy him; he believed that he

[1] Globe, Part I., 2 Sess. 38th Cong., p. 550.

would be better pleased if it was altogether omitted. He was informed that Tennessee had sent a vote as well as Louisiana. The object of the committee was to settle the question before the meeting of the joint convention.[1]

Senator Collamer thought that any law honestly intended to carry into effect the provisions of the Constitution could not be objected to. It could if it opposed or was inconsistent with that instrument. There had been legislation on the subject and additional action by Congress might be necessary. For the resolution he offered the following substitute:

> That the people of no State, the inhabitants whereof have been declared in a state of insurrection by virtue of the fifth section of the act entitled "An act further to provide for the collection of duties on imports, and for other purposes," approved July 13, 1861, shall be regarded as empowered to elect electors of President and Vice-President of the United States until said condition of insurrection shall cease and be so declared by virtue of a law of the United States.[2]

By Mr. Howard the question was regarded as of very great importance not only as a precedent for the future, but "as indicating the opinion of Congress on the subject, to use a familiar term, of 'reconstruction,' or rather the rights of the States in rebellion." He believed it clear that the Vice-President was to open the certificates and that the duty of counting devolved upon the two Houses thus assembled. The act of 1792 seemed so to construe the Constitution.

"The power of counting the votes," he asserted, "and of rejecting votes which are void for fraud or illegality, is, under the Constitution, in the joint convention thus assembled." There was no doubt about it, he declared, because the Houses convened for a great and protective purpose; they were exercising the tutelary authority of the people, in protecting the nation from the imposition of false and fraudulent ballots and

[1] Globe, Part I., 2 Sess. 38th Cong., pp. 550-551.
[2] Ibid., pp. 551-552.

certificates. The inhabitants of the States mentioned in the proclamation of the President were public enemies; therefore they had no political rights under the United States.

"I look upon this measure as necessary," continued Mr. Howard, "as one form in which the sense of Congress ought to be expressed against any hasty attempt to readmit these rebellious States into the Union." For one, he would require the loyalty and friendliness of a majority of the people of the rebellious States to be proved before readmitting any of them. "The theory of our Government," he went on, "is different from that of almost every other government on earth. It is that the will of the majority shall govern; in common phrase, the majority of the people, but practically the majority of the voting population."

In conclusion he declared that it was "the bounden duty of Congress, in every case, to keep out of the Union every one of these eleven seceded States until, in pursuance of our laws, passed or to be passed, it has become perfectly evident to us that there is in such a State a clear, absolute majority of its voting population friendly to the Government of the United States, and willing to proceed in the discharge of their functions as a State; and, until that is done, you may be perfectly sure, so long as I hold a seat in this body, my vote will be given against any such proposal. I never will consent to admit into this Union a State a majority of whose people are hostile and unfriendly to the Government of my country. I prefer to hold them in tutelage (for that is really the word) one year, five years, ten years, even twenty years, rather than run the risk of a repetition of this rebellion, which has cost us so much blood and treasure."[1]

Ten Eyck, considering Louisiana as the strongest case, mentioned it in preference to Arkansas or Tennessee, and, from a paper furnished by a gentleman who was familiar with the

[1] Globe, Part I., 2 Sess. 38th Cong., pp. 553-554.

situation there, was able to state that "eleven thousand four hundred and fourteen votes were polled at this election. The average vote for ten years prior to the rebellion in these parishes was fifteen to sixteen thousand." The same parishes cast their highest vote, 21,000, in 1860. He expressed a wish to save Tennessee also from the effect of the resolution, and declared that he did not see how the Vice-President-elect, an alien, could preside over the Senate. Further, a vote in favor of the resolution prejudged the case of the Senators and the legality of the Legislature which sent them.[1]

Senator Pomeroy did not suppose that States unrepresented in either House could be represented in the Electoral College. He criticised the correctness of the preamble so far as it related to Arkansas. The rebel governor as well as the rebel legislature, he said, was driven out long ago.

"Arkansas," he continued, "has not voted at all in the Presidential election. . . . Under the instructions and impressions that the members from Arkansas received here last session, they distinctly understood that States not represented in either branch of Congress would have no right to vote at the Presidential election. They returned to Arkansas and so reported, and they never had any election; there are no votes here from that State. They have been in suspense awaiting the action of Congress." The resolution itself did not, of course, affect Arkansas, for there were no votes from that State to be counted.[2]

Mr. Cowan, probably adopting a hint dropped by Senator Ten Eyck, noticed the fact that the proclamation of January 1, 1863, exempted from its operations thirteen named parishes of Louisiana because no rebellion existed in them. The validity of that decree had been recognized, while the proclamation of December 8 following invited the people of

[1] Globe, Part I., 2 Sess. 38th Cong., pp. 554-555.
[2] Ibid., pp. 555-556.

Louisiana and other States to resume their rights. The question was whether the arrangements of the President were to be executed in good faith.

It was the duty of the Executive, he continued, " to put down this rebellion, to relieve the people from its oppression, and to restore them precisely to where they were when the rebellion found them. If that is done, in ten days after his proclamation, *eo instanti,* the people resume their rights and functions; and in this case I understand they are not only in possession of the right, but are actually in the enjoyment of it, having a regularly organized government with all the machinery necessary and proper to a government." He believed that men and money were furnished the President to sustain State governments and make them supreme within their own limits.

Concluding this portion of his remarks he said: " Mr. President, this involves a direct conflict between the Legislative and Executive bodies of this Government, and at this time I am of opinion that we cannot afford to enter into that conflict." [1]

Senator Powell, of Kentucky, said that when it was asserted that General Banks did not interfere in the Louisiana election the statement was not true, for there could be no greater interference in the elections of a State than to alter the qualifications of voters. He declared himself " opposed to admitting on this floor persons who are elected under the bayonet influence in any way whatever. I very well know that there was no free expression of the people of Louisiana in these elections. I know that they but obeyed the behests of the military, whatever commanders may say about it. . . . But for its tragical results upon republican liberty it [the election] would be the greatest of farces."

The Kentucky member believed that the rebellious States

[1] Globe, Part I., 2 Sess. 38th Cong., p. 556.

were still in the Union, and when a majority of the people in any of them returned to loyalty, when their governments were organized, their Senators and Representatives should be received.[1]

Cowan, entering again into the discussion, said: " We are bound by the Constitution to preserve the Union and to preserve the rights of the people under the Union; not merely the rights of a majority, but the rights of the people, of all the people, and of any number of the people however small. What are we to do? A minority of the people come forward and say, ' If you aid us for a while we can preserve this State and keep her in the Union.' ' But no,' according to the doctrine advanced here, ' there must be a majority of you before we can recognize you as in the Union.' . . . That will be very poor encouragement for the loyal men of the rebel States to try and bring back their people to reason." The Pennsylvania Senator was one of the few who adhered to the opinion that the masses of men at the South were not disloyal; that it was a leaders' rebellion.[2]

Sherman, of Ohio, described the scene in the joint convention of 1856 when Humphrey Marshall wanted to speak and Mr. Mason, president of the Senate, refused to recognize him. Speaker Banks, however, did recognize him; upon this, Mason and others left the convention, and confusion ensued; that, Mr. Sherman believed, was a reason why the resolution should be disposed of.[3]

Mr. Wade said: " About a year ago Congress, anticipating that such questions as this might arise, in my judgment very wisely framed a law and passed it through both branches with the hope of settling this matter in advance. That law was made upon great deliberation in both bodies of Congress;

---

[1] Globe, Part I., 2 Sess. 38th Cong., pp. 557-558.
[2] Ibid., p. 558.
[3] Ibid.

it received a very large vote in each House. It was very proper in my judgment that Congress should fix the matter then, because everybody could anticipate that a question of the most serious danger to the Republic might arise in the then approaching Presidential election, which might endanger the stability of our Union, and which might under certain circumstances precipitate these Northern States into a civil war. Apprehending that such a question might arise, Congress wisely, in my judgment, provided against it; but the President did not agree with them, and he vetoed their bill, leaving the question open with all its dangers, which, thank God, have not arisen."

The President, added Mr. Wade, chose to pocket the bill, "and, as I suppose, he did it in defence of the proclamation which he had put forth, declaring that whenever a tenth part of the people of a State would come back, he would recognize them as the State and as part and parcel of this Government — a proposition which, with all my respect for the Chief Magistrate, I am bound to say is the most absurd and impracticable that ever haunted the imagination of a statesman. . . . And I must say of that proclamation of the President that it was the most contentious, the most anarchical, the most dangerous proposition that was ever put forth for the government of a free people.

". . . I had a conversation with the now Vice-President-elect of the United States on that subject, and with other gentlemen on the Union side in the Southern States, and I do not know of one of them who was not filled with the deepest apprehension that if this principle should prevail they would be annihilated by the nine tenths." [1]

As to permitting citizens of Louisiana who were serving in the army and navy to vote in the election of February 22, 1864, Mr. Doolittle observed: "We have done the same thing

[1] Globe, Part I., 2 Sess. 38th Cong., pp. 576-582.

in Wisconsin, in Ohio, in Pennsylvania, in New York, all growing out of exigencies which have occurred since this rebellion began, passing laws, authorizing men, although in the Army of the United States, still to take part in the elections, providing that they should not be deprived of their rights of citizenship because they had enlisted in the Army to bear all the sacrifices which are necessary to defend their country in this struggle. And, sir, I maintain that there was nothing wrong in this."[1] Even if it were wrong, only 808 soldiers, he asserted, participated in the election. A separate registry of this vote had been kept by General Banks. So far, therefore, from being a military usurpation it was an attempt of the President to lay down the military power. This he was endeavoring in good faith to do.

After a somewhat excited defence of the Administration by Senator Doolittle, and severe attacks on both President Lincoln and General Banks by Mr. Powell and others, Ten Eyck's motion to strike out Louisiana from the joint resolution was defeated, February 3, 1865, by a vote of 22 to 16.[2] Lane's motion immediately after to strike out the preamble, which would leave only an unmeaning resolution, was lost by a vote of 30 nays to 12 yeas.[3]

Senator Harris proposed to amend Mr. Collamer's substitute by resolving, " That it is inexpedient to determine the question as to the validity of the election of electors in the said States of Tennessee and Louisiana, and that in counting the votes for President and Vice-President the result be declared as it would stand if the votes of the said States were counted, and also as it would stand if the votes of the said States were excluded, such result being the same in either case." By nearly the same majority this proposition also was voted down without much discussion.[4]

[1] Globe, Part I., 2 Sess. 38th Cong., p. 575. [2] Ibid., pp. 576-582.
[3] Ibid., p. 582. [4] Ibid., p. 583.

Reverdy Johnson, who favored the House resolution as amended by the Committee on the Judiciary, did not think the rebellious States were out of the Union, and asserted that there was no power in any branch of Government to declare war against a State. Referring to the Whiskey Insurrection in Washington's administration, he said that Congress passed no act declaring it at an end. The President declared it. It ended itself. The insurrectionists laid down their arms, and expressed willingness to yield obedience to the United States; that ended the insurrection and disbanded the Federal forces, "and that happening, the State of Pennsylvania, every part of it, stood exactly in the relation, for all purposes, in which the State and every part of it stood before the insurrection was commenced."[1]

Mr. Collamer said that the real point in Senator Johnson's argument was whether Congress had anything to do in the reorganization or reëstablishment of those States. Mr. Johnson, continued the Senator from Vermont, seemed to think not. On resuming his speech, February 4, 1865, he inquired: "When will, and when ought, Congress to admit these States as being in their normal condition? When they see that they furnish evidence of it. It is not enough that they stop their hostility and are repentant. They should present fruits meet for repentance. They should furnish to us by their actions some evidence that the condition of loyalty and obedience is their true condition again, and Congress must pass upon it; otherwise we have no securities. It is not enough that they lay down their arms. Our courts should be established, our taxes should be gathered, our duties should be collected in those States; and before they come here to perform their duties or privileges again as members of this Union, they should place themselves in an attitude showing to us that they have

[1] Globe, Part I., 2 Sess. 38th Cong., p. 585.

truly taken that position, and we should pass upon it; and I insist that the President, making peace with them, if you please, by surceasing military operations, does not alter their status until Congress passes upon it. . . . I believe that when reëstablishing the condition of peace with that people, Congress, representing the United States, has power, in ending this war as any other war, to get some security for the future."

The guaranty clause, Mr. Collamer asserted, implied that States were to be kept in the Union; it was inserted for the security of the minority in a State, though there might be but one man there to redeem Sodom. No one State could discharge the United States from a performance of that obligation. To keep it Congress, if it was essential to maintaining a republican form of government, could abolish slavery if that institution stood in the way of performing the guaranty. Before restoring the States, he added in conclusion, the President would need the assistance of Congress, else how could he get rid of the confiscation act.[1]

Collamer's substitute, which shared the fate of the amendment offered by Ten Eyck, could be construed only by an examination of the President's proclamation to ascertain what States were in insurrection.

To the preamble, which stated that four years earlier certain designated States had rebelled, and on the 8th of November preceding were in such condition of rebellion that no valid election for the choice of electors of President and Vice-President could be held there, Senator Pomeroy objected that the rebel governor of Arkansas had been killed, and the entire disloyal government destroyed. When the election was held the real local authorities in that State were Union men. It would not be true, as the preamble declared, that these authorities were in rebellion on November 8. The

[1] Globe, Part I., 2 Sess. 38th Cong., p. 591.

terms of the disloyal officials in Arkansas had expired by limitation; the chief men in that government were not alive to exert any influence if they were disposed to do so. It was not true to say that they made war on the United States on the 8th of November, 1864, or that they were then in condition to do so. Since the rebellion began they never had but one election.

Pomeroy's amendment to substitute for "state of rebellion" the word "condition" was carried by a vote of 26 to 13. The preamble, as thus perfected, declared that certain States had rebelled four years before, and on November 8 were in such "condition" that no valid election was held.[1]

Mr. Lane believed that for the protection of Union men in those States a loyal government was indispensable, and that it did more to demoralize the insurgents and to close out the rebellion than any other act that could be accomplished. It would be worth more than all the victories that could be gained in the field.[2]

Senator Howe in closing the debate observed that four days had been spent in discussing not the passage of the joint resolution, but the reason to be assigned in its preamble for excluding the vote of certain States. It belonged to the legislatures of those commonwealths, he maintained, to declare whether valid elections had been held there. He distrusted that sort of legislation, and in conclusion said: "If you will take hold of the question of the political relations of these communities, and if you will tell what is the truth, and has been the truth since 1861, that there are no State organizations there, no State governments, I am with you. When you establish that, you know what they may and what they may not do."[3]

[1] Globe, Part I., 2 Sess. 38th Cong., p. 593.
[2] Ibid., p. 594.
[3] Ibid., pp. 594 595.

338 LINCOLN'S PLAN OF RECONSTRUCTION

By a vote of 29 to 10 the joint resolution was passed on February 4. In the record the names of Cowan, Doolittle, Harris, Howe, Lane of Kansas, Nesmith, Saulsbury, Ten Eyck, Van Winkle and Willey appear in opposition.[1]

For the purpose of canvassing the electoral votes, both Houses assembled in joint convention four days later, February 8, 1865. The Vice-President in discharge of his duty proceeded to open and hand to the tellers the votes of the several States, beginning with Maine. No one dissenting it was agreed on a suggestion by Senator Wade to dispense with the reading of everything in the certificate except the result of the vote.

When all the votes had been recorded, Cowan said: " Mr. President, I inquire whether there are any further returns to be counted." The Vice-President replied in the negative. To his former question Mr. Cowan then added, " And if there be, I would inquire why they are not submitted to this body in joint convention, which is alone capable of determining whether they should be counted or not." The Vice-President acknowledged that he had in his possession returns from the States of Louisiana and Tennessee, but in obedience to the law of the land " the Chair holds it to be his duty not to present them to the convention." The Pennsylvania Senator thereupon inquired whether the joint resolution had been signed by the President, and was informed that while the official communication of its approval had not been received by either House, the Chair had been apprised that the resolution had received the Executive approval.

Cowan then suggested that, as a motion was not in order, the votes of Louisiana and Tennessee be counted, and that the convention determine the fact. Representative Cox immediately recommended the reading of the joint rule under which both Houses were then acting. On being directed by

[1] Globe, Part I., 2 Sess. 38th Cong.. p. 595.

the Vice-President the secretary complied with this suggestion.

Thaddeus Stevens did not think any question had arisen which required the two Houses to separate, for that, according to the language of the joint resolution, could only occur upon the reading of those returns which had been opened by the president of the convention.

Mr. Cowan did what he could to bring the question before the two Houses, and failing, withdrew it. The result, after some further effort to call up the returns from Louisiana and Tennessee, was then announced. The tellers reported that for President of the United States Abraham Lincoln had received 212, and George B. McClellan 21 votes; that for Vice-President Andrew Johnson had received 212, and George H. Pendleton 21 votes.[1]

On February 10 the president *pro tempore* laid before the Senate the following communication from Mr. Lincoln:

To the honorable the Senate and House of Representatives:

The joint resolution entitled "Joint resolution declaring certain States not entitled to representation in the Electoral College" has been signed by the Executive, in deference to the view of Congress implied in its passage and presentation to him. In his own view, however, the two Houses of Congress, convened under the twelfth article of the Constitution, have complete power to exclude from counting all electoral votes deemed by them to be illegal; and it is not competent for the Executive to defeat or obstruct that power by a veto, as would be the case if his action were at all essential in the matter. He disclaims all right of the Executive to interfere in any way in the matter of canvassing or counting electoral votes, and he also disclaims that, by signing said resolution, he has expressed any opinion on the recitals of the preamble, or any judgment of his own upon the subject of the resolution.[2]

Except for a brief speech by Reverdy Johnson this message was received in silence by the Senate. Mr. Johnson commented upon the extraordinary course of the President, whose

[1] The subject of the counting of the electoral votes will be found in the Congressional Globe, Part I., 2 Sess. 38th Cong., pp. 668-669.
[2] Globe, Part I., 2 Sess. 38th Cong., p. 711.

duty, he said, was clearly to approve or to disapprove, not virtually to read a lecture to the Senate as he had done. The Maryland member did not doubt that the motives of the President were perfectly correct and patriotic, but it was not the first time, he asserted, that that had been done. The bill for the reconstruction of the seceded States passed both Houses by an overwhelming majority; but it was defeated by the President's failure to approve, and the adjournment of Congress before ten days elapsed. In his manifesto or proclamation he approved portions and disapproved others.[1]

Short as this paper was, however, it was entirely characteristic of the President. This little lesson in constitutional law is only another proof that Mr. Lincoln possessed in an eminent degree the faculty of seeing clearly through the most intricate question. His disposal of this difficulty as well as his reflections on Congress remind one of the facility with which he straightened out for General Butler the liquor problem at Norfolk. The succeeding chapter will describe another phase of the controversy between the political departments of the Government.

[1] Globe, Part I., 2 Sess. 38th Cong., p. 711.

X

SENATE DEBATE ON LOUISIANA

AT the opening of its second session, December 5, 1864, the Speaker of the Thirty-eighth Congress laid before the House the credentials of W. D. Mann, T. M. Wells, Robert W. Taliaferro, A. P. Field and M. F. Bonzano, who claimed seats as Representatives from the State of Louisiana. A petition, signed by numerous citizens of that commonwealth, protesting against the admission of these claimants, was referred at the same time on motion of Henry Winter Davis to the Committee of Elections in connection with their credentials, which had already received the same direction. On the 13th this remonstrance was ordered to be printed.

Mr. Dawes on February 11 following reported that "M. F. Bonzano is entitled to a seat in this House as a Representative from the First Congressional District of Louisiana." Six days later he presented a report and resolutions from his committee to the effect that Messrs. Field and Mann from the Second and Third Districts, respectively, were also entitled to seats. These reports with the accompanying resolutions were laid on the table and ordered to be printed.

No further action was taken on the question of their admission, but on March 3, 1865, Chairman Dawes by unanimous consent reported from the Committee of Elections a resolution that there be paid to each of the Louisiana claimants for compensation, expenses and mileage the sum of

$2,000 and a like amount to T. M. Jacks, J. M. Johnson and A. A. C. Rogers, claimants from Arkansas.

The House, however, was not nearly so unanimous as its committee. Mr. Washburne remarked that Congress, by allowing at the last session the sum of $1,500 to one gentleman who claimed a seat, had fixed a sort of rule in such cases. That amount he would, probably, not object to paying to the present applicants; but if large payments, such as the compensation proposed by the resolution, were made to men coming to the Capitol it was feared they might not soon stop.

Representative Johnson, of Pennsylvania, believed that regardless of their right to seats they should be compensated because they had been encouraged to come; they appeared at the Capitol, he asserted, with an honest expectation of getting seats, and in an honest effort to restore popular government to their States.

Mr. Dawes declared that they came not as adventurers but under what they supposed was the policy of the General Government; hence the favorable recommendation of the committee. When he demanded the previous question, Representative Brandegee moved to lay the resolution on the table. Thaddeus Stevens asked to strike out the words " claimants for seats." To this the Massachusetts member offered no objection. " I do not want to recognize the idea," added Stevens, " that anybody on earth thinks that these men are entitled to seats."[1] This request, however, was denied, and the resolution was then adopted.

It was during their three months' sojourn in Washington that one of the claimants, A. P. Field, committed an assault upon Representative William D. Kelley, of Pennsylvania, whom he regarded as the chief obstacle to their admission. This occurrence, which took place on February 20 at the Willard Hotel, was due, no doubt, to the artificial excitement

[1] Globe, Part II., 2 Sess. 38th Cong., p. 1395.

of the Louisiana claimant, but was without influence upon the action of the House.[1]

The General Assembly of Louisiana, as previously related, had chosen Charles Smith and R. King Cutler as United States Senators. With the Representatives-elect these gentlemen also appeared in Washington as claimants for seats. On December 7, two days after Congress assembled, the president *pro tempore* presented certain proceedings of the Louisiana Legislature declaratory of the election of Smith and Cutler. The papers, it was announced, would lie on the table unless otherwise ordered. Just as Henry Winter Davis had done in the House, Senator Wade offered a memorial from Louisiana citizens remonstrating against their admission, and also against the reception of any electoral vote from that State. On his motion it was agreed that all documents pertaining to the subject be printed. On the following day, December 8, the credentials as well as the remonstrance were referred to the Committee on the Judiciary.

Senator Trumbull on February 17 succeeding made a report from his committee, and offered a joint resolution relative to the credentials of Smith and Cutler. At the request of Charles Sumner the resolution was read at length and was as follows:

That the United States do hereby recognize the government of the State of Louisiana, inaugurated under and by the convention which assembled on the 6th day of April, A. D., 1864, at the city of New Orleans, as the legitimate government of the said State, and entitled to the guarantees and all other rights of a State government under the Constitution of the United States.[2]

This resolution was limited to Louisiana because the facts, while in many respects similar, were not identical with those in the case of Arkansas. Besides, when the subject first came

[1] Globe, Part I., 2 Sess. 38th Cong., pp. 971-974.
[2] Ibid., p. 903.

up in committee the Arkansas case had not been presented, though it arose before Louisiana had been disposed of. Trumbull believed it the intention of the committee to act immediately upon Arkansas when the case of Louisiana had been considered.[1]

Sumner moved, February 23, to strike out all of the joint resolution except the enacting clause, and to substitute the following:

> That neither the people nor the Legislature of any State, the people of which were declared to be in insurrection against the United States by the proclamation of the President, dated August 16, 1861, shall hereafter elect Representatives or Senators to the Congress of the United States until the President, by proclamation, shall have declared that armed hostility to the Government of the United States within such State has ceased; nor until the people of such State shall have adopted a constitution of government not repugnant to the Constitution and laws of the United States; nor until, by a law of Congress, such State shall have been declared to be entitled to representation in the Congress of the United States of America.[2]

To this amendment Senator Trumbull objected that it would put it in the power of the President, by refusing to issue his proclamation, to keep a State out forever. Sumner's substitute was promptly defeated by a vote of 29 to 8.[3]

Of the members of the committee Powell alone opposed the resolution offered by Mr. Trumbull. The chief object in recognizing the government of Louisiana at that time, said the Kentucky Senator, was to allow that State to vote for the proposed amendment of the Constitution; to do that effectually those favorable to the resolution desired first to admit her Senators and Representatives; their admission would be the immediate effect of its passage.

A just conclusion on that subject could be reached only by information concerning the action of the President, of the

[1] Globe, Part II., 2 Sess. 38th Cong., p. 1011.
[2] Ibid.
[3] Ibid.

military, and of the people of Louisiana in connection with the election. He opposed the loyal government because it was not formed by the people of that State; however, he did not want to be classed with those who thought Louisiana out of the Union. He believed that something approximating a majority of her people should indicate a willingness to return to the Union, and should participate in the movement for reorganization. The formation of the existing government, he asserted, was controlled and influenced by persons who were not citizens of Louisiana, and, he added, " It is a government formed really and virtually by the military power of the United States, using as instruments delegates who were elected under and by force of the bayonet."

Before Senators could vote for the resolution, he continued, they must maintain the doctrine announced in the President's proclamation of December 8, 1863, when he proposed that one tenth of the loyal voters in a State who would comply with the conditions therein prescribed, could form a State government; they must further maintain that the President, of his own volition, had power by decretal order to alter the constitution of a State; that the President had power to prescribe the qualifications both of voters and candidates for office in the States; finally they must believe that not only did the President possess these powers, but that Major-General Banks, in virtue of his office, possessed them in Louisiana.

Mr. Powell proposed to show that not only did Louisiana people not act of their own volition, but that " they were coerced to do what they did." The constitution of that State, he asserted, was not made by the free suffrage of the people.

The creation of a State government is a purely civil act; the people must act without restraint. He had never heard any Senator say that the President could legitimately exercise the power assumed in his proclamation of December 8, 1863. Mr. Powell objected to the oath which was to be taken as a condition precedent to becoming a qualified elector in one of the revolted States, especially to that portion which promised support of all future proclamations of the President on the question of slavery. " Why, sir," he exclaimed, " the President may proclaim that the negro shall be the master and the white man the slave; that the negro shall be the voter and the white man deprived of the right of suffrage; and yet this oath requires the man taking it to swear in advance that he would support even such a measure as that. . . .

" At the very threshold, then," he continued, " you repudiate the great principle of republican government that majorities shall rule. Here you propose to say not that majorities, but that less than one tenth shall rule." It was intimated by the President that when they made a constitution it must not recognize African slavery. General Banks, carrying out the suggestion of the President, as well as what had been distinctly stated to General Steele in relation to Arkansas, took it upon himself to alter the constitution of Louisiana in that respect.

Whence does the President, it was asked, derive the power to prescribe qualifications for either electors or candidates? The proclamation, the Kentucky Senator asserted, was the basis of the whole proceeding, and those who voted for the resolution endorsed the proclamation.

Mr. Powell then reviewed the acts and read the proclamation of General Banks, whose conduct he denounced for presuming to declare certain parts of the Louisiana constitution no longer applicable to any class of persons in that State, and, therefore, inoperative and void.

He further objected that Banks had no authority to call the convention, for the constitution of Louisiana could be lawfully amended in only the mode pointed out by itself. The President's proclamation, he added, would allow only those to vote who were qualified electors under the fundamental law of the State; those in the army and navy were not, but General Banks in his ukase of February 13, 1864, allowed them to participate in the election.

He also invited attention to the action of the Department Commander in designating provost marshals to take care that the polls were properly opened, in the absence of the sheriffs, and that suitable persons were appointed judges of election and so forth. Of the 11,414 votes he asserted that 808 were cast by soldiers who under the President's proclamation were not legal voters. The fact, added Mr. Powell, that General Banks after the inauguration of Hahn as governor continued to issue proclamations shows that the civil was controlled by the military authority.

Passing on to a discussion of the statement of Banks before the Committee on the Judiciary that the military did not interfere in the election of February 22, Senator Powell quoted the following passages from a proclamation of the Department Commander:

> Those who have exercised or are entitled to the rights of citizens of the United States will be required to participate in the measures necessary for the reëstablishment of civil government. . . . It is therefore a solemn duty resting upon all persons to assist in the earliest possible restoration of civil government. Let them participate in the measures suggested for this purpose. Opinion is free and candidates are numerous. Open hostility cannot be permitted. Indifference will be treated as a crime, and faction as treason.

"Talk to me," exclaimed Mr. Powell, "of freedom of election under such military orders! Why, sir, there was but one free man, in my opinion, in all Louisiana at that time, and that was Major-General Banks; and I do not know that he was free, for he was serving his master at the White House." The fundamental law there was martial law, which is but the will of the commander-in-chief, and under that law he could have beheaded them if they did not vote.

From beginning to end, he continued, the coercive finger

of the military was engaged in the establishment of that government. Under the various proclamations even Unionists, men who had always been loyal, could not vote unless they took the oath required in the President's proclamation. There was a large class of loyal men in Louisiana, he said, who refused to take that oath, for there had been presented to the Judiciary Committee an earnest protest signed by Thomas J. Durant and thirty-one others, influential Union men of that State, against the admission of Senators and Representatives and against counting its electoral vote. Those Senators, he added toward the conclusion of his remarks, who only a few days before opposed the counting of Louisiana's electoral vote should now vote against the resolution acknowledging the government which appointed the Senators that are claiming seats.[1]

Sumner and Davis referred to the resolution as a shadow. To this Mr. Doolittle replied that the vote of Louisiana might be necessary to secure the constitutional amendment, and that the new constitution of that State had struck the shackles from 90,000 slaves not reached by the Emancipation Proclamation.

Mr. Henderson, who favored the resolution, secured the floor, and observed, among other things, that Louisiana and Arkansas did not claim that they were yet strong enough to maintain their governments without the military aid of the nation; but neither was Maryland, West Virginia, Kentucky or Missouri; even Ohio, Indiana or Illinois, he said, could not without national assistance maintain their State organizations for sixty days against the Confederate armies.

"If we would have State governments," said Mr. Henderson, "we must begin somewhere and at some time." It was nonsensical, he argued to talk of restoring the Union, while keeping the loyal people in those States for all time to come

[1] Globe, Part I., 2 Sess. 38th Cong., pp. 1061-1064.

under military domination. "We must declare the right in Congress," he added, "to make and establish these governments for the States, or permit the President, under military law, to set them up, or we must recognize such as the loyal people may set up for themselves." If, as Madison thought, Congress cannot make them, but can only guarantee such as already exist and are found to be republican in form, it must be left with the President, under his power as the head of the army, or to the people of the respective States. If left entirely with the President he might by military force impose upon the State a constitution against the wishes of both the loyal and disloyal. The Senator frankly admitted that neither House would be under any obligation to receive members sent from a State so constituted.

"But," he went on to say, "if the people — the loyal masses, whether a majority or a minority of the whole voting population as formerly known — participated in its creation and acquiesce in the revival of the State government, the case though inaugurated by the President in my judgment would be very different. According to the theory of our Government, and its practice in all its past time in analogous cases, it would seem that whether Congress or the President inaugurated the proceeding, the constitution can only receive its validity and authority from the approval or acquiescence of the people to be affected; and that brings me to consider how the people in the seceded States shall revive their governments, and who are the legally qualified voters for that purpose in these States.

"At the threshold of the inquiry we are met with the objection that the States are now without officers of any kind legally elected, and that of themselves they are powerless to inaugurate any movement to set up a loyal government. It is said they have no officials to superintend the election, to count the votes, and grant certificates of election. However desirable these formalities may be, it has not been the uniform practice of Congress to require them."

In the case of California, continued Mr. Henderson, the first election was called by the military order of a subordinate officer of the army, a delegate convention was chosen, a constitution was framed by that assembly and submitted to Congress. It was accepted as republican in form, and under it a State government was inaugurated that for fifteen years had been administered with the greatest success. The territory, he said, was wholly without civil authorities recognized by the United States. Congress had passed no enabling act, had prescribed no forms of proceeding, had failed to fix the qualifications of voters, had appointed no judges of election or other officers to count and certify the votes; yet the act, however informal, was ratified because the constitution on its face was unobjectionable in form, and it was believed that the people interested acquiesced in the government it established.

If the people of Rhode Island, added Mr. Henderson, had acquiesced in the government set up under Dorr, Congress and the Executive would have recognized it as legitimate. The Senator from Kentucky contended that although a majority of the legal and qualified voters of Louisiana should acquiesce in the new constitution Congress could not admit the State. In support of his view Mr. Henderson pointed to the State government of Missouri, which was the offspring of a movement purely revolutionary.

In the States whose representatives were seeking admission to Congress but one government asked recognition, and what if these organizations were of revolutionary origin? — the revolution was on the side of loyalty. Revolutionary governments had been accepted in time of peace — governments springing up in the midst of anarchy, without the sanctions of regularity; why, he asked, should they be rejected now when they were needed to protect the loyal inhabitants of the respective States and to aid the nation in vindicating its lost authority?

The assertion that on the face of these constitutions they were republican in form Senator Sumner denied. They did not follow out the principles of the Federal Constitution. This general answer was unsatisfactory, and Mr. Henderson said that the only question with him was how could he best get these States performing their legitimate functions in the Union again. If, as the Massachusetts Senator maintained, the act of secession took the States out, why could not the act of loyal men bring them back? If secession, he argued, was potent enough to take a State out, and that was mere revolution, why could not the loyal men perfect a revolution on the side of Government as well as rebels perfect a revolution on the side of secession, outrage and wrong?

The doctrine that secession took the States out of the Union, Sumner objected to have imputed to him. A subsequent remark indicated one ground of his opposition to the government of Louisiana. "If the loyal men, white and black, recognize it, then," he declared, "it will be republican in form. Unless that is done, it will not be."

When asked whether Congress could interfere with the right of suffrage in one of the States, Sumner evaded a candid reply, and concealed his meaning under these words: "It is the bounden duty of the United States by act of Congress to guarantee complete freedom to every citizen, and immunity from all oppression, and absolute equality before the law." No government that does not guarantee these things, he added, can be recognized as republican in form according to the theory of the Federal Constitution, if the United States are called upon to enforce the constitutional guaranty.

Senator Henderson, interpreting this answer in the affirmative, observed that if under the guaranty clause the national Legislature could regulate the suffrage in the States, there was no limitation except the mere discretion of Congress. In support of this position he cited Madison in No. 43 of *The Federalist,* and of course had this part of the argument his own way, for the test of a republican form satisfactory to the Massachusetts Senator would leave few representatives in Congress.

Mr. Henderson denied that the admission of Senators and Representatives from these commonwealths would be a precedent for other States to demand recognition, even with the institution of slavery, thus bringing back the germs of a new rebellion against the Government; because in the constitutions presented involuntary servitude was abolished. With slavery remaining any restoration would be utterly useless. It was against union with the free States that the Southern people had taken up arms, and against restoration that they continued to use them. In that struggle they would employ every moral and material force, including the slave himself, stimulated by the boon of freedom, to resist the return of their States. Whatever the future might bring, it would fail to bring to the doors of Congress seeking admission a State constitution without a positive interdict of slavery.

To the objection that a majority of the people of these States were in rebellion and that to recognize the loyal minority would be to subvert the whole republican system Senator Henderson replied that if it were strictly true that a majority in a particular community "not only shall but must govern," then a majority of legal voters in a State desiring to secede would have the undoubted right to do so. As no principle of the General Government authorized such action, it was not true, he said, that a majority of citizens in a State can govern themselves except in strict obedience to the Constitution of the United States. If a majority proved derelict and undertook to destroy the very Government of which the State is a part, it is right that the minority, who sustain the Government in its entirety, State and national, should institute government for their protection. He admitted that General Banks did a great many things for which there was no legal authority; but the question was whether this constitution was the will of the loyal men of Louisiana. If it was, their representatives had a right to seats on the floor of Congress.

In reply to Sumner, Senator Henderson said he favored the idea that the loyal men should govern a State, and he added, if that be the government of the few it results from the voluntary disloyalty of the many. They, of their own will, had relinquished the right to govern themselves under the Constitution, and as they had no right to govern themselves otherwise they could not govern at all. As to the oligarchy of skin, to which Sumner had referred, Henderson believed that the regulation of the suffrage was a question for the consideration of the States; if they conferred the franchise on the negro, he did not object.

As to the Louisiana constitution the question was whether it embodied the will of those legally entitled to exercise the functions of the State government. If the casting of illegal votes vitiated elections, but few elections, he asserted, would be valid.

If those States were admitted, they could immediately settle all questions of suffrage, and Congress would be relieved of the difficulty in future. He put clearly the difference of opinion prevailing among Senators on this subject when he stated that Mr. Powell objected to the new constitution of Louisiana because negro soldiers were permitted to vote, while Mr. Sumner opposed it because negroes at home did not vote. Concluding this part of his speech, he declared that the Federal Government by recognizing the old organization in Rhode Island against Dorr expressed its preference for a constitution of restricted suffrage.

Without naming his authority Henderson then read from a private letter the opinion of a gentleman whom he regarded as one of the ablest jurists in the United States.[1] The correspondent said in part:

> It must be observed that the civil society, and the political society so to speak, of a State need not necessarily do [be] the same. In other words the basis of *representation* may be the whole population, but the basis of *suffrage* be property, adult years, &c. The power to choose rulers is lodged in the voters, and they may not exceed one tenth of the population. . . . That portion of the population in which political power is lodged, determines who shall fill the respective offices, make laws, etc: Although the members of that society may have possessed every requisite therefor, yet the moment they ceased to be citizens of the United States they ceased to belong thereto.
>
> That rule holds good with respect to every member, and the political society may, by death, disqualification of members, &c., be reduced to a very few persons. To state an extreme case, for illustration of the principle, Massachusetts formerly had a property qualification, and although her population entitled her to, say, thirteen Representatives in the United States House, her voters may not have exceeded fifty thousand. Suppose while that qualification remained, by some financial or other disaster, only one thousand or one hundred citizens retained the necessary income or property, would not the persons chosen to Congress by the few and only remaining voters be duly elected? So with regard to any other element of suffrage, as United States citizenship, if by its loss the voters are reduced to very few in number, do not those few constitute the political or voting power? As to the policy or impolicy of restricted suffrage, we are not now concerned, but are endeavoring to reach a constitutional and legal analysis of our governmental system.
>
> But here is encountered the startling and practical difficulty, " Shall a few persons be permitted to govern a State, despite the wishes of its inhabitants, and without giving them all a voice? Is that republican?"
>
> But it must be remembered that the few voters, say one seventh, or one tenth of the whole population, have always been intrusted with that

---

[1] While this chapter was in press an interesting letter from Senator Henderson informed the author that the Hon. Samuel Treat, of St. Louis, formerly Judge of the United States Court for the Eastern District of Missouri, is the distinguished jurist referred to in the text.

SENATE DEBATE ON LOUISIANA

power. Wisdom has fixed the basis of suffrage, without regard to relative numbers; that is, it has endeavored, under our popular system, to give the right or privilege to as many citizens as were supposed competent to exercise it intelligently. The rules prescribed as to age, sex, citizenship, &c., were deemed essential, right, and proper. Whether many or few come within the rules does not affect their validity. . . . If persons heretofore entitled to a vote chose to commit a felony, and incur thereby, as a penalty, the deprivation of their former right of suffrage, it is not supposed that the loss of such votes is anti-republican. If, then, a majority choose to perpetrate treason, or to expatriate themselves, or in any other way become disqualified, how does that action vitiate the rule? If they, after becoming disqualified, remain in the State, are they not bound to submit to its rulers and laws? If their rulers are chosen without their voice, is it not in consequence of their own voluntary action? Indeed, it often happens that the persons elected to office receive only a meager minority of the votes which could have been lawfully polled, yet that fact has no influence upon the legal result. So a person is often chosen by a minority of the votes actually cast, and is not the majority bound to submit?

The author of this letter appears to have been more familiar with the Constitution, as it was understood by its framers, than almost any member of either House, notwithstanding the presence in Congress of many distinguished statesmen. In the following eight propositions Mr. Henderson then gave a masterly summary of the Presidential plan of reconstruction:

1. I hold that the seceded States are still in the Union and cannot get out of it except through amendment of the Constitution permitting it.
2. The seceded States being still in the Union are entitled to claim all the rights accorded to other States.
3. That each State now in the Union has the right to stand upon the form of its constitution as it existed at the time of its admission. The people of such State may change its constitution, provided they retain a republican form of government; but neither the President nor Congress can reform, alter, or amend such constitution, nor prescribe any alteration or amendment as a condition of association with the other States of the Union. The General Government may properly lend its aid to enable the people to express their will; but any attempt to exercise power constitutionally reserved to the State, beyond what may be demanded by the immediate exigencies of war, will not tend to restore the Union, but rather to destroy our whole system of government.
4. When citizens of a State rebel and take up arms against the General

Government they lose their rights as citizens of the United States, and they necessarily forfeit those rights and franchises in their respective States which depend on United States citizenship.

5. If a seceded State be still in the Union, entitled to recognition as a State, and a majority of the people have voluntarily withdrawn their allegiance, the loyal minority constitute the State and should govern it.

6. Congress should not reject the governments presented because of mere irregularity in the proceedings leading to their reorganization.

7. If Congress has no right to make and impose a constitution upon the people of any State; if its power extends no further than to guaranty preëxisting republican forms of government; if the State still exists, and the loyal men are entitled to exercise the functions of its government, it follows that the only questions to be examined here are, first, is the constitution the will of the loyal men qualified to act? and, second, is it republican in form?

8. The constitutions of Louisiana and Arkansas are thought to be republican in form, and it is admitted that the loyal men of those States respectively acquiesce in them. Hence the duty of Congress to recognize them, and the duty of each House to admit their representatives.[1]

On February 25 debate on Trumbull's resolution was resumed. At this point Mr. Sumner offered an amendment in substance as follows:

That it is the duty of the United States at the earliest practicable moment, consistent with the common defence and general welfare, to reëstablish by act of Congress republican governments in those States where loyal governments have been vacated by the existing rebellion, and thus, to the full extent of their power, fulfil the requirement of the Constitution, that "the United States shall guaranty to every State in this Union a republican form of government."

Sec. 2. *And be it further resolved,* That this important duty is imposed by the Constitution in express terms on "the United States," and not on individuals or classes of individuals, or on any military commander or executive officer, and cannot be intrusted to any such persons, acting, it may be, for an oligarchical class, and in disregard of large numbers of loyal people; but it must be performed by the United States, represented by the President and both Houses of Congress, acting for the whole people thereof.

Sec. 3. *And be it further resolved,* That, in determining the extent of this duty, and in the absence of any precise definition of the term

[1] Globe, Part II., 2 Sess. 38th Cong., pp. 1065-1070.

"republican form of government," we cannot err, if, when called to perform this guaranty under the Constitution, we adopt the self-evident truths of the Declaration of Independence as an authoritative rule, and insist that in every reëstablished State the consent of the governed shall be the only just foundation of government, and all men shall be equal before the law.

Not less important is the declaration in the fourth section that "in the performance of this guaranty, there can be no power under the Constitution to disfranchise loyal people, or to recognize any such disfranchisement, especially when it may hand over the loyal majority to the government of the disloyal minority; nor can there be any power under the Constitution to discriminate in favor of the rebellion by admitting to the electoral franchise rebels who have forfeited all rights and by excluding loyal persons who have never forfeited any right." To allow the reëstablishment of any State without proper safeguards for the rights of all the citizens, and especially without making it impossible for rebels to trample upon the rights of those who are now fighting the battles of the Union, would be, said the succeeding section, for the United States to fail in duty under the Constitution.

More directly in opposition to the resolution reported by the chairman of the Judiciary Committee, however, was the seventh section, which declared "That a government founded on military power, or having its origin in military orders, cannot be a 'republican form of government' according to the requirement of the Constitution; and that its recognition will be contrary not only to the Constitution, but also to that essential principle of our Government which, in the language of Jefferson, establishes 'the supremacy of the civil over the military authority.'"

The resolutions further asserted that a government founded on an oligarchical class, even if erroneously recognized as a "republican form of government," could not sustain itself without national support; that such an organization was not at that moment competent to discharge the duties and execute the powers of a State, and that its recognition would tend to enfeeble the Union, to postpone the day of reconciliation and to endanger the national tranquillity. The ninth section renders clear one ground of Sumner's hostility to the recognition of Louisiana. It asserts that

> Considerations of expediency are in harmony with the requirements of the Constitution, and the dictates of justice and reason, especially now, when colored soldiers have shown their military value; that as their muskets are needed for the national defence against rebels in the field, so are their ballots yet more needed against the subtle enemies of the Union at home; and that without their support at the ballot-box the cause of human rights and of the Union itself will be in constant peril.[1]

It was agreed on motion of Mr. Sumner to have his amendment printed.

Senator Howard, of Michigan, entered at this point into the debate. Much of what he said has already been related in the preceding narration of events leading up to the reinauguration of a loyal government in Louisiana. While admitting that the President's plan had been undertaken for patriotic ends, he could not, he said, recognize in the Executive, without the subsidiary aid of an act of Congress, any right to assure a community, composed of voters numbering one tenth of the electors who participated in the Presidential contest of 1860, that it would be recognized as a legitimate government and entitled to the constitutional guaranty. This, he said, was a stretch of authority beyond any previous attempt, and he thought it time that Congress, in whom, he believed, rested solely the authority of readmitting and reconstructing the rebellious States, "should lay hold

[1] Globe, Part II., 2 Sess. 38th Cong., p. 1091.

of this subject, assert their power, and provide by some statute of uniform application for the reconstruction, as it is called, and readmission of the insurrectionary States. That is their right and their duty; that is not the right, it is not the duty of the President."

A State he defined negatively as not "the geographical superficies," the land, on which population resides, and positively as "a moral person, a political community, possessing the faculty of political government." The land, he said, is the theatre on which the political community moves and acts, but is endowed with no thought, no right, no duty. The thinking beings residing upon it constitute the State.[1]

"A State of the Union or a State in the Union is, therefore, a people yielding obedience to the laws of the Union, that is, the acts of Congress and the national treaties. . . . A people who have a State government which is republican in form; a people who were one of the original thirteen States which formed the United States, or a people who have, since the adoption of the Constitution, been, in the language of that Constitution, 'admitted by the Congress into this Union' as States upon an equal footing with the original States; for this equality of rights and powers as States is plainly implied by the language and the manifest intention of the instrument; and no other people except such original State or admitted State; none but a State which permits the laws of the Union to have full scope and force within its limits; none but a State which sends Senators and Representatives to Congress friendly to the Government itself, willing to vote men and money to support and uphold it, who believe that a person forcibly resisting its authority is a traitor and deserving of death; none but a State which is willing to

[1] In support of this view the Senator cited Penhallow's Case, 3 Dallas, p. 94.

bring to trial, to convict such a traitor, and to punish him for his treason; none but a State whose population is capable of furnishing both the grand jury to indict and the traverse jury to convict such a traitor; none but a State whose population and whose authorities are in favor not only of permitting the laws of the United States relating to civil rights to be executed, but who are willing that the punitive code of the nation, the code of vengeance against its enemies, shall be carried out; none but such are States of the Union. . . .

"To be in fact a State of the Union and in the Union, this will or consent of the people must be in harmony with the Constitution, and its movements subsidiary to it. It must regard the Constitution as its highest political good; its injunctions as the highest human law, its commands as the infallible and final measure of civil duty. In short, to be in the Union is to be actively and willingly coöperating with other States in the performance of all those acts and things without which the Federal Government cannot act or move, cannot perform the functions required of it by the Constitution; it is to elect Senators and Representatives to the Congress of the United States; to permit the courts of the United States to be held within their limits, and its citizens to act as jurors and officers of the court; to permit the judgments and sentences of the court to be executed against its citizens; to permit the United States mail to be carried through the State and its contents distributed according to law; to permit the officers of the United States to collect the Federal revenue whether derived from foreign or domestic products; to permit the United States to manage and control their own property, whether consisting of forts, dockyards, arsenals, mints, or public lands; to make such elections of Senators and Representatives freely and as the means of maintaining itself as a State in the Union; and to permit all these things willingly and freely as rights belonging to the Federal Government with which neither the State government nor the people of the State have any right whatever to interfere. In short, to be a State in the Union is to use all those powers of the State which have a relation to the Federal Government in a manner friendly to that Government, friendly to its existence and continuance, in a manner promotive of the objects of that Government; and to permit without hindrance the exercise within the State of all the powers of the Federal Government."

Though he declined to discuss the question whether a State by omitting to send Representatives and Senators to Congress would on that account cease to be a member of the Union, he gave it as his opinion that mere failure to be represented in Congress would not be followed by such consequences; but if a State not only refused to participate in Federal legislation but went farther, and as a political community made war upon the General Government, he declared that "it would be folly, madness, to say that the State was not our enemy in every sense in which that term can be employed to describe hostile relations between independent communities. . . . No one will pretend that such a community is in the Union in fact, for that would be to make an admission and in the same breath to contradict it. *De facto*, such a community, and, if it be bounded by State lines, such a State, is as completely out of the Union as is Canada or Mexico, from the moment it assumes the attitude of hostility until it is subdued and conquered by our arms, or until it voluntarily lays down its arms, ejects its hostile government and returns *in fact* to its once friendly sentiments and friendly relations to the Federal Government."

"Loyalty," continued Senator Howard, "thus becomes the final test in solving the question, what is a State in the Union? If a State by its overt acts has shown a want of this friendship, it is no longer in the Union *de facto*, and cannot be treated as if it were. The Supreme Court, acting upon the soundest principles of public law, have decided the waging of war by a State, although acting under an illegitimate and revolutionary government, renders her territory enemy's territory, and the people there resident enemies of the United States, in the sense of the laws of war. And their decision could not have been different."

The State, he argued further, was in fact, though wrongfully, out of the Union because its actual government was disloyal and treasonable. Out of it because unsubdued rebellion made it for the time being an independent though unrecognized nation on the earth's surface, throwing off its allegiance to its paramount Government, and assuming by the sword to assert its separate nationality.

"But we are at war with the rebel States, and are told . . . that the Government, so far at least as the rebel States are concerned, is under some peculiar constitutional restraint by which its hands are tied; that we are prohibited from 'subjugating' those States; that all we can do, under the Constitution, is to break up the military array of the rebels, disperse their armed bands, take away their arms, and do that very indefinite duty, *restore order;* that thereupon our task is ended and the rebel States have a constitutional right to come back into the Union and participate in the enactment of Federal laws and the conduct of the Federal Government. And we are menaced both in Congress and out with terrible retributions if we conquer or attempt to conquer, if we subjugate or attempt to subjugate, the rebel States. It is admitted by these our critics that in an international war . . . we should have all the rights and powers of other independent nations, and might rightfully conquer our adversary, . . . that we might make a complete conquest of his people and his territory. . . .

"Now, it is lawful to wage such a foreign war, for

the purpose of effectuating such a complete conquest, and of course lawful to attain it; . . . lawful to substitute the political authority of the United States for that of a hostile foreign nation;" otherwise, he argued, the war could not be a successful one; hence in a war with a member of the Union the United States could substitute for the authority of such hostile commonwealth its own authority. There was no difference between the two cases. The former actual hostile government should be supplanted by the Federal Government. No other government had a right to give the law. Had the conquered rebel people that right? No; for that would be to allow them at once to expel their conquerors by a popular decree, and to deny the supremacy of the Federal Government which had subdued them. Had the old State government, he asked, the once loyal government, the right to govern the conquered people? No; there was no such government. It had long since ceased to exist. "In fact, there is no government there, none at all, which can for a moment be recognized or permitted by the United States, as the party now holding the actual mastery of the country; and like every other case where the possession of a country has arisen from the use of superior force, the will of the conqueror is the law — that is, the will of the United States expressed, in the absence of acts of Congress, by the Commander-in-Chief of the Army, but by the acts of Congress after Congress has spoken.

" . . . No one will deny that we have a right to subdue by arms and to reduce to quietude and submission a rebel State, that is, the people of a State in insurrection. But how absurd to make this concession, and at the same time to deny to us the constitutional power to occupy and hold the territory and its people in our military grasp — an occupation just as necessary to the end in view as the firing of cannon, the charging of cavalry, or any other operation in the field.

" . . . The true objects of the war . . . are the suppression of the rebellion, the reëstablishment of the original Federal authority within the State, and the revival of the loyalty of the people of the State as the sole foundation and condition of all its civil rights as a State of the Union and of the right of its people to be treated as friends and not as enemies. Although the United States have the full and complete right which conquest gives, for the purpose of subjecting these domestic enemies to the exercise of the powers granted by the Constitution to Congress, and for the purpose of restoring to the body-politic its vital blood, loyalty to the Government, yet those purposes, those distinct ends, are without doubt limits beyond which we cannot go. We are restrained by the manifest objects for which the national Government was formed; but restrained by no particular clause of the Constitution. The instrument contains no such clause, and the limitation and restraint are of precisely the same nature as those which any other government is under in subduing an insurrection of its own subjects or citizens; the plain object of the war in both cases being the restoration of legitimate authority and the revival of allegiance. And until this revival of allegiance there must be the same need of military occupation and repression in both cases."

After showing that the existence of the States is indispensable to that of the Federal Government, he proceeded, " it is not permissible by mere interpretation to clothe that Government with a power permanently to abolish the State government by way of punishing or suppressing the rebellion; or to convert the States into mere Territories of the United States, that is, public domain, to be divided up afterward by lines different from those of the States, and again admitted into the Union like matured Territories, with such new geographical limits as Congress may see fit to establish."

Article IV., Section 3, Clause 1 of the Constitution the Senator regarded as an express prohibition to change the boundaries of any State once in the Union without its consent; "its consent in its capacity as a State, freely given by its own Legislature." He believed that the Amnesty Proclamation of President Lincoln indicated that its author held a different opinion.

He rejected the idea that the rebellious States could be converted into Territories. This term, under our system, he added, "implies land never lying in any State, land ceded to the United States either by the old States, or purchased or conquered from foreign nations. The term never has been used to describe a State or any part of a State; and it implies not only the ownership of the soil and right of disposition, but full and complete political jurisdiction in the Federal Government over the people resident there. . . ."

The objects of the conquest being as stated above, such forcible occupation was, he continued, in its very nature temporary and ought to cease the moment those objects were attained. This could not be done without establishing a government to preserve order, life and property — a provisional government, for that is the true historic name to be applied in all cases where an old government has been overthrown; a provisional government instituted by the conqueror, and to be continued just so long as Congress deemed it necessary to continue it for the attainment, and while attaining, those high objects. The occupancy, that is, the possession of all the reins of local government by the Federal authorities would be but temporary, provisional, fiduciary. It should necessarily last until the Federal Government had done its duty in the reëstablishment of order and the revival of loyalty. Until then it was, and should continue, the omnipotent sovereign of the State, holding actually by right of conquest, though for a particular purpose, and being itself necessarily the final judge to determine when its tutelary mission had been accomplished.

He avoided, he said, a discussion of the question whether a State can commit suicide, that is, extinguish its own being by waging a rebellious war against the Federal Government; instead of presenting any such abstract question of political dialectics, the case, he declared, merely presented the usual question which arose whenever and wherever there had been a forcible revolution. What, he inquired, was the duty of the paramount and lawful government in its treatment of insurgent communities? And was not the Government doing its whole duty in punishing the ringleaders in the revolt and restoring the old and constitutional Government over those districts?

The Government, Mr. Howard proceeded, must be the final judge of the duration of this military occupation. It was bound by the plain terms of the Constitution not only to suppress the insurrection, which was done the moment it had obtained firm possession of the whole of the hostile territory, but to guarantee to the conquered State a republican form of government. To perform this high and sacred trust, time of course was necessary; likewise a great variety of means and instrumentalities, " of all which the Government of the United States must, because it has no superior, no equal in the matter, be the sole and final judge. These means may embrace acts of provisional legislation, creating private rights and duties not previously in existence, but existing by law and of a permanent nature, paramount to all subsequent State legislation because arising under the supreme authority of the nation, as, for instance, the giving freedom to slaves; or they may undoubtedly embrace conditions to be performed by the subdued States on taking their places again in the Union, such as would be an ordinance forever abolishing slavery in the State. . . .

"Yet while thus in our military power, awaiting our action, looking to their restoration, nothing is clearer than that the citizens of the rebel States, though owing obedience to all the laws of the United States, possess no political rights under the Constitution except protection. They are not free to act, because their freedom to act would, if indulged, lead them again to draw the sword against the United States. . . . They have no right to send members to this body or to the House of Representatives, much less to participate in the election of President and Vice-President. They are the ward-provinces of the United States, progressing toward the maturity of revived loyalty, but not yet entitled to exercise the elective franchise or to participate in the enactment of laws.

"If I am asked what I mean by the Government of the United States, and whether I mean that the President as Commander-in-Chief has the exclusive power to establish these provisional governments, I answer, I do not. He has the right to regulate military occupation until Congress has acted upon the subject; . . . but the establishment of provisional governments, the quieting of the rebellious province and the reëstablishment of legitimate authority over it, pertains to the sovereign power, that is, the law-giving power of the nation. With us that power is lodged in Congress and not in the President; and in my opinion it is the business of Congress, and Congress alone, to establish and uphold these provisional governments. . . . We need not doubt that whatever we see fit to enact will be approved and carried out by the President. We cannot be more truly anxious than he to fix upon a stable, firm policy for restoring peace and union; but we ought not to shut our eyes to the necessities he will continually be under, to the almost irresistable importunities he will encounter, to provide some sort of civil government for the subdued States or districts; or to the consequences of leaving such mighty questions for him to decide. It is our plain duty to establish a uniform rule on the subject, so that all may be treated alike and the same remedy be applied with a paternal but firm and resolute hand to each delinquent State."

He opposed for two reasons the "scheme" of allowing one tenth or any other minor part of the male citizens of a commonwealth to organize a government and assume to act as a State: first, "because as against the will of an actual majority the government of such a minority must necessarily come to a speedy end and thus invite a renewal of the civil war, in that locality at least; and second, because government by a minority is of evil example and inconsistent with the genius of American liberty. . . . As a Republican I would sooner hazard ten slaveholders' rebellions than risk liberty in a government by a minority." In this connection he assigned an additional motive for his attitude toward the resolution. The will of the friendly element, he said, could prevail only by military support, and such an organization, if intended as a civil government, was not republican in the sense of the Constitution. When such aid was withdrawn the majority, he asserted, would wreak vengeance on the weakened minority.

Concluding this part of his argument, he added: "The measure now before you proposes to acknowledge eight thousand citizens of Louisiana as a State, and to give them the rights and privileges exercised by a voting population of more than fifty thousand in 1860. Eight thousand are thus to give the law or assume to give it to forty-two thousand — to more than five times their number. This they may do so long as their decrees are sustained by the presence and consent of a competent military force; but we all know, both parties there know, the world knows, and, sir, posterity will know, that it is not the eight thousand who govern the State, but the fear of the bayonet, and the fear is inspired solely by the President of the United States, as Commander-in-Chief of the Army and Navy! Disguise it, or attempt to disguise it, as we may, to this complexion doth it come at last. Yes, sir, both the eight thousand and the forty-two thousand voters are governed not by themselves, but by the bayonet! And this is at present the only government in Louisiana. The object of the present measure is to continue this hybrid, unnatural government there. It allows the meager and almost contemptible proportion of less than one sixth of the voting population to govern the whole State, and to have the influence of the whole State in our legislation here, while we know that if the military forces were withdrawn that privileged one sixth part would be swept away like chaff before the hurricane breath of the enraged majority. Sir, such a government is the merest bubble, especially if unsustained by military power. This is too obvious to need further comment."

"All this we might possibly endure," continued Senator Howard, "were it not that the measure before us clothes this mockery of a government, this king of shreds and patches, this mistletoe State *régime* that falls to the earth the moment it ceases to cling around the flag-staff of the national forces, with the high attribute of voting upon and determining questions of legislation, questions of war or peace, questions of prosecuting or ceasing to prosecute the present war, in this Hall and in the Hall of the House of Representatives. This measure introduces here Senators and Representatives whose immediate friends and relatives at home have deliberately aided and assisted to put to death myriads of Union soldiers from the North, and in swelling up that vast debt of more than two thousand million dollars which now rests upon the country. Think you that such Senators and Representatives, whose constituents have already been stripped of their property by the rebel government, and brought down to the depths of poverty; a community without the habits of labor among the intelligent classes; naked, hungry, despondent and sullen; think you that their Representatives would at the present time be safe depositories of the power to tax their constituents to pay this debt? Is it not, on the other hand, the part of prudence to guard against the contingency of having that debt repudiated by such legislators and the still more disgraceful contingency of being, by their votes, aided by a Northern party, finally compelled to pay the rebel debt of $4,000,000,000? And tell me, what right has Louisiana, the majority of whose population is to-day, wherever they are, hostile to this Government and anxious for its overthrow; what right has she, upon any recognized principle of public law or justice, to be represented in Congress?"

The treatment accorded Louisiana would, he feared, be a precedent for the ten remaining States. There would be the expense of holding each for a time in military occupation to bolster up their State governments. He preferred for Louisiana and the other insurgent States a provisional establishment for regulating domestic affairs, but without representation in Congress until the mass of their people plainly perceived their error in attempting to overthrow the General Government.

Congress should, he thought, take the subject of readmission into their own hands. It was for them and not for the President to execute the important guaranty to each State of a republican form of government, and that duty became more and more urgent as the Federal armies swept on from victory to victory. In making good that guaranty the great indispensable necessity, he declared, was loyalty.[1]

Mr. Howard was followed immediately by Reverdy Johnson, of Maryland, who to the great surprise of his fellow-Democrats argued in favor of the resolution. His remarks were introduced by a concise statement of the chief political events occurring in Louisiana between the capture of New

[1] Globe, Part II., 2 Sess. 38th Cong., pp. 1091-1095.

Orleans and the ratification, in September, 1864, of the new constitution. Concluding this part of his speech he said:
"These, sir, are the facts. The Committee on the Judiciary — and in the conclusion to which they came I concurred — were of opinion that under the circumstances in which the State was at the period when these proceedings were had, she could not be recognized as a State of the United States under that constitution adopted in 1864, except by an act of Congress. The committee were of opinion that it was not in the power of the Executive under the circumstances to bring the State back under that constitution. They were of opinion, however, that it was competent for Congress to do so, and the only question before the Committee was, whether, under the circumstances under which the State was at the time, it was not the duty of Congress to bring the State back so as to have her represented in the Union."

His objection to the conclusion of the committee was that the proceedings which led to the adoption of the constitution were instituted at the instance and under the power of the Federal military authorities. The precedent, he admitted, was really a bad one, and the proposition upon which the committee were called to decide was whether, if they were satisfied that the number of votes said to have been cast were in fact cast, and the persons voting were loyal citizens, they should be denied the privilege of being represented in the councils of the nation and subjected to a continuance of military power. Mr. Johnson added: "My impression is that, no matter how the proceedings were instituted, whether it was by the military authority, or by the coming together of the people of the State, if in point of fact the people of the State did act voluntarily and were competent to act under the original constitution, and were authorized to act by being loyal at the time they did act, it is the duty of the government of the United States to receive them back.

"Another objection was that, however true it might be that it would be in the power of all the voters of the State to adopt a constitution for themselves, or to claim the right of coming back to the Union under the constitution existing at the time of the rebellion, it was not true that it was in the power of fourteen [eleven] thousand, four hundred and fourteen voters, when the entire voting population of the State was fifty-one thousand, to take that course. As it seemed to me then, and seems now, there is no evidence to show that a single citizen of Louisiana was excluded from the right of voting."

It was not so certain, he argued further, that the eleven thousand voters who participated were not a large majority of the actual electors in Louisiana, for the war engaged the greater part of the voting population, and nine tenths of those who entered the Confederate service had forfeited their lives upon the battlefield; of those above or below the military age many had gone elsewhere, or if they remained in the State it was as disloyal citizens.

It was not pretended, he said, in discussing the relation of the loyal minority to the General Government, that by the act of secession they ceased to be citizens of the United States. Their fidelity to the Union entitled them to Federal protection. If loyal, they had forfeited no rights belonging to them before the commencement of the rebellion. No Federal law had been violated, no constitutional obligation evaded by them. They could not ask admission into the Union, because to speak such a desire was to subject themselves to punishment; when the protection of the United States was afforded them and they could once more declare their sentiments without hazard they met at their several election polls, organized their government under existing law, and then, wishing to change it, met in convention and adopted the constitution which had been submitted to the Senate.

"Why," inquired Mr. Johnson, " should we not receive it?" The right of eleven thousand citizens to change their constitution was not denied, but their action was questioned because there were others, then in arms against the Government of the United States, who did not join them in asserting it. In examining the question who were to exercise the authority of the State, he argued: " Now, if it be true that the secession ordinance had no operation to carry the State out, and that I understand even the Senator from Massachusetts [Mr. Sumner] admitted last night; if it be true that the State is in the Union notwithstanding the ordinance, then the only question to be considered is, who are the people of Louisiana that are to exercise the sovereign authority belonging to the State of Louisiana? Are they the loyal or the disloyal? There can be but one answer to that inquiry. It must only be the loyal."

Senator Howard admitted, continued Mr. Johnson, that it is not in the power of the United States to change the territorial limits of the States that had gone out, because the Constitution prohibits it. If he had thought for a moment he would have seen that the Constitution equally prohibits any interference on the part of the General Government with the exercise of the right of suffrage in a State. He then combated at some length the intimation of Senators Howard and Sumner that any power without a State had a right to prescribe qualifications for the exercise of the suffrage.

Mr. Powell, too, concurred in this view and asked by what authority General Banks and the President undertook to prescribe the qualifications of voters in Louisiana. The Maryland Senator replied that this question had been anticipated. The eleven thousand four hundred and fourteen voters, according to the proof before the Senate, were all loyal men and entitled to vote by the original constitution of Louisiana, no matter how they were brought together. If, coming together, they did an act which they would have been authorized to do if they had come together voluntarily they ought to be received.

Powell then inquired, what right had the Senate to presume that there may not have been twelve thousand loyal voters in Louisiana who were deprived of the right of suffrage because of this order of General Banks? As the Kentucky Senator understood it, no man could vote "unless he would go forward and take the oath prescribed by the President and swear to support and sustain all proclamations in regard to African slavery already issued and all that might afterward be issued." Mr. Johnson acknowledged this difficulty and admitted that he had always felt it; but they had the same difficulty, he asserted, in his own State, and a much greater one; he would be sorry to think Maryland was not in the Union. "Maryland is in the Union," said Senator Powell. "The constitution," observed Johnson in reply, "which now makes her a State in the Union was adopted the other day. I mean the one which governs her. She has manumitted her slaves by force of that constitution. No man in Maryland seriously contests the obligation of that constitution in that particular or in any other. But it was adopted, in fact, by the exclusion of a good many men who were entitled to vote."

Mr. Johnson at this point became engaged in an argument, not wholly relevant, with Sumner in which he gained some advantage over the Massachusetts Senator. As a specimen of the latter's parliamentary tactics at this time it may not be irrelevant to reproduce a passage from the *Congressional Globe*.

MR. SUMNER. Allow me to ask the Senator [Johnson] whether, in his opinion, the Ordinance governing the Northwest Territory, prohibiting slavery everywhere throughout that Territory, and which was declared to be a perpetual compact, could be set aside by any one of the States in the Territory now.

Mr. Johnson. I certainly think they can, except so far as rights are vested.

Mr. Sumner. The Senator, then, thinks Ohio can enslave a fellow-man?

Mr. Johnson. Just as much as Massachusetts can.

Mr. Sumner. Massachusetts cannot.

Mr. Johnson. Why not?

Mr. Sumner. Massachusetts cannot do an act of injustice.

Mr. Johnson. Oh, indeed! I did not know that. [Laughter.][1]

Notwithstanding this claim for his native State Sumner admitted a moment later that Massachusetts had united in the Convention of 1787 with South Carolina to deny to Congress authority to prohibit the slave trade for twenty years, and he confessed that such action was unjust. His inconsistency was still further exposed by Senator Henderson, who called attention to the fact that the educational qualification imposed by the Massachusetts constitution would exclude from the franchise almost every negro in Louisiana if the provisions were applicable in the latter State.[2]

After this colloquy, not uninteresting to the student of constitutional history, the Maryland Senator resumed his remarks:

"One word more, sir, and I have done. If Congress passes this resolution, and the State is admitted, no court will hereafter be able to decide that she is not a State in the Union, and no court therefore can call in question the validity or effect of any provision to be found in her constitution. One of the provisions of this constitution is that all the slaves of Louisiana are emancipated. Pass this resolution, admit the State, and that provision is effectual at once."[3]

Mr. Sumner, having in mind the fundamental condition imposed by Congress upon the admission of Missouri, offered

[1] Globe, Part II., 2 Sess. 38th Cong., p. 1097.
[2] Ibid.
[3] Ibid., pp. 1095-1098.

the following amendment of the resolution from the Committee on the Judiciary:

> *Provided,* That this shall not take effect except upon the fundamental condition that within the State there shall be no denial of the electoral franchise, or of any other rights on account of color or race, but all persons shall be equal before the law. And the Legislature of the State, by a solemn public act, shall declare the assent of the State to this fundamental condition, and shall transmit to the President of the United States an authentic copy of such assent whenever the same shall be adopted, upon the receipt whereof he shall, by proclamation, announce the fact; whereupon, without any further proceedings on the part of Congress, this joint resolution shall take effect.[1]

Though Senator Clark favored the principle of Sumner's amendment, he opposed it, as it stood, because it affected a resolution which proposed " to recognize the government in the State of Louisiana," which in his judgment was still a State in the Union, " having its constitution overthrown, but desiring and attempting to establish a new " one; and he added, " I hold that we have no power to amend that constitution; and that is the reason why I shall be obliged to vote against it here."

He spoke for the adoption of Trumbull's resolution and, in doing so, traveled some of the ground gone over by Henderson. The government of Louisiana, Mr. Clark believed, belonged to the Union people. He was not aware that any definite number of persons was required to constitute a State, nor did he understand how the majority by going into rebellion could take away the rights of the loyal minority.

The guaranty of a republican form of government was made, he asserted, to meet precisely such a case as had arisen in Louisiana. In this view it became the duty of Congress to protect the government established by the minority.[2]

Mr. Pomeroy, speaking to the principle of Sumner's amend-

[1] Globe, Part II., 2 Sess. 38th Cong., p. 1099.
[2] Ibid., pp. 1101-1102.

ment, declared that he would vote against all measures that looked like Congressional interference with the right to vote in the States. Saulsbury interrupted him to inquire what he would have done had the President, or his Secretary of War, sent armed soldiers to the polls and imposed a test upon voters as was done in Delaware, where Democrats were chased into swamps and compelled in the night time to lie out in the snow. Pomeroy's only reply to this was to relate his own experience under Democratic supremacy in the early days of Kansas. He resumed his remarks on Louisiana, but these had been anticipated by the speakers who preceded him. In conclusion he asserted that there were two reasons for recognizing Arkansas where there was but one in favor of Louisiana.[1]

The Delaware Senator did not fail to call attention to Pomeroy's evasion, and said he was glad to observe a change in the spirit of some of his Republican friends. " I think," he said, " they begin to scent the danger in the distance; that they begin to see that if a Government of law is to be destroyed, and power is to be concentrated in Executive hands, or in the hands of Executive agents, there is an end of liberty in this country. I hail the dawn, therefore, of a better day."[2]

Mr. Henderson again entered into the discussion, and in the course of his remarks drew from Senator Sumner this remarkable statement concerning Louisiana: " It is in and it is not. [Laughter.] The territory is in; but as yet there is no State government that is in." In this discussion Sumner asserted also that when the bill of his friend Senator Wade was before Congress no one questioned its constitutionality though it proposed to interfere in the suffrage and to impose a condition upon States at the time of their reconstruction. Pomeroy dissented from the doctrine that Congress could reconstruct

[1] Globe, Part II., 2 Sess. 38th Cong., pp. 1101-1102.
[2] Ibid., p. 1102.

the insurgent States, and maintained that the only question then was whether they would recognize what the people of Louisiana had done.

Reverdy Johnson pointed out to Sumner the great increase of representation in Congress which the South would acquire by an extension of the suffrage to negroes. The three fifths provision, he said, would be done away with, and he made the further observation that for years to come the entire colored vote of that section would be in the hands of a few white men. He urged recognition of both Louisiana and Arkansas, so that the constitutional amendment would become binding, for unless ratified by three fourths of all the States it would be open to doubt.

The session was drawing rapidly toward its close; it was late in the evening of February 25, and the resolution under discussion was too important to be passed without due consideration. These circumstances offered Mr. Wade, who vehemently opposed the measure, a decent pretext for demanding the "yeas" and "nays" on his motion to postpone the subject till the first Monday of December following, 1865.

Before a vote was reached on this motion, however, Powell spoke again at considerable length. In addition to his former arguments, many of which were repeated, he said that "all the loyal Union men in the State of Louisiana who refused, like supple menials and slaves, to crouch beneath the iron military power of General Banks, and take that oath were excluded from voting," and he added, "I believe to-day there are more men of that description in Louisiana than voted to ratify this constitution."

When asked by Mr. Henderson whether he had heard of any objection to it on the part of the loyal men of Louisiana, Powell answered that Thomas J. Durant and thirty-one others, distinguished, leading, loyal men of that State, had made earnest and powerful protest against it, and remonstrated

SENATE DEBATE ON LOUISIANA 379

against the admission to Congress of Senators and Representatives from Louisiana. They were also opposed to counting her electoral vote. Mr. Durant, he believed, was the first district-attorney appointed in Louisiana by the present Executive. Henderson insinuated by an inquiry that Durant was himself a candidate for office at that election and took the oath prescribed. Powell not being informed on these points, the matter was left in doubt.

The Kentucky Senator took this opportunity to characterize the manner of General Banks in his statement before the Judiciary Committee as that of a " swift witness, to make a case that he thought would cause Louisiana to be admitted." He also called upon some advocate of the resolution to explain a support of the present measure after voting a few days before for the resolution declaring that the electoral vote of Louisiana should not be counted. If Louisiana was then a legitimate government, why, he asked, was she not entitled to cast her electoral vote? He did not then believe it a legitimate government and so opposed the counting of her electoral vote; but the Senator from Maryland [Mr. Johnson] and the Senator from Missouri [Mr. Henderson], who then voted with him, now supported the resolution.[1]

Wade's motion to postpone further consideration of the joint resolution till the first Monday of December was defeated by a vote of 17 to 12.[2]

In the course of the discussions to postpone Sumner said that he would regard its passage as a national calamity. It would be the political Bull Run of that Administration, sacrificing, as it would, a great cause and the great destinies of this Republic. When Trumbull taxed him with intent to postpone discussion by dilatory motions the Massachusetts Senator admitted his opposition and declared that to defeat

[1] Globe, Part II., 2 Sess. 38th Cong., pp. 1106-1107.
[2] Ibid., p. 1107.

the measure he would employ any weapon in the arsenal of parliamentary warfare.

The friends of the Administration endeavored to press their adversaries to take final action on the resolution. The earnestness of the two factions provoked rather sharp censure of Sumner and the few Republicans who acted with him and were attempting by dilatory motions to fatigue the Senate into a postponement. Doolittle was especially severe on them, and particularly on Sumner, who replied with much asperity. He was supported by Howard and Chandler, while Trumbull, Foster and Doolittle undertook a defence of the resolution and its advocates. This wrangling appears to have delighted the Democratic members. Mr. Hendricks, indeed, made no attempt to conceal his satisfaction.

"The discordant elements of the Republican party are exhibiting themselves here," said the Indiana Senator, "and I venture the prophecy that a like exhibition will be witnessed over the country within a very few years. But four years ago, at the Chicago Convention, when Mr. Lincoln was nominated for the Presidency a solemn pledge was made to the people of this country that that party, when it came into power, would not undertake to interfere with the institutions of the States. As soon as the disturbed condition of the country gave the pretext for it, the undertaking was commenced; and now, when, in the judgment of some, it has been accomplished, there comes up the grave question, what is to be done, and what is to be the political condition of the four million negroes when they are set free? And upon that question the real strife of to-night has been witnessed. That is the subject and it need not be disguised. It is growing out of the discordant elements of the party that now governs the country."[1]

Trumbull, in reply to an inquiry of Senator Wade, said that

[1] Globe, Part II., 2 Sess. 38th Cong., p. 1111.

he had voted against receiving the electoral vote of Louisiana because it had not been recognized. Now he proposed to put it in a condition where it could cast electoral votes, and do all other acts belonging to a State.

To this Wade replied that "If the President of the United States, operating through his major-generals, can initiate a State government, and can bring it here and force us, compel us, to receive as associates on this floor these mere mockeries, these men of straw who represent nobody, your Republic is at an end.

"Sir, I have heard a great deal about this pretended election in Louisiana that did not come from Major-General Banks, and I pronounce the proceeding a mockery. It is not pretended that there could be drummed up from the riffraff of New Orleans and sent into the vicinity under the mandate of a Major-General more than about six thousand votes, where over fifty thousand were formerly polled.

. . . .

"Talk not to me of your ten per cent. principle. A more absurd, monarchical, and anti-American principle was never announced on God's earth—— "[1]

At this point Senator Sherman, of Ohio, interposed to obtain consideration for a revenue measure which he had in charge, whereupon his colleague changed somewhat the declamation against the resolution to a denunciation of its advocates, especially Trumbull, upon whom he retorted the charge of retarding legitimate business. Howard resented the charge of radical factiousness and denounced Trumbull with considerable warmth. Sherman suggested that enough had been said on both sides, and in the lighter skirmishing of the breathing-spell which followed, Mr. Sprague, of Rhode Island, hitherto a silent spectator of these exciting scenes, declared that he held in his possession a paper indicating the

[1] Globe, Part II., 2 Sess. 38th Cong., p. 1128.

names of the members of the Louisiana Legislature, and it showed that twenty-five, or twenty-seven or thirty of those gentlemen who constituted that assembly were officeholders of the Federal Government, or the government of the State, which, he said, was the same thing.[1]

While Sherman's measure and Trumbull's resolution were competing for priority of consideration Sumner remarked that during the preceding summer, 1864, he had met a distinguished gentleman just returned from Louisiana; he had been present at some of the sittings of the convention, having been in New Orleans in discharge of important public duties. This gentleman, added Sumner, said compendiously that the convention was "nothing but a stupendous hoax."

When Reverdy Johnson inquired the name of Sumner's informant, Senator Grimes replied that he could furnish a large number of names of persons present in New Orleans when the convention was held, and added: "If the Senate will give a committee I will undertake to prove and I will prove that the voters whose votes were polled in the outlying parishes at Thibodeaux and Placquemines, and other places, were carried in army transports to those places where they polled the votes, being discharged soldiers and persons belonging in New Orleans, and were brought back to New Orleans, and were not residents of the places where they purported to vote."[2]

Sumner, immediately after the uncontroverted statement of Mr. Grimes, added, with more energy than elegance: "The pretended State government in Louisiana is utterly indefensible whether you look at its origin or its character. To describe it, I must use plain language. It is a mere seven-months' abortion, begotten by the bayonet in criminal conjunction with the spirit of caste, and born before its time,

[1] Globe, Part II., 2 Sess. 38th Cong., p. 1129.
[2] Ibid.

rickety, unformed, unfinished — whose continued existence will be a burden, a reproach, and a wrong. That is the whole case; and yet the Senator from Illinois now presses it upon the Senate at this moment to the exclusion of the important public business of the country." [1]

The urgency of the army and navy appropriation bills prevented for the time further consideration of the Louisiana question. The subject, however, was again brought before the Senate on March 2, 1865, by Mr. Doolittle, who had received and had been requested to file with the secretary of the Senate a certificate, under seal of the State of Louisiana, of the election of Michael Hahn as a Senator of the United States from the State of Louisiana for six years from March 4, 1865. Mr. Davis, of Kentucky, opposed its reception. Doolittle's motion to have it laid on the table and filed was, however, agreed to.

Only two days of the session remained; in the temper of the Senate it was impossible that the resolution could pass at that time, and the House had not yet taken it up for discussion. In these circumstances the measure was abandoned, though very reluctantly, by its champions.

[1] Globe, Part II., 2 Sess. 38th Cong., p. 1129.

XI

INCIDENTS OF RECONSTRUCTION

THE Emancipation Proclamation did not affect, as is well known, the status of slaves in the loyal border States or in the excepted parts of Virginia and Louisiana. The State of Tennessee, too, as we have seen, was not named in the edict of freedom; that was published by the President simply as a measure of military necessity, and was not regarded by him or by others as operative to prevent, when war had ceased, a revival of servitude in the insurgent States, for negroes could easily be imported from those loyal commonwealths still tolerating that institution. It was uncertain, too, how the proclamation would affect the status of slaves in those districts not yet overrun by the Union armies. In the border States, in Tennessee and in the excepted parts of Louisiana and Virginia there were probably 2,000,000 men in bondage. In order, then, to abolish universally as well as permanently to prohibit involuntary servitude an amendment of the Constitution was proposed in the familiar language of the sixth section of the ordinance of 1787. Though it passed the Senate, April 8, 1864, it failed at that time to receive in the House the requisite two thirds vote. It has been seen how upon the recommendation of Mr. Lincoln it was reconsidered and passed by the Representatives at a succeeding session, January 31, 1865, and submitted to the States for their action. It was adopted by his own State, Illinois, on the following day. By the close of February sixteen others had followed its example, and before the President's death twenty in all had ratified the Amendment. To Mr. Lincoln, who had long held anti-slavery opinions, this expression of public sentiment was extremely grateful; indeed, less than two months before his assassination he declared his satisfaction at the popular verdict, and his confidence that the States would consummate what Congress had so nobly begun. The Thirteenth Amendment, however, was not announced as part of the organic law until after the Presidential plan of reconstruction had been ignored by the Thirty-ninth Congress. This subject, therefore, need not be further discussed in these pages.

The extraordinary amount of work actually completed by the national Legislature can be comprehended only by considering the degree of perfection to which the committee system has been carried under congressional government. Measures that conduct the reader over vast stretches of the records of Congress occupy but a day or two in the calendar. The discussions described in the two preceding chapters did not, as might be supposed, engage the entire attention of Federal legislators. It was desirable, if, indeed, it was not essential, that the sentiments of the lawmaking body of the nation be authoritatively declared on the question of admitting members to Congress from those States reconstituted under the Executive plan; definitive action in the matter of the electoral votes which they presented was also awaited with not a little interest. Scarcely inferior in importance and more instructive than these measures was the passage of an act, approved March 3, 1865, which created in the War Department a "Bureau of Refugees, Freedmen and Abandoned Lands." As the system of relief then inaugurated was destined to become an important agency in the work of reconstruction a brief account of its origin and institution may not be deemed superfluous.

A former chapter has related how great numbers of "contrabands," by assembling early in the war at Fortress Monroe and Newport News, taxed the ingenuity of even General Butler to provide for their maintenance; it also noticed an attempt under Mr. E. L. Pierce to improve the condition of abandoned slaves in South Carolina, and the friendly interest of Secretary Chase in that experiment. But the hundreds of fugitives within Federal lines in May, 1861, had grown to be millions by the beginning of 1865. Of this army of homeless freedmen the policy of enlisting colored troops provided directly for nearly 200,000 able-bodied males. The women, the children and the large class unsuitable for military service left a multitude still unprovided for. Some relief, it is true, was afforded by the Treasury Department, which undertook to establish on abandoned and confiscated lands colonies of self-supporting negroes, but the ignorance and rapacity of many persons entrusted with the supervision of this work led to its general failure. Here and there, indeed, more satisfactory results were obtained, though these isolated successes seldom reached the point of actual encouragement. The South Carolina experiment may, therefore, be properly regarded as the germ of the Freedmen's Bureau.

The progress of these communities had been watched anxiously by the abolition and the kindred associations which sprang up to continue the work that anti-slavery men had begun. On this subject a committee representing the Freedmen's Aid Societies of Boston, New York, Philadelphia and Cincinnati addressed, December 1, 1863, an able memorial to the President. Without expressing a favorable opinion of the plan suggested by the petitioners, Mr. Lincoln referred the question, as one of great magnitude and importance, to the consideration of Congress. The Freedmen's Aid Societies, however, had been anticipated by Representative Eliot, of Massachusetts, who had offered, January 12, 1863, a bill to establish a Bureau of Emancipation, which was referred to a select committee; but other business, regarded as more urgent, prevented them from reporting at that time a measure which had been prepared. At the succeeding session the proposition was offered again. After numerous efforts to secure favorable action, efforts extending over a period of two years, Congress took the subject into consideration. The House proposed one, the Senate a different measure; a committee of conference suggested something unlike either, though embodying important features of both. This, like every proposition affecting the negro, encountered considerable opposition. The creation of such a bureau, said its adversaries, conceded the very point that pro-slavery men had always maintained; namely, that the negro was incapable of taking care of himself. The extent of its powers, its duration and the cost of its maintenance were successively made grounds of opposition by those hostile to its establishment. Nor did its enemies fail to point out the great temptation to abuse which was offered by the system.

The act established in the War Department, to continue during the rebellion and for one year thereafter, a bureau to which should be committed the management of all confiscated or abandoned lands, and the control of all subjects relating to refugees and freedmen from any district within the territory embraced in the operations of the army, under such regulations as might be adopted by the head of the bureau and approved by the President.

The conduct of the bureau was entrusted to a commissioner appointed by the President with the concurrence of the Senate. In the exercise of his functions he was to be assisted by such clerks as the Secretary of War might assign him; their number, of course, was limited by law. For his compensation the head of the new bureau was to receive a sum fixed at $3,000 per annum. To aid in executing the provisions of the act the President was authorized to select, by and with the advice and consent of the Senate, one assistant commissioner for each of the States declared to be in insurrection, not, however, to exceed ten in number, each to receive an annual salary of $2,500.

The Secretary of War, besides assigning clerks of the several grades mentioned in the law, was authorized to issue, under regulations which he might himself prescribe, such provisions, clothing and fuel as might be deemed needful for the immediate and temporary shelter and supply of destitute and suffering refugees and freedmen as well as their wives and children. Any military officer could be detailed to duty under the act, but without increase of pay or allowances.

It was further provided that the commissioner, " under the direction of the President, shall have authority to set apart, for the use of loyal refugees and freedmen, such tracts of land within the insurrectionary States as shall have been abandoned, or to which the United States shall have acquired title by confiscation or sale, or otherwise, and to every male citizen, whether refugee or freedman, as aforesaid, there shall be assigned not more than forty acres of such land, and the person to whom it was so assigned shall be protected in the use and enjoyment of the land for the term of three years at an annual rent not exceeding six per centum upon the value of said land, as it was appraised by the State authorities in the year 1860, for the purpose of taxation, and in case no such appraisal can be found, then the rental shall be based upon the estimated value of the land in said year, to be ascertained in such manner as the commissioner may by regulation prescribe. At the end of said term, or at any time during said term, the occupants of any parcels so assigned may purchase the land, and receive such title thereto as the United States can convey, upon paying therefor the value of the land, as ascertained and fixed for the purpose of determining the annual rent aforesaid." [1]

[1] Globe, 2 Sess. 38th Cong., p. 141 (appendix).

INCIDENTS OF RECONSTRUCTION

It was made the duty of the assistant commissioners to submit a quarterly report of their proceedings to the commissioner, who in turn was required to report annually to the President before the commencement of each regular session of Congress. Special reports might from time to time be requested of either the head of the bureau or his subordinates.

The bureau thus established was organized principally by officers of the regular army under direction of General Oliver O. Howard, who had been selected by President Johnson as commissioner. It soon grew to vast proportions. At first it was economically managed and beneficent in its influence; subsequently, however, it degenerated into an abuse. Interesting and instructive as would be an inquiry into its operations, the history of this politico-philanthropic experiment does not fall within the limits of this work.

Since the adjournment, February 27, 1861, of the Peace Convention, which had been in session at Washington endeavoring to discover, if possible, a means of avoiding the irrepressible conflict, there was a large class who believed that if only they had been directing the policy of Government the outbreak could have been averted; even when war was flagrant and passions were highest this class, though diminished greatly in numbers, did not altogether despair of effecting a settlement between the sections. Besides these well-meaning patriots there were not a few who were ambitious of notoriety or possessed of an undue opinion of their own importance. Persons of both classes attempted from time to time to bring about an armistice which would facilitate negotiations between the two governments. The efforts of these men have no further bearing on the subject of reconstruction than as they serve to show Mr. Lincoln's views in successive stages of the conflict.

Prominent among these attempts was the Jacquess-Gilmore mission, which has been described in an interesting volume of Rebellion reminiscences by one of the participants.[1] Horace Greeley's career as a diplomat is also a familiar story, which at once illustrates the guilelessness of the editor and the sagacity of the President. Mr. Greeley's failure at Niagara Falls, however, did not discourage a similar undertaking by Hon. Jeremiah S. Black, who, with no greater success, had an interview in Canada with his former friend Jacob Thompson.[2]

More important, because of its consequences, than the work of any of these volunteer commissioners was the visit of Francis P. Blair, Sr., to Richmond. This distinguished politician and editor had in the days of Nullification assisted in shaping the policy of the Government. The bosom friend and confidential adviser of Andrew Jackson, Mr. Blair thoroughly understood Southern feeling, and from long residence in Washington was intimately acquainted with Southern leaders. His political victories in the past encouraged, no doubt, the hope of some notable achievement to crown his maturer years. For some time he had been meditating a plan of reunion which would not only end the strife but contribute to heal the wounds of war. Though anxious to communicate his project to the President, he received no encouragement to do so. By requesting Blair to call upon him after the fall of Savannah Mr. Lincoln evaded a discussion of the subject. That contingency, however, was not remote, and late in December the veteran political leader received from the President a card bearing these words:

> Allow the bearer, F. P. Blair, Sr., to pass our lines, go South, and return.
>
> A. Lincoln.
>
> *December 28, 1864.*

[1] Personal Recollections of Abraham Lincoln, by James R. Gilmore.
[2] Gorham's Life and Public Services of Edwin M. Stanton, Vol. II. pp. 148-153.

INCIDENTS OF RECONSTRUCTION

With this credential Mr. Blair went at once to the camp of General Grant, whence under flags of truce he sent two communications to Jefferson Davis requesting, among other things, permission for an interview. This, after some delay, was granted, and on the 12th of January, 1865, he found himself in Richmond face to face with the Confederate President. What transpired is accurately known from accounts of the meeting by both Blair and Davis. The former admitted frankly that Mr. Lincoln afforded him no opportunity to explain the object of his mission, and, indeed, appeared anxious to avoid an interview on that subject. When he had been assured that the Confederate authorities were under no engagements to European powers that would prevent their entering into arrangements with the Government of the United States Mr. Blair unfolded his plan by reading to Mr. Davis a carefully prepared paper embodying the following suggestions:

Slavery, he said, was doomed, for even the South itself had proposed to employ the slave in winning its independence. That institution, therefore, no longer remained as an obstacle to peace. Louis Napoleon, he continued, had declared publicly that his object was to make the Latin race supreme in the southern part of North America. This, indeed, had been an idea of the Emperor's uncle, who desired at one time to make conquests of territory in the States bordering the Gulf, and the foothold already effected in Mexico was one step in the accomplishment of this grand design. After developing these points Mr. Blair added, "Jefferson Davis is the fortunate man who now holds the commanding position to encounter this formidable scheme of conquest, and whose fiat can at the same time deliver his country from the bloody agony now covering it in mourning. He can drive Maximilian from his American throne, and baffle the designs of Napoleon to subject our Southern people to the 'Latin race.'"

How this was to be accomplished Mr. Blair's paper outlined. President Lincoln's amnesty proclamation looked to an armistice, which could be enlarged to embrace all engaged in the war; then by secret preliminaries to a cessation of hostilities Mr. Davis could transfer to Texas such a portion of the Confederate army as was deemed adequate to his purpose. With a Southern force on the Rio Grande and Juarez conciliated it could enter Mexico and expel her invaders. If these combined forces were insufficient, multitudes from the Federal army, officers and men, would be found ready to engage in the enterprise. Both Republicans and Democrats of the North had declared their adherence to the Monroe Doctrine.

After thus indicating for Mr. Davis a means of escape from his dilemma the adroit politician next appealed powerfully to his desire of fame. "He who expels the Bonaparte-Hapsburg dynasty from our Southern flank," proceeded Mr. Blair, "which General Jackson in one of his letters warned me was the vulnerable point through which foreign invasion would come, will ally his name with those of Washington and Jackson as a defender of the liberty of the country. If in delivering Mexico he should model its States in form and principle to adapt them to our Union and add a new Southern constellation to its benignant sky while rounding off our possessions on the continent at the Isthmus, and opening the way to blending the waters of the Atlantic and Pacific, thus embracing our Republic in the arms of the ocean, he would complete the work of Jefferson, who first set one foot of our colossal Government on the Pacific by a stride from the Gulf of Mexico."[1]

Blair remarked in conclusion, "There is my problem, Mr. Davis; do you think it possible to be solved?" After a little consideration came the reply, "I think so." Touching the

[1] N. and H., Vol. X. pp. 101-102.

INCIDENTS OF RECONSTRUCTION

question of bringing the sections together again Mr. Davis observed that though a spirit of vindictiveness had been engendered by the war, time and events would do something toward its removal. The circumstance of Northern and Southern armies united in a common cause would, he believed, assist greatly in restoring the old feeling. He also acknowledged to his visitor that European powers were pleased to see the sections exhausting their resources in mutual war.

Thus was the Confederate leader persuaded to entertain the bold project of conquering Mexico under pretence of relieving the Monroe Doctrine from its peril. The explanation of this easy conversion, however, lies mainly in the fact that Mr. Davis, however he might endeavor to conceal his convictions, was convinced that the resources of the South were scarcely equal to another campaign. Like other leaders of the Confederacy he was anxious to seize any means of escape from an embarrassing situation. He proposed to Mr. Blair, therefore, the appointment of commissioners, and mentioned Judge Campbell, formerly of the United States Supreme Court, as one qualified by his talents and integrity to undertake such a mission.

During his short sojourn in Richmond Mr. Blair learned from other prominent secessionists the hopelessness of the rebellion, and this, perhaps, was the only tangible result of his celebrated intrigue. To initiate the project Mr. Davis handed him a letter to be shown President Lincoln. That interesting communication was as follows:

RICHMOND, VIRGINIA, 12 *Jany.*, '65.

F. P. BLAIR, Esq.:

SIR: I have deemed it proper, and probably desirable to you, to give you, in this form, the substance of remarks made by me, to be repeated by you to President Lincoln, etc., etc. I have no disposition to find obstacles in forms, and am willing now, as heretofore, to enter into negotiations for the restoration of peace; and am ready to send a commission whenever I have reason to suppose it will be received, or to receive a commission, if the United States Government shall choose to send one. That, notwithstanding the rejection of our former offers, I would, if you could promise that a commissioner, minister, or other agent, would be received, appoint one immediately, and renew the effort to enter into conference, with a view to secure peace to the two countries.

Yours, etc.,
JEFFERSON DAVIS.[1]

Mr. Lincoln's only response to the communication thus brought to his attention was to open a little wider the door for negotiation by sending to Mr. Blair the following letter:

WASHINGTON, *January* 18, 1865.

F. P. BLAIR, Esq.:

SIR: You having shown me Mr. Davis's letter to you of the 12th instant, you may say to him that I have constantly been, am now, and shall continue ready to receive any agent whom he, or any other influential person now resisting the National authority, may informally send to me, with the view of securing peace to the people of our one common country. Yours, etc.,

A. LINCOLN.

With this note Mr. Blair returned to Richmond framing as best he could excuses why President Lincoln rejected the overtures of Jefferson Davis for a joint invasion of Mexico. With the nature of these explanations this essay is not concerned. To cover his retreat from an unsuccessful intrigue the disappointed commissioner then suggested that, perhaps, Grant and Lee could enter into negotiations for peace with more assurance of success than politicians could hope to do. Though Mr. Davis offered no objection to this proposal, Blair was forced soon after to report that military negotiations were out of the question.

The Confederate leader was then compelled to choose between obstinate perseverance in his policy of a war for Southern independence or to accept frankly Mr. Lincoln's

---

[1] N. and H., Vol. X. p. 107.

offer of reunion. Blair's first visit to Richmond did not escape observation, and, when his second conference was known, interest in the purpose of his mission became intense. Without some effort at negotiation Mr. Davis could not afterward satisfy the peace party in the South without subjecting himself to the injurious imputation of preferring war. In these circumstances, and after consultation with his cabinet, he authorized Alexander H. Stephens, John A. Campbell and R. M. T. Hunter to proceed to Washington as a commission for the purpose of informally conferring with Mr. Lincoln " upon the issues involved in the existing war, and for the purpose of securing peace to the two countries." They were burdened with no instructions, and only one condition was insisted upon, that is, an acknowledgment of Southern independence.

Toward the end of January they presented themselves at the Federal military lines near Richmond, and, after an exchange of telegrams with the authorities in Washington, were permitted to pass on to Fortress Monroe. It was the original intention of President Lincoln to intrust the work of the conference wholly to Secretary Seward, and for this purpose he gave him the following written instructions:

EXECUTIVE MANSION,
WASHINGTON, *January* 31, 1865.

Hon. WILLIAM H. SEWARD, *Secretary of State:*

You will proceed to Fortress Monroe, Virginia, there to meet and informally confer wtth Messrs. Stephens, Hunter, and Campbell, on the basis of my letter to F. P. Blair, Esq., of January 18, 1865, a copy of which you have. You will make known to them that three things are indispensable, to wit: *First.* The restoration of the national authority throughout all the States. *Second.* No receding by the executive of the United States on the slavery question from the position assumed thereon in the late annual message to Congress, and in preceding documents. *Third.* No cessation of hostilities short of an end of the war and the disbanding of all forces hostile to the Government. You will inform them that all propositions of theirs, not inconsistent with the above, will be considered and passed upon in a spirit of sincere liberality. You will hear all they may choose to say and report it to me. You will not assume to definitely consummate anything.

Yours, etc.,
ABRAHAM LINCOLN.[1]

    The different if not conflicting statements as to the object of their mission nearly led to a return of the Confederate representatives without any interview whatever. General Grant, fearing the unfavorable influence on the Union cause of such a result, sent to Secretary Stanton a confidential dispatch in which he referred to the evident sincerity of Stephens and Hunter. He also expressed his regret that they were about to return without an expression on the subject of their mission from any person in authority. President Lincoln, who was about to recall Mr. Seward by telegraph, decided, on reading Grant's message, to join his Secretary at Fortress Monroe, for which place he set out at once.

    The famous conference, which took place February 3, 1865, on board a steamer at Hampton Roads, has been treated in detail by nearly every historian of the Rebellion, and, therefore, need only be briefly noticed in these pages. An informal discussion of four hours occurred on the *River Queen*. By a previous agreement no writings or memoranda were made; hence our principal knowledge of what transpired at that celebrated interview is derived from accounts subsequently written out from memory by the Confederate commissioners, and from Secretary Seward's letter to Charles Francis Adams, United States Minister to England.

    Mr. Stephens, who began the discussion, asked whether there was no way of restoring former relations; to this Mr. Lincoln replied, " There was but one way that he knew of, and that was, for those who were resisting the laws of the

---

[1] Letters and State Papers of Lincoln, Vol. II. pp. 644-645.

Union to cease that resistance." Stephens observed that they had been led to believe that both sections might for a time cease their present strife and unite on some continental question until passion had somewhat subsided and accommodation become possible.

To this suggestion Mr. Lincoln replied promptly: "I suppose you refer to something that Mr. Blair has said. Now it is proper to state at the beginning that whatever he said was of his own accord, and without the least authority from me." The President then stated that before the visit to Richmond he had flatly refused to hear Mr. Blair's propositions; he was willing, however, to hear proposals for peace on the conditions expressed in his reply to the letter of Mr. Davis. The restoration of the Union was a *sine qua non* with him, therefore his instructions that no conference be held except on that basis.

Though the Confederate statesmen had resolved not to enter into any agreement that would require their forces to unite in an invasion of Mexico, Mr. Stephens continued to press the subject, and this after Mr. Lincoln had refused even to discuss the question. The President then brought the conversation back to the original object of the meeting, and declared that he could not entertain a proposition looking to an armistice until the paramount question of reunion was first determined.

The terms of reunion were then discussed. On this subject Mr. Lincoln is reported by the commissioners to have said that the shortest way to effect this was to disband the insurgent armies and permit "the National authorities to resume their functions." As to the admission of members to Congress from the seceding States the President believed they ought to be received, and also that they would be; however, he could enter into no stipulations on that subject. By the cessation of resistance, he is alleged to have declared, the

States would be immediately restored to their practical relations to the Union. This sentiment was probably ascribed to him for party purposes.

As the enforcement of the confiscation and other penal laws was left entirely with him he assured them that the Executive power would be exercised with the utmost liberality. The courts could determine all questions involving rights of property, and Congress, after passion had been somewhat composed, would, no doubt, be liberal in making restitution of forfeited property, or would indemnify those who had suffered.

The President refused to promise any modification whatever of the terms of his Emancipation Proclamation. He regarded it as a judicial question. How the courts would decide it he did not know. His own opinion was that as the proclamation was only a war measure, as soon as the war ceased it would be inoperative for the future. It would be held to apply only to such slaves as had come under its operation while it was in active exercise. The courts, however, might hold that it effectually emancipated all the slaves in the States to which it applied at the time. He is reported further to have said that he interfered with slavery to maintain the Union, and then only with hesitation and under pressure of a public necessity. He had always favored emancipation, but not immediate emancipation.

On the same occasion he is said to have stated as his belief that the people of the North were not less responsible for slavery than those of the South; if the war should then cease, with the voluntary abolition of slavery by the States, he would favor, individually, payment by the Government of a fair indemnity for the loss to owners. That feeling, he believed, had an extensive existence in the loyal States. He knew some who were in favor of an appropriation as high as $400,000,000 for that purpose. However, he could enter into no stipulation. He merely expressed his own views and what he believed to be the views of others upon the subject.

Relative to the division of Virginia Mr. Lincoln said he could give only "an individual opinion, which was, that Western Virginia would continue to be recognized as a separate State in the Union."

Seward brought to the notice of the commissioners one topic which to them was new, that is, the passage by Congress three days earlier of the proposed amendment to the Federal Constitution. He is reported to have said that it was passed in deference to the war spirit, and that if the South would agree to immediate restoration its ratification might be defeated. This, however, is doubtful, for the Cabinet as well as the President approved the action of Congress in submitting the Thirteenth Amendment to the consideration of the States; besides, it is not in harmony with Mr. Seward's anti-slavery record.

In urging on Mr. Stephens separate State action to effect a cessation of hostilities, the President said: "If I resided in Georgia, with my present sentiments, I'll tell you what I would do if I were in your place. I would go home and get the Governor of the State to call the Legislature together, and get them to recall all the State troops from the war; elect Senators and Members to Congress, and ratify this constitutional amendment prospectively, so as to take effect — say in five years. Such a ratification would be valid, in my opinion. I have looked into the subject, and think such a prospective ratification would be valid. Whatever may have been the views of your people before the war, they must be convinced now that slavery is doomed. It cannot last long in any event, and the best course, it seems to me, for your public men to pursue would be to adopt such a policy as will avoid, as far as possible, the evils of immediate emancipation. This would be my course, if I were in your place." [1]

The advice was wasted. When the party was on the point of separating, Mr. Stephens again asked the President to reconsider the plan of an armistice on the basis of a Mexican expedition. " Well, Stephens," replied Mr. Lincoln, " I will reconsider it; but I do not think my mind will change." Thus ended the famous Hampton Roads conference.

On their return to Richmond the commissioners made a formal report to Mr. Davis of the failure of negotiations; this he transmitted to the Confederate Congress with an artful letter designed to strengthen the war party in the South, and to silence effectually the adversaries of his administration. To improve this advantage a day was appointed for the purpose of getting a popular expression on the result of the conference. Business was generally suspended, and the people crowded every building in the city suitable for holding large assemblies. Churches, theatres and halls of legislation were engaged for the occasion. Twenty orators, among the ablest in the South, told their hearers of the Northern " ultimatum," not omitting to describe eloquently all the consequences of subjugation. The old war spirit appeared to have been kindled once more; " But," says Mr. Pollard, " it was only the sickly glare of an expiring flame; there was no steadiness in the excitement; there was no virtue in huzzas; the inspiration ended with the voices and ceremonies that invoked it; and it was found that the spirit of the people of the Confederacy was too weak, too much broken to act with effect, or assume the position of

[1] An interesting account of this entire subject will be found in Nicolay and Hay's Lincoln, Vol. X. ch. VI.; see also Raymond's Life of Lincoln, pp. 647-662.

erect and desperate defiance."[1] In March General Lee revealed the weakness of his army at Fort Steadman; Grant's movements around Petersburg followed in April; the rest is a familiar story.

From this brief discussion of topics only allied to the Presidential method of re-union it is time to resume our examination of the main theme.

It is almost a trite observation to remark that President Lincoln's opinions on public questions were formed only after mature deliberation, and that to the conclusions thus reached he adhered with inflexible tenacity. Notwithstanding the sentiments of Congress on the question of reconstruction he evinced a decided preference for his own. This is proved by a number of letters and speeches from which two may be selected both because of the time of their appearance and the station of the persons to whom they were addressed. To General Hurlbut, who had temporarily succeeded Banks in command at New Orleans, the President wrote, November 14, 1864, the following admonitory letter:

> Few things, since I have been here, have impressed me more painfully than what, for four or five months past, has appeared a bitter military opposition to the new State government of Louisiana. I still indulged some hope that I was mistaken in the fact; but copies of a correspondence on the subject between General Canby and yourself, and shown me to-day, dispel that hope. A very fair proportion of the people of Louisiana have inaugurated a new State government, making an excellent new constitution — better for the poor black man than we have in Illinois. This was done under military protection, directed by me, in the belief, still sincerely entertained, that with such a nucleus around which to build we could get the State into position again sooner than otherwise. In this belief a general promise of protection and support, applicable alike to Louisiana and other States, was given in the last annual message. During the formation of the new government and constitution they were supported by nearly every loyal person, and opposed by every secessionist. And this support and this opposition, from the respective standpoints of the parties, was perfectly consistent and

[1] The Lost Cause, pp. 684-685.

logical. Every Unionist ought to wish the new government to succeed; and every disunionist must desire it to fail. Its failure would gladden the heart of Slidell in Europe, and of every enemy of the old flag in the world. Every advocate of slavery naturally desires to see blasted and crushed the liberty promised the black man by the new constitution. But why General Canby and General Hurlbut should join on the same side is to me incomprehensible.

Of course, in the condition of things at New Orleans, the military must not be thwarted by the civil authority; but when the constitutional Convention, for what it deems a breach of privilege, arrests an editor in no way connected with the military, the military necessity for insulting the Convention and forcibly discharging the editor is difficult to perceive. Neither is the military necessity for protecting the people against paying large salaries fixed by a legislature of their own choosing very apparent. Equally difficult to perceive is the military necessity for forcibly interposing to prevent a bank from loaning its own money to the State. These things, if they have occurred, are, at the best, no better than gratuitous hostility. I wish I could hope that they may be shown to not have occurred. To make assurance against misunderstanding, I repeat that in the existing condition of things in Louisiana, the military must not be thwarted by the civil authority; and I add that on points of difference the commanding general must be judge and master. But I also add that in the exercise of this judgment and control, a purpose, obvious and scarcely unavowed, to transcend all military necessity, in order to crush out the civil government, will not be overlooked.[1]

A similar communication, though less peremptory in tone, he felt constrained to send to General E. R. S. Canby, who had been assigned to command in the military division of West Mississippi. Under date of December 12, 1864, he wrote that officer:

I think it is probable that you are laboring under some misapprehension as to the purpose, or rather the motive, of the Government on two points — cotton and the new Louisiana State government.

It is conceded that military operations are the first in importance; and as to what is indispensable to these operations, the department commander must be judge and master.

But the other matters mentioned I suppose to be of public importance also; and what I have attempted in regard to them is not merely a concession to private interest and pecuniary greed.

. . . .

[1] Letters and State Papers of Lincoln, Vol. II. pp. 597-598.

As to the new State government of Louisiana. Most certainly there is no worthy object in getting up a piece of machinery merely to pay salaries and give political consideration to certain men. But it is a worthy object to again get Louisiana into proper practical relations with the nation, and we can never finish this if we never begin it. Much good work is already done, and surely nothing can be gained by throwing it away.

I do not wish either cotton or the new State government to take precedence of the military while the necessity for the military remains; but there is a strong public reason for treating each with so much favor as may not be substantially detrimental to the military.[1]

That Mr. Lincoln never modified these opinions is conclusively proved by the last public utterance of his life. In addressing the citizens of Washington, who were holding a demonstration in consequence of Lee's surrender, the President on the evening of April 11 said:

By these recent successes the reinauguration of the national authority — reconstruction — which has had a large share of thought from the first, is pressed much more closely upon our attention. It is fraught with great difficulty. Unlike a case of war between independent nations, there is no authorized organ for us to treat with — no one man has authority to give up the rebellion for any other man. We simply must begin with and mold from disorganized and discordant elements. Nor is it a small additional embarrassment that we, the loyal people, differ among ourselves as to the mode, manner, and measure of reconstruction. As a general rule, I abstain from reading the reports of attacks upon myself, wishing not to be provoked by that to which I cannot properly offer an answer. In spite of this precaution, however, it comes to my knowledge that I am much censured for some supposed agency in setting up and seeking to sustain the new State government of Louisiana.

In this I have done just so much as, and no more than, the public knows. In the annual message of December, 1863, and in the accompanying proclamation, I presented a plan of reconstruction, as the phrase goes, which I promised, if adopted by any State, should be acceptable to and sustained by the executive Government of the nation. I distinctly stated that this was not the only plan which might possibly be acceptable, and I also distinctly protested that the executive claimed no right to say when or whether members should be admitted to seats in Congress from such States. This plan was in advance submitted to the then Cabinet, and distinctly approved by every member of it. One

[1] Letters and State Papers of Lincoln, Vol. II. pp. 616-617.

of them suggested that I should then and in that connection apply the Emancipation Proclamation to the theretofore excepted parts of Virginia and Louisiana; that I should drop the suggestion about apprenticeship for freed people, and that I should omit the protest against my own power in regard to the admission of members of Congress. But even he approved every part and parcel of the plan which has since been employed or touched by the action of Louisiana.

The new constitution of Louisiana, declaring emancipation for the whole State, practically applies the proclamation to the part previously excepted. It does not adopt apprenticeship for freed people, and it is silent, as it could not well be otherwise, about the admission of members to Congress. So that, as it applies to Louisiana, every member of the Cabinet fully approved the plan. The message went to Congress, and I received many commendations of the plan, written and verbal, and not a single objection to it from any professed emancipationist came to my knowledge until after the news reached Washington that the people of Louisiana had begun to move in accordance with it. From about July 1862, I had corresponded with different persons supposed to be interested [in] seeking a reconstruction of a State government for Louisiana. When the message of 1863, with the plan before mentioned, reached New Orleans, General Banks wrote me that he was confident that the people, with his military coöperation, would reconstruct substantially on that plan. I wrote to him and some of them to try it. They tried it, and the result is known. Such has been my only agency in getting up the Louisiana government.

As to sustaining it, my promise is out, as before stated. But as bad promises are better broken than kept, I shall treat this as a bad promise, and break it whenever I shall be convinced that keeping it is adverse to the public interest; but I have not yet been so convinced. I have been shown a letter on this subject, supposed to be an able one, in which the writer expresses regret that my mind has not seemed to be definitely fixed on the question whether the seceded States, so called, are in the Union or out of it. It would perhaps add astonishment to his regret were he to learn that since I have found professed Union men endeavoring to make that question, I have purposely forborne any public expression upon it. As appears to me, that question has not been, nor yet is, a practically material one, and that any discussion of it, while it thus remains practically immaterial, could have no effect other than the mischievous one of dividing our friends. As yet, whatever it may hereafter become, that question is bad as the basis of a controversy, and good for nothing at all — a merely pernicious abstraction.

We all agree that the seceded States, so called, are out of their proper practical relation with the Union, and that the sole object of the Government, civil and military, in regard to those States is to again get them into that proper practical relation. I believe that it is not only possible,

INCIDENTS OF RECONSTRUCTION

but in fact easier, to do this without deciding or even considering whether these States have ever been out of the Union, than with it. Finding themselves safely at home, it would be utterly immaterial whether they had ever been abroad. Let us all join in doing the acts necessary to restoring the proper practical relations between these States and the Union, and each forever after innocently indulge his own opinion whether in doing the acts he brought the States from without into the Union, or only gave them proper assistance, they never having been out of it. The amount of constituency, so to speak, on which the new Louisiana government rests, would be more satisfactory to all if it contained 50,000, or 30,000, or even 20,000, instead of only about 12,000, as it does. It is also unsatisfactory to some that the elective franchise is not given to the colored man. I would myself prefer that it were now conferred on the very intelligent, and on those who serve our cause as soldiers.

Still, the question is not whether the Louisiana government, as it stands, is quite all that is desirable. The question is, will it be wiser to take it as it is and help to improve it, or to reject and disperse it? Can Louisiana be brought into proper practical relation with the Union sooner by sustaining or by discarding her new State government? Some twelve thousand voters in the heretofore slave State of Louisiana have sworn allegiance to the Union, assumed to be the rightful political power of the State, held elections, organized a State government, adopted a free State constitution, giving the benefit of public schools equally to black and white, and empowering the legislature to confer the elective franchise upon the colored man. Their legislature has already voted to ratify the constitutional amendment recently passed by Congress, abolishing slavery throughout the nation. These twelve thousand persons are thus fully committed to the Union and to perpetual freedom in the State — committed to the very things, and nearly all the things, the nation wants — and they ask the nation's recognition and its assistance to make good their committal.

Now, if we reject and spurn them, we do our utmost to disorganize and disperse them. We, in effect, say to the white man: You are worthless or worse; we will neither help you, nor be helped by you. To the blacks we say: This cup of liberty which these, your old masters, hold to your lips we will dash from you, and leave you to the chances of gathering the spilled and scattered contents in some vague and undefined when, where, and how. If this course, discouraging and paralyzing both white and black, has any tendency to bring Louisiana into proper practical relations with the Union, I have so far been unable to perceive it. If, on the contrary, we recognize and sustain the new government of Louisiana, the converse of all this is made true. We encourage the hearts and nerve the arms of the twelve thousand to adhere to their work, and argue for it, and proselyte for it, and fight for it, and feed it, and grow it, and ripen it to a complete success. The colored man, too, in seeing all united for him, is inspired with vigilance, and energy, and daring, to the same end. Grant that he desires the elective franchise, will he not attain it sooner by saving the already advanced steps toward it than by running backward over them? Concede that the new government of Louisiana is only to what it should be as the egg is to the fowl, we shall sooner have the fowl by hatching the egg than by smashing it.

Again, if we reject Louisiana we also reject one vote in favor of the proposed amendment to the national Constitution. To meet this proposition it has been argued that no more than three fourths of those States which have not attempted secession are necessary to validly ratify the amendment. I do not commit myself against this further than to say that such a ratification would be questionable, and sure to be persistently questioned, while a ratification by three fourths of all the States would be unquestioned and unquestionable. I repeat the question: Can Louisiana be brought into proper practical relation with the Union sooner by sustaining or by discarding her new State government? What has been said of Louisiana will apply generally to other States. And yet so great peculiarities pertain to each State, and such important and sudden changes occur in the same State, and withal so new and unprecedented is the whole case that no exclusive and inflexible plan can safely be prescribed as to details and collaterals. Such exclusive and inflexible plan would surely become a new entanglement. Important principles may and must be inflexible. In the present situation, as the phrase goes, it may be my duty to make some new announcement to the people of the South. I am considering, and shall not fail to act when satisfied that action will be proper.

The promised announcement was never made; for within three days the great career of Abraham Lincoln was brought to a close. The inherent difficulties of reconstruction, as well as the mischievous consequences of faction among Union men, he perceived and acknowledged at the outset. Precisely how he would have removed the one and, without breaking with his party, have avoided the other we can never know. His uniform success in dealing with other embarrassing questions appears to justify the opinion that he would not have failed altogether in solving the greater problem presented by the return of peace. This subject will be further discussed in the succeeding chapter.

XII

CULMINATION OF THE PRESIDENTIAL PLAN

ABLE and candid exponents of public opinion in the South, even those who were a part of the "Lost Cause," are almost unanimous in regarding the assassination of President Lincoln as one of the greatest calamities that befell their section of the Union.[1] Indeed, the writer has heard a distinguished editor ascribe to Jefferson Davis himself the opinion that next to the failure of the Confederacy the untimely death of Mr. Lincoln was the severest blow inflicted on Southern interests.[2] Many of the evils experienced by their States during the early years of Congressional reconstruction would have been avoided, they believe, under a continuance of the wise and considerate policy of the martyr President. While it is true that the confidence which he enjoyed among the masses in the loyal States, his unquestionable integrity and his splendid intellectual powers would have made him a formidable adversary even in a controversy with Congress, yet we have no assurance that these undoubted elements of strength would have enabled him, in the confused times following the Rebellion, to do more than postpone a contest with the Legislative branch in which a desire to discipline the South was even then winning adherents. The passions of the hour would have discovered a weakness in his clemency

[1] Why the Solid South? p. 1.
[2] This recollection has been verified by correspondence with Col. A. K. McClure, the gentleman referred to.—AUTHOR.

to the vanquished, while his very breadth of soul and sense would have been regarded by radical members of his party as only an evidence of his desire to facilitate the restoration to power of red-handed rebels. But it is idle to speculate on what might have been the result of his endeavors to heal the wounds of war, for, by the assassin's bullet, the execution of his policy passed into other hands.

While the terrible tragedy of April 14 was still unknown to a great majority of American citizens, Andrew Johnson was quietly installed in the office of President. As every detail of the simple ceremony in the Kirkwood Hotel is familiar to this generation of readers, that event requires only a passing allusion. In the presence of the constitutional advisers of his predecessor, except Secretary Seward, who had been dangerously wounded by one of Booth's accomplices, the oath of office was administered by Chief Justice Chase, who, with the Attorney-General, had examined the precedents and the law. Besides these officials a few members of Congress, who still lingered at the capital, were in attendance as witnesses.

Something of Andrew Johnson's political career has been related in the chapter on Tennessee. As military governor of that State his high courage, his acknowledged patriotism, his honesty of purpose and principle were evident to all. Traits of character suspected, but not then fully disclosed, were developed by more complex conditions. The problem that confronted him may be briefly stated.

When Mr. Johnson succeeded to the Presidential office Confederate armies somewhat broken, indeed, but still capable of mischief were retarding the victorious march of Sherman's legions. Measures for disbanding the former became necessary when Southern leaders, recognizing the hopelessness of further resistance, made overtures looking to an armistice which took place and to the surrender that subsequently followed. It became necessary to discontinue at once the enlistment of men in the loyal States, and, to economize expense, to muster out of service as expeditiously as possible the grand army of Union volunteers. The energy and promptness with which this task was accomplished were not the least of Secretary Stanton's services to the nation. The perfection to which years of experience had brought the machinery of the War Department enabled the bulk of the Union armies to return without delay to their homes, where, discarding the character of soldiers, they melted insensibly into the civil population and speedily resumed the pursuits of peace. Relations with France were somewhat strained, and, owing to a succession of unfriendly acts, a war with Great Britain was not improbable. The public finances, too, required attention. To provide a revenue adequate to the extraordinary demands of the time was beginning to tax the resources of Government. A satisfactory settlement of even the least of these might well have appeared a serious question. The cessation of hostilities, however, presented a problem far transcending the greatest of them in importance.

Many of the late Confederate States were threatened with anarchy, for in those commonwealths the recent authority had been extinguished and no organizations existed which the Administration could recognize as State governments. The political reconstruction of four of them, it is true, had been commenced under encouragement and direction of the national Executive, but even in those much remained to be done. Before examining the condition of the insurgent States as a whole it may be well, therefore, to summarize the most important events that occurred in Arkansas, Tennessee, Louisiana and Virginia between the institution of loyal governments in those commonwealths and the meeting of the Thirty-ninth Congress in December, 1865.

The General Assembly of Arkansas, though lacking its full membership, convened in March, 1865, and unanimously adopted on April 14 succeeding the proposed amendment to the Federal Constitution. The action of Congress, however, in submitting that proposition to the States had been anticipated by the Union men of that commonwealth, for their organic law had already abolished involuntary servitude; by the same instrument they had repudiated all debts created in the conduct of the war, thereby complying with three of the principal conditions required for restoring their State to the Union.

During the same session an act passed the Legislature disfranchising all citizens who had aided the Confederate cause after the organization, April 18, 1864, of a loyal government. By the adversaries of this measure it was claimed that the lawmaking body exceeded its powers, because the act in effect prescribed qualifications for the suffrage different from those required by the State constitution, and, so far as it attempted to deprive citizens of their privileges without judicial conviction of crime, was contrary to the law of the land. This statute awakened the indifferent, and, as the time approached for holding Congressional elections, excited considerable discussion.

In the mean time the new government silently extended its authority over those parts of the State occupied by Southern soldiers until the cessation of hostilities. Governor Flanigan on retiring suggested that Confederate county officers be continued under his successor. This proposal, however, was promptly rejected and the secession establishment in all its parts completely ignored. Governor Murphy then published a proclamation urging the people in those regions hitherto dominated by the enemy, which comprised nearly half the counties in the State, to assemble and renew their local organizations. His address was favorably received, and his administration soon acquiesced in throughout the commonwealth. Outrages ceased with the disappearance of Confederate soldiers, and by the beginning of July judicial tribunals had been revived in nearly every county. Some of the courts had been in session, and most of them were prepared to meet regularly for the transaction of business. Taxes were collected as quietly as before the war, and civil process could be executed in every part of the State. Hundreds had returned from the South to their former homes and resumed the pursuits of peace. Discontent, so far as any existed in the State, was confined to some ex-Confederate officers and to a few non-combatants who had sympathized with the rebellion. Both classes advised disregard of the disfranchising law, but as a rule the returned soldiers on both sides were quiet and orderly. All accounts concur in representing the pacification of Arkansas as complete toward the end of summer, and by October 13, 1865, the Secretary of State was able to report officially that the new government was in successful operation, the civil organization of every county having been effected. Governor Murphy in approving a circular published near the close of the same month by Brigadier General Sprague, an assistant commissioner of the Freedmen's Bureau, enjoined both civil officers and citizens to give all possible encouragement to the officers and appointees of the bureau.[1]

The President on receiving intelligence of this satisfactory condition of affairs sent to Governor Murphy the following dispatch:

There will be no interference with your present organization of State government. I have learned from E. W. Gantt, Esq., and other sources, that all is working well, and you will proceed and resume the former relations with the Federal Government, and all the aid in the power of the Government will be given in restoring the State to its former relations.[2]

As the time approached for an election of national Representatives, the Governor issued another address in which he advised the choice of persons who could take the oath required

[1] Ex. Doc. No. 70, H. of R., 1 Sess. 39th Cong., p. 78.
[2] Ann. Cycl., 1865, p. 28.

by Congress. Three members were elected, namely: William Ryers, G. H. Kyle and James M. Johnson, who subsequently appeared at Washington and presented their credentials.[1]

The foregoing account of the situation in Arkansas is confirmed by the testimony of General Reynolds, military commander of the department, who had sent officers into all the counties. These reported civil government as everywhere reëstablished. The State, they asserted, had never enjoyed greater tranquillity. There was not a shadow of conflict between the civil and the military authority, for the latter in sustaining the former was careful not to encroach on any of its functions. In short, the restoration of civil law in that State was universally admitted.

In two thirds of the counties, however, great destitution prevailed. Early in the summer the General Government felt compelled to distribute among indigent freedmen and refugees vast quantities of food, and Northern generosity alone, the Governor declared, could prevent great distress during the ensuing winter. Nor was his expectation disappointed. It is a splendid tribute to the character of Americans that one of the most destructive conflicts in history, with all the animosities which protracted civil wars engender, did not perceptibly impair in them the feelings of humanity.

The organization of a Union government in Tennessee has elsewhere been described. The Assembly chosen under its authority met at Nashville on the 2d of April, 1865, and three days later ratified the Thirteenth Amendment. On the 21st the President was requested to proclaim the insurrection at an end in that commonwealth, though a few weeks later he was called upon for troops to guarantee a republican form of government and to protect the State against invasion and domestic violence. Besides appointing executive officers the

[1] Ann. Cycl., 1865, p. 28.

Legislature elected to the United States Senate David T. Patterson and Joseph S. Fowler.

The most important measure of the session, however, was the enactment on June 5 of a severe law affecting the elective franchise. By it the right to vote was restricted, as formerly, to white males who had attained their twenty-first year. To the classes excepted by the Proclamation of December 8, 1863, were added all those who had left seats in the General Assembly, all who were absentees from the United States for the purpose of aiding the rebellion and all who had fled within the Confederate lines with the same intention. These were disfranchised for the period of fifteen years from the passage of the act.[1]

During this session there was presented by the freedmen of the State a petition for the elective franchise. The "colored citizens of Tennessee," as they styled themselves, received no response to their prayer beyond the approval of an order for printing 500 copies of their memorial. The motion for this trifling concession was carried by a vote of 41 to 10.

On June 12 the Legislature adjourned until the first Monday in October. On the same day Governor Brownlow ordered an election to be held on August 2 for Representatives to Congress in each of the eight districts into which the State had just been divided. Vacancies in the General Assembly were directed to be filled at the same time.

The disfranchising act, with the oath required thereunder, had the effect of excluding a large number, probably three fourths, of the citizens from voting. Its adversaries declared the law unconstitutional, and it encountered much opposition, especially in Middle and West Tennessee. Its constitutionality, however, was sustained by one of the State courts in a decision rendered June 29, and the Governor, in a proclama-

[1] Acts of the State of Tennessee, 1865, p. 33.

tion of July 10 succeeding, argued in favor of the statute. Those who should unite to defeat its execution would be "declared in rebellion against the State of Tennessee, and dealt with as rebels." It was further signified that votes cast in violation of the law would not be taken into account by the Secretary of State.

Nor were these idle threats, for the civil officers were instructed " to arrest and bring to justice all persons who, under pretence of being candidates for Congress or other office, are traveling over the State denouncing and nullifying the Constitution and laws of the land, and spreading sedition and a spirit of rebellion." [1]

It was relative to these measures that President Johnson on July 20, 1865, sent the following despatch to Governor Brownlow:

> I hope and have no doubt you will see that the recent amendments to the constitution of the State as adopted by the people, and all the laws passed by the last Legislature in pursuance thereof, are fairly executed, and that all illegal votes in the approaching election be excluded from the polls, and the election for members of Congress be legally and fairly conducted. When and wherever it becomes necessary to employ force for the execution of the laws and the protection of the ballot-box from violence and fraud, you are authorized to call upon Maj.-Gen. Thomas for sufficient military force to sustain the civil authorities of the State. I have received your recent address to the people, and think it well timed, and hope it will do much good in reconciling the opposition to the amendment to the constitution and the laws passed by the last Legislature. The law must be executed and the civil authority sustained. In your efforts to do this, if necessary, Gen. Thomas will afford a sufficient military force. You are at liberty to make what use you think proper of this despatch.[2]

Though no violence marked the election, considerable irregularities, notwithstanding the Governor's precautions, appear to have crept into modes of registration, and he felt com-

[1] Ann. Cycl., 1865, p. 779.
[2] Ibid.

CULMINATION OF THE PRESIDENTIAL PLAN 415

pelled in consequence to reject the ballots of twenty-nine counties. In this contest 61,783 citizens participated, but when those illegally enrolled were disregarded the number was reduced to 39,509. The defective vote, which applied to all the candidates, was thrown out in every county, though it changed the result in only one district. Of the eight Representatives chosen all were Union men; four, however, were conservatives, opposed both to test oaths and measures of disfranchisement.[1] Governor Brownlow because of his action was severely censured, but was supported by a majority of the General Assembly.

In October, when the Legislature reassembled, a bill to render persons of African and of Indian descent competent witnesses in the State courts passed the Senate by the close vote of 10 to 9, but failed altogether to receive the approval of the House. The Representatives of his State declined at that time, by a vote of 35 to 25, to pass a simple resolution endorsing the Administration of President Johnson, but almost unanimously adopted in place of that proposition the following:

Resolved, That we endorse the administration of his Excellency the President of the United States, and especially his declaration that treason shall be made odious, and traitors punished.[2]

A colored convention representing the freedmen of the State was held at the capital during the week succeeding the election. If the Legislature did not grant before December 1, 1865, their petition for the elective franchise, this body re-

[1] This election resulted in the choice of Nathaniel G. Taylor, Horace Maynard, Edmund Cooper, Isaac R. Hawkins, John W. Leftwich, William B. Stokes, William B. Campbell and Dorsey B. Thomas. The last named, however, was affected by the Governor's recount, and Daniel W. Arnell, who was declared the successful candidate, was admitted to Congress with the other Tennessee Representatives on the 24th of July, 1866. See Why the Solid South? pp. 182-183.
[2] Ann. Cycl., 1865, p. 780.

solved to protest against the admission of the Tennessee delegation to Congress. On the question of negro suffrage the Governor in his October message said:

> I think it would be bad policy, as well as wrong in principle, to open the ballot-box to the uninformed and exceedingly stupid slaves of the Southern cotton, rice, and sugar fields. If allowed to vote, the great majority of them would be influenced by leading secessionists to vote against the Government, as they would be largely under the influence of this class of men for years to come, having to reside on and cultivate their lands. When the people of Tennessee become satisfied that the negro is worthy of suffrage, they will extend it, and not before; and I repeat that this question must be regulated by the State authorities and by the loyal voters of the State, not by the General Government.[1]

Apprehending trouble from the antagonism of races Mr. Brownlow advocated the old idea of colonization for the black man. He believed, however, that negroes should be admitted to testify in the courts and argued in favor of conferring such a privilege. Repugnance to their testimony, he declared, was due principally to education and habit.

If the following account from *The Knoxville Whig* of September 27 is trustworthy the freedmen of Tennessee had but a slender claim to the right to vote. That journal said:

> Thousands of free colored persons are congregating in and around the large towns in Tennessee, and thousands are coming in from other States, one third of whom cannot get employment. Indeed, less than one third of them want employment, or feel willing to stoop to work. They entertain the erroneous idea that the Government is bound to supply all their wants, and even to furnish them with houses, if, in order to do that, the white occupants must be turned out. There is a large demand for labor in every section of the State, but the colored people, with here and there a noble exception, scorn the idea of work. They fiddle and dance at night, and lie around the stores and street corners in the day time.[2]

The Governor's message, sent in at this session, was hopeful in tone. He favored some amendment but not a repeal

[1] Ann. Cycl., 1865, p. 781.
[2] Ibid.

of the franchise law. He advised also a " full pardon to the masses — the young and the deluded, who followed blindly the standard of revolt, provided they act as becomes their circumstances." The unrepentant, however, should suffer the period of disfranchisement; while the active leaders, he believed, were entitled " neither to mercy nor forbearance." To some negroes he would give the right of suffrage, but, believing it unsafe, he was opposed to conferring it on them all.

Tennessee, over which advancing and retreating armies had repeatedly passed, suffered even more severely than Arkansas, for besides having been the principal theatre of operations for the contending hosts in the West, her territory had also been in the early rule of Governor Johnson the scene of local strife. Old family feuds that for various reasons had been allowed to slumber were in many instances revived, and the most lawless outrages perpetrated in the face of day. These disorders, however, had practically ceased toward the conclusion of his governorship, and peace reigned once more within the borders of that community. The existence there of a considerable demand for labor assisted greatly in diminishing the burden of the authorities.

The closing months of the war found the loyal government of Louisiana endeavoring with the influence of the Union army to extend its jurisdiction over all the territory that had been brought under Federal control. Notwithstanding its contracted area this commonwealth for certain purposes was treated as a restored member of the Union. Like the Northern States it was affected by the draft which, on February 15, took place in some districts included in the Department of the Gulf. But the great struggle that for four years had employed the attention and tested the resources of the Government soon reached its close, thus rendering unnecessary any field service from the recruits then obtained.

Though the attitude of Congress toward the Banks government has been described in the preceding pages, that was not believed the proper place to examine the nature of the election which was held on September 5, or the *personnel* of the Legislature chosen on that occasion. In connection with the appointment by that assembly of Messrs. Smith and Cutler as United States Senators the subject was noticed incidentally. The action of Congress on the question of admitting members from Louisiana was, however, fully entered into in that relation.

Some additional information affecting the validity of that election is afforded by a proclamation published May 13, 1865, by the acting Governor, J. Madison Wells.[1] This document asserts that the Register of Voters for the city of New Orleans declared officially that there had been enrolled 5,000 persons who did not possess the legal qualifications for electors. To ascertain the political people, therefore, a new registration was thought desirable. Mr. Wells accordingly declared the old records closed from the date of his proclamation. The certificates granted thereon, as well as the enrollment, were pronounced null and void. He then authorized the opening on June 1, 1865, of a new set of books, the enrollment to be made in accordance with the qualifications prescribed by the constitution and laws of Louisiana. The old registration having been made under an order of General Banks this announcement led at once to a difference between the Department Commander and the acting Governor. Many names recorded on the old books were alleged to have been those of colored men, and a circumstance presently to be related tends to support the assertion.

About that time the Confederate Governor, Allen, transferred to Federal officials all the important military records

---

[1] Having been elected United States Senator, Mr. Hahn resigned the governorship on the 4th of March and was succeeded in office by Lieutenant-Governor Wells.

CULMINATION OF THE PRESIDENTIAL PLAN 419

in his possession, and from his capital at Shreveport published a communication in which he announced his administration closed on that day. He said in part: " The war is over, the contest is ended, the soldiers are disbanded and gone home, and now there is in Louisiana no opposition whatever to the Constitution and laws of the United States." [1]

On June 10 an address to the people of thirty-five parishes was issued by the new Governor, who congratulated them on their return to the protection of the national flag. It was not with the past, he reminded them, but with the present and the future that their welfare was bound up. They were exhorted to go manfully to work and reëstablish civil government. The submission to law and the prompt acquiescence of those recently hostile to the United States he regarded as a hopeful sign. Even the soldiers, he said, returned to their homes better and wiser men, promising by a cheerful obedience to law to atone for past errors. All citizens were urged to imitate their example. Provisional appointments to county offices would be made until they could be filled by election. In naming persons for such places the Governor promised to be guided by the recommendation of the people if they selected men of good reputation who had taken the amnesty oath, which would be a prerequisite in every case. If the people did not act promptly he would feel compelled to make appointments upon the best information obtainable. If errors were made, then citizens would be themselves to blame for neglecting promptly to suggest the proper persons. A provisional judiciary would also be constituted.

Important elections, he announced, would take place in the autumn, when Representatives to Congress and members of a Legislature would be chosen. If each parish was provided with the proper officers to open the polls an election for governor and other State officers would take place at the

[1] Ann. Cycl., 1865, p. 510.

same time. The people addressed were informed that in making the new constitution its framers did not intend to deprive them of their rights. The response to this appeal was a local reorganization in nearly all the parishes affected.

Governor Wells, on September 21, in a second order appointed the 6th of November succeeding as the day for holding the election, and also defined the qualifications of voters. White male citizens of the United States who had attained the age of twenty-one years and had resided twelve months in the commonwealth were declared entitled to exercise the suffrage. Evidence was also required of every elector that he had taken the oath of amnesty contained in the proclamation of December 8, 1863, or that prescribed, May 29, 1865, by Mr. Johnson. The excepted classes could vote only upon receiving a special pardon from the President. In other respects the election would be conducted in accordance with the constitution of 1852.

By a Democratic convention, held October 2 in New Orleans, at which twenty-one parishes were unrepresented, Mr. Wells was unanimously nominated for Governor. The preamble to a body of resolutions adopted on that occasion asserts that the issue which for four years had tried the strength of the Government had been made openly and manfully; that the decision having been adverse they now came forward in the same spirit of frankness and honor to support the Federal Government under the Constitution.

The "National Democratic" party they believed to be the only agency by which radicalism, to which they imputed a tendency toward consolidation, could be successfully encountered, and through which the General Government could be restored to its pristine purity. On the subject of reorganization they endorsed President Johnson's policy, which, it was alleged, preserved unimpaired the rights of the States and maintained their equality in the Union.

Noticing a question already assuming importance, they declared that, in accordance with the constant adjudication of the Federal Supreme Court, persons of African descent could not be regarded as citizens of the United States; that under no circumstances could there exist any equality between the white and other races; that as the national Government was instituted by, so it was designed to be perpetuated for the exclusive benefit of, white men. For the time they were content with this oblique reference to the subject of negro suffrage. Another resolution advised the calling of a convention to frame a constitution for the State, that of 1864 being characterized as the creation of fraud, violence and corruption.

This convention, which admitted the effectual abolition of slavery in the South, assumed that those who had sustained loss by the policy of emancipation could rightfully petition Congress for compensation. The repeal was also advocated of those statutes and ordinances not in harmony with the Federal Constitution. Believing it consonant with "the chivalrous magnanimity" of President Johnson the convention earnestly appealed for an early general amnesty and a prompt restitution of property.

Almost a month preceding the meeting of this convention an address was circulated by the "National Conservative Union" party, whose representatives assembled one week later than the Democratic delegates. Its members opposed both an extension of suffrage to negroes and the calling of a new constitutional convention. Like the Democratic delegates they endorsed the reconstruction policy of the President. They approved the attitude of their conservative Northern friends who opposed radicalism and an elevation of the freedmen to political equality with whites. The doctrine of secession was repudiated, and to the payment of all obligations created in carrying on the war they declared themselves inflexibly opposed. They, too, favored the speedy passage of an act of general amnesty as well as a repeal of the confiscation law.

Governor Wells was also the choice of this convention. He accepted both nominations and perceived no inconsistency in doing so, never, he asserted, having been a strict party man. Mr. Wells, who had formerly been a Red River planter, proved his loyalty to the Federal Government by coming within the Union lines as soon as they were established, and bringing with him his slaves, thereby endangering somewhat his ownership.

Though he had not yet returned to his home, the friends of Henry Watkins Allen, the late Confederate executive, named him as their candidate for governor.

In the election, which was held at the appointed time, the entire vote polled was 27,808, of which Governor Wells received 23,312, and ex-Governor Allen, 5,497. In every county except one the Democratic ticket for members of the Legislature was successful.

Perhaps the most instructive incident of this contest was the part played by those known as "Radical" Republicans. These held a mass-meeting in the city of New Orleans on November 13 at which were adopted resolutions claiming the election to Congress of Henry C. Warmoth as territorial Delegate. When he subsequently appeared in Washington his case was brought to the attention of the House by Thaddeus Stevens, who offered, December 20, 1865, what purported to be a certificate of Warmoth's election as Delegate from the "Territory of Louisiana." On request of the Pennsylvania leader this document was referred to the Joint Committee on Reconstruction.[1]

This extreme element, which assumed to regard Louisiana as a Territory, polled 19,000 votes, most of which were alleged

[1] Globe, Part I., 1 Sess. 39th Cong., p. 101.

to have been cast by colored men. It declared the State organization repugnant to the Federal Constitution both in law and effect. The President, it was asserted, could not restore Louisiana by proclamation, for reinstatement could be accomplished in a constitutional manner only by petitioning Congress for admission whenever a majority of the people deemed such a course expedient, and the temper of the whites, nine tenths of whom were disloyal, rendered it inadvisable at that time to take such a step. The meeting rejoiced that the Republican party in the North had triumphed in the recent elections, for these victories pointed to ultimate success. The premature admission of Louisiana Congressmen, by placing the Union people under rebel rule, would be disastrous. However, as loyal citizens they would confine themselves to peaceable means of redress.

Warmoth appears shortly before the end of the war to have gone into Louisiana with the Union army, in which he is said by one authority to have acquired the reputation of a brave soldier and by another to have merited dismissal from its ranks.[1] By organizing the freedmen and insisting upon their political rights he won their confidence; his shrewdness and engaging address retained their gratitude. In this election his adherents not only sought to determine the Federal relations of Louisiana, but also conferred upon negroes the privilege of voting, for there was then no law of either the General or State government investing them with any such right.

The Legislature, which was convoked in special session, assembled at New Orleans on the 23d of November. The Governor's message on that occasion related chiefly to such local objects as required the attention of the lawmaking body. By recommending an election of United States Senators Mr. Wells repudiated the action of the General Assembly, which,

[1] Three Decades of Federal Legislation, p. 429; also Why the Solid South? p. 397.

at the preceding session, had appointed Messrs. Smith and Cutler to represent the State. Acting upon the Governor's suggestion, the latter was again chosen, with Hahn for his colleague. These appointments were intended to fill vacancies caused by the withdrawal, February 5, 1861, of John Slidell and Judah P. Benjamin.

One of the first acts of the lower House was the selection of a committee to consider a resolution which provided for assembling a convention to draft a State constitution. For reasons already assigned the majority report of this committee recommended the calling of a convention and counselled the Governor to order an election in which the question could be voted on by the people. The minority recognized the constitution of 1864 as binding, and on the ground of public economy preferred its amendment, especially as it had already acted favorably on the abolition of slavery. The adoption of the Thirteenth Amendment and the repeal of the ordinance of secession were mentioned by them as conditions essential to the recognition of Louisiana as a State and as indispensable to a restoration of all the privileges which that condition implied.

As early as February 17 preceding the Legislature established under the constitution of 1864 had ratified the Thirteenth Article amending the Constitution. By a vote of two to one the Assembly again approved that action. The session came to an end on the 22d of December.

This commonwealth, a veritable Eden when the strife began, had been sadly changed in its progress. A generous Government, indeed, by repairing the levees protected her fairest parishes from inundation. The same beneficent authority maintained many public institutions of charity that must else have ceased their noble work. Distress and want had already invaded that once prosperous community, and in the city of New Orleans alone 16,000 persons were dependent upon and maintained by Federal bounty. Silence reigned in the great cotton market of the world. The wreck of her public finances has elsewhere been described. Her opulent commerce had been destroyed, agriculture everywhere languished. Plantations that but lately teemed with rich harvests showed the effects of interrupted cultivation, and the mighty river that had annually poured into her metropolis the productions of a dozen States now flowed untroubled to the Gulf.

To show the attitude of Congress toward the Alexandria government events in Virginia have in part been anticipated. The Legislature of the loyal portion of that Commonwealth was composed of members from only ten counties and parts of other counties. It was by delegates from this restricted area that the constitution of 1864 was framed and adopted.

By this instrument the elective franchise was confined to male whites that had attained the age of twenty-one years, who had resided twelve months in the State and were willing to swear support of the Federal Constitution and the restored government; but officials and voters were required in addition to make oath, or affirmation, that they had not, since January 1, 1864, voluntarily given aid or assistance to those in rebellion against the General Government. The Assembly, however, was empowered, when it was deemed safe to do so, to restore to citizenship all who would be disfranchised by this provision of the organic law.

Involuntary servitude was also abolished. While great numbers of negroes were thus set at liberty, nothing was then done to elevate them to the dignity of citizens. The question of making them voters was, of course, still more remote.

The General Assembly was prohibited from making provision for the payment of any debt or obligation created in the name of the Commonwealth by the pretended State authorities at Richmond; and it was also forbidden to permit any county, city or corporation to levy or collect taxes for the discharge of any debt incurred for the purpose of aiding any rebellion against the State or the United States, or to provide for the payment of any bonds held by rebels in arms.[1]

The Confederate capital, long deemed impregnable, fell on the 2d of April. Within a week came tidings of the surrender of Lee's entire army, greatly reduced in numbers, it is true, but hitherto the main reliance of the Confederacy. Mr. Lincoln, apparently, was not altogether without expectation of some such fortunate outcome of the extensive preparations that had been made for ensuring the success of the final campaign, and on the following day, April 10, 1865, he sent from Washington to the executive head of the restored State this telegram:

GOVERNOR PIERPONT, *Alexandria, Virginia:*
Please come up and see me at once.[2]

A. LINCOLN.

Mr. Pierpont, as the writer has been credibly informed, called by request on President Lincoln during the week of his assassination, evidently in response to this telegram, when they spent three hours together in conversation. No third party appears to have been present at their consultation. The topic discussed it is not difficult to imagine. Shortly before his death, which occurred in March, 1899, Governor Pierpont informed his daughter that he never believed Andrew Johnson carried out Mr. Lincoln's idea in the reconstruction of Virginia.[3] That policy, however, had not then, April 10, assumed definitive form in the mind of the President himself, for he expressly stated to Mr. Pierpont that he had no plan for reorganization, but must be guided by events. His

[1] Poore's Charters and Constitutions, Vol. II. p. 1938 *et seq.*
[2] Letters and State Papers of Lincoln, Vol. II. p. 670.
[3] Letter of Mrs. Anna Pierpont Siviter to the author.

last public utterance establishes the correctness of this statement.

Four weeks later President Johnson by executive order recognized the Alexandria establishment, and toward the close of the same month, May 26, 1865, Mr. Pierpont, with other members of his government, arrived in Richmond. The sneer of Thaddeus Stevens that the archives and property of loyal Virginia were conveyed to the new capital in an ambulance affords at least an adequate idea of the feeble condition of the restored State. But notwithstanding the absence of all pomp and his lack of the usual emblems of authority the Governor, we are told, was received in a very flattering manner.

Virginia, which emerged from the struggle crippled by the loss of an important part of her domain, suffered more in the destruction of the elements of wealth than any of her errant sisters, and though entering somewhat reluctantly on a career of rebellion, she was the only member of the Confederacy that was permanently weakened. Industry could never repair the alienation of her territory. While it may appear that the General Government acted harshly toward a State to which the Union owed so much, the preceding pages show clearly that the loss of her trans-Alleghany counties was due chiefly to an unwise administration of her internal affairs. Notwithstanding the statement of Mr. Blaine, the writer does not think that Virginia was singled out for punishment. But even apart from her dismemberment the ravages of war fell most heavily on the Old Dominion. There it was that the Army of the Potomac and the Army of Northern Virginia contended longest for supremacy. Troops in their marches and countermarches foraged liberally on her people, sometimes without distinction of friend or foe. Concrete illustrations will occur to every reader acquainted with the military history of the great conflict.

The devastation of the Shenandoah valley was only a striking example of what was constantly occurring within more restricted areas of the State. Barns and dwelling houses, fences and crops perished in the universal destruction. Cattle were either killed or carried off, and even the implements of husbandry were frequently devoted to the flames. The injury thus sustained by agricultural interests was followed in many districts by an alarming scarcity of food during the ensuing years, and to escape starvation numbers of her citizens fled from once happy homes. Newspaper correspondents in their progress through the State describe scenes of wretchedness and distress. In exploring for their journals wide regions that had recently been the theatre of war they witnessed spectacles of want, hunger and despair. Uncultivated tracts in the wake of the armies contributed to heighten the picture of desolation. Richmond, the centre of so many interesting historical associations, though long exempt from pillage, perished ultimately in a conflagration. In short, nearly every landmark of prosperity was effaced by the calamities of war.

To repair these ravages, to repeople these solitudes, to revive commerce and agriculture, to restore tranquillity and maintain order was the stupendous task before Governor Pierpont, in whose public career it may be regarded as the second stage. After the formation of West Virginia, in which he had acted a conspicuous and honorable part, and one that can scarcely be overrated, his exertions barely sufficed to preserve the continuity of a loyal government in his native State. In the former undertaking he had the coöperation of nearly every person of consideration beyond the Alleghanies. His efforts in Richmond, however, received but indifferent support. Whites of little influence and negroes who were still but prospective citizens made up the greater number of his adherents. A handful of secessionists, it is true, set the example of obedience to the laws, though they found among their late associates but few imitators. It was from such material and in such circumstances that Mr. Pierpont was to reconstruct the grand old Commonwealth. The Governor, however, applied himself at once to the duties imposed by his office. He appointed persons to reorganize the various counties by holding elections for local officers, though in numerous instances he merely authorized to act for the preservation of peace those citizens whom the military officers might select. The difficulties of the situation were such that he summoned the Legislature to meet in special session at Richmond on the 20th of June.

In response to this request the lawmaking body assembled at the appointed time. The Executive message on that occasion related concisely what had been done by the restored government subsequent to June, 1861. It also stated that since his arrival at the capital the Governor had conversed with intelligent men of every shade of political opinion and representing every part of Virginia. He was convinced, he said, that if the test of loyalty prescribed by their constitution was enforced in the election and qualification of officers, it would render organization impracticable in most of the counties. It was folly to suppose that a State could be administered " under a republican form of government where in a large portion of the State, nineteen twentieths of the people are disfranchised and cannot hold office. But, fortunately, by the terms of the constitution, the General Assembly has control of this subject. The restricting clauses of the constitution were devised in time of war. . . . Men accept the facts developed by the logic of the past four years, declare that they have taken the oath of allegiance to the Government of the United States without mental reservation, and intend to be, and remain, loyal to the Government of their fathers. It would not be in accordance with the spirit of that noble Anglo-Saxon race, from which we boast our common origin, to strike a fallen brother, or impose upon him humiliating terms after a fair surrender." [1]

For the oath required by the State constitution he suggested the substitution of that prescribed by the President, or one of similar character; he also recommended the passage of an act to legalize marriage between persons of color, and the appointment of a day for holding elections of Representatives to Congress and for members of the Legislature in those counties where none had been chosen.

The subject of disfranchisement was immediately taken up in both Houses, and the result of their action was to allow the suffrage to those who, upon taking the amnesty oath, had not held office under the Confederacy or its State governments. Those who had done so could neither vote nor hold office. The Legislature submitted to the people, to be determined at the election in October succeeding, the question of removing this restriction upon officeholders.

This action of the Assembly was followed by the appearance of a large number of competitors for office, and considerable interest was awakened. Finding, however, that they would be unable to take the oath required by Congress many of the candidates for the national Legislature withdrew. The President was asked by some citizens of Albemarle County whether, in his opinion, Congress would probably insist upon the oath. The following reply to their inquiry was made by Attorney-General Speed:

> The President has referred to me your letter, dated Charlottesville, Virginia, September, 1865, and I am instructed by him to say that he has no more means of knowing what Congress may do in regard to the oath about which you inquire than any other citizen. It is his earnest wish that loyal and true men, to whom no objections can be made, should be elected to Congress.
>
> This is not an official letter, but a simple expression of individual opinion and wish.[2]

[1] Ann. Cycl., 1865, p. 817. [2] Ibid.

The election was held on October 12, the vote polled being the smallest ever given in the history of the State. In the first eight Congressional districts, however, it exceeded 40,000. The constitutional amendment met with very little opposition, many counties voting unanimously to remove the restriction upon the suffrage.[1] The Assembly then chosen convened at Richmond on December 4, 1865, the time fixed for the meeting of Congress.

While it is true that there were grounds for apprehension regarding the stability of the new governments instituted in these four States, the principal cause of anxiety to the Administration was the disorganized political and social condition of the remaining members of the late Confederacy. It was universally agreed that with the destruction of its military power the authority of that government was completely extinguished. From that moment until the revival within them of Federal laws these commonwealths were destitute of all legislation of a general character. Under our dual principle of government, however, this could be endured temporarily. But the absence of a central organism would soon be evident in the reappearance of those alarming symptoms which marked American political and industrial life in the critical period between the Treaty of Paris, in 1783, and the inauguration, nearly six years later, of the present national system. In that unhappy interval, however, the authority of the various States was ample for the regulation of domestic affairs, while in the deranged and confused times succeeding the Rebellion seven entire commonwealths were left without any general or any particular government. Their territory, indeed, had passed under control of the Union forces, for when the Administration of Jefferson Davis was overthrown the disloyal State establishments, of which it was only an emanation, fell likewise. Though internal progress was not seri-

[1] Ann. Cycl., 1865, p. 817.

ously to be expected in this situation, tolerable order was preserved by Federal soldiers, who occupied the entire region between the Potomac and the Rio Grande, for even in those States reorganized under Executive auspices civil authority was not yet established on a foundation sufficiently secure to maintain itself without assistance from the military power of the nation.

Besides the absence of all civil government there were other elements of discord that tended to increase the confusion in these States. Their population, it need scarcely be observed, was not homogeneous. The decree of emancipation together with the incidents of war had brought freedom to almost the entire slave population of the South. This was soon to be confirmed by the proposed constitutional amendment, which was designed both to place beyond question the status of freedmen and to strike the shackles from the limbs of the last bondman in the loyal as well as in the disloyal States. About the middle of December nearly 4,000,000 negroes bereft of the hand that bestowed their daily sustenance found themselves suddenly dependent for support upon their own exertions. The General Government, it is true, by creating the Bureau of Freedmen and Refugees, diminished considerably the danger from this source, though this relief by no means solved the problem of transforming the recent slave into a useful member of society; besides, the bureau itself subsequently degenerated into a fruitful source of abuse.

Nor were Southern whites by any means unanimous as to the best policy to adopt in the circumstances in which an unsuccessful rebellion had placed them. Between Union men and secessionists there existed a feeling of extreme bitterness. Even among members of the latter class there was considerable difference of opinion, as in North Carolina, where the former Whigs, by the moderation of their views as much as by constantly agitating the question of reconstruction, had

CULMINATION OF THE PRESIDENTIAL PLAN

somewhat embarrassed the Richmond authorities while war was still flagrant. Add to these causes of disorder the discontent of thousands of disbanded soldiers who returned in the gloom of defeat not infrequently to ruined homes and wasted fields. Then, too, there was the disappointment and humiliation naturally felt by a brave and impulsive people who had fought gallantly in support of a cause condemned, indeed, by the civilized world, but believed by them to be not only just but indispensable to their prosperity and happiness.

Though a volume could be profitably employed in describing, town by town and county by county, the extent of destruction inflicted on the South, a few brief paragraphs must suffice to suggest an imperfect idea of the enormous loss of wealth sustained by that section. The wreck of four members of the Confederacy has been noticed in the preceding pages. That rapid sketch, however, took no account of the damage to individuals by the liberation of their slaves, for, except in those instances where negroes left the commonwealth, that was not in any sense a loss to the State. If it were, a community, by reducing to servitude a part of its inhabitants, could at any time increase the amount of its capital. It is only from the slaveholder's point of view, therefore, that emancipation can be regarded as a pecuniary loss. Immense damage was sustained by both North and South in the withdrawal of millions of men from the various fields of production. The energy of these multitudes, which was rapidly making the United States the most opulent and powerful nation on the globe, had exerted itself for four years in the destruction of former accumulations.

Almost at the moment that the star of the Confederacy had begun to decline the imperial State of Georgia, hitherto exempt from punishment, was wasted by fire and sword. Sometimes the Southern, sometimes the Northern army stripped the country of everything capable of supporting life. Crops had been harvested, indeed, but this served only to facilitate their destruction. In the retreat of Johnston and the advance of Sherman toward Atlanta highways had been injured, bridges burned and many lines of railroad completely destroyed. Dwellings, when they interfered with military operations, were levelled by even the Confederate army, and the Union forces could not be expected to show greater consideration for the property of public enemies. General Hood not only wasted the vast stores accumulated in Atlanta but burned habitations when they stood in the way of his fortifications. Though winter was rapidly approaching, the Federal commander deemed it necessary after the capture of that stronghold to expel from their abodes a considerable part of its population. A brief truce, it is true, enabled the miserable inhabitants to remove a part of their effects farther south; thousands, outcasts from their ruined homes, were thus driven to wander among strangers whose bounty had already been taxed by earlier fugitives; both classes were dependent for their maintenance on the precarious charity of an impoverished people. Crowded dwellings forced great numbers in the inclement weather to seek shelter in the neighboring forests, where they found a safe refuge, indeed, but a scanty subsistence. Over the region traversed by Sherman and Johnston the forces of Hood soon after traced a devastating march northward to Dalton. The mischiefs of the great march to Savannah have frequently been described. Its beginning was announced by the blaze of burning buildings, and when the last of the Federal soldiers had set their faces toward the sea the city of Atlanta was little more than a mass of smoking ruins. Though the region traversed was probably the richest in the State, extensive misery accompanied the progress of the army. The meat and the vegetables needed for his command were taken by the Union General. Horses, mules and wagons were freely appropriated; slaves also were

CULMINATION OF THE PRESIDENTIAL PLAN 435

assisted to escape from their masters. Mills and cotton-gins were frequently devoted to the flames. In Milledgeville factories, storehouses and public buildings were destroyed. The principal edifices of Macon perished about the same time. Indeed, Augusta was the only considerable place in the State that escaped serious harm. The people in northwestern Georgia were in the utmost destitution, large families being frequently for whole days without food; venerable persons of both sexes, sinking under the weight of years and infirmities, often walked fifteen and even twenty miles to procure food enough to prevent starvation. The injury to all the usual means of transportation greatly increased the difficulty of bringing relief. When the conflict had ended, however, Federal officers did what they could to alleviate the almost universal distress, and their magnanimity was not without influence on the future conduct of many an ex-Confederate veteran.

South Carolina, the fatal State that woke the sword of war, did not suffer greatly in the earlier stages of the conflict, though even then her foreign commerce was extinguished and her agriculture interrupted along the coast. Before its close, however, she was destined to experience most of its horrors. A restless generation of agitators had assiduously inculcated the notion that the South was ruthlessly oppressed by Yankee avarice. This teaching bore fruit, and the people of South Carolina, coming to regard themselves as little better than tributary slaves, were easily persuaded to resort to the wager of battle. With the progress of the contest this proud State was growing weaker within, hostile pressure was constantly increasing from without. Time at length and the fortunes of war had brought round their revenge, and when the veterans of Sherman turned northward from Savannah the Palmetto State was powerless to prevent, or seriously to retard, their advance. Transportation was greatly embarrassed by the destruction of the bridges as well as the tracks of almost every important railway within the State. Immense quantities of cotton and numbers of cotton warehouses, uncounted dwellings and depots, machine shops and foundries, as well as several sailing vessels and steamboats were consumed by flames. Besides these blackened memorials of disaster and defeat, the stately cities of Charleston and Columbia were almost simultaneously laid in ruins by great conflagrations. The inability of the civil authorities to furnish food for his army constrained General Sherman to forage for supplies. In this manner all the cattle, hogs, sheep and poultry, even the little stores of meal, treasured as the last barrier against want, were consumed, and the people left entirely without subsistence. To prevent general starvation the Confederate commander was compelled to distribute the rations of his soldiers among the wretched inhabitants. From various causes many ancient and wealthy families found themselves suddenly reduced to a condition of beggary, and so low was the condition of the public treasury that the Legislature as early as the mid-summer of 1865 had already begun seriously to discuss the question of repudiation.

With some slight alterations this picture of South Carolina's ills will serve for that of her northern and more deserving sister, so far at least as concerns those parts overrun by the contending hosts. The cessation of hostilities stopped the carnival of death and silenced the engines of destruction before half of North Carolina's territory had been crossed. From the first years of the war there were numerous instances of privation among the loyalists of that State. Toward its close the more favored classes also began to feel the pressure of want. The negroes required and received assistance from the Freedmen's Bureau. The whites, refugees as well as secessionists, were aided by the commanders of the rival forces.

Florida, fortunately for her people, was so remote from

the principal scenes of war that she felt few of its evils. Battles, it is true, occurred within the State, but they were as skirmishes compared to the bloody engagements which took place elsewhere. The same observations are substantially true of Texas. A fringe of Mississippi's territory, too, had been swept by the furnace-blast of war. The extensive movements around Corinth, Iuka, Vicksburg, Jackson and Port Hudson will suggest the extent of destruction that visited the northern half of that State. There existed considerable privation in that section, though no general distress as in other members of the Confederacy.

All the Gulf States, however, were not equally fortunate. Though long impending, the fate of Alabama came swiftly. Almost in the same hour she was invaded from the north and menaced from the south. A large portion of her material resources was already exhausted when the cavalry raids of General Wilson spread terror and devastation through the interior counties. The city of Selma was laid in ashes; smaller towns and villages were likewise consumed by flames; schools and colleges, private buildings and public edifices perished in the universal wreck. Monuments of ruin were everywhere conspicuous throughout a region the most productive, probably, in all the South. Silence and desolation reigned where but lately stood proud and hospitable mansions. Nor was the destruction of wealth or its elements the only injury sustained, for industry would soon repair the losses of capital. Labor itself had been severely crippled. Of the army of 122,000 soldiers which Alabama furnished to the cause of secession 35,000, it was estimated, had been left on the field of battle, and at least an equal number had been disabled for life. Mobile, enriched by the cotton trade, was silent as some ancient necropolis. Her splendid commerce was ruined; her stately ships were gone, and the wave broke unheeded on the shores of her deserted harbor.

438 LINCOLN'S PLAN OF RECONSTRUCTION

This hurried summary conveys only a very inadequate notion of the complex problem which Mr. Johnson was forced to consider. His arduous duty was to repair the ravages of military violence, to evoke order from the discord of civil strife, to heal the wounds which the imperious power of slavery had inflicted upon industries and institutions; in a word, to restore the harmony of that Republic founded by the wisdom of Washington and preserved by the policy of Lincoln. The sentiments of the Chief Magistrate who was about to attempt this difficult but indispensable task it is now time to consider. His deliberate conclusions and his spontaneous utterances are best examined, it is believed, in something like chronological order.

On June 9, 1864, almost a year before his accession to the Presidency, he had said in addressing the people of Nashville:

But in calling a convention to restore the State, who shall restore and reëstablish it? . . . Shall he who brought this misery upon the State be permitted to control its destinies? If this be so, then all this precious blood of our brave soldiers and officers so freely poured out will have been wantonly spilled. . . .

Why all this carnage and devastation? It was that treason might be put down and traitors punished. Therefore I say that traitors should take a back seat in the work of restoration. If there be but five thousand men in Tennessee loyal to the Constitution, loyal to freedom, loyal to justice, these true and faithful men should control the work of reorganization and reformation absolutely. I say that the traitor has ceased to be a citizen, and in joining the rebellion has become a public enemy. He forfeited his right to vote with loyal men when he renounced his citizenship and sought to destroy our Government. . . . If we are so cautious about foreigners who voluntarily renounce their homes to live with us what should we say to the traitor, who, although born and reared among us, has raised a parricidal hand against the Government which always protected him? My judgment is that he should be subjected to a severe ordeal before he is restored to citizenship. . . . Before these repenting rebels can be trusted, let them bring forth the fruits of repentance. . . . Treason must be made odious, and traitors must be punished and impoverished. Their great plantations must be seized, and divided into small farms, and sold to honest, industrious men. The day for protecting the lands and negroes of these authors of the rebellion is past. It is high time it was.[1]

Though he had never been accustomed to conceal his opinions on questions of public interest, and though there was no reason for supposing that his views on reorganization had changed in the months intervening between the Nashville speech and his inauguration, there was considerable curiosity, if not indeed impatience, to learn his sentiments on the paramount issue before the nation. Even the unparalleled excitement and profound regret occasioned by the assassination of Mr. Lincoln could not make men forget the grave questions which the changed conditions of the Union presented for the consideration of statesmen. Therefore the brief remarks addressed by the new Executive to those who were present at his inauguration were eagerly scrutinized for some indication of the principles which he was likely to adopt in the conduct of his Administration. The absence, however, of even a hint on that interesting subject gave universal disappointment, and anxious patriots were not reassured by his failure to announce any expression of a purpose to continue the policy of his predecessor. By his intimate friends this omission was construed as an intention to pursue in dealing with the South a less generous course than, it was believed, Mr. Lincoln had marked out.

Among the more extreme "Radicals" this surmise occasioned little regret, for they did not object to the accession of an Executive made, as they believed, of sterner stuff than the late incumbent. From his fierce denunciation of secessionists both while military governor of Tennessee and subsequently, it was generally understood that more stringent methods would be adopted by Mr. Johnson than had hitherto been employed. Among other things he said in his inaugural: "As to an indication of any policy which may be pursued by me

[1] McPherson's Hand-Book of Politics, 1868, p. 46.

in the administration of the Government, I have to say that that must be left for development, as the administration progresses. The message or declaration must be made by the acts as they transpire. The only assurance that I can now give of the future, is by reference to the past." [1]

Delegations of citizens who waited upon him to tender their cordial support were assured in the most explicit terms that his past course was an indication of what his future policy would be. Three days after entering upon the duties of his office a deputation of distinguished persons called on Mr. Johnson under circumstances at once unusual and touching. The remains of the late President still lay in the White House. Before the sad procession of the dead left the national Capital for Springfield, Governor Oglesby, with other gentlemen from Illinois, called to assure the new Executive of their respect and confidence. His record, they declared, gave assurance to their State that in his hands they could safely trust the destinies of the Republic. The President responded in a speech discussing a far wider range of topics than he had treated in his inaugural. Appropriate reference to his predecessor, the tragical close of whose career was scarcely alluded to in his first address, was made in this more extended discourse. He spoke with unaffected and profound emotion. " The beloved of all hearts has been assassinated," said he, " and when we trace this crime to its cause, when we remember the source whence the assassin drew his inspiration, and then look at the result, we stand yet more astounded at this most barbarous, most diabolical act. . . . We can trace its cause through successive steps back to that source which is the spring of all our woes. No one can say that if the perpetrator of this fiendish deed be arrested, he should not undergo the extremest penalty of the law known for crime: none will say that mercy should interpose. But is he alone guilty? Here,

[1] Ann. Cycl., 1865, p. 800.

gentlemen, you perhaps expect me to present some indication of my future policy. One thing I will say: every era teaches its lesson. The times we live in are not without instruction. The American people must be taught — if they do not already feel — that treason is a crime and must be punished. . . . When we turn to the criminal code we find arson laid down as a crime with its appropriate penalty. We find theft and murder denounced as crimes, and their appropriate penalty prescribed; and there, too, we find the last and highest of crimes,— treason. . . . Let it be engraven on every mind that treason is a crime, and traitors shall suffer its penalty. . . . I do not harbor bitter or resentful feelings towards any. . . . When the question of exercising mercy comes before me it will be considered calmly, judicially — remembering that I am the Executive of the Nation. I know men love to have their names spoken of in connection with acts of mercy, and how easy it is to yield to that impulse. But we must never forget that what may be mercy to the individual is cruelty to the State."

Commenting on this speech Mr. Blaine, from whom it is quoted, says that it "was reported by an accomplished stenographer, and was submitted to Mr. Johnson's inspection before publication. It contained a declaration intimating to its hearers, if not explicitly assuring them, that 'the policy of Mr. Lincoln in the past shall be my policy in the future.' When in reading the report he came to this passage, Mr. Johnson queried whether his words had not been in some degree misapprehended; and while he was engaged with the stenographer in modifying the form of expression, Mr. Preston King, of New York, who was constantly by his side as adviser, interposed the suggestion that all reference to the subject be stricken out. To this Mr. Johnson promptly assented. He had undoubtedly gone farther than he intended in speaking to Mr. Lincoln's immediate friends, and the correction — inspired by one holding the radical views of Mr. King — was equivalent to a declaration that the policy of Mr. Lincoln had been more conservative than that which he intended to pursue." [1]

To a deputation of New Hampshire citizens he said in part: "This Government is now passing through a fiery, and, let us hope, its last ordeal — one that will test its powers of endurance, and will determine whether it can do what its enemies have denied — suppress and punish treason." Though he had been urged, he asserted, by friends whose good opinion he valued, he refrained from foreshadowing in a public manifesto the policy which would guide him. He further observed on this occasion: "I know it is easy, gentlemen, for any one who is so disposed, to acquire a reputation for clemency and mercy. But the public good imperatively requires a just discrimination in the exercise of these qualities. . . . To relieve one from the penalty of crime may be productive of national disaster. The American people must be taught to know and understand that treason is a crime. . . . Treason is a crime, and must be punished as a crime. It must not be regarded as a mere difference of political opinion. It must not be excused as an unsuccessful rebellion, to be overlooked and forgiven. It is a crime before which all others sink into insignificance; and in saying this it must not be considered that I am influenced by angry or revengeful feelings." He added, that to those who had been deluded and deceived by designing men, to those who had been only technically guilty of treason, he would accord amnesty, leniency and mercy. On the instigators of rebellion, however, should be visited "the full penalty of their crimes." [2]

Replying, April 21, to an address of Governor Morton, who introduced a delegation from Indiana, he said: "Mine has

[1] Twenty Years of Congress, Vol. II. pp. 9-11.
[2] Ann. Cycl., 1865, p. 800.

been but one straight-forward and unswerving course, and I see no reason why I should depart from it. . . .

"I hold it as a solemn obligation in any one of these States where the rebel armies have been driven back or expelled — I care not how small the number of Union men, if enough to man the ship of State — I hold it, I say, a high duty to protect and secure to them a republican form of government. This is no new opinion. . . . In adjusting and putting the government upon its legs again, I think the progress of this work must pass into the hands of its friends. If a State is to be nursed until it again gets strength, it must be nursed by its friends, and not smothered by its enemies."[1] To this delegation he declared himself not less opposed to consolidation than to dissolution and disintegration. In a brief reply on the same day to a deputation from Ohio he added nothing of value to these observations, and on the 24th of April he addressed in a similar strain a body of exiles from the South.

"The colored American asks but two things," said the spokesman of a negro delegation about the same time, "that he have, first, complete emancipation, and secondly, full equality before American law." To this the President replied, among other things, that he feared leading colored men did not "understand and appreciate the fact that they have friends on the south side of the line. They have, and they are as faithful and staunch as any north of the line. It may be a very easy thing, indeed popular, to be an emancipationist north of the line, but a very different thing to be such south of it. South of it, it costs a man effort, property, and perhaps life."[2]

Two months later, June 24, in replying to an address of a South Carolina committee, he said in part: "The friction

[1] McPherson's Pol. Hand-Book, 1868, pp. 45-46.
[2] Ann. Cycl., 1865, pp. 801-802.

of the rebellion has rubbed out the nature and character of slavery. The loyal men who were compelled to bow and submit to the rebellion should, now that the rebellion is ended, stand equal to loyal men everywhere. Hence the wish of reconstruction, and the trying to get back the States to the point at which they formerly moved in perfect harmony." He reminded them that as an institution slavery was gone, and said there was no hope that the people of South Carolina would be admitted into either the Senate or the House of Representatives until by their conduct they had afforded evidence of this truth. In their circumstances the true policy was to restore the State government, not through military rule, but by the action of the people.[1]

Desiring to relieve all loyal citizens and well-disposed persons from unnecessary trade restrictions, and to encourage a return to peaceful pursuits, the President removed, April 29, 1865, the interdict on all domestic and coastwise intercourse in that portion of the late Confederate States east of the Mississippi and within the lines of national military occupation. From this order, however, certain named articles contraband of war were excepted. Military and naval regulations in conflict with his proclamation were revoked. On May 22 following he announced that ports in the same district would be reopened to foreign commerce after July 1, 1865, though certain places in Texas were still denied this privilege.

The insurrection hitherto existing in Tennessee was declared at an end on June 13, 1865. The authority of the United States, this Proclamation asserted, was unquestioned within the limits of that commonwealth, and duly commissioned Federal officials were in undisturbed exercise of their functions. All disabilities attaching to the State and its inhabitants were therefore removed; but nothing contained in

[1] Ann. Cycl., 1865, p. 802.

CULMINATION OF THE PRESIDENTIAL PLAN 445

the order was to be construed as affecting any of the penalties and forfeitures for treason which had previously been incurred.

Ten days later, June 23, the blockade of Galveston and other ports beyond the Mississippi was rescinded. These were to be opened to foreign trade on the 1st of July succeeding. It was ordered, August 29, 1865, that after September 1 all restrictions upon internal, domestic and coastwise commerce be removed, so that even articles contraband of war might be imported into and sold in the late insurgent States, the necessity for prohibiting intercourse in those articles having in great measure ceased.

In an order dated May 9, 1865, the President declared null and void all acts and proceedings of the military and civil organizations of Virginia which had been in rebellion against the General Government; also that all persons who should exercise or attempt to exercise any authority, jurisdiction or right under Jefferson Davis, and his confederates, or under John Letcher or William Smith,[1] and their confederates, or any pretended commission or authority issued by them, or any of them, since April 17, 1861, would be deemed and taken as in rebellion against the United States, and dealt with accordingly. By the same order the authority of the United States was revived within the geographical limits known as Virginia, and the heads of the several Executive Departments were instructed to enforce therein all Federal laws the administration of which belonged to their respective offices.

To carry into effect the constitutional guaranty of a republican form of government and "afford the advantage and security of domestic laws, as well as to complete the reëstablishment of the authority of the laws of the United States, and the full and complete restoration of peace within the limits aforesaid, Francis H. Pierpont, Governor of the State of

[1] Letcher and Smith were Governors of Virginia during the war.

Virginia," was assured of such assistance from the Federal authorities as was believed necessary in any lawful measures that he might adopt for extending the State government throughout that Commonwealth.[1]

The Secretary of the Treasury was directed to nominate without delay assessors of taxes and collectors of customs and internal revenue, and such other officers of his Department as were authorized by law, to execute the revenue laws of the United States. Preference in making appointments was to be given to qualified loyal residents of the districts in which their respective duties were to be performed; but if suitable persons could not be found residing there, then citizens of other States or districts should be named.

In the matter of appointments similar instructions were given to the Postmaster-General, who was empowered to establish post offices and post routes, and to enforce the postal laws of the United States in the State of Virginia.

The heads of the remaining Executive Departments, State, War, Navy and Interior, were likewise ordered to enforce the acts of Congress pertaining to their respective offices. The judge of the United States District Court for Virginia was directed to hold courts in that Commonwealth, while it was made the duty of the Attorney-General to instruct the proper officers to libel and bring to judgment, confiscation and sale, property subject to confiscation, and to provide for the administration of justice within the said State in all matters of which the Federal courts had cognizance.

It was this recognition of his government, and this assurance of support, that induced Mr. Pierpont less than three weeks afterward to remove his capital from Alexandria. An account of this event as well as of the nature of the Governor's duties in his enlarged jurisdiction, has been anticipated.

In recognizing Mr. Pierpont as Governor of Virginia,

[1] McPherson's Pol. Hand-Book, 1868, p. 8.

President Johnson merely concluded to retain for reconstruction what had already been accomplished by the loyal minority of that Commonwealth. Nor is it easy to perceive why, by rejecting what had been done, he should have increased the difficulties of a situation even then sufficiently complicated. While military governor of Tennessee he had executed, and, so far as appears, without remonstrance, all the measures recommended by Mr. Lincoln, so that when he succeeded to the Presidency he was to some extent committed to the policy of his predecessor. He preserved his consistency by endeavoring to maintain that system in which he had formerly acquiesced, and in sustaining the reconstructed governments of Louisiana, Arkansas, Tennessee and Virginia it is somewhat hazardous to affirm that he acted unwisely. More than this the adherents of President Lincoln could not reasonably have expected. Mr. Johnson was not, however, required by any consideration of moment to apply that mode of restoration to the seven remaining States; nor is it by any means certain that he had a legal right to do so. With President Lincoln the problem was to preserve the Union. To effect that object he believed it necessary to institute loyal governments, and his action in so doing appears to have been clearly within his powers as Commander-in-Chief. Had his course been unwise or even prejudicial to national interests, the reorganization of those States was still a legitimate war measure to which his discretion undoubtedly extended. When Andrew Johnson became President, however, the nature of the problem had greatly changed, for even though no proclamation had yet announced the termination of the Rebellion, hostilities had entirely ceased before he issued the first of his orders on reconstruction. It was only by something like a legal fiction, therefore, that the war powers could longer be exercised. It is believed that his failure to recognize the different circumstances was an error of judgment. The danger of a renewal of the conflict was not sufficiently real to justify a continuance of the unlimited authority that might be deemed necessary in time of war. He was aware that Congress had refused to admit representatives or to count electoral votes from those States reorganized during the Rebellion, when the action of the Executive rested on the firm, if somewhat undefined, foundation of the war powers. After a majority, even in these circumstances, had pronounced against that system, on what ground could the new President base his expectation of success? Without first assuring himself of the coöperation of the Legislative branch he should not have undertaken the arduous task of reviving Union governments in those commonwealths where even the very image of civil authority had been effaced. Perhaps he had been convinced that the method of restoration was analogous to the process of terminating war with a foreign power in which the initiative is to be taken by the Executive Department of Government. On this subject Mr. Blaine acutely remarks, that, "There is nothing of which a public officer can be so easily persuaded as of the enlarged jurisdiction that pertains to his station."[1] It was while executing his measures of reconstruction that Mr. Lincoln discovered the real sentiments and, to his surprise, no doubt, encountered the determined opposition of Congress. In the case of his successor the same excuse cannot be urged, for he was aware of the temper of the Republican majority, and appears to have consulted only his courage in espousing a cause already condemned by many of the most influential leaders of the party to which he principally owed his election.

As the order recognizing the Alexandria government marked no distinct Executive policy, speculation could still amuse or employ itself on the expected announcement by the new President. The first step in that momentous undertaking was the appointment, May 29, 1865, of William W. Holden

[1] Twenty Years of Congress, Vol. II. p. 70.

as Provisional Governor of North Carolina. The order promulgating that measure was as follows:

Whereas the fourth section of the fourth article of the Constitution of the United States declares that the United States shall guarantee to every State in the Union a republican form of government, and shall protect each of them against invasion and domestic violence; and whereas the President of the United States is, by the Constitution, made commander-in-chief of the army and navy, as well as chief civil executive officer of the United States, and is bound by solemn oath faithfully to execute the office of President of the United States, and to take care that the laws be faithfully executed; and whereas the rebellion, which has been waged by a portion of the people of the United States against the properly constituted authorities of the Government thereof, in the most violent and revolting form, but whose organized and armed forces have now been almost entirely overcome, has, in its revolutionary progress, deprived the people of the State of North Carolina of all civil government; and whereas it becomes necessary and proper to carry out and enforce the obligations of the United States to the people of North Carolina, in securing them in the enjoyment of a republican form of government:

Now, therefore, in obedience to the high and solemn duties imposed upon me by the Constitution of the United States, and for the purpose of enabling the loyal people of said State to organize a State government, whereby justice may be established, domestic tranquillity insured, and loyal citizens protected in all their rights of life, liberty, and property, I, Andrew Johnson, President of the United States, and Commander-in-Chief of the army and navy of the United States, do hereby appoint William W. Holden, Provisional Governor of the State of North Carolina, whose duty it shall be, at the earliest practicable period, to prescribe such rules and regulations as may be necessary and proper for convening a convention, composed of delegates to be chosen by that portion of the people of said State who are loyal to the United States, and no others, for the purpose of altering or amending the constitution thereof; and with authority to exercise, within the limits of said State, all the powers necessary and proper to enable such loyal people of the State of North Carolina to restore said State to its constitutional relations to the Federal Government, and to present such a republican form of State government as will entitle the State to the guarantee of the United States therefor, and its people to protection by the United States against invasion, insurrection, and domestic violence; *Provided,* that in any election that may be hereafter held for choosing delegates to any State convention, as aforesaid, no person shall be qualified as an elector, or shall be eligible as a member of such convention, unless he shall have previously taken the oath of amnesty, as set forth in the President's proclamation of May 29, A. D. 1865, and is a voter qualified as prescribed by the Constitution and laws of the State of North Carolina, in force immediately before the 20th day of May, 1861, the date of the so-called ordinance of secession; and the said convention when convened, or the Legislature that may be thereafter assembled, will prescribe the qualifications of electors, and the eligibility of persons to hold office under the Constitution and laws of the State, a power the people of the several States composing the Federal Union have rightfully exercised from the origin of the Government to the present time.

And I do hereby direct:

First. That the military commander of the Department, and all officers and persons in the military and naval service aid and assist the said Provisional Governor in carrying into effect this proclamation, and they are enjoined to abstain from, in any way, hindering, impeding or discouraging the loyal people from the organization of a State Government, as herein authorized.

Then followed instructions, similar to those contained in the order of May 9, relative to Virginia, directing the heads of the several Executive Departments to enforce those Federal laws in North Carolina of which the administration belonged to their respective offices.

Somewhat earlier on the same day was published an Amnesty Proclamation, renewing in effect the provisions of that issued by Mr. Lincoln on the 8th of December, 1863. It increased, however, the number of classes excepted from the benefits of the original offer by adding the following:

All persons who have been or are absentees from the United States for the purpose of aiding the rebellion.

All military and naval officers in the rebel service, who were educated by the Government in the Military Academy at West Point or the United States Naval Academy.

All persons who held the pretended offices of governors of States in insurrection against the United States.

All persons who left their homes within the jurisdiction and protection of the United States, and passed beyond the Federal military lines into the pretended confederate States for the purpose of aiding the rebellion.

All persons who have been engaged in the destruction of the commerce of the United States upon the high seas, and all persons who have made raids into the United States from Canada, or been engaged in destroying the commerce of the United States upon the lakes and rivers that separate the British Provinces from the United States.

All persons who, at the time when they seek to obtain the benefits hereof by taking the oath herein prescribed, are in military, naval, or civil confinement, or custody, or under bonds of the civil, military, or naval authorities, or agents of the United States, as prisoners of war, or persons detained for offences of any kind, either before or after conviction.

All persons who have voluntarily participated in said rebellion, and the estimated value of whose taxable property is over twenty thousand dollars.

All persons who have taken the oath of amnesty as prescribed in the President's proclamation of December 8, A. D. 1863, or an oath of allegiance to the Government of the United States since the date of said proclamation, and who have not thenceforward kept and maintained the same inviolate.[1]

The proclamation provided, however, that persons belonging to the excluded classes could make special application for pardon, when such liberal clemency would be exercised by the President as was deemed consistent with the facts in each case, and with the peace and dignity of the United States.

Secretary Seward, who attested the proclamation, approved its general tenor as well as its details. At first he appears to have opposed the "Twenty-thousand-dollar exclusion," but finally yielded to the arguments of the President, who by this description had hoped to include a numerous class that did not come under any of those specified. In this respect it possessed the comprehensive as well as the convenient character of a general warrant. All attempts to fix responsibility for secession have proved futile, and it is difficult to explain the President's attitude toward Southern men of property unless, indeed, he meant to humiliate a class that he personally disliked, or, perhaps, he intended to act upon the principle that to be mild it is necessary first to appear cruel. Precisely why the other classes were excepted from the offer of indemnity the reader of Rebellion literature need not be

[1] McPherson's Pol. Hand-Book, 1868, pp. 10-11.

informed. The amnesty proclamation applied to all the insurgent States.

Like the "Louisiana plan," the order appointing Mr. Holden was based on that clause of the Federal Constitution which guarantees " to every State in this Union a republican form of government." It was in his character of Commander-in-Chief of the Army and Navy, as well as Executive, that he assumed to appoint a provisional governor. The Rebellion, which in its progress had " deprived the people of the State of North Carolina of all civil government," he described as having been " almost entirely overcome." This condition rendered it necessary to fulfill the Federal obligation to secure to the people of that State a republican form of government. The order being self-explanatory, it only remains to observe that none but " loyal people " were to participate in electing delegates to the convention, which it was made the duty of the Governor to convoke. The term " loyal people " included all who would take the oath and receive the pardon provided for in the proclamation. These were required to be qualified voters under the laws in force immediately before the act of secession. By this provision the negroes of the State were excluded from the electoral people, and the work of reconstruction left entirely in the hands of the whites. The convention chosen by these citizens, or the Legislature that might be thereafter assembled, was authorized to " prescribe the qualifications of electors, and the eligibility of persons to hold office under the constitution and laws of the State, a power," added the order, which " the people of the several States composing the Federal Union have rightfully exercised from the origin of the Government to the present time."

Governor Holden in a proclamation of June 12, 1865, announced his appointment and declared his purpose to order an election of delegates to a State convention, the object of calling which was briefly noticed. He also made known his

CULMINATION OF THE PRESIDENTIAL PLAN

intention to commission justices of the peace for the purpose of administering the oath of allegiance and opening the polls. He urged the people to resume their accustomed pursuits; refugees were encouraged by an offer of protection to return to the State, and freedmen were instructed in the duties peculiar to their altered circumstances.

By a second proclamation, dated August 8, the choice of delegates to the proposed convention was fixed for September 21 succeeding. Some delay in appointing a date for holding the election was occasioned by a desire to afford the people an opportunity of enrolling their names and obtaining the required certificates.

By such voters as were not included in any of the excepted classes, together with the few who had been able to procure the Presidential pardon, full delegations were chosen in all but three counties. The details of this election accessible to the writer are exceedingly meagre. Owing much to the timely publication and the admirable character of the orders of General Schofield, who had exercised the functions of military governor until superseded by Mr. Holden, the contest appears to have been free from unusual violence, though newspaper correspondents, it is true, reported disturbances at several polling places and mention rumors of rioting.

The convention, which assembled at Raleigh on October 2, was composed for the most part of members who had either openly opposed or reluctantly joined the secession movement. There were few, however, who had not given aid and comfort to the enemy. In other words, they were Whigs and conservative Democrats. Every representative readily took the oath to support the Constitution of the United States. The convention organized by electing Edwin G. Reade, an ex-member of the Thirty-fifth Congress, as president. On taking his seat Mr. Reade made an appropriate and conciliatory address.

The Provisional Governor also submitted to the members of the convention a brief message in which he observed that their duties were too plain to require any suggestions from him. North Carolina, he said, attempted in May, 1861, to separate herself from the Union. That attempt involved her in protracted and disastrous war. She entered the rebellion a slaveholding and emerged from it a non-slaveholding State. "In other respects," he declared, "so far as her existence as a State and her rights as a State are concerned, she has undergone no change."[1] He assumed that the convention would insert in the organic law a provision forever prohibiting involuntary servitude in North Carolina. The language abolishing that institution, the form of the resolution abrogating the ordinance of secession and the nature of the action to be taken on the war debt were the most important questions before the convention.

On October 7 the repealing ordinance was passed unanimously in the following terms:

The ordinance of the convention of the State of North Carolina, ratified on the 21st day of November, 1789, which adopted and ratified the Constitution of the United States, and also all acts and parts of acts of the General Assembly ratifying and adopting amendments to the said Constitution, are now, and at all times since the adoption and ratification thereof, have been, in full force and effect, notwithstanding the supposed ordinance of the 20th of May, 1861, declaring the same to be repealed, rescinded, and abrogated; and the said supposed ordinance is now, and at all times hath been, null and void.[2]

The resolution abolishing slavery, reported on the following day, was adopted on the 9th of October, and is as follows:

Be it declared and ordained by the delegates of the people of the State of North Carolina in convention assembled, and it is hereby declared and ordained, That slavery and involuntary servitude, otherwise than for

[1] Ann. Cycl., 1865, p. 626.
[2] This ordinance was ratified by a vote of 20,506 to 2,002; Poore's Charters and Constitutions, Vol. II. p. 1419n; also Three Decades of Federal Legislation, p. 385.

crimes, whereof the parties shall have been duly convicted, shall be, and is hereby, forever prohibited within the State.[1]

Not without some reluctance there was also adopted a resolution prohibiting any future Legislature from assuming or paying any State debt created directly or indirectly for the purpose of aiding the Rebellion. There seems to have been in the convention a strong element opposed to the passage of such a measure, or at all events who preferred to refer it to a popular vote. The decision of the convention on this subject appears to have been influenced by a telegram from the President to Governor Holden, in which the former says:

> Every dollar of the debt created to aid the rebellion against the United States should be repudiated finally and forever. The great mass of the people should not be taxed to pay a debt to aid in carrying on a rebellion which they in fact, if left to themselves, were opposed to. Let those who have given their means for the obligations of the State look to that power they tried to establish in violation of law, Constitution, and will of the people. They must meet their fate. It is their misfortune, and cannot be recognized by the people of any State professing themselves loyal to the Government of the United States and in the Union. . . .[2]

The convention adjourned October 19 to reassemble on the fourth Thursday of May, 1866. Judge Reade, its president, previously delivered a farewell address, in which he said: " Our work is finished. The breach in the Government, as far as the same was by force, has been overcome by force; and so far as the same has had the sanction of legislation, the legislation has been declared to be null and void. So that there remains nothing to be done except the withdrawal of military power when all our governmental relations will be restored, without further asking, on the part of the United States. The element of slavery, which so long distracted and

[1] Ratified by 19,039 to 3,970 votes. Poore's Charters and Constitutions, Vol. II. p. 1419n.
[2] McPherson's Pol. Hand-Book, 1868, p. 19.

divided the sections, has by an unanimous vote been abolished. Every man in the State is free. The reluctance which for a while was felt to the sudden and radical change in our domestic relations — a reluctance which was made oppressive to us by our kind feelings for the slave, and by our apprehensions of the evils which were to follow him — has yielded to the determination to be to him, as we always have been, his best friends; to advise, protect, educate and elevate him; to seek his confidence, and to give him ours, each occupying appropriate positions to the other. . . . It remains for us to return to our constituents and engage with them in the great work of restoring our beloved State to order and prosperity." [1]

An election, fixed for November 9, was ordered by Mr. Holden for the choice of Governor, members of a General Assembly, county officers and Representatives in Congress. On the same occasion the people were to vote on the ordinance abolishing and prohibiting slavery. The action of the convention on the Confederate debt being final, that subject was not referred to the popular judgment.

On behalf of the convention the president and other delegates soon after adjournment proceeded to Washington to acquaint Mr. Johnson with the result of their deliberations. They related to him what has already been placed before the reader. As the convention had yielded what was involved in the war, President Johnson was requested to declare on the part of the Federal authorities that the governmental relations of North Carolina had been reconciled. Notwithstanding what had been done they feared that their State delegation would be excluded from Congress by the imposition of a test oath which few men in that commonwealth could take. The convention, therefore, petitioned Congress, through Mr. Johnson, to repeal the requirement. The President, after expressing his satisfaction with what North Carolina had done,

[1] Harper's New Monthly Magazine, Vol. XXXII., p. 127.

reminded the delegates that to make restoration practicable one thing still remained to be accomplished, namely, their acceptance of the amendment abolishing slavery throughout the United States.

The ordinances submitted to the people were ratified at the November election, when Jonathan Worth was chosen Governor over Mr. Holden by a majority of 6,730, in a total of 58,554 votes. The repeal of the secession ordinance was ratified by a vote of 20,506 to 2,002, and that prohibiting slavery by 19,039 against 3,970.

In a dispatch of November 27, President Johnson, thanking the Provisional Governor for the efficient manner in which he had executed his duties, said that the result of the election was greatly to damage the prospects of the State in the restoration of its government, that if the action and spirit of the Legislature were in the same direction it would greatly increase the harm already done, and might prove fatal. He hoped the mischief would be repaired.[1]

Meanwhile the Legislature during a brief session ratified, with only six dissenting votes, the Thirteenth Amendment, and elected John Pool and William A. Graham United States Senators. Seven Representatives in Congress had been previously chosen.

Mr. Holden, who continued to perform the functions of his office until the inauguration of his successor on the 15th of December, probably owed his appointment to his reputation as a Democratic editor. Though his rise to political prominence was similar to that of the President, he had not the latter's inflexibility of principle. A secessionist in 1856, when the success of Fremont appeared probable, he soon began to recede from that position, and in 1859 was opposed to disunion; subsequently he drifted with the popular current and even went so far in an advanced stage of the Rebellion as to

[1] Ann. Cycl., 1865, p. 628.

advocate a "last-dollar-and-last-man" resolution. But even this, together with the expression of extreme opinions, did not restore him to public confidence, and before the end of the war the *Standard,* which he edited, became the organ of the disaffected. Notwithstanding this wavering and inconsistent career the fact that he was generally regarded as an enemy of secession singled him out as the proper person to reorganize the government of North Carolina.

Though the President was not indifferent to the demoralized condition of his native State, that consideration alone does not appear to have induced him to begin the process of reconstruction with that commonwealth. There is strong testimony to prove that Mr. Lincoln had prepared a similar proclamation for restoring the former relations of North Carolina, and on July 8, 1867, General Grant testified before the Joint Committee on Reconstruction that he had twice heard read at meetings of Mr. Lincoln's Cabinet a paper embodying the same provisions as that published by President Johnson.

Before taking the second step a brief interval elapsed; perhaps the President was hesitating; however this may be, he informed Hon. George S. Boutwell that "the measure was tentative." The fears of the Massachusetts statesman and his concern for harmony in the Republican party, of which he was an able and honored leader, induced him, in company with Senator Morrill, of Vermont, to call on the President. During their conversation Mr. Johnson, when the dangers of his policy were indicated, assured his visitors "that nothing further would be done until the experiment had been tested."[1]

Notwithstanding this deliberate assurance, the President at that time appears to have almost determined on the system that he intended to adopt, for scarcely two weeks had passed when he appointed, by a proclamation similar to that for North

[1] McClure's Magazine, Dec., 1899, p. 174.

Carolina, William L. Sharkey, Provisional Governor of Mississippi. Within a month from the date of Mr. Holden's appointment others were made for all the remaining States except Florida, the order for reorganizing which was delayed till July 13.[1]

The origin and development of the Executive plan having now been traced with some degree of minuteness, it is not the design of this essay to pursue circumstantially the institution of that system in the six remaining States. By proclamations almost identical with that issued in the case of North Carolina, provisional governors were appointed in all of those commonwealths before the middle of July. Though the method of reorganization in these States presented similar features, several were distinguished in some respects from the others. Observations on those differences will employ nearly all that remains to be said on Reconstruction under President Johnson.

The appointment of Mr. Holden alarmed Republican leaders; the successive proclamations for restoring the other States directed public attention to the questions involved in reconstruction. Seeing that Congress was not in session, that the President had assumed an expectant attitude, and that every plan of reunion proposed was liable to serious objection, it is not a matter of wonder that the recent Confederate authorities attempted of themselves to restore Federal relations.

These were among the considerations that induced Governor Clarke, of Mississippi, to summon the Legislature of that State to meet on May 18. In his address convoking the disloyal assembly he urged the people, in order to remove the necessity for sending Federal troops among them, to restore

[1] The Provisional appointments were made in the following order: June 13, 1865, William L. Sharkey, Mississippi; June 17, James Johnson, Georgia, and Andrew J. Hamilton, Texas; June 21, Lewis E. Parsons, Alabama; June 30, Benjamin F. Perry, South Carolina; July 13, William Marvin, Florida.

and preserve peace. The Legislature came together accordingly, and, among other measures, provided for the election, on June 19, of delegates to a State convention. Before that date, however, the President had appointed William L. Sharkey, an eminent jurist, Provisional Governor, thus ignoring both the measures of Mr. Clarke and the insurgent assembly. The latter was dispersed by a military order, while the Governor was carried off to a fortress in Boston harbor.

Mr. Sharkey, in a dutiful and able address, appointed August 7 as the day for holding an election of delegates to a State convention which was to meet at the city of Jackson one week later. In this proclamation, he said: " The negroes are now free — free by the fortunes of war — free by proclamation — free by common consent —free practically, as well as theoretically, and it is too late to raise questions as to the means by which they became so."[1] Though the Governor, to avoid the delay of separate county organization, had appointed many local officials who had held their posts during the Rebellion, he required all of them to take the oath of allegiance prescribed by the President.

The convention, which assembled at the appointed time, declared the ordinance of secession null and void, prohibited slavery and made it the duty of the next Legislature to provide for the protection of the person and the property of freedmen. The lawmaking body was also to take measures for guarding both the negroes and the commonwealth against any evils that might arise from sudden emancipation. The first Monday in October was appointed for the election of State officers and members of Congress. A memorial was also adopted urging the President to remove the colored troops from the State. The members, acting apparently in their individual capacity, united in a petition for the pardon of Jefferson Davis and of Governor Clarke. The amendment of the State con-

[1] Ann. Cycl., 1865, p. 580.

stitution abolishing slavery was adopted by the decisive vote of 86 to 11. After South Carolina, Mississippi contained the greatest proportion of slaves, and was thus very deeply involved in the system.

While the convention was in session the President sent to Governor Sharkey a telegram in which he made the following remarkable suggestion:

> I am gratified to see that you have organized your convention without difficulty. . . . If you could extend the elective franchise to all persons of color who can read the Constitution of the United States in English and write their names, and to all persons of color who own real estate valued at not less than two hundred and fifty dollars and pay taxes thereon, you would completely disarm the adversary and set an example the other States will follow. This you can do with perfect safety, and you would thus place Southern States in reference to free persons of color upon the same basis with the free States. I hope and trust your convention will do this, and as a consequence the radicals, who are wild upon negro franchise, will be completely foiled in their attempts to keep the Southern States from renewing their relations to the Union by not accepting their Senators and Representatives.[1]

From the view point of practical politics this recommendation was undoubtedly a wise one, but it will scarcely be contended that it was the suggestion of enlightened statesmanship. The South, distrusting the President's sincerity, refused to adopt his suggestion. The communication is reproduced, not to show that the President was not always impelled by the highest motives so much as to show that even before Congress had assembled he had already come to regard as "the adversary" those whose exertions secured his election.

In his proclamation appointing a date for the election of delegates Governor Sharkey advised the people, when it might be necessary in consequence of the remoteness of a military force, to form a county patrol for the apprehension of offenders. Information having reached him that in many parts of

[1] Ann. Cycl., 1865, p. 581.

the State organized bands had been robbing and plundering, and that the Federal troops were insufficient to suppress these disorders, he urged citizens, especially the young men who had "so distinguished themselves for gallantry," to organize promptly in each county volunteer companies, one of cavalry and one of infantry if practicable, to assist in detecting, punishing and preventing crime.

From his headquarters at Vicksburg, General Slocum, the Federal commander, immediately published an order to prevent the proposed reorganization of the militia. The contemplated force, he said, would be numerically superior to his own, and, as many of the Union troops on duty in Mississippi were freedmen, collisions would be unavoidable. The crimes referred to by Mr. Sharkey were, the General asserted, committed against Northern men, Government couriers and negroes. Southerners, it was true, had been halted by these marauders, but were promptly released and informed that they had been stopped by mistake. Citizens who recognized the persons were unwilling to disclose the names of these lawless members of the community. The State, too, he declared, had not yet been relieved from the attitude of hostility which she assumed against the General Government. Those engaged in attempts to organize the militia would be arrested.

Fearing that the President would not support General Slocum, Carl Schurz, who had been sent South on a mission to assist in carrying out the Administration policy, expressed in a communication to the President some doubt as to the wisdom of the Governor's action. To this the President, in a reply of August 30, said he presumed that General Slocum, without first consulting the Government, would issue no order interfering with Mr. Sharkey in his effort to restore the functions of the State government. In the matter of organizing patrols Mr. Johnson took the same view as the Governor, and in that connection said, " The people must be trusted with their government, and, if trusted, my opinion is that they will act in good faith and restore their former constitutional relations with all the States composing the Union." [1]

The lapse of fifteen months had worked a revolution in the opinions of the President. Circumstances, it is true, had changed since the delivery of his Nashville speech; the main question, however, had not greatly altered, for it was still important to determine the political people of the late insurgent States. From declaring that " rebels " must take a back seat in the work of restoration, the President had come to believe that " the people must be trusted with their government." It is not to convict Mr. Johnson of inconsistency that his opinions are here brought into juxtaposition, but rather to inquire whether every important consideration for ignoring secessionists in 1864 had disappeared by 1865.

On representation from the Provisional Governor that the Federal commander interfered to prevent the execution of his proclamation for reorganizing the militia, the President on September 2 required General Slocum to revoke his military order. Under instructions somewhat peremptory in tone, that officer two days later rescinded his proclamation.

The condition of the freedmen, as well as their exact legal status, became about this time the subject of much discussion in Mississippi. While many continued in the service of their old masters, numbers roamed about the country in idleness, and nearly all of them had very extravagant notions of their newly acquired rights and privileges. Though the whites admitted of necessity the complete freedom, they were for the most part unprepared to grant equal rights to negroes. Between them and their employers, however, there occurred but little serious trouble. All labor was contracted for, and owners of plantations, apprehensive that labor would be difficult

[1] Ann. Cycl., 1865, p. 583.

to secure at the beginning of the season, were anxious to make contracts for the year 1866. Toward the close of September the assistant commissioner of the Freedmen's Bureau turned over to the civil authorities all the business of his court. To get rid of military tribunals, Governor Sharkey promised that in all cases involving the rights of negroes their testimony would be accepted.

In the election, which was held on October 9, General Benjamin G. Humphreys, late of the Confederate army, was chosen Governor; immediately thereafter he was pardoned by the President. Five Representatives in Congress were also elected. By the Legislature, which convened and organized one week later, Governor Sharkey was appointed United States Senator to fill the unexpired term of Jefferson Davis. For the long term, Mr. J. L. Alcorn was elected. The legislation relative to freedmen will be subsequently considered.

Besides his complaint to the President relative to the interference of General Slocum with the proposed reorganization of the militia, Governor Sharkey expressed dissatisfaction with the military authorities who refused to obey writs of *habeas corpus* issued by local judges. To this Secretary Stanton replied that the grant of a provisional government did not affect the proper jurisdiction of military courts, and that this jurisdiction was still called for in cases of wrong done to soldiers, whether white or colored, and in cases of wrong done to colored citizens, and where the local authorities were unable or unwilling to do justice, either from defective machinery, or because some State law declared colored persons incompetent as witnesses. Mississippi was to a considerable extent still under military law, and the suspension of the writ of *habeas corpus* had not been revoked. To a similar remonstrance the Secretary of State replied that, the commonwealth being still under martial law, the military power was supreme.

On receiving tidings of General Johnston's surrender, Gov-

CULMINATION OF THE PRESIDENTIAL PLAN 465

ernor Brown, of Georgia, called a session of the Confederate Legislature, but General Gilmore, who commanded the department including that commonwealth, issued a counter-proclamation annulling the late Executive's order. General Wilson, in writing the ex-Governor, used expressions that were needlessly harsh, and whether the language was his own or that of the President, to whom the commander ascribed it, the style was neither dignified nor magnanimous. Whoever may have been responsible for the phraseology, the Union General appears to have believed in a rigorous exercise of the rights of conquest. With the defeat of this attempt of the recent authorities to restore their commonwealth to its old status, Georgia remained in military hands till the appointment, June 17, of James Johnson as Provisional Governor.

In the work of reconciling the people of that State the Provisional Executive was assisted by a sensible address of ex-Governor Brown, and by the support of many leading secessionists. Now that the "irrepressible conflict" had been settled, the people appeared anxious for the reorganization of their State. The 4th of October was early fixed as the date for holding an election of delegates. The suffrage of citizens was solicited and received by candidates of ability and character. These were pledged to advocate the necessary measures for restoring their commonwealth.

The convention assembled at Milledgeville on October 25, was called to order by the Provisional Governor, and elected Herschel V. Johnson as its president. Instead of declaring the nullity of the secession and kindred ordinances the convention "repealed" them. On the question of repudiating the war debt the vote stood 133 to 117 in favor of the proposition. This resolution, however, was not carried until November 7, and appears even then to have been passed only after considerable pressure from Washington, whence the President directed or assisted by telegraph the proceedings in all the reconstruction conventions. The war debt thus declared void amounted to $18,135,775. The necessity for this action is evident; the hardships occasioned thereby can be easily imagined.

The State constitution, which was thoroughly revised, recognized the changes that had occurred in civil and social affairs. In that instrument the freedom of slaves was expressly declared, and the Legislature was required to make regulations respecting the altered relations of this class of persons. The constitution as thus amended was unanimously adopted by the convention.

Though Georgia was not the most loyal supporter of Jefferson Davis in the time of his prosperity, now that adversity had overtaken him, the convention, in a memorial to President Johnson, invoked the Executive clemency in behalf of their late chief. The convention assumed for the people their share in the crime for which Mr. Davis and a few others were undergoing punishment.

As in the case of Mississippi, the President approved the organization of "a police force" in the several counties, for the purpose of arresting maurauders, suppressing crime and enforcing authority.

The Legislature, which was elected November 15, assembled at Milledgeville on the 4th of December following. With its proceedings we are not now concerned more than to observe that the Thirteenth Amendment was adopted by that body five days subsequently.[1] The measures of the Georgia Assembly were not before Congress when it convened.

Like the chief magistrates in several other Southern States, the Confederate Governor of Texas, when convinced after the surrender of General Kirby Smith that the war had ceased, took steps toward bringing his commonwealth into its old practical relations with the Union. He accordingly ordered

[1] Constitution of the United States, by Francis N. Thorpe, p. 49.

an election of delegates to a convention to be held on June 19, but was anticipated by President Johnson, who two days earlier had appointed Andrew J. Hamilton Provisional Governor. Though the latter did not promptly appoint a day for holding the election, he announced his intention of doing so at an early date. There was probably in the minds of the less intelligent Texans a notion that emancipation was to be gradual, or that it was not yet an accomplished fact. To dispel any such idea the new Executive circulated an address which informed the public that if, " in the action of the proposed convention, the negro is characterized or treated as less than a freeman," Senators and Representatives from Texas would vainly seek admission to the halls of Congress. The choice of delegates having been fixed for January 8, 1866, an account of the convention or of the proceedings in the Assembly subsequently organized in that State does not fall within the scope of this work. In the interval justice was administered by officers temporarily commissioned for that purpose.

The negro population, which, because of the influx from other Southern States, had doubled since 1860, presented a difficult problem in the reorganization of Texas. They knew little of the uses of freedom and were kept systematically at work only by the candid admonitions of General Granger and the Governor. Toward the close of December, however, a better feeling prevailed among them; but it appears to have been a serious problem to have kept the freedmen of Texas steadily at work. Planters throughout the State lost heavily by their inability to engage or to retain in their service laborers enough to gather the standing cotton crop. The full consideration of this subject is inseparable from an analysis of Texan legislation relative to freedmen. Though well advanced, the reconstruction of Texas under the Executive plan was not completed before the meeting of the Thirty-ninth Congress.

Nothing in the reorganization of Alabama or of South Carolina calls for especial mention. The same is true of Florida. Both the spirit and tendency of Southern legislation, however, require to be noticed, and with that examination a brief recapitulation will complete this investigation.

Before concluding this inquiry two related topics require briefly to be noticed, namely, the character of the reconstruction conventions, and the *personnel* as well as the spirit of the legislatures organized under their authority. As to the former it may be observed that there were several modes in which constitutional conventions could have been assembled; all, however, were objectionable because of an element of irregularity. Considering them chronologically, rather than logically, the first was the method employed by the Union men of western Virginia. The Wheeling convention of June, 1861, was composed of delegates chosen at elections called, not by the constituted authorities, for they were already committed to a policy of rebellion, but by a spontaneous popular movement inaugurated by loyal and influential leaders. The work of this body, even though revolutionary, or at least irregular in its origin, was acquiesced in by the people affected and subsequently approved by the General Government. So few, however, were the loyalists of the insurgent States generally, that it was not practicable elsewhere in the South to reorganize governments in a similar manner.

A second mode was that adopted by Mr. Lincoln. Under this method, the President, as Commander-in-Chief, protected Union minorities in their efforts to reëstablish local governments in harmony with the Federal Constitution. This plan, it is evident, could be justified merely as a military measure, and, therefore, was lawful only during the continuance of the Rebellion. On the return of peace all such provisional schemes would disappear unless tolerated by the neglect or confirmed by the legislation of Congress. The conventions held under this theory rested on the authority of the commanding officer, who was himself acting by Executive direction. In reorganizing the government of Louisiana, General Banks, it will be remembered, declared that the fundamental law of that commonwealth was martial law, which was no more than his arbitrary will. In purging the electoral people and amending the constitution of that State he acted in strict conformity with that assumption. If in the preceding pages the reconstruction measures of Mr. Lincoln have been characterized as legitimate, it must not be supposed that it was intended to assert that they would have been lawful in time of peace, for under the American system it has never been deemed competent for the national Executive to call a convention. Though the establishments instituted under his authority, except in the case of Tennessee, never received the permanent sanction of Congress, the conventions which organized these governments stand on a foundation somewhat different from those assembled by the appointees of President Johnson, for in the summer of 1865 the plea of military necessity could no longer be urged. If, therefore, the conventions held in Louisiana, Arkansas and Tennessee were tainted with irregularity, those assembled in the remaining States were undoubtedly revolutionary. Technically, however, the conventions of both classes stand on the same footing. Governor Perry, of South Carolina, regarded as revolutionary the body which he convoked to reorganize his commonwealth, and for that reason, as he alleged, dissolved the convention before it had taken final action on the important question of the Southern debt.

The course of the Confederate governors of Mississippi, Georgia and Texas, who summoned the insurgent legislatures of their respective States for the purpose of calling conventions, suggests a third mode in which the machinery of government could have been set in motion. This plan, however, presented an evident difficulty, inasmuch as these assemblies could not have been recognized without admitting in some sort the validity of the secession and kindred ordinances. Mr. Lincoln, it is true, intended, before hostilities had ceased, to permit the members of the Virginia Legislature to meet as influential individuals for the purpose of recalling their State troops from the Confederate army. The surrender of Lee occurring soon after, and the President's action having been misunderstood, he withdrew this permission, and did it the more readily as the necessity which suggested it had passed completely away. The department commanders prevented any response to the proclamations of the Executives in the three States named above, and President Johnson by his prompt appointment of provisional governors ignored or anticipated their action. To say nothing of the revolutionary course contemplated by the ex-Confederate governors, the success of their plan required the approval or at least the connivance of Federal authorities.

Still another manner of proceeding was for Congress, by calling or authorizing conventions, to inaugurate the movement for reconstruction; but the power of the national Legislature extends only to the passage of enabling acts for Territories, and these commonwealths appear to have been neither constitutional Territories nor constitutional States. However, as some irregularity was inseparable from any system of reorganization, the Legislative branch of Government was the authority least objectionable for controlling informal changes in the nature of the Union. If powers not conferred by the Constitution must be assumed, it is better in the interests of civil liberty for the representatives of the people to transcend the organic law.

The second mode, it need scarcely be observed, was that embodied in the Executive plan. The conventions which assembled under encouragement and direction of President Johnson had an opportunity unequaled since the formation of the Constitution of winning the gratitude of the nation. By adopting an enlightened and humane policy they could have furnished an example of patriotism that would serve to influence the deliberations not only of the first assemblies to meet under the new order, but of all future legislatures in those States. It is well known that they did not prove equal to this emergency; the concessions to Northern opinion were not gracefully yielded, and lost much of their merit by having been extorted from the fears of the delegates. In some instances the conventions, by assuming functions of the ordinary legislative character, transcended their powers, and many of them "repealed" the ordinances without condemning the principle of secession. They amended and even adopted constitutions that were never submitted to the people. The civil rights of the negro were abandoned to the mercy of those who had fought to perpetuate human servitude. No provision was made for freedmen in the fundamental law, it having been assumed that the new legislatures could be trusted to extend justice equally to all classes in the community. In a word, those were disappointed who had expected from the conventions a display of civic virtues commensurate to the occasion.

The remaining topic, that is, the character of the reconstructed governments as well as the spirit and tendency of their legislation, may in this place be briefly dismissed. Not, indeed, that the subject is unimportant, for it was mainly upon this question that the Thirty-ninth Congress justified its refusal to admit members from the South, and vindicated its rigorous treatment of the subjugated States. While an investigation of public opinion in that section is essential to a correct understanding of legislative action, the full consideration of the subject belongs properly to a treatise on

Congressional reconstruction, a theme to which this essay is only introductory. For the present purpose, therefore, a brief outline must suffice.

Though the reconstruction conventions were correctly regarded as revolutionary, that character would not affect the legislatures instituted by their authority if the people concerned acquiesced in their proceedings. Americans of that day were not altogether indifferent to the sacred right of revolution, even if the principle was not so highly esteemed as formerly. An objection far more serious than the irregular origin of these conventions was the spirit which animated Southern legislators.

When the Thirty-ninth Congress convened at its first session members had before them only the merest fragments of the mass of testimony subsequently reported by the Joint Committee on Reconstruction, though even then they possessed evidence of the temper of the Southern mind sufficient, they believed, to recommend the most deliberate procedure. It would not be difficult to collect from contemporary literature proofs of hostility to the General Government sufficient to justify the attitude of Congress when it assembled on the 4th of December, 1865. From various sources the Northern people had caught glimpses of the actual condition of affairs within the late Confederacy. These manifestations of unfriendliness to the Union were enough to excite suspicion, and, in a matter affecting the future welfare of a great and powerful nation, suspicion is a just ground for inquiry.

The alacrity with which the Southern people rushed to battle, as well as the vigor with which they prosecuted the war, was a phenomenon not more remarkable than the unanimity and promptness with which they apparently acquiesced in the result. It was long before the people of the North could believe that the rebellion was anything more than a leaders' insurrection, and they could not easily be persuaded after its close that those who had fought so desperately to destroy, were sincere in their professions of loyalty to, the Union. It was not unnatural, therefore, that the late adversaries of the South would look with suspicion on her instant submission. With few exceptions Southern statesmen seemed desirous of effecting an early reunion. While various reasons might be assigned to explain this dutiful and almost unlimited obedience, it is certain that the argument chiefly relied upon by the provisional governors was that it was only by such a course that they could hope soon to be relieved of the presence among them of Yankee soldiers. Apprehension that more burdensome conditions might be imposed by Stevens and other radical leaders in Congress was, perhaps, not altogether without influence in producing this general acquiescence in the policy of the President.[1] As every citizen who engaged in rebellion had forfeited both his life and his estate, it would be prudent temporarily to conceal any feeling of resentment, or any desire of revenge. These considerations were not without influence on the conduct of both the leaders and the people. With the quick upgrowth, however, of a feeling of personal safety, encouraged, no doubt, by a lavish distribution of pardons, and with an expectation, not unfounded, that reconciliation would speedily be followed by either a restoration of, or indemnity for, confiscated property, this policy of conformity would vanish. Thus under exterior tranquillity rankled bitter memories of disaster and defeat nourishing a state of unrest which even the unquestioned influence of their late commanders could not always keep from expressing itself in acts of violence. However, as Henry Winter Davis had foretold, the Southern population generally put on the seemly garb of peace and observed the form of holding elections.

[1] See Why The Solid South? pp. 9-10, for an ingenious explanation of the unanimity and promptness with which the Presidential policy of reconstruction was accepted by the South.

Notwithstanding that many of their most enlightened citizens recommended, and that their most trusted leaders enjoined, submission to the new order, the transition from a state of hostility was marked even at the outset by acts of the highest indiscretion. Nor were these confined to irresponsible individuals whose utterances might have been justly regarded as the momentary inspiration of passion. Some of the acts referred to were the deliberate convictions of legislative bodies, and, as these measures appear to have escaped criticism, they may fairly be supposed to reflect the sentiments of the South. In the circumstances this was especially unfortunate, postponing as it did the day of peace and reconciliation; it afforded also a decent pretext to the "Radicals," if they desired one, for excluding the Southern delegations from Congress. It justified inquiry, and investigation was fatal to Southern claims of universal submission.

Though the exclusion of representatives undoubtedly intensified, it did not occasion the change in Southern feeling, for the Mississippi measures, presently to be noticed, were passed before the meeting of Congress. Acts of frequent occurrence tended to confirm the worst fears of that body, and long before the Joint Committee had completed their labors they were supplied with new species of violence if any description of outrage was lacking to crown their indictment. With due allowance for the fact that during many years preceding the war outrages were much more numerous in the slave than in the free States, it soon became apparent that it was unsafe to leave to the justice of Southern courts either the few Unionists who had remained faithful in that section or the recently enfranchised slaves. The estimation in which the former were held appears in the fact that in competition for office they were uniformly defeated by ex-Confederate candidates, sometimes by unpardoned, and even unrepentant ones. The feeling toward

CULMINATION OF THE PRESIDENTIAL PLAN

freedmen was one of extreme bitterness. Overlooking scattered acts of violence and outrage of which negroes were generally, though not always, the victims, Southern hostility toward them found unmistakable expression in the November legislation of Mississippi. On the 22d of that month was enacted a law regulating the relation of *master* and *apprentice* in the case of " freedmen, free negroes and mulattoes." Among other things this statute provided:

> That it shall be the duty of all . . . civil officers . . . in this State to report to the probate courts of their respective counties, semiannually, . . . all freedmen, free negroes, and mulattoes, under the age of eighteen, within their respective counties, beats or districts, who are orphans, or whose parent or parents have not the means, or who refuse to provide for and support said minors, and thereupon it shall be the duty of said probate court to order the clerk of said court to apprentice said minors to some competent and suitable person, on such terms as the court may direct, having a particular care to the interest of said minors: Provided, That the former owner of said minors shall have the preference, when in the opinion of the court, he or she shall be a suitable person for that purpose.
>
> Sec. 2. . . . That the said court shall be fully satisfied that the person or persons to whom said minor shall be apprenticed shall be a suitable person to have the charge and care of said minor, and fully to protect the interest of said minor. The said court shall require the said master or mistress to execute bond and security, payable to the State of Mississippi, conditioned that he or she shall furnish said minor with sufficient food and clothing, to treat said minor humanely, furnish medical attention in case of sickness, teach or cause to be taught him or her to read and write, if under fifteen years old, and will conform to any law that may be hereafter passed for the regulation of the duties and relation of master and apprentice: Provided, that said apprentice shall be bound by indenture, in case of males until they are twenty-one years old, and in case of females until they are eighteen years old.
>
> Sec. 3. . . . That in the management and control of said apprentices, said master or mistress shall have power to inflict such moderate corporeal chastisement as a father or guardian is allowed to inflict on his or her child or ward at common law: Provided, That in no case shall cruel or inhuman punishment be inflicted.
>
> Sec. 4. . . . That if any apprentice shall leave the employment of his or her master or mistress, without his or her consent, said master or mistress may pursue and recapture said apprentice, and bring him or her

before any justice of the peace of the county, whose duty it shall be to remand said apprentice to the service of his or her master or mistress; and in the event of a refusal on the part of said apprentice so to return, then said justice shall commit said apprentice to the jail of said county, on failure to give bond, until the next term of the county court; and it shall be the duty of said court, at the first term thereafter, to investigate said case, and if the court shall be of opinion that said apprentice left the employment of his or her master or mistress without good cause, to order him or her to be punished, as provided for the punishment of hired freedmen, as may be from time to time provided for by law, for desertion, until he or she shall agree to return to his or her master or mistress: Provided, that the court may grant continuances, as in other cases; and provided further, that if the court shall believe that said apprentice had good cause to quit his said master or mistress, the court shall discharge said apprentice from said indenture, and also enter a judgment against the master or mistress, for not more than one hundred dollars, for the use and benefit of said appprentice, to be collected on execution, as in other cases.

Sec. 5. . . . That if any person entice away any apprentice from his or her master or mistress, or shall knowingly employ an apprentice, or furnish him or her food or clothing, without the written consent of his or her master or mistress, or shall sell or give said apprentice ardent spirits, without such consent, said person so offending shall be deemed guilty of a high misdemeanor, and shall, on conviction thereof before the county court, be punished as provided for the punishment of persons enticing from their employer hired freedmen, free negroes or mulattoes.[1]

In the matter of apprenticing minors it will be observed that the former owner, when a person satisfactory to the court, was to have the preference; in the event of his death his widow or other member of his family was, if deemed suitable, to have the preference in re-apprenticing the minor. When there was no record testimony of the date of birth, judges of county courts were empowered to fix the age of the minor. The act was to go into force immediately after its passage.[2]

The act of November 25, conferring civil rights on emancipated slaves, provided:

[1] **Laws of** Mississippi, pp. 86-88. [2] Ibid., pp. 89-90.

CULMINATION OF THE PRESIDENTIAL PLAN

That all freedmen, free negroes and mulattoes may sue and be sued, implead and be impleaded in all the courts of law and equity of this State, and may acquire personal property and choses in action, by descent or purchase, and may dispose of the same, in the same manner, and to the same extent that white persons may; Provided, that the provisions of this section [1] shall not be so construed as to allow any freedman, free negro or mulatto, to rent or lease any lands or tenements, except in incorporated towns or cities in which places the corporate authorities shall control the same.

. . . .

Sec. 5. . . . That every freedman, free negro and mulatto, shall, on the second Monday of January, one thousand eight hundred and sixty-six, and annually thereafter, have a lawful home or employment, and shall have written evidence thereof, as follows, to wit: if living in any incorporated city, town or village, a license from the mayor thereof, and if living outside of any incorporated city, town or village, from the member of the board of police of his beat, authorizing him or her to do irregular and job work, or a written contract, as provided in section six of this act, which licenses may be revoked for cause, at any time, by the authority granting the same.

Sec. 6. . . . That all contracts for labor made with freedmen, free negroes and mulattoes, for a longer period than one month shall be in writing and in duplicate, attested and read to said freedman, free negro or mulatto, by a beat, city or county officer, or two disinterested white persons of the county in which the labor is to be performed, of which each party shall have one; and said contracts shall be taken and held as entire contracts, and if the laborer shall quit the service of the employer, before the expiration of his term of service, without good cause he shall forfeit his wages for that year, up to the time of quitting.

Sec. 7. . . . That every civil officer shall, and every person may arrest and carry back to his or her legal employer any freedman, free negro or mulatto, who shall have quit the service of his or her employer before the expiration of his or her term of service without good cause, and said officer and person shall be entitled to receive for arresting and carrying back every deserting employee aforesaid, the sum of five dollars, and ten cents per mile from the place of arrest to the place of delivery, and the same shall be paid by the employer, and held as a set-off for so much against the wages of said deserting employee: Provided, that said arrested party after being so returned may appeal to a justice of the peace or member of the board of the police of the county, who on notice to the alleged employer, shall try summarily whether said appellant is legally employed by the alleged employer and has good cause to quit said employer; either party shall have the right of appeal to the county court, pending which the alleged deserter shall be remanded to the alleged employer, or otherwise disposed of as shall be right and just, and the decision of the county court shall be final.

Sec. 8. . . . That upon affidavit made by the employer of any freedman, free negro or mulatto, or other credible person, before any justice of the peace or member of the board of police, that any freedman, free negro or mulatto, legally employed by said employer, has illegally deserted said employment, such justice of the peace or member of the board of police, shall issue his warrant or warrants, returnable before himself, or other such officer, directed to any sheriff, constable or special deputy, commanding him to arrest said deserter and return him or her to said employer, and the like proceedings shall be had as provided in the preceding section; and it shall be lawful for any officer to whom such warrant shall be directed to execute said warrant in any county of this State, and that said warrant may be transmitted without indorsement to any like officer of another county, to be executed and returned as aforesaid, and the said employer shall pay the cost of said warrants and arrest and return, which shall be set off for so much against the wages of said deserter.

Sec. 9. . . . That if any person shall persuade or attempt to persuade, entice or cause any freedman, free negro or mulatto, to desert from the legal employment of any person, before the expiration of his or her term of service, or shall knowingly employ any such deserting freedman, free negro or mulatto, or shall knowingly give or sell to any such deserting freedman, free negro or mulatto, any food, raiment or other thing, he or she shall be guilty of a misdemeanor, and upon conviction shall be fined not less than twenty-five dollars and not more than two hundred dollars and the costs, and if said fine and costs shall not be immediately paid, the court shall sentence said convict to not exceeding two months' imprisonment in the county jail, and he or she shall moreover be liable to the party injured in damages: Provided, if any person shall, or shall attempt to persuade, entice, or cause any freedman, free negro or mulatto, to desert from any legal employment of any person with the view to employ said freedman, free negro or mulatto, without the limits of this State, such person, on conviction, shall be fined not less than fifty dollars and not more than five hundred dollars and costs, and if said fine and costs shall not be immediately paid, the court shall sentence said convict to not exceeding six months' imprisonment in the county jail.

This arbitrary and cruel act, wholly inconsistent with a state of personal freedom, by forbidding the lease to freedmen, free negroes and mulattoes of either lands or tenements outside of cities, not only made of the emancipated slaves a landless and homeless class, but deprived them of all hope of rising out of that condition. On the second Monday of

CULMINATION OF THE PRESIDENTIAL PLAN

January, 1866, less than two months after the passage of this act, and annually thereafter, they were required to have a lawful home or employment, and to possess written evidence thereof. This requirement extended to the doing of even irregular and job work, and a written contract for all labor for a longer period than one month. If the laborer, without good cause, left the service of his employer before the expiration of his term, he forfeited all wages for that year up to the time of quitting. As the freedmen were wholly without representation in the State judiciary, the master class could in every instance determine the sufficiency of the cause. The intermarriage of the races was made a felony, and the white or the black person convicted of that crime was to be confined in the State penitentiary for life.[1] Southern whites had no objection to the personal attendance, even in first-class railway coaches, of colored servants, but as other than a servant, the freedman was considered exceedingly obnoxious, and this sentiment was enacted immediately before either of the statutes mentioned, into a law which excluded negroes from riding in cars of the first class.[2]

There was some apprehension lest this and similar legislation would lead to bloody outbreaks. The colored race generally was growing distrustful and discontented. The fear of violence was probably not unconnected with the passage of a law approved November 29, which provided:

Sec. 1. . . . That no freedman, free negro or mulatto, not in the military service of the United States Government, and not licensed so to do by the board of police of his or her county, shall keep or carry fire-arms of any kind, or any ammunition, dirk, or bowie-knife, and on conviction thereof, in the county court, shall be punished by fine, not exceeding ten dollars, and pay the costs of such proceedings, and all such arms or ammunition shall be forfeited to the informer, and it shall be the duty of every civil and military officer to arrest any freedman, free

[1] Laws of Mississippi, 1865, pp. 82-86.
[2] Ibid., p. 231.

negro or mulatto, found with any such arms or ammunition, and cause him or her to be committed for trial in default of bail.

Sec. 2. . . . That any freedman, free negro or mulatto, committing riots, routs, affrays, trespasses, malicious mischief and cruel treatment to animals, seditious speeches, insulting gestures, language or acts, or assaults on any person, disturbance of peace, exercising the function of a minister of the Gospel without a license from some regularly organized church, vending spirituous or intoxicating liquors, or committing any other misdemeanor, the punishment of which is not specifically provided for by law, shall, upon conviction thereof, in the county court, be fined not less than ten dollars and not more than one hundred dollars, and may be imprisoned, at the discretion of the court, not exceeding thirty days.

Sec. 3. . . . That if any white person shall sell, lend or give to any freedman, free negro or mulatto, any fire-arms, dirk or bowie-knife, or ammunition, or any spirituous or intoxicating liquors, such person or persons so offending, upon conviction thereof, in the county court of his or her county, shall be fined, not exceeding fifty dollars, and may be imprisoned at the discretion of the court, not exceeding thirty days. . . .

Sec. 4. . . . That all the penal and criminal laws now in force in this State, defining offences, and prescribing the mode of punishment for crimes and misdemeanors committed by slaves, free negroes or mulattoes, be and the same are hereby re-enacted, and declared to be in full force and effect, against freedmen, free negroes and mulattoes, except so far as the mode and manner of trial and punishment have been changed or altered by law.

Sec. 5. . . . That if any freedman, free negro or mulatto, convicted of any of the misdemeanors provided against in this act, shall fail or refuse, for the space of five days after conviction, to pay the fine and costs imposed, such person shall be hired out by the sheriff or other officer, at public outcry, to any white person who will pay said fine and all costs, and take such convict for the shortest time.[1]

Though the General Government was solemnly pledged to guarantee the entire freedom of the negro, he was completely disarmed by these statutes, which were to be administered by men who had been but recently serving the Confederate cause. The purpose of the last measure is rendered clear by Section 4, which reënacted against freedmen all the penal and criminal laws that had applied to slaves. It revived, in short, the black code of *ante bellum* times.

[1] Laws of Mississippi, 1865, pp. 165-167.

Persons convicted of vagrancy, under an amendatory act, approved November 24, 1865, were subject to a fine not exceeding one hundred dollars and costs, besides a maximum imprisonment of ten days. The first section, which defined who were vagrants, was general in its application. The provisions especially affecting freedmen were the following:

Sec. 2. . . . That all freedmen, free negroes and mulattoes in this State, over the age of eighteen years, found on the second Monday in January, 1866, or thereafter, with no lawful employment or business, or found unlawfully assembling themselves together either in the day or night time, and all white persons so assembling with freedmen, free negroes or mulattoes, or usually associating with freedmen, free negroes or mulattoes on terms of equality, or living in adultery or fornication with a freedwoman, free negro or mulatto, shall be deemed vagrants, and on conviction thereof shall be fined in the sum of not exceeding, in the case of a freedman, free negro or mulatto, fifty dollars, and a white man two hundred dollars, and imprisoned at the discretion of the court, the free negro not exceeding ten days, and the white man not exceeding six months.

. . . .

Sec. 5. . . . That all fines and forfeitures collected under the provisions of this act shall be paid into the county treasury for general county purposes, and in case any freedman, free negro or mulatto, shall fail for five days after the imposition of any fine or forfeiture upon him or her for violation of any of the provisions of this act, to pay the same, that it shall be, and is hereby made the duty of the sheriff of the proper county to hire out said freedman, free negro or mulatto, to any persons who will, for the shortest period of service, pay said fine or forfeiture and all costs: Provided, a preference shall be given to the employer, if there be one, in which case the employer shall be entitled to deduct and retain the amount so paid from the wages of such freedman, free negro or mulatto, then due or to become due; and in case such freedman, free negro or mulatto cannot be hired out, he or she may be dealt with as a pauper.[1]

. . . .

No extended knowledge of human affairs is necessary to perceive that, by a rigorous enforcement of these laws, the great mass of freedmen could be easily restored to a state of practical servitude during the season when their labor was

[1] Laws of Mississippi, 1865, pp. 90-93.

desirable, and that for the remainder of the year their condition would be little better than that of the pauper. That the two races were regarded as equal before the law will scarcely be contended. An act approved December 1 made it a misdemeanor in certain cases for either a white or a black man to hunt hogs or other stock upon any lands other than his own; the white man was liable, on conviction, to a fine of from $100 to $500, or imprisonment from one to three months in the county jail, or both, at the discretion of the court. For the same offence no imprisonment was provided in the case of freedmen, and the fine was fixed between $10 and $20. The latter, however, could be hired at public outcry to the lowest bidder who would pay the fine and cost. The employer, it was provided, was to have the preference in hiring.[1]

The Legislature first to meet under the reformed government not only expressed for the people of Mississippi no profound regret for resisting the Federal authority, but left no doubt in what estimation it held those who fought for Southern independence by releasing ex-Confederate soldiers from indictments for misdemeanors committed before the war.[2] In perfect harmony with the spirit of this act of oblivion was one which changed the name of Jones County to that of Davis, and the name of Ellisville in the same county to Leesburg.[3] This, it should be observed, was only three days before the meeting of Congress.

This legislation, by no means the most severe enacted under the new governments, marks in Southern sentiment a reaction no less unexpected than the complete and almost instantaneous submission following the surrender of Johnston. The sudden change in opinion has been ingeniously and even

[1] Laws of Mississippi, 1865, pp. 199-200.
[2] Ibid., pp. 210-211.
[3] Ibid., p. 240.

CULMINATION OF THE PRESIDENTIAL PLAN 483

absurdly accounted for. In the latter class of explanations may be included the notion that the people of the South were exasperated by the interference of Congress, that body, as already mentioned, not having convened till after the passage of the obnoxious laws. On the other hand, it was not generally known, even in Mississippi, that the President in the work of reorganization had resolved to ignore the coördinate political branch of Government; he had, indeed, fairly signified to Governor Sharkey the position that he intended to assume, but his communication to that official, which was never designed for publication, was not immediately circulated through the State; the knowledge, therefore, that the Executive had concluded to oppose the policy of Congress could not have been a factor in disturbing the brief repose of the seceding States, and we must seek elsewhere for the cause.

In many of the insurgent commonwealths rebellion had involved almost every citizen in the guilt of treason, almost every estate in the liability to confiscation. The President and his advisers hoped by a generous distribution of pardons to win the esteem and confidence of this numerous and influential class, and to leave to " Radical " members of Congress the ungrateful office of punishment. This policy contributed to awaken the undaunted spirit of the South, and was, no doubt, an element in unsettling the conditions that prevailed after the surrender. Northern magnanimity, which was content to regard the defeat of secession as sufficient discipline for the rebellious States, and the attitude of the Democratic party were also important influences in misleading the South. More responsible for the reaction, however, than any of these was the unsatisfactory administration of the Freedmen's Bureau. The testimony of General Grant can be cited to prove that, while accomplishing much that was desirable, this institution was retarding somewhat the progress of reconstruction. In a hurried tour of the late Confederate States he had observed that it was not conducted with good judgment or economy, and remarked in his report to the President that "the belief widely spread among the freedmen of the Southern States, that the lands of their former owners will, at least in part, be divided among them, has come from the agents of this bureau. This belief is seriously interfering with the willingness of the freedmen to make contracts for the coming year. . . . Many, perhaps the majority, of the agents of the Freedmen's Bureau advise the freedmen that by their own industry they must expect to live. To this end they endeavor to secure employment for them, and to see that both contracting parties comply with their engagements. In some instances, I am sorry to say, the freedman's mind does not seem to be disabused of the idea that a freedman has the right to live without care or provision for the future. The effect of the belief in division of lands is idleness and accumulation in camps, towns, and cities." [1]

Though its management was open to criticism, the necessity for the existence of the bureau, to afford at least temporary protection to the newly enfranchised, was perceived and acknowledged by the General. It probably accorded well with the political aspirations of bureau agents to create in the minds of freedmen a belief that the Government would give to each of them " forty acres of land and a mule "; for this expectation would be a pledge of allegiance to the Federal representative, without the approval of whom no negro could seriously hope to secure so enviable a start in his career of freedom.

That confusion would follow the violent overthrow of a long-established industrial system was to be expected, and it was not unnatural for the South to ascribe to the influence of bureau agents much of the mischief inseparable from immediate emancipation. While the complaints of the late in-

[1] Ann. Cycl., 1866, p. 132.

CULMINATION OF THE PRESIDENTIAL PLAN 485

surgents were commonly considered with deference, it was scarcely to be expected that they would not sometimes be despised, and it would be easy to impute to their discontent every outrage reported to the officers of the bureau or the commanders of the posts. Though Federal representatives as a rule labored faithfully to restore and preserve order, it would be singular if some of them, assuming the arrogant manner of conquerors, did not occasionally depart from that system of conciliation which the generous nature of Mr. Lincoln had adopted.

These were among the causes of the Southern reaction. It is no justification of these severe and even cruel enactments to show, as Mr. Herbert has done, that similar laws disgraced the statute books of many Northern States. In the settlement then in progress the Southern people conceded nothing of importance that was not won in the war, and if they were as sincere in their desire for reunion as some writers contend, they should not have feared the paradox of improving by their example the ancient legislation of the free States, or have been alarmed at the innovation of reducing to practice the principles of the Declaration of Independence.

It is not to be denied that there was considerable ground for complaint because of the influence of many employees of the bureau in demoralizing the Southern system of labor, but the further punishment of a race that had been trodden down by oppressive generations does not commend itself as either a humane or an enlightened remedy; besides, the South was greatly indebted to the fidelity of the negro, who during the war possessed, without abusing, the opportunity as well as the capacity for mischief. On the other hand, there was some obligation to Northern men for their magnanimity, and under wiser counsels their wishes, and even their prejudices, would have been respected. In the victorious section public opinion, then in the formative stage, was watching anxiously the progress and the proceedings of the new governments. Except a few extremists, the voters of the loyal States did not dream at that time, as was persistently asserted at the South, of forcing negro suffrage on the rebellious States. They did, however, desire to see embodied in the new State constitutions such provisions as would establish before the law the equality of all classes.

While the policy of President Johnson did not altogether escape criticism at the South, so general and so prompt was the acquiescence in his plan, that when Congress convened nearly all the States recently in rebellion had remodeled their governments and elected members of Congress who were at the national capital waiting to be admitted to seats. Without separately considering the new establishments, they may be described concisely and with sufficient accuracy as governments differing but little from those extinguished by the fall of the Confederacy. The members of the former, it is true, had taken an oath of allegiance, and the influence of that act upon their conduct will presently be noticed. Though it certainly was not the original intention, and appears never to have become the fixed purpose of Mr. Johnson to entrust to enemies of the Government the work of restoring the insurgent States, the result of his endeavors was that reconstruction was left almost exclusively in the hands of those who had attempted to destroy the Union. It was precisely such a contingency that Mr. Lincoln had in mind when he declared in his message of December 8, 1863, that, "An attempt to guarantee and protect a revived State government, constructed in whole or in preponderating part from the very element against whose hostility and violence it is to be protected, is simply absurd." [1]

This deliberate statement, as well as the subsequent administrative acts of Mr. Lincoln, sufficiently disposes of the no-

[1] Ann. Cycl., 1863, pp. 780-781.

tion that he favored a rather loose system of reconstruction. Without attempting to distinguish between theories really identical, there was still a considerable difference in the reorganization effected under the two Executives. The conditions which confronted the President and Congress in December, 1865, could have arisen only from disregarding the principle laid down by Mr. Lincoln. From his solemn and reiterated declarations there can be little doubt that he would have rejected without hesitation any system of which the first fruits were little more than a nullification of his decree of emancipation.

Notwithstanding his tireless threats of severity, we can easily perceive in the reorganization directed by Mr. Johnson, a noticeable falling back from the Executive plan of December, 1863, as announced and enforced by his predecessor. Nor did this retrogression proceed from the greater humanity, but rather from the greater weakness of the new President. Even in the matter of fealty there was a difference; for while the conflict was still doubtful, the taking of an oath of allegiance to the General Government was a serious step for the Southern Unionist, because the record thereafter singled him out, if not for destruction, at least for annoyance, or for punishment by the friends of secession, and, perhaps, the oath then effected some such object as it was designed to accomplish. When war had ceased, however, there was no longer a choice of sides, and thenceforth universal swearing as an instrument of government became practically worthless. It was not regarded, at all events, as an efficient security for the future. Mr. Johnson probably continued to exact oaths of allegiance because they were formerly of value in distinguishing the friends from the enemies of the Government. Though professing the same general opinion on the subject of amnesty, the principles on which the two Presidents granted pardons were sufficiently distinct.

We have seen that President Johnson, who had once declared that "rebels" should take a back seat in the work of reconstruction, so far changed his opinion that he subsequently said the people must be trusted in the restoration of their governments; he likewise modified his early impressions as to the permanence of the establishments instituted under his predecessor, for it was his original opinion that those governments were merely provisional in their nature, and would require the confirmation or the approval of Congress. Ultimately, however, he came to regard himself as the judge of their sufficiency. The evidence of this is conclusive. In a telegram of July 14, 1865, to Governor Sharkey, Secretary Seward said:

"The government of the State [Mississippi] will be provisional only until the civil authorities shall be restored, with the approval of Congress. Meanwhile military authority cannot be withdrawn." [1]

If it be contended that Mr. Seward made this important declaration upon his personal responsibility the argument fails, because in a dispatch to Governor Marvin, of Florida, dated September 12, 1865, nearly two months later, the Secretary of State repeated the substance of the message in language even more explicit. On that occasion he said: "It must, however, be distinctly understood that the restoration to which your proclamation refers will be subject to the decision of Congress." [2]

The determination of President Johnson to retain the members of Mr. Lincoln's Cabinet would indicate his original intention of applying to the subjugated States the system adopted by his predecessor. The influence which led to the modification of the method of enforcing without abandoning the principles underlying that plan it is not easy to discover.

[1] Gorham's Life of Stanton, Vol. II. p. 255.
[2] McPherson's Pol. Hand-Book, 1868, p. 25.

His change of attitude toward the South has been variously explained. By Mr. Blaine it has been ascribed to the flattery of Southern leaders, as well as to the personal influence of Secretary Seward, whose wide culture, and consequent humanity, would favor a policy of conciliation. Without intending to underestimate the insinuating address of the New York statesman it may be observed that his powers of persuasion appear to have exerted themselves with most success in the direction of the President's inclination. The attention of Southern leaders, a class of men by whom the President had hitherto been ignored, deserves, however, to be noticed in any enumeration of even the probable cause of the change. Another theory has it that Mr. Johnson both feared and hated several of the leading Republicans, because of their connection with a movement to procure his resignation from the Vice-Presidency, a station which, they believed, he had disgraced by appearing in an intoxicated state to take the oath of office. His desire to punish those who had constituted themselves custodians of the national dignity, it is asserted, was a principal motive in his surrender to the South. A more reasonable explanation of the change which occurred in the President's attitude toward his own section is that offered by Dr. Chadsey, who regards Mr. Johnson as an inconsistent advocate of State Sovereignty.[1] In this principle he believed as firmly as Jefferson Davis himself, though unlike the Confederate chieftain he refused, by stopping short of secession, to accept its logical results. Nearly all his administrative acts are those which might have been expected from a Democrat of the strict construction school, and Andrew Johnson never professed allegiance to any other political party.

The governments of which the reorganization has been described in the preceding pages continued in operation until suspended by the Reconstruction Act of March 2, 1867.

[1] President Johnson and Reconstruction, pp. 33-34.

Except Texas all these establishments, as previously observed, had sent members to the Thirty-ninth Congress. Their claims to seats, it is well known, were completely ignored, and a select body, consisting of nine members from the lower and six from the upper House, was appointed to investigate the condition of the late Confederate States, and to report whether any of them were entitled to representation in either branch of Congress. With the conclusions of the celebrated Joint Committee this essay is not concerned further than to observe that on the recommendation of the majority the Tennessee delegation was admitted on the 24th of July, 1866. Long before that event, however, the task of restoring the Union had been taken altogether out of Executive hands.

If we reflect how much swifter in a political organism is the progress of ruin than that of repair, and consider that four years had been abandoned to the destruction and disorders of civil war, we cannot but be surprised at the attempt of the President, single-handed, to adapt and execute in less than three months a series of measures designed to restore tranquillity and revive prosperity among the impoverished inhabitants of a wasted country. In this view his failure in the work of reconstruction can excite little astonishment. One reason for this precipitate action was a desire to reunite the sections before the meeting of Congress, and it was so far a praiseworthy if not a prudent course to adopt. But had he proceeded ever so leisurely there would still have existed undoubted obstacles to success. To say that he was lacking in the tact of his predecessor, that he was naturally of an obstinate and even of a combative disposition, and that he possessed defects, both of temper and judgment, would be merely to repeat a few trite observations.[1] Conditions were rapidly changing, but with Mr. Johnson, conditions

[1] In this connection his repudiation of the Sherman-Johnston agreement will occur to the reader.

CULMINATION OF THE PRESIDENTIAL PLAN 491

passed for almost nothing, though in reality circumstances make legislative acts beneficial or otherwise. Like the measures of the Thirty-eighth Congress for restoring the Union, those of Mr. Johnson may be carefully examined without discovering any considerable traces of originality. Indeed, if we except President Lincoln, this entire period seems to have been somewhat lacking in constructive statesmanship, though no branch of the public service was without officials of integrity, judgment and ability.

In the course of the preceding pages the inaugurals, the messages, the letters and other communications of Mr. Lincoln have been freely quoted to show his opinions on all of the principal and most of the subordinate phases of reconstruction. To complete the design of this inquiry, there remains to be considered but a single topic related to the main theme, namely, the limitations of the Presidential plan for restoring the Union. Many of these defects having been incidentally noticed, a general recapitulation does not appear to be required, and the subject, it is believed, may be appropriately concluded by an examination of those features of the Executive system which the narrative has not hitherto sufficiently emphasized.

This summary disclaims, however, any intention of attempting the absurdity of testing the statesmanship of Abraham Lincoln by contrasting a method of reconstruction proposed in 1863 with that deemed adequate by Congress to meet the changed conditions of 1867. We may, indeed, fairly and even profitably compare the sentiments of the two political departments in the summer of 1864, when, for the first time during the war, they were arrayed in opposition on a fundamental policy of civil administration. Because of its variance with received notions of representative government, the so-called "ten *per cent.* principle" will be first considered.

The proportion of the political people that Mr. Lincoln

offered to recognize as constituting a State encountered, probably, more opposition than any single feature of his plan. While its merits and its defects were equally evident, the latter, as might be expected, were given by its adversaries the place of prominence in all their criticisms. Exception was taken as well to the legality as to the expediency of the principle. The former has been fully discussed, and on that subject all that need be observed is that President Lincoln believed it constitutional to preserve the Union, and every measure conducive to that end he regarded as lawful.

On the question of expediency, however, several considerations suggest themselves. Apart from its repugnance to the American idea of majority rule, its palpable weakness was that governments founded on the consent of a minimum proportion of the electors would require the support of Federal power. Here occurs the question, did the forces thus engaged so greatly impair the efficiency of the main armies as sensibly to retard the work of destroying the enemy? It cannot be denied that there were occasions when a few additional regiments could have been employed to advantage; but neither the reverses nor the disasters of the Union armies were caused by lack of numbers so much as by the need early in the war of commanders of military genius. On the other hand, the troops who sustained the new governments, besides weakening the Confederacy, were affording protection to organizations that otherwise could not have been recruited. There is record of not less than sixty-five regiments furnished by the States restored during the Presidency of Mr. Lincoln.[1]

But even more important than this gratifying result was the influence which the reinstatement of four seceding commonwealths exerted on the attitude of those European powers

[1] Strait's Roster of Regimental Surgeons and Assistant Surgeons, p. 314. This estimate includes all the troops furnished by the new State of West Virginia.

which had proved early in the conflict their hostility to the United States. The "Johnson governments," so-called, were never required to furnish any such unquestioned evidence of reviving loyalty, and that fact should not be overlooked in any comparison of the results accomplished by the two Executives.

Notwithstanding the general existence of a strong opposition to minority rule, the revolutionary proceedings in western Virginia were sanctioned by every department of Government. Members from the loyal eastern counties were at first admitted to seats in both branches of Congress; their successors, however, were in turn refused this indulgence until there was presented the novel spectacle of a single Senator representing the diminished glory of the Old Dominion. Louisiana, too, which for a few days was heard in the lower House, was subsequently excluded altogether by the changing views of Congress. The revived bill of Wade and Davis provided in one of its many forms for recognizing that State as well as Arkansas, and even when the extremists obtained control of Congress the loyal government organized in Tennessee was approved by avowed opponents of the Executive plan. Mr. Lincoln, indeed, clearly perceived the inherent weakness of his system, and no one could have been more anxious than he to secure a wider constituency. These facts seem to indicate that between him and Congress there was not then so wide a gulf as, for partisan purposes, is sometimes represented. It is true that there was a difference of principle between the two departments; that there was a powerful party in Congress who believed that reconstruction was essentially a work of peace and, therefore, pertained exclusively to the national Legislature. The holders of this view were, doubtless, confirmed in their opinion by a conviction that the Executive was encroaching on a coördinate branch of government.

The Presidential system as well as the contemporary theory of Congress restricted the suffrage of whites, by whom it was almost universally engrossed at the foundation of the Republic. On the ground of justice and to encourage the cultivation of civic virtues among the negroes, Mr. Lincoln would admit those qualified to exercise this important privilege. His successor acknowledged in a private communication that for party purposes he favored some extension of the elective franchise to freedmen. Though Congress advanced rapidly toward negro suffrage, the first essay of that body in the work of reconstruction included no provision for conferring on the colored race a right to participate in government. By Wade and Davis it was not then deemed necessary even as a defensive power. Only a few bold innovators, considered almost fanatic on the question, were in favor of bestowing the right to vote on the multitudes maintained by the Freedmen's Bureau; it was not then deemed within the commission of the general Government, the teachings of political science were still respected by the majority in Congress, and the fruits of victory, it was hoped, could be secured without a resort to radical measures.

The form of an oath to support the proclamations and laws respecting slavery appeared in the Presidential plan as a condition indispensable to reinstatement. On this subject the difference between the Executive and Congress was merely one of degree; for the Wade-Davis bill, doubtless in imitation of the Presidential system, imposed terms precedent, and the new constitutions were to repudiate the rebel debt, abolish slavery and prohibit the higher insurgent officials, civil as well as military, from holding the office of governor, from serving in the State legislatures and even from voting.

By its adversaries the plan of Mr. Lincoln was condemned for its failure to exact any security for the future beyond the oath of allegiance, the telegraphic supervision by the Pres-

CULMINATION OF THE PRESIDENTIAL PLAN

ident and the power of Congress over the admission of members. This defect the legislative theory endeavored to supply, but even the guardianship proposed by Wade and Davis could give no assurance that the rebellious communities would not, after reinstatement, eliminate by constitutional amendment the conditions imposed on their readmission.[1]

[1] The author believes himself fortunate in being able to place before his readers a letter from the pen of Hon. J. B. Henderson, the only surviving Senator who participated in the debates summarized in chapter X., and, so far as the writer is informed, the only living member who served in the United States Senate during that eventful period. Coming, as it does, from one who supported many of Mr. Lincoln's most cherished measures, the letter will be welcomed as a valuable historical document. It contrasts forcibly the Presidential plan with the theory of Senator Sumner, and though written on August 21, 1901, more than a generation after the occurrence of the principal events discussed in this book, it is characterized by the clearness and the energy of expression which marked even the unpremeditated addresses of the Senator's Congressional career. On the subject of reunion he writes as follows:

"Time, in my judgment, has stamped its approval on Mr. Lincoln's views touching the questions of reconstruction during the Civil War. He was always calm and judicial. He was philosophical in periods of the most intense excitement. He never lost his head, but under all circumstances preserved his temper and his judgment. He was not the buffoon described by his enemies. On the contrary, he was a wise statesman, a learned lawyer, and a conscientious patriot; and, better than all, an honest man.

"The infirmity in Mr. Sumner's theories of reconstruction came from the great exuberance of his learning. He ransacked history, ancient and modern, for precedents growing out of civil wars. But these precedents all antedated the American Constitution. They grew out of monarchical systems of government, and had no relation to the republican forms created by our Constitution. Under our system there can be no suicide of a State. Individual citizens by rebellion and disloyalty may forfeit their political rights, but the State as an entity commits no treason and forfeits no rights to existence. Under our Constitution the State cannot die. It is the duty of the Federal Government to see that it does not die—that it shall never cease to exist. If the State be invaded from without, the duty of the General Government is to protect and defend it. If domestic violence threatens the subversion of the local government, the nation's duty is to intervene and uphold the hands of

However crude we may now consider Mr. Lincoln's system it should not be forgotten that with him the paramount consideration was the overthrow of the Confederacy. With that purpose all his measures harmonized, and it is scarcely critical to examine them from any other point of view. How far necessity, which had originally suggested, would subsequently have modified his plan it is now impossible to state. Without detracting a particle from his well-won fame it may be admitted that his method, which could not have foreseen the rapid succession of changes following his death, was but indifferently adapted to solve the problem with which Congress those who maintain the laws. The trustee of an express trust cannot excuse himself to a minority of the beneficiaries because the majority repudiate his agency.

"'The United States shall guarantee to every State in this Union a republican form of government.' No State government is republican in form that does not acknowledge the supremacy of the Federal Constitution. This is the essential test of republicanism. No State can enter the Union without conforming its Constitution to this supreme organic law. And whenever by force or violence, a majority of its citizens undertake to withdraw the State from its obedience to Federal law and to repudiate the sovereignty of the Federal Government, it at once becomes the duty of Congress to act.

"This duty of Congress is not to destroy the State or to declare it a suicide, and proceed to administer on its effects. On the contrary, the duty clearly is to preserve the State, to restore it to its old republican forms. Its duty is not to territorialize the State and proceed to govern it as a conquered colony. The duty is not one of demolition, but one of restoration. It is not to make a Constitution, but to guarantee that the old Constitution or one equally republican in form, and made by the loyal citizens of the State, shall be upheld and sustained.

"If a majority of the people of a State conspire to subvert its republican forms, that majority may be, and should be, put down by the Federal power, while the minority, however few, sustaining republican forms may be constitutionally installed as the political power of the State.

"These, as I understand, were the views of Mr. Lincoln; and they were not the views of Mr. Sumner, as enunciated in his resolutions of 1862 and advocated by him in his subsequent career in the Senate.

"A departure from these views gave us the carpet-bag governments of the Southern States, and brought upon us divers other evils in our ideas and theories of government, whose effects are yet visible."

was compelled to deal in 1867; but the measure of permanent success which attended the deliberate legislation of that body by no means justifies the conclusion that some other system would have proved a total failure. With all its immaturity the plan of the President was not without its advantages. It aimed to restore with as little innovation as possible the Union of the Fathers; with some exceptions the natural leaders of Southern society were to participate in the work of reorganization, and the author of this simple plan approached his difficult task in a generous and enlightened spirit.

On the life and character of Abraham Lincoln an admiring generation has exhausted the language of panegyric; the terms of censure have been reserved almost exclusively for his method of restoring the Union; but neither the critic's ken, nor the ambitious phrase of eulogy, nor all the thoughts that since his death have dropped from poets' pens affords that clear insight into his nature which is unconsciously revealed in the simple and beautiful exhortation that concludes his last inaugural. The sentiments which immortalize that celebrated state paper could have proceeded only from the depths of a noble soul—a soul that would have imposed silence on the voice of vengeance and would never have consented to the revenge of section upon section. In this book an endeavor has been made fully to discuss his plan of reconstruction; the spirit in which he approached that difficult task is best stated in his own generous and patriotic words, with which may be fittingly closed this long though interesting inquiry: " With malice toward none; with charity for all; with firmness in the right, as God gives us to see the right, let us strive on to finish the work we are in; to bind up the nation's wounds; to care for him who shall have borne the battle, and for his widow, and his orphan—to do all which may achieve and cherish a just and lasting peace among ourselves, and with all nations." [1]

[1] N. & H., Vol. X., p. 145.

THE END.

APPENDIX A

THIRTY-SEVENTH CONGRESS

SENATE

First session, July 4, 1861, to August 6, 1861. Republicans (31) in Roman, Democrats (10) in *Italics*, Unionists (7) in SMALL CAPITALS, vacancies 2.

Second session, Dec. 1, 1862, to Mar. 4, 1864.

CALIFORNIA.—*Milton S. Latham* and *James A. McDougall* (vice E. D. Baker, who died).
CONNECTICUT.—James Dixon and Lafayette S. Foster.
DELAWARE.—*James A. Bayard* and *Willard Saulsbury*.
ILLINOIS.—Lyman Trumbull and Orville H. Browning.
INDIANA.—Henry S. Lane and *Jesse D. Bright* (expelled Feb. 5, 1862, and was succeeded by *David Turpie*).
IOWA.—James W. Grimes and James Harlan.
KANSAS.—James H. Lane and Samuel C. Pomeroy.
KENTUCKY.—*Lazarus W. Powell* and GARRETT DAVIS (vice *John C. Breckenridge*, expelled).
MAINE.—Lot M. Morrill and William Pitt Fessenden.
MASSACHUSETTS.—Charles Sumner and Henry Wilson.
MARYLAND.—ANTHONY KENNEDY and *James A. Pearce* (died Dec. 20, 1862, and was succeeded by THOMAS H. HICKS).
MICHIGAN.—Zachariah Chandler and Jacob M. Howard.
MINNESOTA.—*Henry M. Rice* and Morton S. Wilkinson.
MISSOURI.—JOHN B. HENDERSON (vice Trusten Polk, expelled) and ROBERT WILSON (vice Waldo Porter Johnson, expelled).
NEW HAMPSHIRE.—John P. Hale and Daniel Clark.
NEW YORK.—Preston King and Ira Harris.
NEW JERSEY.—John C. Ten Eyck and *John R. Thomson* (died Sept. 12, 1862, Richard S. Field was temporarily appointed to fill the vacancy, and James W. Wall was subsequently elected for the unexpired term).
OHIO.—Benjamin F. Wade and John Sherman (vice Salmon P. Chase, who resigned Mar. 6, 1861).
OREGON.—Edward D. Baker (died Oct. 21, 1861, and was succeeded by BENJAMIN F. HARDING) and *James W. Nesmith*.
PENNSYLVANIA.—Edgar Cowan and David Wilmot (vice Simon Cameron, who resigned in March, 1861).
RHODE ISLAND.—Henry B. Anthony and James F. Simmons (resigned. SAMUEL G. ARNOLD elected to fill the unexpired term).

VERMONT.—Solomon Foot and Jacob Collamer.
VIRGINIA.—WAITMAN T. WILLEY and JOHN S. CARLILE.
WISCONSIN.—James R. Doolittle and Timothy O. Howe.

HOUSE OF REPRESENTATIVES

CALIFORNIA.—Aaron A. Sargent, Timothy G. Phelps, Frederick F. Low.
CONNECTICUT.—Dwight Loomis, *James E. English*, Alfred A. Burnham, *George C. Woodruff*.
DELAWARE.—GEORGE P. FISHER.
ILLINOIS.—Elihu B. Washburne, Isaac N. Arnold, Owen Lovejoy, William Kellogg, *William A. Richardson, James C. Robinson, Philip B. Fouke, John A. Logan*.
INDIANA.—*John Law, James A. Cravens*, William McKee Dunn, *William S. Holman*, George W. Julian, Albert G. Porter, *Daniel W. Voorhees*, Albert S. White, Schuyler Colfax, William Mitchell, John P. C. Shanks.
IOWA.—James F. Wilson, William Vandever.
KANSAS.—Martin F. Conway.
KENTUCKY.—JAMES S. JACKSON (died in 1862 and was succeeded by GEORGE H. YEAMAN), HENRY GRIDER, AARON HARDING, CHARLES A. WICKLIFFE, GEORGE W. DUNLAP, ROBERT MALLORY, JOHN J. CRITTENDEN, WILLIAM H. WADSWORTH, JOHN W. MENZIES, SAMUEL L. CASEY (*vice* Mr. Burnett, expelled).
MAINE.—John N. Goodwin, Charles W. Walton (resigned. Thos. A. D. Fessenden elected to fill vacancy), Samuel C. Fessenden, Anson P. Morrill, John H. Rice, Frederick A. Pike.
MARYLAND.—JOHN W. CRISFIELD, EDWIN H. WEBSTER, CORNELIUS L. L. LEARY, *Henry May*, FRANCIS THOMAS, CHARLES B. CALVERT.
MASSACHUSETTS.—Thomas D. Eliot, James Buffinton, Benjamin F. Thomas (sometimes classed as a Unionist), Alexander H. Rice, Samuel Hooper, John B. Alley, Daniel W. Gooch, Charles R. Train, Goldsmith F. Bailey (died May 8, 1862, and was succeeded by Amasa Walker), Charles Delano, Henry L. Dawes.
MICHIGAN.—Bradley F. Granger, Fernando C. Beaman, Francis W. Kellogg, Rowland E. Trowbridge.
MINNESOTA.—Cyrus Aldrich and William Windom.
MISSOURI.—Francis P. Blair, jr. (resigned in 1862), JAMES S. ROLLINS, WILLIAM A. HALL, *Elijah H. Norton*, THOMAS L. PRICE, *John S. Phelps, John W. Noell*.
NEW HAMPSHIRE.—Gilman Marston, Edward H. Rollins, Thomas M. Edwards.
NEW JERSEY.—John T. Nixon, John L. N. Stratton, *William G. Steele, George T. Cobb, Nehemiah Perry*.
NEW YORK.—*Edward H. Smith, Moses F. Odell, Benjamin Wood, James E. Kerrigan*, William Wall, Frederick A. Conkling, *Elijah*

APPENDIX A

Ward, Isaac C. Delaplaine, Edward Haight, Charles H. Van Wyck, *John B. Steele*, Stephen Baker, Abraham B. Olin, *Erastus Corning*, James B. McKean, William A. Wheeler, Socrates N. Sherman, *Chauncey Vibbard*, Richard Franchot, Roscoe Conkling, R. Holland Duell, William E. Lansing, Ambrose W. Clark, Charles B. Sedgwick, Theodore M. Pomeroy, Jacob P. Chamberlain, Alexander S. Diven, Robert B. Van Valkenburg, Alfred Ely, Augustus Frank, Burt Van Horn, Elbridge G. Spaulding, Reuben E. Fenton.

OHIO.—*George H. Pendleton*, John A. Gurley, *Clement L. Vallandigham, William Allen*, James M. Ashley, *Chilton A. White*, RICHARD A. HARRISON, Samuel Shellabarger, *Warren P. Noble*, Carey A. Trimble, Valentine B. Horton, *Samuel S. Cox*, Samuel T. Worcester, Harrison G. Blake, *Robert H. Nugen*, William P. Cutler, *James R. Morris*, Sidney Edgerton, Albert G. Riddle, John Hutchins, John A. Bingham.

OREGON.—George K. Shiel.

PENNSYLVANIA.—*William E. Lehman, Charles J. Biddle*, John P. Verree, William D. Kelley, William Morris Davis, John Hickman, *Thomas B. Cooper* (died April 4, 1862, and was succeeded by John D. Stiles), *Sydenham E. Ancona*, Thaddeus Stevens, John W. Killinger, James H. Campbell, HENDRICK B. WRIGHT, *Philip Johnson*, Galusha A. Grow, James T. Hale, *Joseph Baily*, Edward McPherson, Samuel S. Blair, John Covode, *Jesse Lazear*, James K. Moorhead, Robert McKnight, John W. Wallace, John Patton, Elijah Babbitt.

RHODE ISLAND.—GEORGE H. BROWNE, WILLIAM P. SHEFFIELD.

TENNESSEE.—HORACE MAYNARD.

VERMONT.—Ezekiel P. Walton, Justin S. Morrill, Portus Baxter.

VIRGINIA.—CHARLES H. UPTON, EDMUND PENDLETON, WILLIAM G. BROWN, JACOB B. BLAIR, KILLIAN V. WHALEY, JOSEPH E. SEGAR.

WISCONSIN.—John F. Potter, Luther Hanchett (died Nov. 24, 1862, and was succeeded by Walter McIndoe), A. Scott Sloan.

DELEGATES FROM TERRITORIES

COLORADO.—Hiram P. Bennett.
DAKOTA.—John B. S. Todd.
NEBRASKA.—Samuel G. Daily.
NEVADA.—*John C. Cradlebaugh.*
NEW MEXICO.—John S. Watts.
UTAH.—*John M. Bernhisel.*
WASHINGTON.—James H. Wallace.

APPENDIX B

THIRTY-EIGHTH CONGRESS

SENATE

First regular session, Dec. 7, 1863, to July 4, 1864.
Second session from Dec. 5, 1864, to March 3, 1865.

CALIFORNIA.—John Conness and *James A. McDougall.*
CONNECTICUT.—James Dixon and Lafayette S. Foster.
DELAWARE.—*Willard Saulsbury* and *George Read Riddle (vice* Senator *Bayard,* who resigned).
ILLINOIS.—*William A. Richardson* and Lyman Trumbull.
INDIANA.—*Thomas A. Hendricks* and Henry S. Lane.
IOWA.—James Harlan and James W. Grimes.
KANSAS.—Samuel C. Pomeroy and James H. Lane.
KENTUCKY.—GARRETT DAVIS (Senator DAVIS is sometimes mentioned as a Democrat) and *Lazarus W. Powell.*
MAINE.—Lot M. Morrill and William Pitt Fessenden (resigned in 1864, and was succeeded by Nathan A. Farwell).
MASSACHUSETTS.—Charles Sumner and Henry Wilson.
MARYLAND.—REVERDY JOHNSON and THOMAS H. HICKS (died Feb. 13, 1865).
MICHIGAN.—Zachariah Chandler and Jacob M. Howard.
MINNESOTA.—Alexander Ramsey and Morton S. Wilkinson.
MISSOURI.—John B. Henderson (sometimes mentioned as a Unionist) and B. Gratz Brown (*vice* Waldo Porter Johnson, expelled, Robert Wilson having been appointed *pro tem.*).
NEW HAMPSHIRE.—Daniel Clark and John P. Hale.
NEW JERSEY.—*William Wright* and John C. Ten Eyck.
NEW YORK.—Edwin D. Morgan and Ira Harris.
OHIO.—Benjamin F. Wade and John Sherman.
OREGON.—Benjamin F. Harding and *James W. Nesmith.*
PENNSYLVANIA.—*Charles R. Buckalew* and Edgar Cowan.
RHODE ISLAND.—William Sprague and Henry B. Anthony.
VERMONT.—Solomon Foot and Jacob Collamer.
VIRGINIA.—LEMUEL J. BOWDEN and JOHN S. CARLILE (sometimes mentioned as a Democrat).
WEST VIRGINIA.—Waitman T. Willey and Peter G. Van Winkle.
WISCONSIN.—James R. Doolittle and Timothy O. Howe.
NEVADA.—James W. Nye and William M. Stewart.

HOUSE OF REPRESENTATIVES

CALIFORNIA.—Thomas B. Shannon, William Higby, Cornelius Cole.
CONNECTICUT.—Henry C. Deming, *James E. English*, Augustus Brandegee, John H. Hubbard.
DELAWARE.—Nathaniel B. Smithers.
ILLINOIS.—Isaac N. Arnold, John F. Farnsworth, Elihu B. Washburne, *Charles M. Harris*, Owen Lovejoy (died Mar. 25, 1864, and was succeeded by Ebon C. Ingersoll), Jesse O. Norton, *John R. Eden*, *John T. Stuart*, *Lewis W. Ross*, *Anthony L. Knapp*, *James C. Robinson*, *William R. Morrison*, *William J. Allen*, *James C. Allen*.
INDIANA.—*John Law*, *James A. Cravens*, *Henry W. Harrington*, *William S. Holman*, George W. Julian, Ebenezer Dumont, *Daniel W. Voorhees*, Godlove S. Orth, Schuyler Colfax, *Joseph K. Edgerton*, *James F. McDowell*.
IOWA.—James F. Wilson, Hiram Price, William B. Allison, J. B. Grinnell, John A. Kasson, A. W. Hubbard.
KANSAS.—A. Carter Wilder.
KENTUCKY.—Lucien Anderson, GEORGE H. YEAMAN, HENRY GRIDER, AARON HARDING, ROBERT MALLORY, Green Clay Smith, Brutus J. Clay, William H. Randall, WILLIAM H. WADSWORTH.
MAINE.—*Lorenzo D. M. Sweat*, Sidney Perham, James G. Blaine, John H. Rice, Frederick A. Pike.
MARYLAND.—John A. J. Cresswell, Edwin H. Webster, Henry Winter Davis, Francis Thomas, *Benjamin G. Harris*.
MASSACHUSETTS.—Thomas D. Eliot, Oakes Ames, Alexander H. Rice, Samuel Hooper, John B. Alley, Daniel W. Gooch, George S. Boutwell, John D. Baldwin, William B. Washburn, Henry L. Dawes.
MICHIGAN.—Fernando C. Beaman, Charles Upson, John W. Longyear, Francis W. Kellogg, *Augustus C. Baldwin*, John F. Driggs.
MINNESOTA.—William Windom, Ignatius Donnelly.
MISSOURI.—FRANCIS P. BLAIR, jr. (seat successfully contested by Samuel Knox of St. Louis), Henry T. Blow, *John G. Scott*, Joseph W. McClurg, Sempronius H. Boyd, *Austin A. King*, Benjamin F. Loan, *William A. Hall*, *James S. Rollins*.
NEW HAMPSHIRE.—*Daniel Marcy*, Edward H. Rollins, James W. Patterson.
NEW JERSEY.—John F. Starr, *George Middleton*, *William G. Steele*, *Andrew J. Rogers*, *Nehemiah Perry*.
NEW YORK.—*Henry G. Stebbins* (resigned in 1864 and was succeeded by *Dwight Townsend*), *Martin Kalbfleisch*, Moses F. Odell, *Benjamin Wood*, *Fernando Wood*, *Elijah Ward*, *John W. Chanler*, *James Brooks*, Anson Herrick, *William Radford*, *Charles H. Winfield*, *Homer A. Nelson*, *John B. Steele*, *John V. L. Pruyn*, *John A. Griswold*, Orlando Kellogg, Calvin T. Hulburd, James M. Marvin, Samuel F. Miller, Ambrose W. Clark, *Francis Kernan*, DeWitt C. Littlejohn, Thomas T. Davis, Theodore M. Pomeroy, Daniel Morris, Giles W. Hotchkiss, Robert Van Valkenburg, Freeman Clark,

Augustus Frank, *John B. Ganson*, Reuben E. Fenton (resigned Dec. 10, 1864).

OHIO.—*George H. Pendleton, Alexander Long*, Robert C. Schenck, *J. F. McKinney, Frank C. Le Blond, Chilton A. White, Samuel S. Cox, William Johnson, Warren P. Noble*, James M. Ashley, *Wells A. Hutchins, William E. Fink, John O'Neill, George Bliss, James R. Morris, Joseph W. White*, Ephraim R. Eckley, Rufus P. Spaulding, James A. Garfield.

OREGON.—John R. McBride.

PENNSYLVANIA.—*Samuel J. Randall*, Charles O'Neill, Leonard Myers, William D. Kelley, M. Russell Thayer, *John D. Stiles*, John M. Broomall, *Sydenham E. Ancona*, Thaddeus Stevens, *Myer Strouse, Philip Johnson, Charles Dennison*, Henry W. Tracy, *William H. Miller, Joseph Bailey, Alexander H. Coffroth, Archibald McAllister*, James T. Hale, Glenni W. Scofield, Amos Myers, *John L. Dawson*, James K. Moorhead, Thomas Williams, *Jesse Lazear*.

RHODE ISLAND.—Thomas A. Jenckes, Nathan F. Dixon.

VERMONT.—Frederick E. Woodbridge, Justin S. Morrill, Portus Baxter.

VIRGINIA.—Had Senators but no Representatives. JOSEPH SEGAR, LUCIUS H. CHANDLER and BENJAMIN M. KITCHEN, claimants for seats, were not admitted.

WEST VIRGINIA.—Jacob B. Blair, William G. Brown, Killian V. Whaley.*

WISCONSIN.—*James S. Brown*, Ithamar C. Sloan, Amasa Cobb, *Charles A. Eldridge, Ezra Wheeler*, Walter D. McIndoe.

DELEGATES FROM TERRITORIES

ARIZONA.—Charles D. Poston.

COLORADO.—Hiram P. Bennett.

DAKOTA.—William Jayne (seat successfully contested by John B. S. Todd).

IDAHO.—William H. Wallace.

MONTANA.—Samuel McLean.

NEBRASKA.—Samuel G. Daily.

NEVADA (admitted as a State).—Gordon N. Mott (Henry G. Worthington was elected Representative when Nevada became a State).

NEW MEXICO.—Francisco Perea.

UTAH.—*John F. Kenney*.

WASHINGTON.—*George E. Cole*.

* The West Virginia Representatives took their seats Dec. 7, 1863.

INDEX

INDEX

A

ABOLITION societies, Southern, ended by new industrial era, 5
Adams, Charles Francis, 50
Alabama, in Federal control, 50; Arkansas Legislature addressed by commissioner from, 77; insurrection in, 314; injury sustained by, 437
Alabama, The, 50, 288
Albemarle, The, destruction of, 288
Alexandria, capital of loyal Virginia, 129; convention meets at, 130; blockade of, rescinded, 133; Legislature assembles at, 137; ceases to be capital, 446; recognition of government of, marks no distinct Executive policy, 448
Alleghany Mountains, Virginia divided by, 96
Allegiance, oath of, 24; Governor Johnson's modification of, 27; registration of, 28; required of Louisiana voters, 45; value of, 487
Allen, Henry Watkins, end of administration of, 418; mentioned for governor of Louisiana, 422
Amendment, Thirteenth, Hampton Roads conference refers to, 399; adoption of, by Georgia Legislature, 466
Amnesty and Reconstruction, Lincoln's proclamation of, 23, 24, 25, 224; authority for, 24; classes excepted from benefits of, 25; explanation of, 28; applied in Louisiana, 61; Howard's reference to, 365; Johnson's proclamation of, 450; Seward's approval of, 451; all insurgent States affected by, 452. See Reconstruction
Anthony, Lieutenant-Colonel, arrest of, 169
Antietam, Md., Lee defeated at, 186
Arkansas, effect of Union victories in, 10; enrolling agent sent to, 27; loyal part of, 77; Alabama commissioner addresses Legislature of, 77; position of, 77; interests of, 77; opposition to separate State action in, 77; convention bill passed by, 77; conditional secession defeated in, 78; influence of President's inaugural in, 78; secession of, 78; secession favored by Governor of, 78; military preparations in, 78; confiscation ordinance of, 78; Confederate Congress admit delegates from, 79; convention conflicts with government of, 79; military division of, 79; dissatisfaction among soldiers of, 80; troops of, in Confederate army, 80; indifference of Germans and Irish, 80; bonds of, 81; Union sentiment in, 81; menaced by Federal troops, 81; flight of Governor, 82; troops sent to Corinth from, 82; John S. Phelps, military governor of, 82; regiments furnished Union army by, 83; return of leading secessionists, 83; Federal reverses in, 84; reconstruction of, 85; amended constitution of, 88; Confederate debt repudiated by, 88; division among Union men of, 88; Lincoln's letter on reconstruction in, 89; Gen. Steele's address to people of, 90; election in, 90; adoption of amended con-

stitution for, 90; Congressman elected in, 91; Congress excludes Representatives from, 91; no Presidential election in, 92, 195; legality of government of, maintained by Lincoln, 195; loyal government in, 286; insurrection in, 314; Reverdy Johnson favors recognition of, 378; Thirteenth Amendment ratified by, 409; slavery abolished by constitution of, 410; disfranchising act of, 410; loyal government acquiesced in, 410; pacification of, 411; destitution in parts of, 412
Arnell, Daniel W., election of, 415
Arnold, Isaac N., resolution introduced by, 170
Army of the United States, Provost Court of, 40; discontinuance of enlistments for, 408; mustering out of volunteers in the, 409
Ascension, parish of, vote in, 74
Ashley, James M., reconstruction bill reported by, 289; proposal to confer suffrage on negro soldiers and sailors, 294; no provision for education of negroes in bill of, 298; effects of reconstruction bill of, 302; substitute introduced by, 304; remarks on reconstruction by, 304; motives for compromise offered by, 306; reconstruction bill of, tabled, 311; revived bill of, 312; explanation of inconsistency of, 312; reconstruction bill of, tabled, 313; remarks on reconstruction by, 313
Atlantic Monthly, The, Sumner's article in, 200

B

BAKER, JOSHUA, member-elect from Louisiana, 56
Baldwin, Augustus C., reconstruction bill opposed by, 241
Baltimore convention, Lincoln renominated by, 32; Lincoln did not openly influence, 34; adjournment of, 277
Bancroft, George, relief meeting presided over by, 150; address of, 151; letter of, to Lincoln, 151; Lincoln's letter to, 152
Banks, N. P., expedition of, 43; at Port Hudson, 49; plans for invasion of Texas, 51; petition of New Orleans convention to, 59; intention of ordering an election, 61; Free State General Committee's attack of, 61; decides against Free State Committee, 64; Gen. Shepley's disagreement with, 64; Lincoln's letter to, 65; reconstruction letter of, 66; Lincoln appreciates services of, 67; urged by President to reconstruct Louisiana, 67; date for election fixed by, 67; Shepley's registration approved by, 68; proclamation by, 69; order of, relative to election, 69; letter to Lincoln, 70; date of delegate election fixed by, 74; before Congressional committee, 75; Boutwell's defence of, 255; Powell's criticism of, 346; Governor Wells not in harmony with, 418
Bates, Edward, Attorney-General, letter to A. F. Ritchie, 105; on admission of West Virginia, 123; on Norfolk affairs, 135; letter to Marshal McDowell, 147
Batesville, Gen. Curtis's occupation of, 82
Baton Rouge, secession convention in, 36
Baxter, Elisha, election of, 91
Bayard, James F., 103; admission of West Virginia Senators opposed by, 193
Bell, Joseph M., 40
Bell and Everett, vote for in Louisiana, 37
Belmont, August, Lincoln's letter to, 39
Benjamin, Judah P., resignation of, 76, 424
Bent, Charles, 12
Berkeley County, provision for annexing to West Virginia, 110; annexation of, 127
Bingham, John A., debate on West Virginia closed by, 119

INDEX

Black, Jeremiah S., diplomatic mission of, 390
Blaine, James G., 73; existence of schism in Republican party ignored by, 313; quotation from, 441; Johnson's change of policy explained by, 489
Blair, Francis P., Sr., Lincoln interviewed by, 390; camp of Gen. Grant visited by, 391; Jefferson Davis interviewed by, 391; plan of reunion proposed by, 391; Mr. Davis's letter to, 393; Lincoln's letter to, 394; mission a failure, 394
Blair, Montgomery, on admission of West Virginia, 123; time of emancipation deemed inopportune by, 188; reply to Sumner by, 208
Bliss, C. C., 88
Blockade of Louisiana ports, 37
Blow, Henry T., remarks on reconstruction by, 301
Bonzano, M. F., election of, 76; seat in Congress claimed by, 341; report by Committee of Elections on, 341
Bordeaux, visit of Confederate naval agent to, 50
Border States, Lincoln supported by delegates from, 1; Cotton States expected aid from, 161; Lincoln interviewed by Congressmen from, 163, 171; interests of South bound up with, 171; majority reply of Congressmen from, 173; emancipation proclamation did not affect status of slaves in, 383
Boreman, Arthur I., 100, 128, 129
Bouligny, John E., 43
Boutwell, George S., reconstruction speech of, 254; President Johnson visited by, 458
Bowden, Lemuel J., 131, 138
Boyers, J. E., 128
Bradley, General, 79
Bragg, General, raid of, 19
Brandegee, Augustus, 342
Brazos, battle of, 50
Breckenridge, John C., election of, 316
Bright, Hon. John, Sumner's letters to, 200, 290

Brooks, James, inquiry of, 225
Brown, B. Gratz, substitute of, 264; amendment of, 272
Brown John, 142
Brown, William G., bill of, 113; remarks on admission of West Virginia, 114
Brownlow, William G., 7; unites in call for convention, 21, 29; nomination of, 31; election of, 32; Mr. Johnson's dispatch to, 414; remarks on negro suffrage, 416; policy recommended by, 417
Brownson, Orestes, theory of State suicide summarized by, 210
Bryant, William Cullen, 150
Buchanan, James, election of, 316
Buell, General Don Carlos, army of, 3, 10, 19; treatment of fugitive slaves by, 158
Bullett, Cuthbert, Lincoln's letter to, 39
Bureau of Refugees, Freedmen and Abandoned Lands. See Freedmen's Bureau
Burke, Edmund, 200
Burnside, General Ambrose E., 150
Butler, General Benjamin F., 33; investigation of, 38, 39; relieved from command, 40; Lincoln's letter to, 44; new department assigned to, 133; Pierpont criticised by, 134; Attorney-General criticised by, 135; Lincoln's letter to, 136; department of Virginia commanded by, 143; fugitive slaves arrive at camp of, 144, 147; legal defence of attitude toward slaves, 146

C

CALDWELL, A. B., 128
California, Upper, 12; admission of, 13; first election in, 350
Cameron, Simon, Butler's treatment of slaves approved by, 146
Campbell, John A., commissioner to Hampton Roads conference, 393, 395
Campbell, William B., election of, 415

INDEX

Canby, General E. R. S., Lincoln's letter to, 402
Carey, John B., fugitive slave law pleaded by, 144
Carlile, John S., 98; election of, 103; admission of, to United States Senate, 104; speech on admission of West Virginia, 111; term expires, 131; reconstruction speech of, 267
Chadsey, Charles E., President Johnson's surrender to the South explained by, 489
Chandler, Lucius H., Representative-elect from Virginia, 131; remarks of, 132; exclusion of, 133
Chandler, Zachariah, interest in reconstruction bill, 274; Sumner's opposition to Trumbull's resolution supported by, 380
Chase, Salmon P., on admission of West Virginia, 121; authorized to organize labor of abandoned slaves, 160, 386; emancipation favored by, 180; quotation from diary of, 186; conservatism of Lincoln observed by, 275; Andrew Johnson takes oath of office before, 408
Chattanooga, 4; taken by Federal forces, 22
Clark, Daniel, remarks on reconstruction by, 376
Clarke, Governor Charles, insurgent legislature convoked by, 459; imprisonment of, 460; petition for pardon of, 460
Clarke, Isaac E., 43
Cleveland, Tennessee, 4
Colfax, Schuyler, on admission of West Virginia, 115
Collamer, Jacob, on admission of West Virginia, 111; substitute of, 328; amendment of substitute, 334; defeat of amendment of, 334; defeat of substitute of, 336; remarks on electoral vote of Louisiana by, 328, 335
Colonization, suggested by Lincoln, 153; resolutions of Baltimore Union Convention on, 167; message of Governor Brownlow on, 416

Colored troops, Lincoln urges raising of, 20, 22; General Hunter recommends raising of, 180; policy of enlistment of, 386
Committee, Central Executive of Louisiana, 53
Committee, Free State General of Louisiana, 47, 54, 59, 61; controversy of, with General Banks, 62; confers with General Shepley, 63; friends of, protest against election, 70
Confederate army, Louisiana troops in, 37; Arkansas troops in, 80; driven from western Virginia, 98
Confederate Government, offer of Arkansas to, 80; Arkansas not aided by, 81, 82; hold of, weakened in Arkansas, 83; aid from border States expected by, 171
Confederate officers, disfranchisement of, 236
Confederate States, theory that disunionists were in a minority in, 192; functionaries in, not bound by oaths, 204; governments of, vacated, 205; governments could be organized by Congress in, 206; Constitution the only law in, 206; power of Congress over, 210; people of, unable to plead Constitution, 212; original idea relative to reorganization of, 213; Stevens's idea of status of, 214; status of, 260; approaching disruption of, 286; rights of citizens in, 366; political rights of people in, 367; no foreign engagements entered into by, 391; anarchy threatens many of, 409, 431; Federal troops preserve order in, 432; obstacles to restoration in, 432; blockade of, 444; importance of understanding public opinion in, 471; legislation of, 472; prompt acquiescence of, 472; sentiments of citizens of, 474; Congress excludes delegations from, 474; reaction in, 482; Northern example no defence of legislation in, 485; reconstructed not very different from disloyal govern-

ments of, 486; States represented at opening of 39th Congress, 489; Congress ignores claims of members from, 490
Confiscation, in Arkansas, 78
Congress, amnesty authorized by, 24; President disclaims authority to admit members to, 26; electoral vote of Tennessee excluded by, 35; Representatives from Louisiana admitted to, 46; Louisiana elects members to, 55; organization of, 55; Louisiana not redistricted by, 57; A. P. Field denied admission to, 60; Louisiana elects members to, 76; government of Louisiana not recognized by, 76; electoral vote of Louisiana excluded by, 76; Arkansas elects members to, 91; consents to transfer of Virginia counties, 127; resolution on compensated emancipation passed by, 167; slavery in Territories abolished by, 170; confiscation act of, 179; restored Virginia recognized by, 191; President in agreement with, 191; slavery in rebellious States should be ended by, 197; power possessed over seceding States by, 206; doctrines of Stevens abhorrent to members of, 216; unanimity of, 221; reconstruction discussed by, 224; form of State government should be determined by, 228; reconstruction bill passed by, 273; Lincoln's contest with, 284; President disclaims right to admit members to, 287; constitutional amendment passed by, 288; exclusion of electoral votes by resolution of, 338; protest against admission of members to, 341; power to readmit States resides in, 358; authority over rebellious States possessed by, 365; desire to discipline South winning adherents in, 407; Johnson's distrust of, 461; why reconstruction conventions should have been called by, 470; Southern States reorganized at meeting of, 486; Johnson intended to be guided by, 488; Presidential system suspended by legislation of, 489; Southern members not admitted to, 490; reconstruction assumed by, 490; suffrage in the first reconstruction measure, 494
Confederate Congress, 36; admission of Arkansas delegates to, 79
Contrabands, multitudes of, in camp of General Butler, 147
Constitution, The, those who repudiate cannot plead provisions of, 212, 213; ceases to be a restraint on Government, 213; State in rebellion not embraced by, 214; scope of not contracted by secession ordinances, 218; necessity as an interpreter of, 222; number of States necessary to ratify amendment of, 232; Georgia adopts Thirteenth Amendment of, 466
Constitutional Union men, attitude of, 7
Convention bill, defeated by popular vote in Tennessee, 8
Convention, Lincoln nominated by the Chicago, 1; Southern commercial held at Knoxville, 6; the Greeneville, 9; the Nashville, 30; meeting of the Louisiana constitutional, 75; the Arkansas constitutional, 87; the Richmond secession, 93; the Wheeling, 99, 104; ordinances of the Wheeling, 100; the Wheeling votes on dismemberment, 101; the Wheeling adjourns, 101, 107; the Wheeling authorizes formation of new State, 105; slavery in the Wheeling, 107; meeting of the Baltimore Union, 167; revolutionary character of the Wheeling, 468
Conventions, the reconstruction, character of, 468; irregularity of those called under Presidential plan, 469; why Congress should have called, 470; character and work of those called

INDEX

by President Johnson, 470; origin would not affect work of, if acquiesced in, 472
Conway, Martin, speech on West Virginia by, 113
Cooper, Edmund, election of, 415
Cooper Union, Lincoln's address in, 1; relief meeting in, 150
Cottman, Thomas, 48; election of, 56; Lincoln's letter to, 64
Cotton States, aid from border States expected by, 161
Cowan, Edgar, on admission of Mr. Segar, 139; remarks on electoral vote of Louisiana, 330, 332; inquiry of, concerning electoral votes, 338
Cox, Samuel S., reconstruction speech of, 252
Crane, Samuel, 128
Cravens, James A., reconstruction speech of, 249
Creole, The, 6
Crisfield, John W., interview with Lincoln reported by, 163
Crittenden, John J., speech on West Virginia by, 116
Crittenden Resolution, introduction of, 220; Mr. Strouse refers to, 249
Cruisers, Confederate, 50
Curtin, Governor Andrew G., 98
Cutler, R. King, Senator-elect from Louisiana, 76, 343, 424

D

DAVIS, GARRETT, admission of West Virginia Senators opposed by, 128; resolutions of, 210
Davis, Henry Winter, remarks on Louisiana election, 58; amendment of, 225; chairman of Committee on Rebellious States, 226; reconstruction address of, 226; on Southern loyalists, 231; on modes of establishing republican governments, 232; Thirteenth Amendment approved by, 232; policy of Lincoln criticised by, 232; protest of against policy of Lincoln, 279; character of, 283;

defeat of, for renomination, 284; postponement of Ashley's bill opposed by, 295; reconstruction speech of, 307; last reconstruction speech in Congress, 310; alliance with Stevens, 311; motion relative to Louisiana, 341
Davis, Jefferson, Blair's interview with, 391; proposal for joint invasion of Mexico entertained by, 392; letter to Mr. Blair, 393; on Lincoln's assassination, 407; members of Mississippi convention intercede for, 460; Georgia convention invokes Executive clemency in behalf of, 466
Davis-Wade Bill, passed by House, 262; passed by Senate, 273; Lincoln's action on, 273; proclamation concerning, 277; no provision for negro suffrage in, 494
Dawes, Henry L., on Louisiana Representatives, 56; on admission of West Virginia, 116; report on Mr. Segar's election, 131; on election of Mr. Chandler, 132; reconstruction speech of, 295; Mr. Davis's criticism of, 306; bill of Representative Wilson criticised by, 312; report on election of Mr. Bonzano, 341; remarks of, 342
Delaware, slave interest in, 155; Lincoln's bill for compensated emancipation in, 155; Federalist party in, 157; Federal interference in, 377
Democratic party, defeat of, 1; vote of, in West Virginia, 129; reconstruction theory of, 218; attitude on reconstruction, 220; negro suffrage opposed by New Orleans convention of, 421; South misled by attitude of, 483
Dennison, Charles, reconstruction speech of, 247
Dennison, William, 32
Dickinson, Daniel S., 33
District of Columbia, slaves not allowed to depart from, 148; colored persons liable to arrest

INDEX

if found in, 152; compensation to owners of slaves in, 167
Dix, General John A., 33; treatment of fugitive slaves by, 149
Donnelly, Ignatius, reconstruction speech of, 245
Doolittle, James R., credentials of Mr. Underwood offered by, 141; reconstruction bill opposed by, 273; on electoral vote of Louisiana, 324, 326, 333; remarks on Louisiana, 348; policy of Administration supported by, 380; credentials of Mr. Hahn offered by, 383
Doubleday, General Abner, treatment of fugitive slaves by, 159
Douglas-Lincoln debates, 1
Dorr, Thomas W., government under, 350
Dunlap, George W., admission of West Virginia opposed by, 214
Durant, Thomas J., 47; Attorney-General of Louisiana, 48; registry conducted by, 51; spokesman of planters, 53; enrollment by, satisfactory to Lincoln, 63; disagreement with General Banks, 65; protest of, against election, 348; recognition of Louisiana opposed by, 378
Durell, E. H., 75

E

EAST, E. H., 28
Edgerton, Joseph K., reconstruction speech of, 219, 301
Election, Presidential, loss of a pretext for secession, 1; in Tennessee, 29; in Arkansas, 92; in West Virginia, 129; electoral votes in, 338; result of, 339
Elections, Committee of, report on Louisiana Representative, 56
Electoral College, bill on representation in, 314
Eliot, Thomas W., amendment to reconstruction bill offered by, 289; reconstruction speech of, 292; Stevens's interruption of, 294; Davis's criticism of, 306; bill for bureau of emancipation introduced by, 386

Emancipation, in Tennessee, 22; East Tennessee convention favors immediate, 29; Lincoln's proclamation of, 47; proclamation of not to be revoked, 52; vote on, in West Virginia, 110; in West Virginia constitution, 125; Lincoln suggests compensated, 155; Lincoln considering, 178; discussion in Cabinet, 180; draft of proclamation of, 181; urged by Chicago clergymen, 184; not hastened by deputations, 186; Lincoln reads proclamation of, 187; Sumner proposes to convert proclamation of, into law, 272; effect of proclamation on status of slaves, 384; discussed at Hampton Roads Conference, 398; Lincoln favored gradual, 398
Emancipation, compensated, Lincoln prepares bill on, 155; message refers to, 161; New York Tribune favors, 164; resolution of Congress on, 167; Baltimore Union convention's resolution on, 167; House of Representatives appoints committee on, 168
Emancipator, The, 5
England, Cromwell's division of, 200
Europe, the civil war pleasing to powers of, 393

F

FEDERALIST, The, 269
Fellows, John Q. A., nomination of, 69; defeat of, 70
Fishback, William M., Lincoln's letter to, 89; election of, 91
Fisher, George P., interest in compensated emancipation, 155
Flanders, Benjamin F., election of, 46; Lincoln's letter to, 52; vote received by, 60; interview with Lincoln, 63; nomination of, 69; defeat of, 70; hostility of Congress toward Louisiana said to have been promoted by, 73
Florida, martial law proclaimed over, 168; unworthy of a place

in the Union, 256; insurrection in, 314; damage sustained by, 436; nature of reorganized government of, 488
Florida, The, capture of, 288
Forfeiture, State, idea of, 204
Forrest, General, 15
Fort Donelson, General Grant in possession of, 10
Fort Henry, Federal occupation of, 10
Fortress Monroe, fugitive slaves at, 144, 385
Foster, Lafayette S., reconstruction policy of Lincoln supported by, 380
Fowler, Joseph S., election of, 413
France, relations with, 409
Franchise, elective, in Tennessee to be fixed by Legislature, 30; free negroes of Louisiana petition for, 55; States have always exercised right to confer, 452
Franchise, negro, Lincoln's opinion concerning, 73. See Negroes
Frederick City, 184
Frederic County, provision for annexing to West Virginia, 110
Freedmen, no provision for education of, 298; Brownlow would admit testimony of, 416; character of, 416; Southern feeling toward, 475; Mississippi legislation relative to, 475
Freedmen's Aid Societies, Lincoln memorialized by, 386
Freedmen's Bureau, act of Congress relative to, 385, 387; germ of, 386; duties of commissioner of, 387; Governor of Arkansas coöperates with, 411; influence in producing Southern reaction, 483; political aspirations of agents of, 484
Fremont, General John C., proclamation concerning slaves, 148; Lincoln's letter to, 148; reply to Lincoln, 149
Fugitive slaves, repeal of acts for rendition of, 144; exclusion from Department of Washington, 148

G

GANTT, GENERAL E. W., secession abjured by, 83
Garrison, William Lloyd, 7
Georgia, martial law proclaimed over, 168; Boutwell would exclude from restored Union, 256; insurrection in, 314; injuries sustained by, 433; Governor Brown's efforts at restoration of, 465; appointment of provisional governor for, 465; leading ex-Confederates aid governor, 465; reconstruction convention of, 465; convention repeals secession ordinance, 465; war debt repudiated by, 465; slaves freed by constitution of, 466; Executive clemency in behalf of Jefferson Davis invoked by convention, 466
Germans, The, indifferent to secession, 80
Gilmore-Jacquess mission, 389
Gooch, Daniel W., reconstruction address of, 250
Government, a republican form guaranteed by reconstruction proclamation, 26; perfection of Congressional system, 385
Grant, General Ulysses S., in possession of Forts Henry and Donelson, 10; martial law proclaimed by, 10; at Mission Ridge and Lookout Mountain, 23; Lee driven back by, 288; Blair visits camp of, 391; influence in bringing about Hampton Roads Conference, 396; movements by army of, 401; management of Freedmen's Bureau criticised by, 484
Great Britain, relations with, 409
Greeley, Horace, 390
Greeneville, Tennessee, 4, 9
Grimes, James W., remarks on Louisiana election, 382
Gulf, Department of, Butler relieved from command in, 40; General Banks in command of, 49

INDEX

H

HAHN, MICHAEL, election of, 46; Lincoln's letter to, 52; vote of, 60; nomination of, 69; election of, 70; oath of, 72; Lincoln's letter to, 73; election of delegates authorized by, 74; election called by, 75; credentials filed in U. S. Senate, 383, 418, 424
Hall, Ellery R., 107
Hall, John, 107
Hale, John P., on admission of West Virginia, 111; on electoral vote of Louisiana, 325
Halleck, General H. W., Tennessee included in department of, 20; General Buell instructed by, 21; General Banks instructed by, 51; order on surrender of fugitive slaves, 158
Hamilton, Andrew J., appointment of, 467
Hampton Roads Conference, 396; Confederate commissioners to, report failure, 400; results of, 400
Harris, Ira, remarks on Crittenden resolution by, 222; remarks on electoral vote of Louisiana, 323, 334; amendment offered by, 334
Harris, Isham G., authorized to appoint commissioners, 8; Legislature convoked at Memphis by, 15
Harlan, James, bill of, 195
Hawkins, Isaac R., election of, 415
Hay and Nicolay, account of Lincoln's message by, 24; quotation from history of, 273
Helena, Arkansas, Union occupation of, 82, 86
Henderson, John B., reply to Lincoln's appeal, 177; reconstruction bill opposed by, 273; recognition of Louisiana favored by, 348; inconsistency of Sumner exposed by, 375, 377; inquiry concerning Louisiana loyalists, 378; letter on reconstruction, 495
Hendricks, Thomas A., Republican factiousness agreeable to, 380
Hiestand, Judge J., appointment of, 41
Holden, William W., appointment of, 448; proclamation of, 450; message of, 454; President Johnson's telegram to, 455; public career of, 457; Republican leaders alarmed at appointment of, 459
Holman, William S., resolution introduced by, 222
Hood, General J. B., 30
Hooker, General Joseph, treatment of fugitive slaves, 158
Howard, Jacob M., on electoral vote of Louisiana, 328; on recognition of Louisiana, 358; Sumner's opposition to Trumbull's resolution supported by, 380
Howard, Oliver O., General, Freedmen's Bureau organized by, 389
Howe, Timothy O., speech on Ten Eyck's amendment, 321
Howell, Rufus K., 41
Hughes, Augustus de B., 43
Humphreys, Benjamin G., election and pardon of, 464
Hungary, similarity of ideas lacking in, 237
Hunter, General David, freedom of slaves proclaimed by, 168; authority to arm negroes requested by, 180
Hunter, Robert M. T., authorized to act as commissioner, 395
Hurlbut, General S. A., on reorganization of Tennessee, 21; Lincoln's letters to, 84, 401

I

ILLINOIS, amendment abolishing slavery adopted by, 384
Indiana, troops from, assist western Virginians, 98
Intelligencer, The National, 61
Ireland, unsuccessful campaign of James II in, 203; similarity of ideas lacking in, 237
Irish, The, indifference to secession, 80

INDEX

J

JACKS, T. M., Congressman-elect, 91; proposed compensation to, 342
Jackson, General Andrew, new industrial era marked by inauguration of, 5; invasion by way of Mexico expected by, 392
Jacquess-Gilmore mission, 389
James II, King, abdication of, 202
Jefferson County, provision for annexation of, 110; annexation of, 127
Jefferson, Thomas, declaration of, 357
Johnson, Andrew, 12; in Thirtieth Congress, 14; people of Nashville addressed by, 15; activity of, 18; Nashville saved by, 19; Lincoln's opinion of, 19; addresses of, 19; urged to raise negro troops, 20; Lincoln's letter to, 22; enlarged authority of, 23; Nashville meeting called by, 27; election of county officers authorized by, 27; proclamation of, 31; nomination of, for Vice-Presidency, 32; Nashville address of, 32; letter of, to Mr. Dennison, 32; popularity in the North, 33; credentials of West Virginia Senators presented by, 103; resolution offered by, 221; election of, as Vice-President, 339; installation of, as President, 408; problem confronting, 408; letter to Governor Murphy, 411; despatch to Governor Brownlow, 414; reconstruction policy endorsed by National Democratic party, 420; Lincoln's policy alleged to have been changed by, 426; Pierpont's government recognized by, 427; Nashville speech of, 438; forecast of policy of, 439; addresses of, 440; visit of Illinois delegation to, 440; visit of Indiana delegation to, 442; visit of negro delegation, 443; South Carolina delegation addressed by, 443; blockade partly raised by, 444; blockade of trans-Mississippi ports rescinded by, 445; work done for reconstruction retained by, 447; Lincoln's policy need not have been adopted by, 447; at inauguration sentiments of Congress already known to, 448; results of attempting reunion without coöperation of Congress, 448; reconstruction of North Carolina begun by, 448; amnesty proclamation of, 450; cases excluded from benefits of amnesty, 450; reconstruction plan of, based on guaranty clause of Constitution, 452; telegram to Governor Holden, 455; visit of North Carolina delegation to, 456; North Carolina election unsatisfactory to, 457; interview of Boutwell and Morrill with, 458; William L. Sharkey appointed Provisional Governor by, 459; appointment of provisional governors by, 459; telegram to Governor Sharkey, 461; attitude of Congress characterized by, 461; Governor Sharkey's reorganization of militia approved by, 462; Mississippi people trusted by, 463; change in sentiments of, 463, 488; General Slocum directed to revoke order by, 463; proceedings in reconstruction conventions directed by, 465; organization of a police force for Georgia approved by, 466; policy toward Congress unknown in the South, 483; prompt acquiescence of South in policy of, 486; reconstruction theory similar to Lincoln's, 487; falling back from Lincoln's plan, 487; Lincoln's Cabinet retained by, 488; change of attitude of, 489; influence of Seward upon, 489; movement to procure resignation from Vice-Presidency, 489; limitations of, 490; reconstruction work of, not marked by originality, 491; negro suffrage, 494
Johnson, Bradish, 48

INDEX

Johnson, Herschel V., election of, 465
Johnson, James, appointment of, 459, 465
Johnson, James M., election of, 91; proposed compensation to, 342; election of, 412
Johnson, Reverdy, in New Orleans, 38; on electoral vote of Louisiana, 335; on President's message, 339; remarks on recognition of Louisiana, 370; Sumner's argument with, 374; remarks on negro suffrage, 378; recognition of Arkansas and Louisiana favored by, 378
Johnson, R. W., secession of, 91
Johnston, General Joseph E., retires to Murfreesboro, 11
Jones, Hon. Ira P., 12
Jordan, Warren, 27

K

KANAWHA, proposed State of, 105; change in name of, 107
Kearney, General Stephen W., 12
Kelley, William D., reconstruction speech of, 252, 291; proposes amendment of Ashley's bill, 312; Field's assault of, 342
Kernan, Francis, bill of Mr. Wilson criticised by, 312
Kimball, General, 86
King, Preston, Mr. Johnson influenced by, 441
Kingwood, Va., Union meeting at, 99
Kitchen, Benjamin M., Representative-elect, 131; denied admission to Congress, 133
Knoxville, early capital of Tennessee, 4; Southern Commercial Convention held at, 6; taken by Federal forces, 22
Kyle, G. H., election of, 412

L

LAMONT, GEORGE D., 43
Lane, James H., on electoral vote of Louisiana, 337
LeBlond, Frank C., reconstruction speech of, 300
Lee, General Robert E., Maryland invaded by, 183; repulse of, 186; driven back by Grant, 288; weakness of, 401; surrender of, 426
Leftwich, John W., election of, 415
Letcher, Governor John, United States could not recognize, 205, 445
Lieber, Dr. Francis, 150, 151; Sumner's letters to, 199, 289
Lincoln, Abraham, Cooper Union address of, 1; conservatism of, 1; nomination of, 1; border State delegations support of, 1; popular vote received by, 1; peer of tried Republican leaders, 1; policy of, 2; sympathy for Tennessee loyalists, 3, 10; Andrew Johnson appointed by, 11; in Thirtieth Congress, 14; authority for appointing military governors, 14; view of their utility, 20; letter to Governor Johnson, 20, 22; authority of Johnson enlarged by, 23; reply to General Rosecrans, 23; proclamation issued by, 23; authority to admit members to Congress disclaimed by, 26; enrolling agents sent to Tennessee, Arkansas, and Louisiana by, 27; renomination of, 32; declined to interfere in nominating convention, 34; reply to protest of McClellan electors, 35; letter to Cuthbert Bullett, 39; letter to August Belmont, 39; Court of Record for Louisiana constituted by, 42; letter to General Butler and others, 44; restoration of Louisiana urged by, 44; letter to General Shepley, 44; Emancipation Proclamation published by, 47; requested to order an election, 48; reply to Louisiana committee, 48; more advanced ground taken by, 49; letter to General Banks and others, 51; urges restoration, 51; enrollment of Durant approved by, 63; willingness to recognize part of Louisiana, 63; letter to Thomas Cottman,

64; letter to General Banks, 65; General Banks's letter to, 66; Banks's services appreciated by, 67; authority conferred on General Banks by, 67; Banks on Louisiana election, 70; letter to Governor Hahn, 73; authority of Mr. Hahn enlarged by, 73; letter to General Hurlbut, 84; letter to General Steele, 89; letter to William M. Fishback, 89; result of Arkansas election gratifying to, 91; requests opinion of Cabinet on admission of West Virginia, 119, 124; approves bill for admission of West Virginia, 125; proclamation concerning West Virginia, 126; letter to General Butler, 136; slavery in first inaugural of, 143; letter to General Fremont, 148; General Fremont instructed by, 149; Bancroft's letter to, 151; letter to Mr. Bancroft, 152; emancipation and colonization suggested by, 153; advance in position of, 154; arming of slaves opposed by, 154, 180; bill for compensated emancipation drafted by, 155; Mr. Pierce's interview with, 160; compensated emancipation proposed by, 161; further advance in position of, 162; letter to Henry J. Raymond, 163; border State Congressmen interview, 163; letter to James A. McDougall, 165; proclamation of General Hunter rescinded by, 168; Sumner's letter concerning, 170; border State Congressmen appealed to, 171; emancipation proposed by, 178; confiscation act approved by, 179; draft of emancipation proclamation read by, 181; rebellious citizens warned by, 183; Chicago clergymen interview, 184; resolves to issue postponed proclamation, 186; meeting of Cabinet, 186; emancipation proclamation read by, 187; first inaugural of, 190; central idea of reconstruction plan of, 190; confidence in ultimate success, 191; Congress substantially agrees with, 191; change in policy of, 193; only one plan of reconstruction proposed by, 194; remarks on Blair-Sumner controversy, 208; reconstruction plan of, criticised by Henry Winter Davis, 232; Mr. Donnelly's character of, 245; Mr. Boutwell defends reconstruction policy, 254; treatment of reconstruction bill by, 273; Sumner's opinion of, 275; proclamation on reconstruction bill, 277; Wade-Davis manifesto concerning action of, 279; result of contest with Congress, 284; reëlection of, 286; silence as to controversy with Congress, 286; no right over admission of Congressmen claimed by, 287; adoption of more vigorous measures hinted at, 287; resolution relative to electoral votes approved by, 339; electoral votes received by, 339; popular approval of Thirteenth Amendment pleasing to, 385; Freedmen's Aid Societies appeal to, 386; Mr. Blair's visit to, 390; Blair's mission not officially sanctioned by, 391; letter to Mr. Blair, 394; letter to Secretary Seward, 395; conference opposed by, except on basis of reunion, 397; last speech on reconstruction, 403; assassination of, a calamity to the South, 407; policy would have saved South from many evils, 407; telegram to Governor Pierpont, 426; Pierpont's interview with, 426; attitude toward Confederate legislatures, 470; a loose system of reconstruction opposed by, 487; reconstruction theory of, similar to Johnson's, 487; President Johnson retains Cabinet of, 488; constructive statesmanship of, 491; a wide constituency favored by, 493; conditions on returning States imposed by, 494; Mr. Henderson's views on, 495

Lincoln-Douglas debates, 1
Little Rock, seized by Confederate troops, 79; threatened by Federal forces, 82; capture of, 83; loyal newspaper published in, 83; Union convention at, 87
Liverpool, abandoned by Confederate naval agent, 50
Longyear, John W., reconstruction address of, 244
Lookout Mountain, battle of, 23, 224
Louisiana, effect of Union victories in, 10; enrolling agent sent to, 27; secession spirit in, 36; secession of, 36; prosperity at the beginning of the war, 36; treasury of, 37; citizens of, in Confederate army, 37; blockade of ports in, 37; attitude toward Richmond government, 37; loyalists of, 37; secessionists of, intimidated, 38; activity of Unionists in, 38; necessity of courts in, 40; courts established in, 41; court of record for, 42; Supreme Court of, 43; Lincoln urges restoration of, 44; Union associations request an election, 45; proclamation for an election in, 45; members of Congress elected in, 46; vote cast in, 46; admission of Representatives to Congress, 46; named as one of the rebellious States, 47; parishes excepted from emancipation proclamation, 47; disagreement among Unionists of, 47; enrollment of citizens in, 48; Lincoln visited by committee from, 48; reorganization interrupted, 49; portion covered by Union arms, 50; Lincoln urges reconstruction of, 52; condition of, 53; amended constitution of 1852 destroyed by rebellion, 54; voting in, 55; franchise asked by free negroes, 55; credentials of Representatives from, 56; suppression of election in, 56; constitution altered by General Shepley, 58; citizens from, in Union army, 60; General Banks to order an election in, 61, 64;

Banks on reconstruction in, 66; Banks fixes date of election for, 67; constitution modified by proclamation of General Banks, 68; provision for voting of loyalists in, 69; election in, 70; protest against election in, 70; Hahn inaugurated Governor, 72; civil subordinate to military power, 73; Free State leaders unite with Radicals in Congress, 74; election in, 74; vote on constitution, 75; Legislature chosen in, 76; Presidential electors appointed for, 76, 195; Senators elected by, 76; government of, not recognized by Congress, 76; electoral vote of, 129, 314; radicals propose to recognize government of, 290; insurrection in, 314; amendment to except from joint resolution, 315; Ten Eyck's speech on electoral vote of, 318; Howe's speech on electoral vote of, 321; Trumbull's speech on electoral vote of, 321; highest vote cast in, 323; remarks of Harris on electoral vote of, 323; speech of Doolittle on electoral vote of, 324; remarks of Hale on electoral vote of, 325; remarks of Collamer on electoral vote of, 328; Howard's speech on electoral vote of, 328; Cowan's remarks on electoral vote of, 330; Powell on electoral vote of, 331; Wade's remarks on electoral vote of, 332; loss of Ten Eyck's amendment concerning, 334; Johnson's remarks on electoral vote of, 335; Pomeroy's amendment, 337; passage of joint resolution, 338; Cowan's inquiry, 338; Senate debate on recognition of, 341; Representatives-elect from, 341; protest against admission of members from, 341; compensation to claimants from, 341; United States Senators chosen in, 343; Trumbull's resolution relative to, 343; Powell opposes recognition of, 344; Henderson favors recognition of, 348; recognition of, would enfeeble Union, 358; Howard's speech on recognition of, 358; governed by bayonet, 367; Howard characterizes government of, 369; Reverdy Johnson's argument on recognition of, 370, 377; Sprague's remarks on election in, 381; Grimes's remarks on election in, 382; slavery in parts of, not affected by emancipation proclamation, 384; draft in, 417; election in, 418; Mr. Wells chosen Governor, 422; Warmoth elected as Territorial Delegate, 422; United States Senators chosen, 424; Thirteenth Amendment ratified by, 424; injuries which rebellion inflicted on, 424

Lovejoy, Owen, resolution offered by, 132; resolution of, relative to emancipation, 170; doctrines of Thaddeus Stevens repudiated by, 217

Lundy, Benjamin, Genius of Universal Emancipation published by, 5

Lyon, General Nathaniel, 79

M

MADISON, parish of, 75
Malhiot, E. E., 48
Mallory, Robert, yeas and nays on Ashley's bill demanded by, 311; bill of Mr. Wilson criticised by, 312
Manassas, battle of, 183
Mann, W. D., Representative-elect from Louisiana, 76; seat in Congress claimed by, 341
Manumission Intelligencer, The, 5
Marcy, William, Secretary, 12
Marvin, Governor, Seward's message to, 488
Maryland, attitude on emancipation, 165
Mason, James M., 103
Mason, Richard B., 13, 14
Massachusetts, sentiments on slavery, 375
Maynard, Horace, 9, 10; joins in call for convention, 21; emancipation policy of Lincoln approved by, 177; election of, 415
Memphis, Legislature convenes in, 15
Mexico, 12, 13; French interests in, 50; invasion of, a part of Napoleon's policy, 391; proposal for joint invasion of, 392
Mileage, allowed to Arkansas claimants, 91
Military commissions, 12
Military Governor, office of, 11, 12, 14, 193
Minority, loyal, rule by, inconsistent with American principles, 205, 217; should institute government for their own protection, 353; further examination of, 491
Mission Ridge, battle of, 23, 224
Missouri, provisional government appointed in, 10; origin of government of, 350
Mississippi, State of, in Federal control, 50; insurrection in, 314; injury sustained by, 437; Provisional Governor for, 459; Governor Clarke summons insurgent Legislature of, 459; secession ordinance declared null and void, 460; slavery abolished in, 460; people advised to form a patrol, 461; disorder in, 462; General Slocum prevents organization of militia in, 462; freedmen of, 463; election in, 464; conflict of civil and military authorities, 464; supremacy of military in, 464; November legislation of, 475; practical revival of black code in, 480; spirit of reconstructed Legislature, 482; character of reorganized government, 488
Monroe Doctrine, Northern Democrats and Republicans adhere to, 392; Mexico to be conquered under pretence of defending, 393
Morrill, Justin S., President Johnson visited by, 458
Morton, Oliver P., Governor, President Johnson interviewed by, 442

McClellan, electors, protest of, 34; ticket in Tennessee withdrawn, 35

McClellan, George B., General, proclamation concerning slaves, 145; instructions to, 152; collapse of Richmond campaign of, 178; Union army again commanded by, 184; Lee defeated by, 186; vote for Presidency received by, 339

McCulloch, General, 79

McDougall, James A., on admission of Mr. Segar, 139; Lincoln's letter to, 165-166

McDowell, General Irwin, treatment of fugitive slaves by, 144

McDowell, J. L., inquiry concerning fugitive slaves, 147

N

NAPOLEON III, 50; policy of, 391

Nashville, occupation of, 10; panic in, 11; occupied by General Nelson, 15; Governor Johnson arrives in, 15; Governor Johnson addresses people of, 15; mayor and council imprisoned, 17; press under restraint, 17; treatment of clergymen in, 17; Union convention at, 21; action of convention, 21; public meeting at, 27; convention at, 29; convention of January, 1865, 30; Legislature meets at, 32

National Conservative Union party, negro suffrage opposed by, 421; reconstruction policy of Mr. Johnson endorsed by, 421; Mr. Wells nominated for governor by, 422

Navy, proportions of, 286

Negroes, free, elective franchise asked by, 55; North Carolina denies franchise to, 452; condition of, in Mississippi, 463; testimony of, 464; numbers in Texas, 467

Nelson, General, enters Nashville, 15

Nelson, Thomas A. R., 9

New Hampshire, President Johnson addresses citizens of, 442

New Mexico, 12

New Orleans, State troops from, seize Federal property, 36; enthusiasm in, 37; bankruptcy of, 37; importance to Confederacy, 38; capture of, 38; results of Federal occupation of, 39; members of court of record arrive in, 43; excepted from emancipation proclamation, 47; menaced by General Taylor, 49; General Shepley forbids election in, 56; amount of taxes paid by, 58; without civil government, 58; extent of the State of Louisiana, 75; constitutional convention in, 75; unqualified voters enrolled in, 418; new registration in, 418; J. Madison Wells nominated by convention held in, 420

Newport News, fugitive slaves arrive at, 144, 386

New York, electoral vote not counted in Washington's election, 326

Nicolay and Hay. See Hay and Nicolay

Noell, John W., on admission of West Virginia, 118; inquiry of, 164

Norfolk, Va., destitution in, 133

North Carolina, Union victories in, 10; secession spirit in, 150; insurrection in, 314; injuries sustained by, 436; Provisional Governor appointed for, 448; "loyal people" of, 452; suffrage withheld from negroes of, 452; nearly all counties choose delegates, 453; ordinance of secession repealed by, 454; abolition of slavery in, 454; payment of rebel debt prohibited by, 455; adjournment of convention, 455; convention ordinances ratified, 457; election unsatisfactory to President Johnson, 457; Thirteenth Amendment ratified by, 457; Congressmen chosen by, 457; why President began reconstruction policy with, 458

O

OGLESBY, GOVERNOR, President Johnson visited by, 440
Ohio, western Virginians assisted by troops of, 98
Olin, Abraham B., on admission of West Virginia, 116
Olustee, battle of, a result of administration policy, 253
Orange, William, Prince of, 203
Orleans, courts established in, 41

P

PAINE, COLONEL, arrest of, 169
Parker, Granville, anti-slavery work of, 108
Parliament, absolute power vested in, 203
Patterson, David T., election of, 413
Patterson, General, proclamation relative to slaves, 145
Peabody, Charles A., appointment of, 42
Peace and Constitutional Society, in Arkansas, 81
Pea Ridge, battle of, 82
Pendleton, George H., reconstruction speech of, 257; votes received by, for Vice-Presidency, 339
Pensacola, Florida, Louisiana soldiers vote at, 70
Perry, Nehemiah, reconstruction address of, 250
Phelps, General John S., alleged opposition to rule of, 38; military governor, 82
Pierce, E. L., labor of abandoned slaves organized by, 160, 386; Lincoln interviewed by, 160
Pierpont, Francis Harrison, chosen Governor of restored Virginia, 101; inauguration of, 101; views of the Constitution, 102; message of, 109; address of, 128; elected Governor, 129; duties of, 133; protests against military interference, 134; application for assistance, 191; Lincoln's telegram to, 426; Lincoln visited by, 426; reception at Richmond, 427; the problem confronting, 428
Plaquemines, voting in parish of, 56; vote of, 74
Poland, similarity of ideas lacking in, 237
Polk, President James K., message of, 13
Pollard, E. A., quotation from "Lost Cause" of, 400
Pool, John, election of, 457
Pomeroy, Samuel C., on electoral vote of Louisiana, 330; amendment offered by, 337; remarks on reconstruction by, 376; extent of Congressional power over reconstruction stated by, 377
Port Hudson, General Banks at, 49; fall of, 49
Portsmouth, Va., Union vote in, 132; destitution in, 133
Powell, Lazarus W., remarks on Louisiana, 331; recognition of Louisiana opposed by, 344; General Banks denounced by, 346; proclamation of Banks quoted by, 347; remarks on Trumbull's resolution by, 373
Property, Federal, seizure of, in Baton Rouge, 36

R

RALEIGH, convention assembles at, 453
Raymond, Lincoln's letter to, 163
Reade, Edwin G., North Carolina convention presided over by, 453; farewell address of, 455
Reconstruction, in Tennessee, 1; Lincoln's proclamation of, 23; in Louisiana, 36, 44, 61; loyal minority authorized to restore States, 25; Lincoln's plan not indispensable to, 26; interrupted in Louisiana, 49; Lincoln's letter relative to, 51; President urges in Louisiana, 52; Banks's plan of, 66; proposed for Arkansas, 85; Lincoln's letters on, 89; in Louisiana connected with war powers of President, 36; emancipation introduced

into, 189; theories and plans of, 190; central idea of Lincoln's plan, 190; both parties agree on Presidential plan, 193; great number of theories and plans of, 193; difficulties of, increased by abolition, 194; Lincoln propounded only one plan of, 194; " Louisiana plan " and negro suffrage, 195; sensation caused by Sumner's scheme of, 198; final work of, influenced by Sumner's resolutions, 199; Stevens's theory of, 211; first act of, a modification of Stevens's theory, 212; theory held at commencement of rebellion, 213; Democratic theory of, 217; Edgerton's speech on, 219; attitude of Democratic party toward, 220; conservative views of Senators on, 220; House of Representatives on, 220; resolution of Thaddeus Stevens concerning, 224; resolution of Henry Winter Davis, 225; address of Mr. Davis, 226; of Southern States premature, 230; President's plan criticised by Mr. Davis, 232; address of Representative Scofield on, 236; address of Representative Williams on, 238; indemnity, security and punishment, elements of, 240; bill opposed by Mr. Baldwin, 241; address of Representative Thayer on, 242; remarks of Representative Yeaman on, 243; address of Representative Longyear on, 244; speech of Ignatius Donnelly on, 245; speech of Representative Dennison, 247; remarks of Thaddeus Stevens on, 247; bill opposed by Representative Strouse, 249; opposition of Mr. Cravens, 249; Representative Gooch on, 250; Representative Perry's remarks on, 250; Fernando Wood's opposition to bill for, 251; remarks of William D. Kelley on, 252; speech of S. S. Cox on, 252; Mr. Boutwell's speech on, 254; speech of George H. Pendleton, 257; bill for, unconstitutional, 258; Representatives pass bill on, 262; provisions of bill on, 262; Senator Wade on, 264; Senator Carlile's speech on, 267; Congress passes bill on, 273; Lincoln's treatment of bill on, 273; interest of Mr. Chandler in bill on, 274; Lincoln's proclamation concerning bill on, 277; notice of in annual message, 286; progress of, 287; forced upon attention of Congress by Union victories, 288; Mr. Ashley reports bill on, 289; Representative Eliot offers amendment to bill on, 289; provisions of Ashley's bill, 289; revived bill recognizes Louisiana and Arkansas, 289; new bill a substitute for Wade-Davis bill, 290; Kelley's speech on, 291; Eliot's speech on, 292; consideration of bill postponed, 295; Mr. Dawes resumes debate on, 295; power conferred on President by bill, 296; remarks of Fernando Wood on, 300; speech of Mr. LeBlond on, 300; remarks of Representative Blow, 301; speech of J. K. Edgerton, 301; Edgerton's summary of bill, 302; substitute for Ashley's bill, 304; further remarks of Ashley on, 305; Ashley explains compromise, 306; Henry Winter Davis speaks on, 306; Mr. Davis's last words in Congress on, 310; Mr. Wilson's bill, 311; revival of Ashley's bill on, 312; defects of Presidential plan of, 358; Howard's speech on, 358; Reverdy Johnson's remarks on, 370; Sumner proposes conditions of, 376; remarks of Senator Clark, 376; remarks of Senator Pomeroy, 377, 378; Presidential plan of, ignored by Congress, 385; Lincoln's conditions for effecting, 395, 397; Lincoln's letter to General Hurlbut on, 401; Lincoln's letter to General Canby, 402; Lincoln's last words on, 403; culmination of Presidential

plan of, 407; President Johnson's policy of, endorsed by Democratic convention, 420; views of Louisiana Republicans on, 422; Andrew Johnson's views of, in 1864, 438; Johnson under no obligation to accept Lincoln's plan of, 447; Mr. Johnson's policy of, 449; steps to, in Mississippi, 458; obstacles to, in Texas, 467; conventions called under Presidential plan, 468; course of Confederate governors relative to, 469; Lincoln's intention to employ Confederate legislatures in work of, 470; expected results of, 473; prediction of Henry Winter Davis relative to, 473; enemies of Union entrusted with, 486; Lincoln opposed a loose system of, 486; Lincoln's and Johnson's theories identical, 487; organizations effected under Lincoln different from "Johnson governments," 487; Johnson's original policy of, 488; acts of Congress suspend governments established under Presidential plan, 489; Joint Committee on, 490; Presidential plan examined, 491; the suffrage in the Presidential system of, 494; precedent conditions for returning States, 494; Senator Henderson's letter on Lincoln's plan, 495
Rector, Governor, call for troops, 81; threat of seceding from Confederacy, 82; flight of, 82
Red River, General Taylor retires to, 50
Republican electoral ticket, none offered for suffrage of Tennesseans in 1860, 7
Republican form of government, Sumner's resolutions relative to, 196; position that war was fought to fulfil guaranty of, untenable, 209; Henry Winter Davis on, 228; duty of Congress to guarantee, 228; Mr. Davis on modes of establishing, 232; Fernando Wood on, 251;

Pendleton on, 259, 260, 261; Carlile on, 268, 269; cannot originate in military orders, 357; military government not republican under the Constitution, 368
Republican party, radical members of, unite with Free State leaders, 74; Sumner's resolutions disavowed by leaders of, 199; relations of Stevens to, 216; change in attitude of, 220; revolutionary policy of, 257; beginning of division in, 273; some radical members of, opposed controversy with President, 289; schism in, 313; change in sentiments of, 377; Hendricks on factiousness of, 380; mass-meeting in New Orleans held by radical members of, 422
Representation, basis of, 354
Representatives, House of, committee on compensated emancipation appointed by, 168; reconstruction views of, 220; reconstruction bill passed by, 262; Ashley's reconstruction bill tabled by, 311, 312; resolution of Mr. Wilson introduced into, 314; measure excluding electoral votes of certain States passed by, 314; constitutional amendment abolishing slavery passed by, 384
Revenue, surplus of 1837, distribution of, 157
Revolution, American, legal forms not ignored in effecting, 206
Revolution, English, 202
Reynolds, General, report on government of Arkansas, 412
Rhode Island cases, 228
Richmond, Arkansas messenger sent to, 80; secession convention meets in, 93; work of convention denounced, 100; fall of, 426
Richmond government, offers concessions to western Virginia, 97; resistance to, 97
Riddell, John Leonard, certificate from, 56
Riley, General Bennett, 13

INDEX

Ritchie, A. F., letter to Attorney-General Bates, 105
Rogers, A. A. C., Congressman-elect, 91; proposed compensation of, 342
Rosecrans, General W. S., inactivity of, 21; suggestion to Lincoln, 23; removed from command, 23, 224
Ryers, William, election of, 412

S

SAULSBURY, WILLARD, 103; on admission of Mr. Segar, 139; admission of West Virginia Senators opposed by, 193; Administration criticised by, 377
Schenck, General, 251
Schofield, General, Governor Holden assisted by, 453
Schurz, General Carl, Governor Sharkey criticised by, 462
Scofield, Glenni W., address of, 236
Sebastian, William K., resignation from United States Senate, 85; return to loyalty, 85
Secession, in Tennessee, 8; Tennessee abrogates act of, 30; spirit of, in Louisiana, 36; ordinance of, 36; in Arkansas, 78; Germans and Irish of Arkansas indifferent to, 80; in Virginia, 93; western Virginia refuses to acquiesce in, 97; war powers unlocked by, 213; attitude of Democratic party toward, 218; Henry Winter Davis on, 227; Pendleton on acts of, 259; Henderson on potency of, 351; Sumner denies that States were taken out of Union by, 351
Secessionists, in Arkansas, 77
Segar, Joseph E., on admission of West Virginia, 118; remarks of, 131; Committee of Elections reports concerning, 131; denied admission to Congress, 133; election to United States Senate, 138

Senate, The United States, reconstruction bill in, 264; exclusion of States from Electoral College, 315; Trumbull's resolution abandoned by, 383; amendment abolishing slavery passed by, 384
Seward, William H., on admission of West Virginia, 120; General McClellan instructed by, 152; Lincoln broaches emancipation to, 178; postponement of emancipation recommended by, 182; Lincoln's letter to, 395; injuries prevented attendance at inauguration of Mr. Johnson, 408; message to Governor Marvin, 488; President Johnson influenced by, 489
Sharkey, William L., appointment of, 459; address of, 460; Johnson's telegram to, 461; conduct of, criticised by Carl Schurz, 462; negro testimony to be considered by, 464
Shelbyville, Tenn., Andrew Johnson's address at, 19
Shenandoah Valley, discontent of, 96; proposed annexation to West Virginia, 109
Shepley, General George F., appointment of, 39; system of courts established by, 41; Lincoln's letter to, 44; requested to hold an election, 45; proclamation for an election issued by, 45; plan of Louisiana Free State Committee approved by, 48; Attorney-General for Louisiana appointed by, 48; orders an enrollment of loyal citizens, 53; election prohibited by, 56, 58; conference of Free State Committee with, 63; disagreement with General Banks, 64, 65; General Banks approves registration of, 68; Norfolk proclamation of, 134
Sheridan, General Philip H., at Mission Ridge and Lookout Mountain, 23; a Confederate army destroyed by, 288
Sherman, John, on election of Mr. Segar, 140; on electoral vote of Louisiana, 332

Sherman, General Thomas W., instructions of War Department to, 149
Sherman, General William Tecumseh, projected march of, 286; safety of, 288
Shreveport, movement toward, 51; ceases to be capital of Louisiana, 419
Slavery, abolition of, in British colonies, 6; to be ignored in reconstruction, 27; Nashville convention urges abolition of, 29; amended Tennessee constitution abolishes, 30; constitution of Arkansas abolishes, 88; introduction into Virginia, 94; in the Wheeling convention, 107; Lincoln's views of, 143; Congress claims no right to interfere with, 167; advance of Northern opinion on, 167; abolished in District of Columbia, 167; not possible for negroes freed by war, 194; reconstruction rendered more difficult by abolition of, 194; ceases to exist when State ceases to exist, 197; duty of Congress to put an end to, 197; recognition of, by a Federal officer analogous to treason, 197; government should protect persons in a state of, 198; Chicago platform on, 207; Emancipation Proclamation not necessary to abolish in seceding States, 207; destruction of, not an end of the war, 222; the one subject of estrangement in the Union, 237; theory of the Fathers concerning, 237; anti-slavery amendment recommended to consideration of Congress, 287; Congress passes joint resolution relative to, 288; restoration useless with, 352; sentiments of Massachusetts and South Carolina on, 375; not affected by emancipation proclamation in certain States, 384; Congress passes anti-slavery amendment, 384; amendment ratified by 20 States, 384; Arkansas abolishes, 410; Virginia abolishes, 425; abolition an injury to slave owners, 433; North Carolina abolishes, 454; Mississippi abolishes, 460; Georgia abolishes, 466

Slaves, bred in Virginia, 94; number in Virginia, 94; in western Virginia, 95; policy of commanders relative to fugitive, 144, 145, 158, 159; declared contraband of war, 146; compensated emancipation of, 153; colonization of, 153; abandoned by masters, 160; to organize labor of abandoned, 160; General Hunter proclaims freedom of, 168; Lincoln asserts right to emancipate, 168; employment of, 169; confiscation of property in, 179; proposed emancipation of, 182; Stevens on employment of, against United States, 212; abandoned lands to be colonized by, 385

Slidell, John, resignation from United States Senate, 423

Slocum, General, organization of Mississippi retarded by, 462; orders of, revoked by President, 463

Smith, Caleb B., resignation of, 119

Smith, Charles, Senator-elect from Louisiana, 76, 343

Smith, General E. Kirby, 50

Smith, Governor William, nullity of acts of, 445

Snow, William D., election of, 91

Society, civil not necessarily identical with political, 354; political liable to reduction, 354; political may be reduced by loss of citizenship, 354

South Carolina, martial law proclaimed over, 168; Stevens on secession ordinance of, 215; Boutwell would exclude from restored Union, 256; insurrection in, 314; sentiments on slavery, 375; damage sustained by, 435; Mr. Johnson receives citizens of, 443; revolutionary character of convention, 469

Southern States, reorganization of, premature, 230; black code of,

INDEX 527

293; an asylum for broken-down politicians, 297; proposed taxation of, 297; power of Congress over, 362; not convertible into Territories, 364. See Confederate States
Speed, Attorney-General, reply to Albemarle County voters, 430
Sprague, William, remarks on Louisiana election, 381
Stanton, Edwin M., aids western Virginians, 98; on admission of West Virginia, 122; disbanding of army by, 409
State, indestructibility of, 192; suicide of a, 197, 201, 209; effect of termination of, 197; slavery terminated by termination of, 197; Federal restraints upon action of a, 198; difficulty of defining, 201; basis of suicide theory, 208; levying war changes status of, 217; the people of, constitute the, 218; constitutions must be formed by people of, 218; only successful revolution can unmake, 218; attitude of Democratic party on suicide of, 219
St. Bernard, parish of, voting in, 56
Steele, General Frederick, Lincoln's letters to, 85, 86, 89
Stephens, A. H., peace commissioner, 395; Lincoln's advice to, 399
Stevens, Thaddeus, on admission of West Virginia, 117, 214; reconstruction theory of, 211; characteristics of, 211; consistency of, 212; remarks on slaves employed in hostility to Government, 212; taxation of seceding States proposed by, 213; secession discussed by, 215; relations to his party defined by, 216; conquered province theory of, 217; remarks on minority government, 217; resolution relative to President's message, 224; on constitutional amendments, 232; reconstruction speech of, 247; distributing President's message, 288; Mr. Eliot interrupted by, 294; remarks of, 342; credentials of Warmoth offered by, 422; sneer at Pierpont's government, 427
Stokes, William B., election of, 415
Strouse, Myer, reconstruction speech of, 249
Suffrage, Representative Kelley on, 291; provisions of Ashley's bill on, 294, 304; a restricted electorate favored by Government, 354; basis of, 354; qualifications for, in Massachusetts, 354; proposal to confer on negroes, 358; Reverdy Johnson on, 378; negroes petition for, 413; Brownlow opposes conferring on negroes, 416; National Conservative party on, 421; provision of Virginia constitution on, 425; North did not intend to force on South, 486
Sumner, Charles, on admission of West Virginia, 110; letter on policy of Lincoln, 170; faith of, 191; resolutions of, 196; sensation produced by restoration scheme of, 198; letters to Francis Lieber, 199, 289; public character of, 199; letters to John Bright, 200, 290; article in Atlantic Monthly, 200; Mr. Blair replies to, 208; preamble to resolutions of, 210; proposal relative to emancipation proclamation, 272; estimate of Lincoln, 275; substitute offered by, 344; amendment offered by, 356; Reverdy Johnson's argument with, 374; inconsistency of, 375; conditions of reunion proposed by, 376; remarks on Trumbull's resolution, 379, 382; Howard and Chandler support position of, 380; remarks on Louisiana election, 382
Sumter, influence of fall, on Arkansas, 78
Supreme Court, The United States, opinion in Cross vs. Harrison, 13; decision relative to rebellious States, 362

T

TALIAFERRO, ROBERT W., seat in Congress claimed by, 341
Taney, Roger B., Chief Justice, quoted by Mr. Davis, 228
Tarr, Campbell, 98, 128
Taylor, Nathaniel, attitude of loyal Tennesseeans defined by, 7; election of, 415
Taylor, General Richard, 37, 49, 50
Ten Eyck, John C., reconstruction bill opposed by, 273; amendment offered by, 315; remarks in support of amendment, 318; defeat of amendment offered by, 334
Tennessee, Presidential reconstruction in, 1; no Republican electoral ticket in, 7; league with Confederacy authorized by, 8; turns military force over to the Confederacy, 8; secession of, 8; activity of loyalists in, 9; proposed dismemberment of, 9; Confederates losing hold of, 10; derangement of government in, 10; Legislature assembles at Memphis, 15; Andrew Johnson appointed military governor of, 15; condition in the Union, 16; judges imprisoned, 18; reprisals on secessionists, 18; lawlessness of, 18; citizens in Union army, 20; included in department of General Halleck, 20; ready for restoration, 21; free from armed insurrectionists, 22; emancipation in, 22; excluded from effects of emancipation proclamation, 22, 384; enrolling agent sent to, 27; county elections in, 27; returns, 28; reconstruction in, 29; Presidential election in, 29, 195; amended constitution of, 30; abrogates act of secession, 30; bonds of disloyal government, 30; constitution ratified by, 31; slaves emancipated in, 31; meeting of loyal Legislature, 31; McClellan electors, 35; electoral vote of, 35, 76, 129; Lincoln maintains legality of government in, 195; Mr. Davis on Unionists of, 230; insurrection in, 314; electoral vote of, 334; exclusion of electoral votes, 338; Cowan's inquiry concerning vote of, 338; Thirteenth Amendment ratified by, 412; United States Senators chosen by, 413; disfranchising act of, 413; irregularities in election, 414; negroes and Indians made witnesses, 415; harshness to traitors favored by, 414; franchise demanded by freedmen of, 415; ravages of war in, 417; insurrection ended in, 444; Joint Committee recommend admission of, 490
Tennessee, Bank of, notes of, irredeemable, 30
Tennessee, East, slavery in, 3; loyalty of, 3; services in Revolution, 4; resources of, 4; anti-slavery journals in, 5; abolition movement in, 5; a thoroughfare to the south-west, 6; Yancey agitates in, 7; treatment of loyalists in, 9; importance of, 21; convention of, revived, 29
Tennessee, West, politics influenced by industries of, 4; martial law in, 15
Texas, expedition into, 50, 51; insurrection in, 314; damages sustained by, 437; blockade of, 444; appointment of Provisional Governor for, 467; obstacles to restoration in, 467; negro population of, 467; reconstruction incomplete, 467; not represented at opening of Thirty-ninth Congress, 490
Thayer, General, 89
Thayer, M. Russell, reconstruction address of, 242
Thomas, Dorsey B., counted out, 415
Thomas, General George, at Mission Ridge and Lookout Mountain, 23; a Confederate army crippled by, 288
Thompson, Jacob, Mr. Black's visit to, 390
Thompson, General Jefferson, 245

INDEX

Treat, Hon. Samuel, excerpt from letter of, 354
Tribune, The New York, emancipation favored by, 164; protest of Wade and Davis printed in, 279
Trumbull, Lyman, on admission of Mr. Segar, 139; remarks on Crittenden resolution, 221; reconstruction bill opposed by, 273; speech on Ten Eyck's amendment, 316; on electoral vote of Louisiana, 321, 327; resolution offered by, 343; Sumner's offer to amend resolution of, 356; Howard's speech on resolution of, 358; Wade moves postponement of resolution, 378; Powell's speech on resolution of, 378; consistency of, 380; resolution recognizing Louisiana abandoned, 383
Tyng, Rev. Doctor, 151

U

UNDERWOOD, JOHN C., Senator-elect from Virginia, 141
Union, dismemberment of, 1; admission of new States into, 207
Union army, Arkansas troops in, 83; troops of restored Virginia in, 109
Union associations, demand an election in Louisiana, 45; delegates appointed by, 47
Unionists, importance of Southern, 3; in Louisiana, 37, 38, 47; Lincoln's advice to, 38; numbers in Arkansas, 77; loyalty in Arkansas, 88; conflicting views of, 88; difficulty of enlisting in Virginia, 133; oath of allegiance taken by, in North Carolina, 150; Henry Winter Davis on Southern, 231
Union party, vote of, in West Virginia, 129
United States, The, policy toward conquered provinces, 12; Tennessee promised republican form of government by, 16; oath of allegiance required of Louisiana voters, 45; policy toward loyal minorities, 105, 349; policy toward South after rebellion, 190; number of States not diminished by secession, 192; republican governments obligatory on members of, 208; duty of each to be represented in Congress, 208; union of, perpetual, 218, 219; Chase's dictum concerning nature of, 219; Government not to interfere in affairs of States, 220; authorized to impose conditions on returning States, 366; demand for revenue felt by, 409; disloyal governments not recognized by, 409
Universal Emancipation, The Genius of, 5
Upshur County, emancipation favored by citizens of, 108

V

VAN WINKLE, P. G., election of, 128
Vicksburg, surrender of, 49
Virginia, rebel government abrogated in, 10; loyalists without civil government, 93; secession of, 93; opposition to secession in, 94; physical features of, 94; slavery introduced into, 94; slaves in, 94; historical part of, 94; birthplace of many illustrious Americans, 94; settlement of trans-Alleghany region, 95; population of western, 95; sympathy of people in western, 95; representation in Legislature, 96; taxation in, 96; power in hands of slaveholders, 96; dismemberment of, discussed, 96; danger of insurrection in, 96; change of representation in, 96; expenditure of revenue, 96; concessions to western, 97; western refuses to acquiesce in secession, 97; the disloyal in, 97; State officials favor secession, 97; Federal Government aids western, 98; ravages of war in western, 98; movement for dismemberment, 98; secession denounced by Clarksburgh

meeting, 99; State government reconstituted, 100; Legislature of restored government, 102; election of United States Senators, 102; State of Kanawha to be erected in, 105; dismemberment ratified, 107; convention of, 107; Legislature meets, 109; Legislature consents to formation of new State, 110; Assembly consents to transfer of Berkeley County,. 126; act annexing counties to West Virginia, 127; transfer of Berkeley and Jefferson counties, 127; opposition to transfer, 127; removal of capital, 129; Legislature passes convention bill, 130; who were voters in, 130; amended constitution of, 130; civil in conflict with military authorities, 134; Legislature meets, 137; attitude of Congress and army toward, 138; feebleness of restored government, 138; admission of Senators from, 141; disloyal government discusses emancipation, 162; United States should protect loyalists of, 191; electoral vote from restored government, 314; slavery in parts of, excepted from emancipation proclamation, 384; division permanent, 399; constitution of 1864, 425; suffrage in, 425; slavery abolished in, 425; prohibitions on Legislature, 425; President Johnson recognizes government of Pierpont, 427, 445; ravages of war in, 427; steps to restoration of, 428; election in, 431; acts of secession authorities void, 445; acts of Congress to be enforced in, 446; Alexandria ceases to be capital of, 446

W

WADE, BENJAMIN F., bill for admission of West Virginia reported by, 110; remarks on admission of West Virginia, 111; reconstruction bill reported by, 264; address of, 264; protest of, with Henry Winter Davis, 279; character of, 283; on electoral vote of Louisiana, 333; remonstrance offered by, 343; postponement of Trumbull's resolution moved by, 378; motion to postpone, defeated, 379; Louisiana election criticised by, 381

Wade-Davis bill, House of Representatives passes, 262; Senate passes, 273; President's action on, 273; President's proclamation concerning, 277; revival of, 290; no provision for negro suffrage in, 494

War, expenses of, 161; condition of cessation of, 161, 397; obligations between States abrogated by, 214; Crittenden resolution on objects of, 221; objects of, 364; vindictiveness engendered by, 393

Ward, Artemus, 186

War Department, application of part of contingent fund of, 43

Warmoth, Henry C., election of, 422; elements of political strength possessed by, 423

Washburne, Elihu B., remarks of, 342

Webster, Daniel, prediction of, 126

Welles, Gideon, on admission of West Virginia, 122; Lincoln broaches emancipation to, 178; quotation from diary of, 178; narrative of, 188

Wells, J. Madison, proclamation of, 418; General Banks not in harmony with, 418; address of, 419; qualifications of voters defined by, 420

Wells, T. M., seat in Congress claimed by, 341

Wellsburgh, meeting at, 97; appointment of commissioners by, 98; arms and ammunition stored at, 98

West Virginia, Congress admits Senators from, 104, 193; prosecution of war favored by, 104; stay law passed by, 104; of revolutionary origin, 105; convention for, 107; slavery in,

INDEX

107; vote on constitution, 109; vote on emancipation, 110; Senate bill for admission of, 110; allotment of Representatives to, 110; Sumner on admission of, 110; proposal to prohibit slavery in, 111; Senate on admission of, 110; Senate passes bill to admit, 113; House bill for admission of, 113; House on admission of, 113; House passes bill for admission, 119; Lincoln approves bill for admission of, 125; constitutional amendment, 125; convention approves constitution, 126; constitution ratified by voters, 126; becomes a State, 126; Berkeley County transferred to, 126; proposal to annex counties to, 127; election in, 128; inauguration of, 128; United States Senators chosen by, 128; opposition to admission of Senators from, 128; Democrats alienated by President's recognition of, 193; Stevens finds no warrant in constitution for admission of, 214; strong enough to maintain a loyal government, 230

Wheeling, delegate convention at, 99; resolutions adopted by convention of, 100; adjournment of convention, 101; convention reassembles at, 104

Whiskey Insurrection, effects on status of Pennsylvania, 335
White, R. T. J., 88
Whittaker, John S., 41
Wickliffe, Charles A., Lincoln interviewed by, 165
Willey, Waitman T., election of, 103, 128; admitted to seat, 104; on admission of West Virginia, 112; remarks on credentials of Mr. Segar, 138, 140
Williams, General, treatment of fugitive slaves by, 159
Williams, Thomas, reconstruction address of, 238
Wilson, Henry, on recognition of restored Virginia, 140
Wilson, James F., previous question on Ashley's bill demanded by, 295; reconstruction bill introduced by, 311; joint resolution introduced by, 314
Wisconsin, electoral vote of, 316
Wood, Fernando, reconstruction bill opposed by, 251; remarks on Ashley's bill, 300; remarks on Wilson's bill, 312

Y

YANCEY, WILLIAM L., 7
Yeaman, George H., reconstruction address of, 243